MANAGERIAL ECONOMICS FOR DECISION MAKING

MANAGERIAL economics
for Decision Making

John Adams and Linda Juleff

palgrave
macmillan

First published 2003 by
PALGRAVE MACMILLAN
Houndmills, Basingstoke, Hampshire RG21 6XS and
175 Fifth Avenue, New York, N.Y. 10010
Companies and representatives throughout the world

PALGRAVE MACMILLAN is the global academic imprint of the Palgrave Macmillan division of St. Martin's Press, LLC and of Palgrave Macmillan Ltd. Macmillan® is a registered trademark in the United States, United Kingdom and other countries. Palgrave is a registered trademark in the European Union and other countries.

Transferred to Digital Printing 2008

ISBN 978-0-3339-6111-7

This book is printed on paper suitable for recycling and made from fully managed and sustained forest sources. Logging, pulping and manufacturing processes are expected to conform to the environmental regulations of the country of origin.

A catalogue record for this book is available from the British Library.

A catalogue record for this book is available from the Library of Congress.

Editing and origination by Aardvark Editorial, Mendham, Suffolk

Printed in Great Britain by
Cpod, Trowbridge, Wiltshire

Contents

contents

List of figures

List of tables

Preface

Welcome to this textbook.

It has been written specifically for students who are undertaking intermediate and postgraduate courses in business, commerce and management. The text is essentially an economics one but it presumes little or no prior knowledge of economics or economic analysis. It is aimed at those students who as part of a business studies, business management or MBA course need to study some of the fundamental aspects of business decisions within an economic context. The text draws mainly from the field of managerial economics but it is not a traditional text in managerial economics. There are many excellent texts in this field and we see this textbook as supplementing those. This approach has been taken on the basis of many years of experience of teaching business students – many of whom find the traditional texts to be too technical and less focused on the problems of managerial decision making. It is also different in style. We have made an explicit attempt to make the text as friendly and readable as possible without oversimplifying fundamental concepts, tools and arguments.

Key Features

This textbook contains a number of features that we believe will enable you to understand economic concepts and to apply them in a clear and straightforward way. It is also written within the context of the European Union – where most of the readers will reside. The text contains numerous Self-Assessment Questions (SAQs) to enable you to test your understanding as you work your way through the material. You can do this by comparing your answer to the SAQs with the answers provided in the text. Some of the individual chapters contain Case Studies and these are explicitly linked to the theoretical concepts discussed in the text. The text also contains a Case Study that runs through several chapters providing a continuing application of many key concepts.

The text is also broken into three distinct parts. These are:

- *Part I:* The Macroeconomic Environment

- *Part II:* The Theory of the Firm and Competitive Strategy

- *Part III:* Investment Decisions

This provides a set of themes and enables you to plan your study according to the particular course or module you may be engaged in at any given time.

Part I

The Macroeconomic Environment

In Part I we begin with a discussion of the process and concept of globalisation. In other words, the text starts at the macro level and gradually moves down to key microeconomic decisions which business managers in the private and public sectors need to consider. The first chapter introduces you to a brief history of globalisation, what it means and how it can be measured. The second chapter in Part I moves down in scale from the global economy to a national economy and develops a simple model of how an individual economy can be analysed in terms of its implications for managerial decision making. The level of mathematics required is basic and students who prefer to avoid this can easily do so and still fully grasp the main implications of the model. In Chapter 3 we move on to the measurement of economic performance at the macroeconomic level and this is directly linked to consideration of performance at the level of business. Part I of the text is thus designed to give you a clear overview of the links between global economic processes, national economy performance and the fortunes of the private and public sector.

Further Reading for Part I

Chapters 1, 2 and 3

Baldwin, R. (1994) 'Towards an Integrated Europe', Centre for Economic Policy Research Paper, London.

Crafts, N. and Toniolo, G. (eds) (1996) *Economic Growth in Europe since 1945*, Cambridge University Press.

European Commission (1996) *First Report on Economic and Social Cohesion*, ECU 14, Luxembourg.

Ferguson, P., Ferguson, G. and Rothschild, R. (1993) *Business Economics*, Macmillan – now Palgrave Macmillan, Basingstoke.

Henley, A. and Tsakalotos, E. (1993) *Corporatism and Economic Performance*, Edward Elgar, Aldershot.

HM Treasury *Economic Trends* (monthly).

Mankiw, G. (1990) 'A Quick Refresher Course in Macroeconomics', *Journal of Economic Literature* **28**(4): 1645–60.

Porter, M.E. (1990) *The Competitive Advantage of Nations*, Macmillan – now Palgrave Macmillan, Basingstoke.

Temple, P. (1997) 'The Performance of UK Manufacturing', London Business School Discussion Paper No. DP 14–97.

1 Globalisation

■ 1.1 Introduction

If asked the question 'what does globalisation mean to you?', most people would be able to give some kind of answer, even if based only on what they have read in newspapers or seen on television news items. However, there would be a very wide array of answers – the term itself has yet to be consistently defined and there will continue to be strong disagreement over what it actually means. This chapter will introduce you to the 'globalisation debate' by focusing on what the term is most likely to mean in practice and how the process itself might be identified and measured. The discussion then moves on to an assessment of what globalisation may imply for policy-makers, business and management decisions.

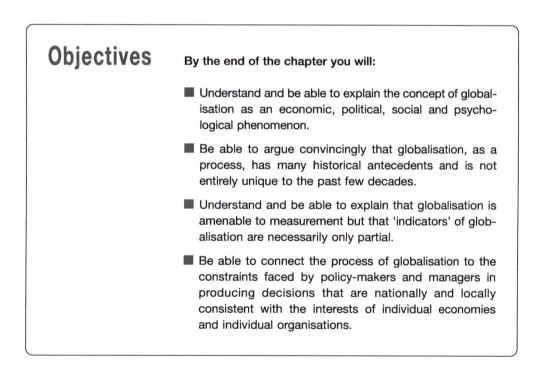

Objectives

By the end of the chapter you will:

■ Understand and be able to explain the concept of globalisation as an economic, political, social and psychological phenomenon.

■ Be able to argue convincingly that globalisation, as a process, has many historical antecedents and is not entirely unique to the past few decades.

■ Understand and be able to explain that globalisation is amenable to measurement but that 'indicators' of globalisation are necessarily only partial.

■ Be able to connect the process of globalisation to the constraints faced by policy-makers and managers in producing decisions that are nationally and locally consistent with the interests of individual economies and individual organisations.

■ 1.2   A Brief History

The EU economies have become increasingly open ones since the end of the Second World War. The EU has always contained many trading economies, but prior to the 1960s the trade was dominated by export activity while imports represented a much smaller fraction of total GDP. In the late 1990s, although export levels were lower relative to that 'golden age' they still represented nearly a quarter of EU GDP and imports represented nearly 30 per cent of GDP. Taken together, over half of the EU's economic activity was based on trade as the economy began the twenty-first century. This development was, however, not confined to EU economies.

All industrialised economies in the world and many of the newly industrialising ones share in a very large trade volume compared with 40 years ago. The development of containerisation, 'super' ships, faster communications and easier currency transfers has enabled trade volumes globally to increase by over 900 per cent in four decades. Alongside this massive growth in global trade volumes has been an 'explosion' in foreign direct investment (FDI), mainly between the industrialised countries, although in the last decade this has increasingly involved developing and newly industrialising countries. Taken together, the growth in trade volumes and in FDI has produced not only a global economy, in a very real sense, but also the 'global' firm. In fact the growth in trade volumes and the emergence of the global firm are closely related: many economies in the world still operate restrictions on imports of one type or another, the EU included, and this has made it necessary for large firms to locate production in foreign markets. In addition the implementation of the General Agreement on Tariffs and Trade (GATT) in 1947 which sought to ease trade restrictions also enables trade volumes between countries to be 'negotiated' so that if firms wish to sell more output than 'negotiated' they must locate production facilities closer to or actually in the receiving economy. So, why has globalisation happened, why has the global firm emerged and what are the implications for EU business? There are many reasons:

- GATT/WTO

- Aggregate demand

- Market access

- Currency convertibility

- Strategic 'thinking'

- Vertical integration

- Geopolitical interests

The GATT simply made it much easier for trading economies to develop closer ties without the restrictions which dogged trade prior to 1945. In other words, a great deal of potential trading had simply been 'smothered' for a whole variety of political, social and economic reasons specific to different economies. The advent of the GATT enabled the potential to be released and further developed. However, this could only take place in the context of growing aggregate global demand for industrial and especially consumer products. Much of the increase in aggregate demand experienced by the developed economies after 1945 was inspired by reconstruction, a need to satisfy 'pent-up' demand after years of rationing, and a realisation that higher trade volumes would more closely integrate these economies politically as well as economically.

However, the rapid development in FDI was mainly market driven, and not cost driven, although in recent years cost has assumed a greater importance than before. Under GATT it was simply not possible to export all of a firm's non-domestic consumption output; in many cases therefore it became necessary to locate production facilities abroad. This improved market access, in terms of both production and exports, lies at the root of the philosophy of the WTO – increased market access is the very bedrock of the multilateral trading system today.

It could be argued that this has become even more essential for trade growth in the future given the advent of economic blocs such as the EU and NAFTA (North American Free Trade Area) which strictly controlled the level of imports negotiated in each round of the GATT agreement. Thus, the sale of computers produced in the EU by a US firm to Germany now represents output for domestic consumption, whereas prior to GATT they were more than likely to have to be imported from the US. However, it could be argued that the development of these economic blocs runs counter to the philosophy of the WTO since they tend to offer protection to their own firms, often negating WTO rules. For many developing countries this is particularly the case in agricultural products. This process of 'regionalisation' is continuing with the expansion of the EU to possibly 25 countries by 2005, further development of the ASEAN bloc (South-East Asian economies), SADCC in Africa and regional groupings in South America. Indeed, the process of 'globalisation' is developing in parallel with increasing regionalisation across the world.

The introduction of the Treaty of Rome in 1957 went a very long way to achieving full convertibility of EU currencies and the US dollar, principally at the insistence of US investors. Hence US FDI anywhere in the EU area would not be exposed to currency risks. This in tandem with growing consumer demand led to the development of a more strategic approach to business planning in which the restrictions implied by the 'need' for local sourcing, controlled use of technology and other aspects of operating outwith the home economy came to be viewed as much less of a problem than in the past.

Management methods were developed to cope with greater diversification of products and greater vertical integration of business so that the 'strategic' firm could guarantee not only sources of input supply but also markets to sell its

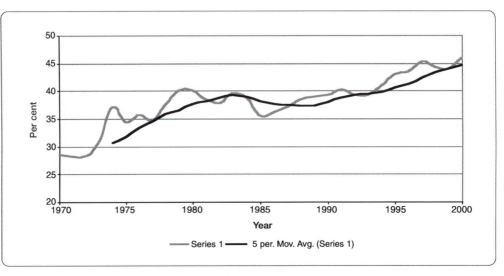

Figure 1.1 Global trade as percentage of global GDP
Source: Constructed from World Bank Tables

output to. The development of production, logistics and financial planning techniques accelerated more in the past three decades than at any other time in business history. All of the above developments enabled the emergence of the global firm; however, the environment in which these developments took place was also amenable, that is, the emergence of new and stronger geopolitical interests on the part of the Western economies ensured that the political environment for such developments was welcoming. However, although GATT has enabled long-term growth in global trade volumes these have fluctuated considerably over the decades. Growth was well above its 5-year moving average throughout the 1970s and early 1980s but fell below its trend for much of the 1980s. It accelerated again in the 1990s, especially from 1994/95, coinciding with the advent of the World Trade Organization (WTO) in 1995. Whether this was merely coincidental or simply a reflection of other global trends is a difficult question to answer. Figure 1.1 traces this growth since the 1970s.

This continues to be the case at the beginning of the twenty-first century. Indeed it is difficult to imagine the major economies of the world and the newly industrialising economies once again retreating into fortress Germany, America, France, UK or Japan.

■ ■ ■ Self-Assessment Question ■ ■ ■ ■ ■ ■ ■ ■ ■ ■ ■ ■

Q1 What might 'globalisation' mean for the competitive stance taken by a small EU firm?

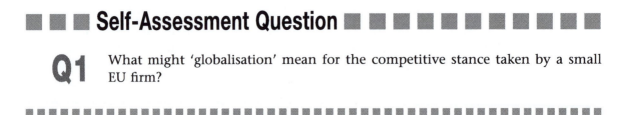

Before we consider what all this might mean for business, business decisions, EU governments and EU citizens we need to take a step back and consider exactly what we mean by globalisation because it is not at all clear and it does not necessarily apply across all sectors of an economy. We need a definition, we also need to 'measure' it and we need to be able to assess what this definition of globalisation and its component indicators can tell us about the probable economic environment EU firms and citizens will face in the future.

■ 1.3   What Is Globalisation?

At its simplest level, globalisation could be defined as a process which increases the share of trade in global GDP, as per Figure 1.1. Or we could define it as a process which leads to an increasing share of FDI as a proportion of global investment. There are many other economic and financial ratios we could use to define the term or the process of globalisation. However, none of these would be sufficient on their own as they are very uni-dimensional. This is because globalisation, whatever it really is, is most certainly multi-dimensional. It is not simply about trade or investment – it involves an acceleration in the process of change which has been ongoing for hundreds, perhaps even thousands, of years. These changes involve all facets of social, political and economic relations which appear to have culminated in connecting billions of people (whether they know it or not) around the world. If you drink tea you are connected with the farmer in China or Sri Lanka; if you drink coffee you are connected with the farmer in Colombia or Kenya; if you wear a designer T-shirt you have a connection with a factory worker in Singapore, Mauritius or the UK. The list of products and an associated list of country connections goes on and on. So, globalisation also involves people: their place of work, their work conditions, their wages, who they work for and how they live their lives are all affected by globalisation.

It could be argued that, in the above sense, these connections are not really that different from the ones created by earlier societies. We know for example that the Romans were trading goods and labour 2000 years ago across Europe, Africa, the Middle East and Asia Minor. The Minoan civilisation based on Crete traded across three continents over 3500 years ago. The Vikings are thought to have been involved in trade across the Atlantic and as far east as the Ural mountains. There is also evidence of trade across the vast expanse of the Indian Ocean between East Africa, Indonesia, Polynesia and even Western Australia occurring thousands of years ago. These were all developed societies (in their terms) and they all engaged in trade over large distances in the context of what was effectively the known world to them. So, if globalisation is to be defined in terms of trade alone then there really is nothing new about it – it has just become larger in scale in terms of the known world today. Of course it is not just about trade – it is more about the nature of trade today, how it is conducted and the speed with which it is conducted. This is the essential difference today – speed of movement and the speed of the flow of information.

Another key difference is in the content of trade – much of it today does not involve physical goods at all. It involves the trading of information, finance, legal and many other services which, even in the nineteenth century, were rarely the subject of international trade. Indeed trade in services has grown so large in recent decades that the GATT now has a parallel in GATS (General Agreement on Trade in Services) which covers almost all types of service, including education itself. The EU has already signed up to GATS inclusive of trade in knowledge and knowledge acquisition – in just a few years it will be possible for universities in over 100 countries to offer their courses in any other country by attendance at class. Thus the very nature of what is traded today, how it is traded and the speed of trade essentially define globalisation as something different from what has gone before. And, in addition to this, we now have a trading 'architecture' – a system of rules most countries are expected to follow under the multilateral trading agreements monitored by the WTO.

In some ways it could be argued that globalisation has also become an attitude of mind as well as a system of economic relations – these days people are not surprised by where a product or service comes from – indeed they are more likely to be surprised if it is made in their own country. But there is another aspect of today's globalisation process which is distinct from similar processes in history – that is the progressive reduction in the ability of the nation state to command its own economic affairs. It is now more difficult than ever for a single country to determine its own economic policy since multinational companies and international financial service companies can move production facilities and money very rapidly across borders to take advantage of differences in tax regimes, labour costs and exchange and interest rates. Hence the trend discussed above towards regional blocs designed to act as larger and therefore stronger economic bargaining units. The world of finance is possibly the most glaring example of globalisation today in terms of scale, speed of movement and cross-border versatility. But even this 'financial globalisation' still has many aspects which do not fit well with the purist view of a wholly globalised world economy. For many, financial globalisation is the forerunner of a wholly integrated world economy. But there are many question marks as to just how globalised even finance has become (Lewis, 1995).

The clearest way to illustrate this is to describe what financial globalisation is not. It is not simply the expansion of net or gross international capital flows; it is not the expansion of individual economies' external financial transactions per se and nor is it the increasing entry of large financial institutions into non-home-based markets. These are all aspects of the *internationalisation* of capital and, as we already know, are subject to significant cyclical fluctuations. Were these the key elements of financial globalisation it would be irrefutably logical to talk of periods of 'deglobalisation' such as in the 1930s and 1950s. In addition there remains a strong tendency for investors and their portfolios to retain a very strong 'home bias' and for wealth in all its forms to be predominantly held within investors' home countries. This home or domestic bias is likely to decline with time, but it is an indication that the completely 'globalised' financial world is still some way off. It seems clear therefore that cyclical fluctuations in cross-border capital transactions can neither conceptually nor empirically form the basis of what is effectively a relatively new and even 'populist' concept. Instead we need a clear and unambiguous theoretical rationale which is capable of providing deeper insights into a process which we *believe* is under way but as yet do not fully understand. As Shirakawa et al. argue:

> globalisation refers to [a situation] where each country's economy, including its financial markets, becomes increasingly integrated resulting in development towards a *single world market.*

In other words, financial market globalisation will not and cannot proceed in the absence of the globalisation of all production relations, including labour itself. Using the definition given above it is possible to delineate stages of the globalisation 'process' and to categorise what these stages mean in terms of both the 'real' economy and the financial markets. Consider Figure 1.2. This is a 'model' which posits a world of only two economies, A and B, in which there are two broadly defined sectors – the goods and services market (GSM) and the financial services market (FSM). In Stage 1 there is no trade between A and B but there is synergy between the GSM and FSM within each economy. In Stage 2 GSM trade between A and B is completely dominant but supported by the FSM within each economy only. The degree of integration between the GSM and the FSM domestically is expanding over time during this stage but does not yet involve cross-border integration in any significant sense.

As GSM trade increases it becomes increasingly necessary for the FSMs in each economy to support it bilaterally since the GSM demand for capital is outstripping the supply of loanable funds domestically (Stage 3). Credit creation and financial economies of scale and scope enable this. With increasing integration there is a greater (parallel) need for coordinated policy action between the authorities in A and B to 'manage' their respective domestic economies. This point (Stage 3) is effectively where the 'global' economy is at the present time – although a high degree of integration has already taken place it is still characterised by a strong 'home' bias in the financial markets.

The shift to the next level (Stage 4), an integrated global economic system in which all sectors are reciprocally and fully integrated within and between each economy, represents a fundamental structural change in the nature of international production relations. So much so as to effectively produce the globalised economy in the Shirakawa et al. sense. In terms of Figure 1.2 the completely globalised economy develops on the path between Stages 3 and 4. The key policy issues along this path are those which relate to increased liberalisation of trade and of financial markets, both of which represent a continued threat to a

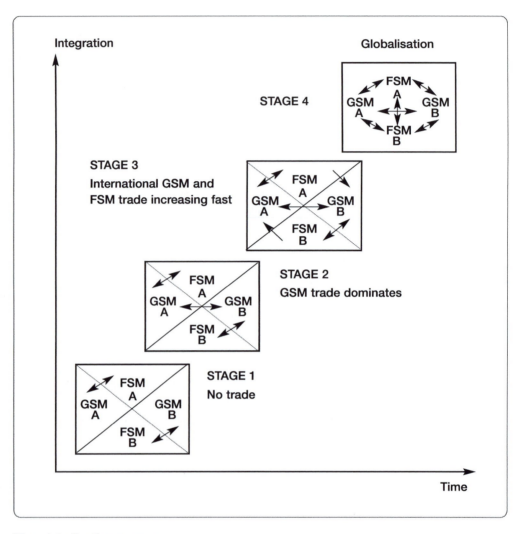

Figure 1.2   The globalisation process

nation's or a group of nations' control over economic policy. For many firms it potentially represents a threat to their own domestic markets – they increasingly face competition from similar firms often located in different continents. For the public provision of services there is also increased competition from private sector service providers since they are, and increasingly in the future will be able to compete to deliver public services. This is especially true of services which are expensive to provide such as health, education and transport. If increased globalisation of trade and of firms is the likely future for many economies, what are the implications for firms in the EU? We can analyse these in terms of possible advantages and disadvantages.

Advantages

A main advantage claimed for EU firms of the emergence of the global firm is the *demonstration* effect. The importation to the EU by foreign firms of new technologies, new management methods, new products and a more dynamic approach to business has enabled EU firms to become more competitive, more attuned to consumers, more cost conscious, more quality conscious and generally more effective in the domestic and global economies.

Many of these advantages have been the result of FDI using local sourcing of inputs supplied by domestic EU firms. In addition, the employment of EU managers by many of these global firms has been an 'education' for EU management in general and this has had spillover effects into EU-managed firms.

Disadvantages

A main disadvantage of the growth in global trade and in FDI to many EU firms has simply been that it came in a period when many EU businesses were not capable of competing effectively, the result being that many EU sectors are now dominated by foreign firms. The claim that local sourcing has enabled many EU firms to develop further is not as strong as first appears since many FDI firms source globally – thus driving down the price a local firm can expect to get for its sales to a global firm. In addition, the introduction of management methods such as just in time, 'outsourcing' and 'strategic' (local) suppliers has meant EU firms need to make investments which 'tie' them into a single customer, thus raising their risk exposure.

Whether the advantages or disadvantages discussed above are perceived or real probably depends on the experience of individual EU firms in competing with or working with the FDI firm. Nevertheless it is quite clear that there are serious threats to domestic EU firms from further globalisation and further development of the global firm. The point is that these need to be recognised and countered using the most modern management methods available and continuing to meet the requirements of customers which are becoming more demanding every year. Although the EU has a significant number of global firms of its own, most employment in the EU is still in the context of small and medium-sized enterprises. These are particularly at risk in the globally competitive market place. The quality of the workforce, the product and above all the management in such enterprises will be the key to long-term survival and development – and not necessarily the minimisation of costs, a strategy which has not been particularly successful for EU firms in the past. However, as a regional economic bloc the EU has already taken a major step towards positioning itself so that its firms and its workers can compete in a globalising economy. This step was the introduction of monetary union. Although only a few countries within the EU have yet to join, there is clearly an advantage to

EU firms in terms of internal reductions in costs in trading within the EU and in the development of a currency to compete with the dollar and the yen. Why should European monetary union (EMU) be a likely benefit to EU firms in terms of globalisation?

1.3.1   EMU and Globalisation

Given that over half of the EU's economic activity involves trade whether as final goods and services or as intermediate inputs, it is quite clear that 15 exchange rates within the EU are a crucial factor in determining not only the volume of intra-European trade but also its value to businesses and to the economy. We already know that globalisation of trade and the emergence of very large multinational corporations have significant implications for EU business but these take on even more significance in the context of EMU. The very first point to make even though it seems obvious is that non-exporting and non-importing firms in the EU will be as much affected by EMU as those involved in intra-EU trade and extra-EU trade. If a family never takes an overseas holiday they will still be as much affected as those who do! In other words, if EMU is eventually implemented as planned in all EU member states its effects on all EU economies will be ubiquitous.

What is EMU?

It is simply the distillation of 15 currencies into one, the euro. This process has already taken place in the USA (after the Civil War), Germany (after reunification) and in the former Soviet Union, although in the latter the process has since been reversed. Thus, integrating several different currencies into one is not a new idea nor will it be a 'first' event. Some would argue that the circumstances are not that different either: in the cases of the three examples above the overriding motivation for a single currency was political integration and the creation of 'nationhood' – and hence in the global economy of today this is exactly what Europeans are striving for although few politicians would openly say so. Whether the motivation for EMU is mainly political or not we are concerned here with its economic implications for EU business in a globalising economy.

The criteria for entry to EMU are, on the surface, fairly reasonable, practicable and straightforward. They are as follows:

1. Low inflation

2. Low nominal interest rate

3. Stable nominal exchange rate

4. Fiscal deficit ≤ 3 per cent of GDP

5. Debt/GDP ratio ≤ 60 per cent

The first three criteria are monetary while the last two are fiscal. That is, a country is required to balance as closely as possible its government 'books' between taxation and expenditure, and the restriction on the debt to GDP ratio is a key instrument in enabling that. The first three criteria are very much monetary in that they are linked to money supply control by the government which in turn is linked to interest rate levels. The requirement for a stable exchange rate (in the 2 years up to membership) is in turn a function of money supply management and interest rates. Thus, all five criteria are interdependent and all five must therefore be achieved if an EU economy is to enter the single currency. Although there have been accusations that the criteria have been relaxed to enable some countries to enter, the point is nevertheless that these five criteria do make sense in terms of seeking a stable, strong and sustainable single currency in the face of increasingly fiercer global competition.

We used the phrase earlier that 'on the surface' these are reasonable criteria for the development of a single currency. This is because they are actually critical to the economic fortunes of all EU economies. In fact it is the criteria for entry which themselves provide the debate over whether an economy should or should not enter EMU.

What are the Implications for EU Business?

Firms which require imported inputs and/or are involved in exporting intermediate or final goods and services currently incur transactions costs associated with currency conversion. In addition, they also face a currency risk in that contracts are often agreed on the basis of either the current rate of exchange or a future rate of exchange, say 3 months ahead. Both of these carry the risk that adverse exchange rate movements will result in a lower than expected price receivable or a higher than expected price payable. Avoidance of these risks can be accommodated using various insurance schemes (which are a cost) and in some cases by using the export credit guarantee schemes operated by many EU governments – in which case the taxpayer carries the risk. The point is clear: trading arrangements on the basis of bilateral exchange rates (between two economies) can be costly and risky. In theory therefore it ought to be in the interests of EU firms to be dealing in a single European currency.

The transactions costs of trade can be significant. An extreme example of this is the movement of people within the EU as tourists! Suppose someone from the UK wished to visit all of the other 14 member states before the introduction of the euro and let us suppose he/she took two wallets – one with £1000 for converting and to live on and one with £1000 simply to convert into the currency of each member state when they arrived there. Using the nominal exchange rates which applied in 1999 within the EU, the second £1000 would be reduced to £723 on return to the UK. That is, having bought absolutely nothing but merely changing from one currency to the next and back to sterling (15 changes) the transaction cost is £277! Although imported and exported goods will never go through 15 currency conversions, nevertheless many EU firms trade with several EU economies and therefore used to incur significant transactions costs. These would still apply to firms and people based in the euro area had the euro not been implemented.

Membership of the single currency reduces these types of cost to zero, a very significant advantage to firms based in the euro area.

■ ■ ■ Self-Assessment Question ■ ■ ■ ■ ■ ■ ■ ■ ■ ■ ■ ■ ■

Q2 Is there a potential conflict of interest between the needs of business in EMU and the needs of the individual national economies?

It could also be argued that past interest and exchange rate management by many EU governments merely protected inefficient firms rather than enabled them to become more competitive. Hence, the creation of EMU helps to enable EU firms to compete more effectively not only with their continental counterparts but also with the rest of the world.

Of course the development of the single currency carries transitory risks but in the long term, as a result of full economic convergence, such risks will be reduced to zero or close to it. However, the benefits of a stronger single currency (relative to the rest of the world) and a stronger pan-European economy in the long term far outweigh transitory risks and changeover costs. Indeed with the advent of the Asian 'tiger' economies, the continued economic power of Japan and the USA and the rapid development of China, Brazil and India, the potential costs of not developing a single currency and hence a single economic bloc could be enormous. How many of the EU's smaller and medium-sized firms would be able to compete with the latter countries in the future if they continue to operate in a 'domestic' system of 15 currencies? EMU is just one lever to help them do so. This is a complex issue and only some of the (main) arguments are represented here. The political, social and cultural advantages/disadvantages of EMU have not been touched upon. However, it is likely to be the case that these will eventually have more sway in which member states join the euro in the future than the more technical economic arguments.

If we consider the five criteria for membership of EMU it is quite clear that these are also highly relevant to becoming and remaining more competitive as the world moves towards Stage 4 as described in Figure 1.2. Firms in the EU will simply not be able to compete, especially with 'low cost' suppliers in other parts of the world, in the absence of low inflation, low nominal interest rates and a stable nominal exchange rate for the single currency. In addition the 'rules' on the fiscal deficit and the debt/GDP ratio for each member state will help to reduce the burden of taxation on business and workers below what it might otherwise have been. This leaves more money in business and in people's pockets so that they can make their own decisions on investment and consumption. It has often been argued by economists that the most vibrant and fast growing economies in the world are characterised by generally lower business and personal taxes than traditionally applies in EU economies. This has certainly been true of the USA, the 'tiger' economies of South-East Asia, India and Brazil. It is also true of China which entered the WTO in 2001 and seems poised to expand at growth rates larger than those achieved by Japan in the 1960s and 70s.

The process of globalisation thus has major implications for business, government and citizens in the EU. Decisions on product pricing, investment, personal consumption, public service provision and many other 'micro-economic' aspects of the day-to-day management of firms, households and government services are themselves influenced by globalisation, even in the smallest way, and in addition, influence how the EU economy itself will progress as globalisation itself progresses.

Now that we have a much clearer idea of what globalisation is (and what it is not), how it relates to business and people and government and what it may mean for all types of economic and managerial decisions, we are in a better position to attempt to measure it. If we can identify a set of 'indicators' of glob-alisation then business and government will be in a better position to judge which investment options, pricing and marketing options and economic policy options are more likely to succeed than others.

■ 1.4 Measuring Globalisation

As discussed above, the concept of globalisation is multi-dimensional and this makes its measurement difficult – no one 'indicator' could possibly be sufficient to describe it, explain it or predict its future path. What we can do, however, is conceptualise what it might mean in terms of Figure 1.2. Whether some countries or no countries are already at Stage 4 cannot be determined precisely because we do not, at present, have a good enough set of indicators of where we are in the globalisation process. This is partly because, as discussed above, there is widespread disagreement on what globalisation actually is. As already mentioned, it could be thought of as a 'state of mind' in which people around the world are either well aware or just notionally aware of the connections between them and the rest of the world. Goods and services are items which can be 'globalised' in the sense of production, sales, sourcing, supply chains, information and strategy. However, it is not so straightforward to measure the globalisation of social 'norms', ideas, consumer behaviour and other non-tangible aspects of a process which some argue is leading to 'sameness' across the world. At the moment, however, we can measure some of the tangible aspects of the globalisation 'process'.

We do know, from our previous discussion, that financial globalisation is certainly not complete and that this is likely to be the key element in the continued globalisation of goods and services towards Stage 4 in Figure 1.2 and also in the Shirikawa et al. sense. It thus follows that despite claims to the contrary, the globalisation of goods and services themselves cannot be complete. However, we can identify a few 'obvious' measurements of globalisation and test these against what has gone before. Three of these are:

■ Global exports and imports (volume)

■ FDI as a proportion of global GDP

■ FDI as a proportion of global direct investment

These three 'indicators' are useful because they give us a picture of the trends involved and also show us whether these trends really are new, are significant and are qualitatively different from trends in the past. Let us consider the growth in global trade in terms of exports and imports as described in Figure 1.3.

The graph spans a period of 20 years at the end of the last century. It shows that the expansion of exports and imports was very rapid in the second half of the 1980s and even faster in the 1990s. A world recession in the early 1990s significantly arrested both trends. We can find the same trends for these indicators from the 1950s right through the 1960s and 70s – however they were not as pronounced. The speed of expansion in the latter part of the twentieth

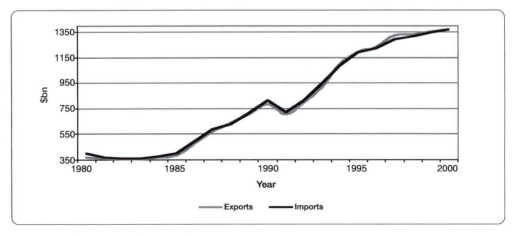

Figure 1.3   Global exports and global imports

century coupled with the scale of trade in terms of volume was quite different from previous periods. Indeed it was this scale and speed of expansion which led to the current notion of globalisation in the populist sense. We can reasonably conclude from this that if the very rapid growth of this period was to continue for the foreseeable future then the world (or large parts of it) will rapidly enter Stage 4 in Figure 1.2. What about our other 'indicators' of globalisation? It has been argued that the real basis of globalisation is not trade per se but the development of 'stateless' corporations which can invest or disinvest 'at will' across the globe in order to maximise the benefits to them of differentials in tax regimes, exchange and interest rates and in regulatory frameworks between different countries.

Again we can clearly detect a sea change in the rate of growth of FDI relative to global GDP first in the mid-1980s and again, but even faster, in the 1990s (Figure 1.4). The troughs in the cyclical pattern of this correspond almost exactly with major economic recessions in the 1970s, 80s and early 1990s when FDI went below its 5-year moving average. This may be another indication of the 'home bias' which we discussed in relation to financial globalisation – when recession occurs there is a strong tendency for investors (corporations and individuals) to reduce planned investments abroad first. This also suggests that the perceived risk of such investment is higher than with domestic investment. Economic uncertainty therefore plays a significant role in arresting, at least temporarily, the process of globalisation in goods, services and finance. It would appear that even large corporations prefer to continue to compete more strongly in their domestic markets than elsewhere when such uncertainty arises. In addition it should be noted that, despite the clear trend of greater

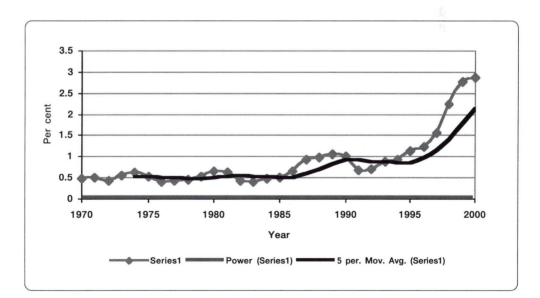

Figure 1.4   FDI as a proportion of global GDP

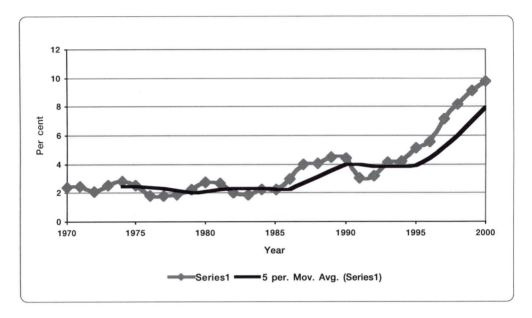

Figure 1.5   FDI as a proportion of global direct investment

investment abroad in the 1990s, the global proportion relative to GDP was still very low by the end of the century at less than 3 per cent. It could be argued that such a low proportion is hardly indicative of a rapidly globalising world economy and in fact is just another, albeit more rapid, phase of foreign investment growth. In other words, some of the 'wilder' claims of a globalising world economy simply do not match the evidence of a very obvious indicator of the process. Another way to look at the foreign investment issue is to consider how it has developed relative to global investment itself rather than global GDP. This is depicted in Figure 1.5.

The same pattern we described in Figure 1.4 is also evident here. As a proportion of global direct investment, foreign investment was significantly above its 5-year moving average only in the latter half of the 1980s and for most of the 1990s. Prior to this period it hardly deviated from its trend. In addition, even by the end of the century only about 10 cents in every invested dollar were actually invested outside domestic economies and the 5-year average was less than 8 cents in every dollar. What can we conclude from this? We know that the most 'movable' commodity, finance and financial services, tends to be seen as the most globalised yet it is still dominated by a very strong 'home bias'; we also know that global trade in terms of exports and imports has certainly accelerated in the past 20 years and would suggest rapid globalisation; but we also know that a fundamental aspect of globalisation as a concept, FDI, has increased rapidly but is still a very small proportion of both global GDP and global investment. In addition to this, such investment expansion is quite easily arrested and sometimes actually reduced by recession and economic uncertainty (Obstfeld and Taylor, 1997).

The evidence is therefore very mixed using these indicators. Indeed it can quite easily be argued that very few economies, if any, are anywhere near Stage 4 as described in Figure 1.2 earlier. This leaves us with an alternative explanation – that 'globalisation', as discussed above, is more to do with faster communications, easier access to information on a global scale and a 'state of mind' than with actual recent history of economic development per se. This does not mean that it is not happening – it does mean that we are still a very long way from Stage 4 in the conceptual model of globalisation. The evidence does suggest that the world has become more of an economic 'unit' than it used to be but still much less of an economic unit than the nation state continues to be! If globalisation is happening then it is developing much more slowly than many commentators and pressure groups suggest. But even at a slower pace of development it still contains many significant implications for national governments and for businesses, wherever they are located. We will consider this in the next section.

■ 1.5　National and Business Implications of Globalisation

Even if developing more slowly than currently assumed, the process of globalisation will have major and profound effects on how individual economies are managed and how individual businesses, large and small, manage their resources and plan their future. At the national level (including regional blocs such as the EU) a number of key macroeconomic management tools are likely to become less effective in addressing the needs of individual economies. These include:

- Regulation of business
- Environmental policy
- Taxation policy
- Trade policy
- Exchange rate management
- Financial regulation
- Central bank functions

Business regulation is commonly associated with competition policy and the achievement of a set of standards in relation to the quality, safety and selling of goods and services. These regulations tend to be domestically defined but can be in contravention (or appear to be) of international or regional bloc rules and agreements such as in the case of the WTO and the EU. There is thus a trend towards the standardisation of such regulation across borders which reduces the ability of domestic governments to determine their own standards and rules. It may be the case that domestic firms' costs will need to rise to meet 'standardised' regulations thus making them less competitive. In other words, changes or enhancements to existing business regulation will inevitably give a competitive edge to firms able to absorb these extra costs. This will have implications for those firms which are slow to react or fail to anticipate future regulatory change. Increasingly the domestic government cannot be relied upon to produce predictable and locally relevant regulation since it is likely to be superseded by an international agreement.

The same analysis can be forwarded in terms of environmental policy where regional or even global agreements will increasingly impose additional costs on business at the local level – even where this may not be locally appropriate in many cases. On taxation the difficulties for domestic government could be even greater. Differentials in corporation tax between countries, even within regional blocs, will increasingly influence the direction of FDI or the decision by a domestic based firm to move its facilities across borders. This has many implications for employment, tax revenue and domestic GDP growth. Although most economies are members of the WTO and regional blocs they still have some room for determining domestic trade policy and the level of protection they give to domestic industry, for example through subsidies. But domestically produced trade 'rules', including protection, increasingly come into conflict with agreements already in existence or are often seen to be by other countries. Increased globalisation is likely to make it even more difficult for domestic trade policy to be 'out of line' with international or regional agreements. The increasing globalisation of financial services makes the management and targeting of an appropriate exchange rate increasingly more difficult. This affects the ability of a domestic government to achieve a 'competitive' exchange rate for its currency and to achieve an interest rate which is consistent with the competitive stance of the businesses operating within its borders. In addition, the possibility of a financial crisis in one country being transmitted to another (financial contagion) has increased significantly, making financial management tools of economic policy even less effective than before. Finally the role and functions of central banks, including the European Central Bank, have now become more complex and more difficult to manage. All of the above add up to an inevitable conclusion – the ability of the nation state or regional economic bloc to determine its own economic future has definitely been reduced and is likely to be reduced further in the future. In the next chapter we consider how the nation state can be understood as an economic system by applying some basic economic analysis.

❏ ❏ ❏ End of Chapter SUMMARY ❏ ❏ ❏ ❏ ❏ ❏ ❏ ❏ ❏ ❏ ❏

In this chapter there are a number of key concepts and relationships with which you should now be familiar. In particular:

- The historical antecedents of globalisation

- The different definitions of globalisation

- The type of indicators of globalisation and their drawbacks

- The key drivers of globalisation

- The relationship between the global economy and the local economy

- The constraints faced by decision makers imposed by globalisation

In addition you should be able to explain clearly that globalisation is not just an economic phenomenon – it is as much driven by political and social developments and by individual perceptions of the 'world order'. The notion that globalisation could be considered as a 'state of mind' is a very powerful one and helps to explain the increasing polarisation of opinion as to the benefits and dis-benefits of the process itself.

References

Lewis, K. (1995) 'Puzzles in International Financial Markets' in Grossman, G. and Rogoff, K. (eds) *Handbook of International Finance* Vol. III, pp. 1913–71.

Obstfeld, M. and Taylor, A. (1997) 'The Great Depression as a Watershed: International Capital Mobility over the Long Run', NBER Working Paper No. 5960.

Shirakawa, M., Okina, K. and Shiratsuka, S. 'Financial Market Globalisation: Present and Future', Bank of Japan Discussion Paper, No. 97-E-11, Tokyo.

▨ ▨ ▨ ANSWERS to Self-Assessment Questions ▪ ▪ ▪ ▪ ▪ ▪ ▪

Q1 It could mean many things! First, the small firm may need to consider the investment it needs to make in order to meet the quality levels and delivery constraints imposed by the global firm. Second, it could mean that the small firm's real competitior(s) are not located within the domestic economy at all – they are as likely to be located in economies both within and outwith Europe. This is very much the case for small high technology (niche) firms in the EU – many of their competitors are in Australia, the USA and the Far East. But because of minimal transport costs (relative to production costs) these competitors might as well be next door!

Q2   There is a potential conflict here. Not all EU firms are significantly engaged in exporting or importing. Therefore the benefits of zero transaction costs to them will be zero. This also applies to employees of such firms. However, the removal of the 'option' to manage interest rates and taxation may well be a hindrance to many sectors in the different member states of the EU, and not just the tradable goods sector.

2 The economic environment

■ 2.1 Introduction

This chapter aims to provide you with an understanding and appreciation of the general economic environment within which business must operate and management must make decisions. It focuses mainly on macroeconomic concepts and variables, some of which you may already be familiar with from the media. In later chapters in the book you will be referred back to Chapter 2 as representing the economic environment within which managerial (micro-economic) decision making is undertaken. The overall view of an economy, presented here, therefore gives you the context and background within which to better understand managerial economics as a set of concepts, tools and techniques. The main topics addressed in the chapter are as follows:

Section 2.2   The Economic Framework
Section 2.3   A Simple Model of the Economy
Section 2.4   Using the Model
Section 2.5   The Economic Environment and Business

Since the chapter deals mainly with the general economic environment you may sometimes find it difficult to relate some of the concepts directly to your own job and organisation. However at appropriate junctures the key relationships which exist between business and the general economic environment will be pointed out and explained in some detail.

In addition you will be asked, using self-assessment questions, to identify some of the relationships yourself and to assess the strength of the connections between the general economic environment and business.

A Note of Caution
This chapter in the book utilises a number of mathematical concepts and techniques in order to enable you to better understand the nature of the relationships between macroeconomic variables. The mathematics used do not assume any previous knowledge of a high level of mathematics. They are presented clearly and in sequence to aid your understanding. It is NOT the purpose of this chapter to teach mathematics but rather to use it as a tool in economic analysis.

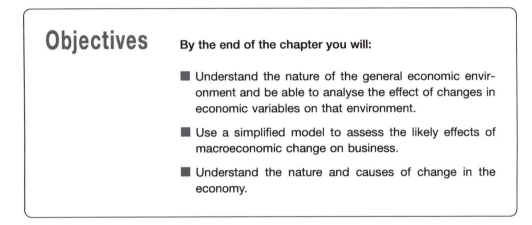

Objectives

By the end of the chapter you will:

■ Understand the nature of the general economic environment and be able to analyse the effect of changes in economic variables on that environment.

■ Use a simplified model to assess the likely effects of macroeconomic change on business.

■ Understand the nature and causes of change in the economy.

■ 2.2 The Economic Framework

Imagine the task you would face in being asked to put together the pieces of a jigsaw numbered in the millions. To make matters worse none of the pieces of this framework have a straight edge! Of course, like us you would not even know where to start and if by some stroke of luck you did manage to get started you would certainly never finish it. This is because of another feature of this particular jigsaw – its total shape and the shapes of many of its individual pieces can and do change – all the time!

What we have just described to you is probably a reasonable description of the nature of the economic environment within which you and we and billions of other people live and work. Its complexity is staggering and yet day in and day out it appears to work as if, as Adam Smith put it in 1776, it is guided by some 'invisible hand'.

How well it works for you or us or anyone else depends very much on where we live, how we earn a living and what we choose to spend our earnings on. In other words, many individuals make up the pieces of the economic framework and what each does must ultimately affect the whole picture. The economic behaviour of individuals engaged in working, consuming goods and services, saving, lending and enjoying leisure brings with it a myriad of economic consequences for themselves, others, organisations, government policy and even trade balances.

Sometimes it is difficult to see the connection between an individual action and the larger economic process but it will certainly be there, however small. By now you are probably wondering why anyone should even wish to become involved in the study of something so obviously complex.

But of course no one actually attempts to complete the framework we described earlier – instead it is simplified down into what appear to be the main pieces and once this is achieved it becomes a much easier task to put the framework together. This simplifying process unfortunately extracts a price – the loss

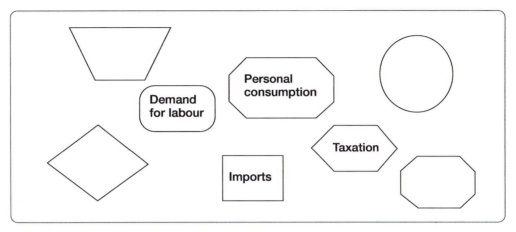

Figure 2.1   A simplified economic framework

of total accuracy. This is because, once simplified, we no longer have the true economic framework but instead as realistic a *model* of it as possible.

You have probably seen and used models of many kinds yourself. For example, the 'map' of the London underground is just a simplified represent-ation of the true layout of the system, that is, a simplified model. If you have ever had to make a journey (not necessarily by Tube) you probably made an estimate of how long the trip would take and what time you expected to arrive at your destination. In making your estimate you must have made some simpli-fying assumptions, for example constant speed, traffic levels, no breakdowns and so on. The whole process is in fact a model of the journey time.

Similarly when you plan your expenditure for a forthcoming holiday you also make estimates of how much you think you will need to spend, what your savings will be by the time the holiday comes round and how much leeway you are likely to have in terms of spare cash. Again this represents a simplifying process, loaded with assumptions and bereft of nitty-gritty detail, that is, it is just another form of model.

Constructing such models in order to help us understand the world around us is something we all do most of the time even though we are often unaware that we are actually doing it. So, how can this process of simplifying the world by constructing a model help us to simplify the complex economic framework we described earlier? As we said above, it is first necessary to identify the main pieces of the framework. We have done this in Figure 2.1 but left some pieces blank for you to fill in from the list below. Select those pieces of the framework which could reasonably be included in the simplified version (Figure 2.1):

Government spending	Investment	Exports	Labour supply
Interest rates	Price of bread	Your income	Rail fares

If you made the correct selections then you must have noticed something about both the pieces already filled in and the list above. Yes, those already filled in are very general in nature while only some in the list are general. These are: government spending, interest rates, investment, labour supply, exports.

Although the price of bread and your income are themselves important they represent only individual cases of the multitude of prices and personal incomes which exist at any one time. The crucial point about understanding the economic environment is that it can be reduced to a manageable number of important and interconnected economic variables, each of which is defined to represent the general level of what is being measured, described or analysed.

You will also have noticed in Figure 2.1 that it would be very difficult to fit together even the limited (reduced) number of pieces accurately. That is, if put together there would still remain blank spaces in-between the pieces – the spaces would represent the simplifying assumptions we have implicitly made in constructing our model of the economic environment.

But this is not a major problem since the pieces which we have included seem to represent a reasonable and sensible set of economic variables for what is, after all, meant to be a simple model.

Our model is not yet complete, however. We have to somehow make connections between each of the pieces of the framework in order to obtain as integrated a picture of the economic environment as possible so that we can begin to understand it and be able to *use* it in a sensible and meaningful way. To do this we need first establish why the pieces in our simplified economic frame-work should be connected at all. That is, we require a *theoretical justification* for their interconnection. It is only on the basis of theory that we can put these apparently unconnected pieces together. This will be done in the next section.

■ 2.3   A Simple Model of the Economy

As we said at the end of section 2.2, we need a theory to enable us to connect up the pieces of the simplified economic framework represented in Figure 2.1. This means, in practice, that we need to hypothesise about the nature of the relationships which we would expect ought to exist between these generalised economic variables. For example, it seems reasonable to hypothesise that the level of personal consumption of goods and services must, in some fashion, be related to an individual's personal disposable income *and* to the level of prices he/she must pay to obtain a given quantity of those goods and services. Immediately we can make a reasonable hypothesis:

personal consumption is a function of (that is, depends on) a person's income level and the prices he/she faces. Now, if this is true for all individuals (and there is no reason to suppose it is not) then we can make the more general statement that:

Total personal consumption in the economy is a function of the total level of income and the general price level. This is more often written in symbol form as:

$$C = f(Y, P) \qquad\qquad\qquad \text{[Eq. 2.1]}$$

which reads as … consumption (C) depends on income (Y) and prices (P). Or alternatively, consumption (C) is a function (f) of income and price levels.

The obvious question now of course is – what kind of function is represented by f? We will come to this later. In the meantime we should continue with the establishment of reasonable hypotheses for our main economic variables. Remember that labour appeared in two separate pieces of our simplified framework – the demand for labour and the supply of labour. What other pieces in the framework might these be related to?

Well, from an employer's point of view it seems reasonable to hypothesise that the demand for labour, that is, number of workers, will depend on the going wage rate for workers who have a particular skill. This wage rate will be the one which both attracts the required number of workers to an employer and retains them with that employer. Similarly the supply of labour (that is, willingness to work) will depend on the wage rate offered. So we can write that:

$$D_L = f(W) \qquad\qquad\qquad \text{[Eq. 2.2]}$$

the demand for labour depends on the wage rate and,

$$S_L = f(W) \qquad\qquad\qquad \text{[Eq. 2.3]}$$

the supply of labour depends on the wage rate.

In terms of Figure 2.1, we have identified the hypotheses that consumption is connected to income and prices and that wages (that is, incomes) are connected to the supply and demand for labour. This leaves the following economic variables to be connected up: savings, investment, interest rates, exports, imports and government spending. We would like you to try and do this with two of them.

■ ■ ■ Self-Assessment Questions ■ ■ ■ ■ ■ ■ ■ ■ ■ ■ ■ ■

Q1 Write down, in words, what you think savings and investment are related to (in Figure 2.1) and then write your answers in the format of a function. Number these functions as (4) and (5).

Q2 Do you think there may also be a connection between savings and investment? Explain what this might be.

We can now complete the connections of the three remaining economic variables in our simplified framework, that is, exports, imports and government spending. Taking exports first, it is clear that these simply represent goods and services produced in the UK but purchased by consumers living in other countries. The amount of goods and services which foreign countries buy from the UK will therefore depend (mainly) on three things – their level of income, the price of the UK good or service and the price of similar goods and services produced in their own economy or imported from other countries. We will make the simplifying assumption that currency exchange rates remain constant (under a single EU currency this is more likely).

Let us also assume that the demand for UK exports cannot be affected by anything UK firms or citizens do. Given these assumptions then exports from the UK to other countries are said to be independent of all the other variables which make up the UK's own economic environment. In our terminology, therefore, exports are not a function of anything – they are just given. This helps to make our model manageable.

■ ■ ■ Self-Assessment Questions ■ ■ ■ ■ ■ ■ ■ ■ ■ ■ ■ ■

Q3 Identify the main weakness in the statement that exports are not a function of anything (for model purposes).

Q4 Which, if any, economic variables in Figure 2.1 might exports be connected to? Are there any other factors (not in the diagram) which could influence exports?

Can we treat imports in the same way? The answer is no, since we are trying to produce a simple model of a single economy's economic environment and it has already been established that consumption is connected to income. In the same way, imported goods and services will also be connected to income since, as output in the economy rises (and so income) it follows that the UK will draw in more imported goods and services to cope. Thus we can write that

$$M = f(Y) \qquad \text{[Eq. 2.6]}$$

that is, imports to the UK depend on UK income.

(Note that your savings and investment functions are Equations 2.4 and 2.5 respectively.)

Finally we come to government spending. Can the level of this be related to any other variable in our simplified framework? Clearly the level of such spending must have an upper limit – all the incomes in the economy plus all the savings must be that upper limit! Of course no government could feasibly spend everyone else's total income and use all the savings available. Therefore the level of government spending will, in practice, be restricted to how much tax revenue the government chooses to raise plus how much it chooses to borrow at any one time.

Notice we deliberately used the word 'chooses' – this is because governments actually *choose* how much to spend on the basis of their own policies, not on the basis of income, savings or prices. These variables obviously impose limits on government spending but, fundamentally, the level of spending will depend on a government's policy programme. So, government spending can be treated in the same way as exports – it is independent of all the other variables in the framework.

We have now established the main connections within the economic framework and we are now in a position to put the pieces together in a clear and unambiguous way. That is, we can produce our simple model of the economic environment.

The level of exports and government spending, although independent of other factors, will still influence the demand for labour. This demand will in turn influence wage rates in the economy and hence the supply of labour. The outcome is the generation of incomes. Some income will be spent on consumption, some on imports and the remainder on savings from which firms will borrow to invest. The amount saved by households and the amount borrowed by firms will in turn depend on the interest rate. Note that prices themselves are influenced by interest rate levels since interest payments on borrowed funds represent a cost of production to firms.

Notice also that although prices help to determine the level of consumption in the economy they are also partly influenced by that level. Similarly government spending and investment by firms also partly influence prices. This is simply due to the fact that consumption by individuals, import spending, government spending, and investment spending all represent the demand for goods and services generated in the domestic economy. Exports from the UK economy, on the other hand, represent demand from other countries. If we add up all the sources of demand for goods and services then we get the *aggregate* level of demand in the economy. This will be composed of some of the functional relationships identified earlier, but not all.

For example, we will not include the demand for labour since this is just a consequence of the demand for goods and services which labour produces. Similarly we do not need to include savings since all savings will be invested – otherwise interest could not be earned. So, we can write down the components of *aggregate demand* in the economy as:

$$AD = C + I + G + (X - M) \qquad \text{[Eq. 2.7]}$$

where AD is aggregate demand, C is consumption, I is investment, G is government spending, X is exports and M is imports.

Notice that import demand is deducted from export demand to give net export demand, which would be negative if imports exceed exports. It follows that for the economy as a whole the following *identity* must hold:

National Income = AD = National Expenditure

Now our simple model of the economic environment is complete and we can begin to use it to help us understand why the economy behaves in the way it does and of course to relate this behaviour to business itself. But first we need to go back to our functional relationships. Can you remember what these were?

$$C = f(\ ) \quad I = f(\ ) \quad M = f(\ ) \quad D_L = f(\ ) \quad S_L = f(\ ) \quad S = f(\ )$$

In keeping with our model we need only concentrate on the first of these. Let us begin with consumption.

Imagine your own situation. Your personal consumption depends on your income and the prices you face for the goods and services you prefer to buy. If your income rises and prices stay constant then your consumption would probably rise too (and/or your savings). Similarly if your income were to fall and prices stayed constant your consumption level would probably fall or you would run down your savings to try and maintain your consumption level. If your income stayed constant but prices fell or rose the result would be the same in each case.

Now suppose your income fell to zero. Would your consumption also fall to zero? Obviously the answer is no. This is because you would maintain some (reduced) level of consumption by using savings and when they ran out you would be supported by the social welfare system – in fact you would probably need to do both at the same time! But the important point is this: even if your income fell to zero your consumption level would still be some positive amount. Only as your income rose above zero would your consumption level also rise.

This means we can treat consumption as if it were dependent on just one variable – that is, we can combine income (Y) and prices (P) to create a new economic variable (Y/P) which we will call *real income*, that is, the true purchasing power of a person's income. Thus consumption is dependent on real income which is written as

$$c = f(y) \qquad \text{[Eq. 2.8]}$$

where the lower-case letters refer to real consumption and real income. If we do not measure these variables in *real* terms (volume) then they only refer to *nominal* (monetary) units of measurement.

We have already established that even where income is zero there will still be a positive (probably minimum) level of consumption – let us describe this minimum level by a. Now we can specify the type of function which relates consumption to income and prices, that is, to real income

$$c = a + b(y)$$ [Eq. 2.9]

which says consumption is equal to a minimum amount plus some proportion of real income. What is missing from Equation 2.9? Yes, taxation! No one (legally) gets all his/her income to spend – the government sees to that! So we can rewrite Equation 2.9 more realistically by including tax. All we do is define real income to be disposable real income, that is, net of income tax. Now we get

$$c = a + b(yd)$$ [Eq. 2.10]

this is known generally as the consumption function. If we were to draw a sketch of c against yd it would look like the one illustrated in Figure 2.2.

As you can see from the sketch we have the intercept on the consumption axis at a, that is, the level of consumption when disposable real income is zero and as yd increases so does consumption. The 45° line equates every point on the consumption axis to every point on the disposable income axis. Where the consumption line cuts this 45° line we have a balance between disposable income and consumption.

Write down what you think b represents in Equation 2.10.

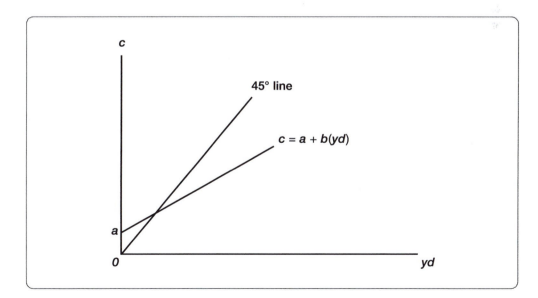

Figure 2.2   The consumption function

If you consider what we have already said about the way consumption behaves as real disposable income rises and falls and if you interpreted the sketch properly, you will have realised that the symbol b represents the proportion by which consumption rises as income rises. The 45° line should have given you the clue that b is a proportion which is less than 100 per cent, that is, the slope of the consumption function drawn from a is less than 1. This means that if income rises by 1 consumption rises by less than 1. So, we can interpret b as representing the proportionate addition to consumption arising out of increased income. The symbol b, and what it represents, is more commonly referred to as the *marginal propensity to consume* (or MPC) out of extra income. The word 'marginal' is used to refer to the fact that we are talking about increases or decreases in consumption which occur even with small increases or decreases in income.

Suppose the MPC is 80 per cent then this means that an increase in income of £1 will lead to a rise in consumption of 80 pence and an increase in income of £50 will lead to a rise in consumption of £40, that is (40/50)*100 = 80 per cent. The opposite is also generally true: if income falls by £40 then consumption will fall by £32.

But what about the other 20 per cent of an increased or reduced income? If it is not being spent on domestic or imported goods and services then it must be getting saved and therefore invested. You now should have a good understanding of the nature of consumption, that is, what controls it, and be able to use the consumption function to determine whether spending will rise and by how much given a change in income. We will now turn to another component of our aggregate demand equation – *investment* – and consider how it is related to both savings levels and the rate of interest.

We have already explained that investment levels depend on the prevailing rate of interest and that investment always equals savings. This is because at the prevailing rate of interest (that is, the price of/return from borrowing/lending money), people will plan to save a given amount and firms will plan to invest a given amount.

As interest rates fall it becomes cheaper to borrow money for investment but it also becomes less attractive to save money! So, a rate of interest will be established which finally equates the two. Suppose firms wanted to borrow an amount equal to £X for investment purposes – they could not do this unless the quantity of loanable funds (savings) at least equalled £X. If we assume savings are less than this then this can only be as a result of *low* interest rates, that is, lack of incentive to save. In order for savings to reach the level of £X the rate of interest has to rise. But as the rate of interest rises it can become too expensive for some firms, thus causing a surplus of saving over investment, and eventually the rate of interest would fall back to the equilibrium level we started with. What this simple analysis shows us is that, by definition, investment will always equal savings because the price of money (the interest rate) controls both. Therefore, at any given level of savings in the economy an equilibrium interest rate must exist. So, our equation for investment demand does not require the interest rate to be involved because it must be the case that

$$y - c = s \qquad \text{[Eq. 2.11]}$$

that is, income minus consumption equals saving and since by definition $i = s$ then $y - c = i$.

So, like export demand and government expenditure demand, investment demand is taken as given in our simple model.

Imports on the other hand tend to behave rather like consumption. Remember we said imports (M) are dependent on UK income levels. If you think about it, as income levels rise the quantity of imports into the UK will rise too – this is because people will want to buy goods and services which either are not produced at all in the UK or are preferred to the UK brand. In addition, even if consumers do spend some of their increased income on UK-produced goods the firms in the UK will need to import more raw materials and spare parts to cope. Thus, as UK income levels rise, the amount of imports must rise. It is also the case therefore that the UK needs a minimum level of imports even at zero income. That is, imports, like consumption, will still be a positive amount even at zero national income. So, we can write our import function as

$$m = d + z(y) \qquad \text{[Eq. 2.12]}$$

that is, imports in real terms (lower-case m) rise as real national income rises. The letter z represents the *marginal propensity to import*.

At this point we want to remind you of the components of aggregate demand, that is, national income. And remember that lower-case letters refer to an economic variable as being measured in real terms, that is, taking account of prices. The components are:

$c = a + b(yd)$	consumption demand equals a basic level plus a proportion of real disposable national income
$+ i$	investment demand
$+ g$	government expenditure demand
$+ x$	export demand
$+ m = d + z(y)$	import demand equals a basic level plus a proportion of real national income

Thus:

$$AD = y = c + i + g + x - m \qquad \text{[Eq. 2.13]}$$

Thus, as we said earlier, aggregate demand is identical to national income which is identical to national expenditure. The components of aggregate demand are what goes into the calculation of an economy's national accounts every year. In the next section we are going to develop a more detailed picture of our simple model of the economic environment.

■ 2.4 Using the Model

Before we look at how our simple model of the economic environment tells us how the economy behaves as any single component of aggregate demand changes, we want to introduce a slight complication while we develop a more detailed version of our model so far. The consumption function relates to real disposable national income, but aggregate demand relates to real gross national income. We want to use a single definition of real national income so we have to get rid of one of these. We will retain the gross version since this will allow us to treat taxation separately from consumption. The procedure is quite straightforward – it is just income minus total taxation. That is, $yd = y - ty$. So, we can take account of this in the consumption function as follows:

$$c = a + b(y - ty)$$ [Eq. 2.14]

where b is the MPC and t represents the taxation rate. Multiplying out the bracketed term gives:

$$c = a + by - bty$$ [Eq. 2.15]

which reads as: consumption equals a basic level plus some proportion of gross real income minus some proportion of gross real income. For example, suppose real national income in 1998 (using 1990 as a base year) is £400 billion, the MPC is 80 per cent (that is, 0.8) and the tax rate is 25 per cent (that is, 0.25) – this includes all allowances and national insurance). Let us also suppose that the basic consumption level a is £60 billion.

Then consumption demand, that is, consumer spending, will be:

$$c = 60 + (0.8 * 400) - (0.8 * 0.25) * 400$$
$$= 60 + 320 - 0.2 * 400$$
$$= 380 - 80$$
$$= 300$$

that is, consumption is £300 billion.

So, out of a real national income of £400 billion consumers spend £300 billion, the government takes £80 billion in taxation and £20 billion remains.

■ ■ ■ Self-Assessment Question ■ ■ ■ ■ ■ ■ ■ ■ ■ ■ ■ ■ ■

Q5   Explain what it means if the MPC is equal to 1 and 0.1 respectively.

The above example illustrates another important point. Real national income (y) must equal the total value of aggregate demand, that is, it must equal the expenditure represented by all the sources of aggregate demand if the economy is to be in balance between the demand for goods and services and the income available to be spent on those goods and services. This level of real national income which is just sufficient to enable aggregate demand to be met is called the *equilibrium level of national income*. We can use our aggregate demand equation to find this level and to find out by how much it will change if any of the components change. Remember that AD = $y = c + i + g + x - m$ [Eq. 2.13]. We will write this out in full now by replacing c and m with their respective equations. This gives:

$$y = (a + by - bty) + i + g + x - (d + zy)$$ [Eq. 2.16]

and collecting all the common terms on each side, that is, we want the terms which include y on one side and the terms which do not include y on the other, we get:

$$y - by + bty + zy = a + i + g + x - d$$ [Eq. 2.17]

and to simplify this we need only factor out the ys on the left-hand side to give:

$$y(1 - b + bt + z) = a + i + g + x - d$$ [Eq. 2.18]

You can check this for yourself by multiplying the terms in the bracket in Equation 2.18 by y and this brings you back again to Equation 2.17. Now, we want to make national income y the subject of the analysis so we can rearrange this last expression to get our final equation which connects the main pieces of the economic framework and gives us our simple model in mathematical terms:

$$\bar{y} = \frac{a + i + g + x - d}{(1 - b) + bt + z}$$ [Eq. 2.19]

Notice we put a bar (–) over the y. This is to indicate that y is the *equilibrium* value of real national income. Equation 2.19 represents our simplified economic environment in symbols. We are going to use Equation 2.19 and the graphs associated with it to analyse first what happens to the economy when any of the aggregate demand components change, and second to relate such events to their possible impact on the business industry. This will be done in the next section.

■ ■ ■ **Self-Assessment Question** ■ ■ ■ ■ ■ ■ ■ ■ ■ ■ ■ ■

Q6

(a) Why is consumption positive even when income is zero?

(b) Why is the marginal propensity to consume less than 1?

(c) If we subtract the MPC from 1 what should we call the number which remains?

(d) What is measured by the slope of the consumption function in Figure 2.2?

Using the simple model of the economic environment we want you to consider Equation 2.19 carefully – after all it *is* our model of the economic environment. First, consider the components of aggregate demand in the numerator (that is, the elements *a*, *i*, *g*, *x* and *d*).

Together or individually some of these could change, thus causing a change in real national income. But they can change independently of each other and are often referred to as the *autonomous* components of aggregate demand. This means they can change independently of the level of national income. So they are the variables in the model. The denominator of Equation 2.19 contains only three elements, the MPC (*b*), the tax rate (*t*) and the marginal propensity to import out of extra income (*z*). Each of these is known as a parameter, that is, they control by how much national income will change given a change in

Table 2.1   Variables and parameters of the model

Variable/parameter	Definition	Changeable
a	Autonomous consumption demand	No*
i	Investment demand	Yes
g	Government expenditure demand	Yes
x	Export demand	Yes
d	Minimum import demand	No*
z	Marginal propensity to import	No*
t	Taxation rate	Yes
b	Marginal propensity to consume	No*

* Only changeable in the longer term

any of the autonomous components of aggregate demand. The parameters of our model are fixed. Table 2.1 sets out which elements are changeable in the national income model.

Only over long periods of time do all the elements in Table 2.1 change. In terms of the foreseeable future (which is quite short in economic terms) only four are subject to any significant change. Nevertheless, taken together, it is easy to see why the behaviour of a whole economy is subject to much fluctuation – even in our simple model four of the eight elements of the model are subject to change!

■ ■ ■ Self-Assessment Question ■ ■ ■ ■ ■ ■ ■ ■ ■ ■ ■

Q7 Explain the effect on national income given:

(a) a rise in autonomous export demand

(b) a rise in taxation rates

(c) a fall in government expenditure

(d) a fall in investment spending

(e) a rise in investment spending and a fall in export demand

(f) a rise in interest rates.

Now we can consider an example of the model at work. We will use a numerical example and we will also be asking you to undertake some numerical work given a series of changes in the components of aggregate demand. Imagine an economy with the following levels of its main economic aggregates:

(Note: B = billions of £)

$c = 257.9B$ $i = 48.4B$ $g = 66.9B$

$x = 80.6B$ $m = 101.4B$

So, AD in this economy amounts to 351.7B.

Assume the MPC is around 88 per cent so b will take the value 0.88 and the MPI is 28 per cent, so z will take the value 0.28. The average tax rate is about 21 per cent so t will have the value 0.21. Before we can show whether or not the model described in Equation 2.19 works we still have to find the value of a in the consumption function. We know the values of c, y, b and t so to find a we will just substitute these values into the consumption function. Remember the consumption function is written as $c = a + by - bty$, thus:

$257.2 = 0.88 * 351.7 - (0.88 * .21) * 351.7 + a$

$257.2 = 309.5 - 65.00 + a$

$257.2 = 244.5 + a$

Hence $a = 12.7$

Now we need to find the value of d in the import function. Remember $m = d + z(y)$, thus:

$101.4 = 0.28 * 351.7 + d$

$101.4 = 98.48 + d$

Hence $d = 2.92$

Now we can put all the data into Equation 2.19 to check if in fact national income is sufficient to support the level of aggregate demand in this economy:

$$351.7 = \frac{12.7 + 48.4 + 66.9 + 80.6 - 2.92}{(1 - 0.88) + 0.88 * 0.21 + 0.28}$$

$$351.7 = \frac{205.68}{0.5848} = 351.7$$

Quite clearly the level of national income is sufficient to meet all the sources of aggregate demand and equally clearly our simple model works well! Of course it is no accident that national income should equal aggregate demand since, by definition, they are the same thing.

■ ■ ■ Self-Assessment Question ■ ■ ■ ■ ■ ■ ■ ■ ■ ■ ■ ■

Q8 What would be the equilibrium level of national income by the end of the following year if:

(a) Exports rose by 10 per cent, average taxation fell to 16 per cent and investment fell by 20 per cent at the start of the year?

(b) The MPI rose to 32 per cent at the start of the year?

(c) The MPC fell to 80 per cent at the start of the year?

We can now look at the national income data more closely. This will help you to further understand the nature of the main variables in the economic environment. Is there a connection between changes in any of the autonomous components of aggregate demand and subsequent changes in its level? This is a key question for economic policy and clearly for business planning.

There is indeed – a change to aggregate demand will result in a new level of national income which is exactly 3.28 times the change to demand in each case. To see why this should be the case let us return to our simplified model.

When we are only dealing with consumption and investment together and not including g, x or m then the model simply becomes:

$$y = \frac{a + i}{(1-b) + bt} = \frac{12.7 + 48.4}{(1-0.88) + 0.88 * .21} = \frac{61.1}{0.3048} = 200.46B \qquad \text{[Eq. 2.20]}$$

Now, if we rearrange the above as

$$y = \frac{1}{(1-b) + bt} * (a + i) \text{ then we get } y = \frac{61.1}{0.3048} = 200.46B \qquad \text{[Eq. 2.21]}$$

that is, it is just the same equation and it gives the same answer. We can simplify it even further to get:

$$\bar{y} = \frac{1}{0.3048} * 61.1 \text{ and so } y = 3.28 * 61.1 = 200.46B$$

Thus, the elements $1/[(1 - b) + bt]$ have the value 3.28. Now let us see if we get the same answer when we add $g + (x - m) = 46.1$. In this case the model becomes:

$$y = \frac{a + i + g + (x-m)}{(1-b) + bt} = \frac{12.7 + 48.4 + 46.1}{0.3048} = \frac{107.2}{0.3048} = 351.7B \qquad \text{[Eq. 2.22]}$$

which is just the same as: $y = 3.28 * 107.2 = 351.7B$ and $46.1 * 3.28 = 151.66B$ which is the *addition* to national income over the 200.46B calculated above.

This number has therefore multiplied the addition to aggregate demand in each case to give the higher level of national income which we observe in the calculations. For this reason it is known as the *expenditure/tax multiplier*. But we want you to notice something about the above equation – it treats imports (m) as if they were similar to exports, that is, just given and not in fact as a function of national income.

We already know that imports are a function of national income and we took explicit note of that fact in developing our simplified model, that is, Equation 2.19. So, if we go back to our complete model, that is to treating imports as a function of national income will we get the same multiplier effect? The answer is no, since imports represent a *withdrawal* of demand from the UK economy and therefore any increase in AD will not result in such a large multiplying effect on national income as 3.28. What will the effect be? Using Equation 2.19 we can find out. Remember our model (Equation 2.19) says that:

$$\bar{y} = \frac{a + i + g + x - d}{(1 - b) + bt + z}$$

and if we rearrange this in the way we did above we get:

$$\bar{y} = \frac{1}{(1 - b) + bt + z} * (a + i + g + x - d) \qquad \text{[Eq. 2.23]}$$

Now if we put our values for the MPC, t and the MPI and for the sources of autonomous aggregate demand into the equation we get:

$$\bar{y} = \frac{1}{(1 - 0.88) + 0.88 * 0.21 + 0.2} * (12.7 + 48.4 + 66.9 + 80.6 - 2.92)$$

$$= \frac{1}{0.5848} * 205.68 = 1.71 * 205.68 = 351.7B$$

Now the value of the multiplier is only 1.71! This is because it now includes the MPI which has the effect of reducing the multiplying effect of a rise in AD. Let us summarise what all this means: if there is no taxation in the economy or imports then the multiplier will simply be:

$$k_1 = \frac{1}{1 - b} \quad \text{(the expenditure multiplier)}$$

If taxation is introduced the multiplier will be:

$$k_2 = \frac{1}{(1-b) + bt} \quad \text{(the expenditure/tax multiplier)}$$

And if imports are introduced and hence the MPI the multiplier will be:

$$k_3 = \frac{1}{(1-b) + bt + z} \quad \text{the open economy multiplier}$$

Where k is the symbol for the multiplier and the subscripts refer to the type of multiplier it represents. Quite obviously, the higher the multiplier then the greater the increase in national income resulting from an increase in any of the components of autonomous aggregate demand, that is, $[a + i + g + x - d]$. Now since the UK is most definitely an *open* economy, that is, it imports and exports, then the relevant multiplier must be k_3, that is, the open economy multiplier.

■ ■ ■ Self-Assessment Question ■ ■ ■ ■ ■ ■ ■ ■ ■ ■ ■ ■

Q9 Use k_3 to calculate the effect on real national income of the events below, assuming our imaginary economy is the UK. Do this as one change followed by the other:

(a) a rise in investment of 12B

(b) a fall in exports of 30B

(c) a rise in government spending of 10B

(d) a rise in autonomous consumption of 10B.

Now we want briefly to summarise what we have said in the last few pages:

1. Personal consumption (*c*) out of real national income (*y*) rises as real national income rises, and the amount by which it rises depends on the marginal propensity to consume (*b*).

2. Government spending, investment spending and export demand are all independent of the level of real national income, but a change in any of these will affect the future level of real national income.

3. Import demand (*m*) rises as real national income rises. The amount by which import demand rises is dependent on the marginal propensity to import (*z*).

4. Three different multipliers have been identified, but in an open economy such as the UK it is always the open economy multiplier which is relevant.

5. The multiplier acts to increase national income by more than the increase in any one of the components of autonomous AD.

Now that we have used our model to investigate how the economy behaves in very general terms we think it is time to use it for a more specific purpose: to analyse change at the economy-wide level and to relate such change to business.

■ 2.5   The Economic Environment and Business

What follows by no means covers all the relationships which exist or may exist between the macroeconomic environment and business, but it will allow you to see in more detail how the two interconnect through some of the main

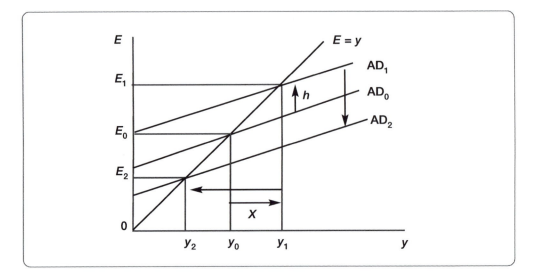

Figure 2.3   Output effects of changes in government spending

economic variables already discussed above. We will use a more general scenario first in order to let you get a 'feel' for the kind of analysis which can be more specifically applied to most sectors of business.

Suppose that a single event occurs – the government begins to increase its spending on social welfare provision because it has accumulated a larger than expected budget surplus (that is, its tax revenue is bigger than planned expenditure) and politically it believes this is the appropriate thing to do with the unexpected surplus money. Thus the tax rate itself does not have to change to fund the extra expenditure.

What does our model of the economic environment predict will be the likely outcome for real national income? We will not use numbers this time but rather a sketch of the situation (Figure 2.3). In this diagram we have drawn the AD line *prior* to the increase in government spending as AD_0, corresponding to the equilibrium real national income of y_0 and real national expenditure (that is, AD) of E_0.

So, the economy is in equilibrium since the level of aggregate demand reflected in the expenditure level of E_0 is supported by the level of national income, y_0. But once the government spends the extra amount on social welfare the AD line will shift vertically upwards to AD_1 which is consistent with a new (higher) level of national income and expenditure – at E_1, y_1. Note we have dispensed with the bar (–) above y since by now you should know that any level of y associated with the 45° line is an equilibrium level as long as it intersects with the AD line.

Now in moving to y_1 national income has risen by the amount (X) which is greater than the increase in government spending (h) – this of course is just the multiplier at work again. So, with the extra money pouring into the pockets of many consumers they obviously will spend as much as their MPC dictates.

This higher spending will raise the demand for labour to produce the extra goods and services and to distribute and retail them. This is essentially what the multiplier does. In the process almost everyone connected to the economic framework experiences a rise in incomes so national income rises. The move to AD_1 then is the first effect. But what is AD_2? Do you remember what the demand and supply for labour depended on? Yes – wage rates. Now if the demand for labour rises because consumption is rising as a result of more money in the economy, the effect is for the price of that labour to be pulled up since the supply of labour will not rise unless the wage rate rises. You already know that the DL is a negative function of wages so as wages are pulled up generally the DL will eventually begin to fall since the higher wages will feed into prices and consumer demand will begin to fall back again. The effect on the demand for labour could be even greater if wage rates refuse to fall back to their previous level – people do not like a wage cut.

If this happens then total employment could be less than it was before the extra government spending. This effect combined with higher prices must therefore reduce consumer spending and so aggregate demand falls to AD_2. The amount by which y rises in the first instance and falls in the second depends on the size of the multiplier and on the ability of firms to adjust to increases or decreases in AD in a relatively short period of time. For example, increases in productivity during the period of instability could help to absorb the higher wage costs and so offset the need to raise prices. Unfortunately, not all firms operate in circumstances which make this kind of adjustment possible.

■ ■ ■ Application Exercise ■ ■ ■ ■ ■ ■ ■ ■ ■ ■ ■ ■ ■ ■

Using your knowledge of how national income is likely to react to any given change in autonomous demand undertake the following. Sketch and explain the outcome of the following events:

(a) a rise in exports

(b) an increase in investment followed by a rise in autonomous imports.

Note: Put your answers on separate paper and keep them for future reference.

You can by now see that a single economic event, working through the multiplier effect, can have both positive and negative effects on the value of real national income. Clearly the business sector is not immune from these effects, but it is still worthwhile for you to analyse more closely the main connections between business and the economic environment as a whole. Before doing so it is sensible to identify those components of aggregate demand which are likely to exert a rapid and significant effect on business if they were to change. So, which components of aggregate demand will fall into this category? It seems reasonable to suppose that changes in personal consumption will have a rapid and significant effect on business, since a downturn in high street spending is very quickly evident in the build-up of stock at both retail and wholesale centres. The level of saving in the economy will also be important to business – if people are saving more then they are also spending less – assuming incomes have not risen enough to allow them to raise both saving and consumption.

As you already know, if interest rates rise then many consumers may prefer to save rather than spend and so will actually reduce their spending. Alternatively, if interest rates fall this will encourage some people to borrow more and increase their spending. So, we will concentrate on the effect of consumption, savings, and interest rate changes on business.

Two of these variables are components of AD (that is, consumption and saving) while the third is the price of money (that is, interest rates). Remember that saving is a component of AD since it is identical to investment, that is, $y = c + s$ and $s = i$ therefore $y = c + i$. Now we can investigate how business is likely to be affected by changes in these important economic variables. Once again, we will base the analysis on a sketch (Figure 2.4). As the vehicle for the analysis we will consider the possible impact on business of a series of changes in consumption over time. In graphs (A) and (B) the vertical axis represents

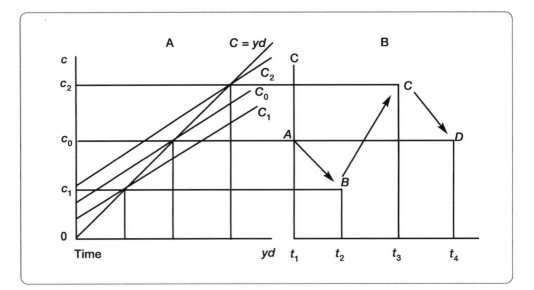

Figure 2.4   Business effect of a rise in interest rates

consumer expenditure, while the horizontal axis in graph (A) measures disposable income but in (B) it measures time. Thus in graph (B) what we have is consumer spending per period of time, for example quarterly periods in a year.

Beginning at the initial consumption line c_0 at time (t_0) consumer spending is equal to A. Now, suppose an increase in interest rates occurs – this will have the effect of raising savings and hence reducing consumption at every level of disposable income. So the consumption line will shift down to its new position of (c_1). As a result consumer spending will fall rapidly to B between period t_1 and t_2. The effect on retail firms could be quite marked, while it will simply be a matter of time before the wholesale and manufacturing sectors experience the same (negative) effect.

Now, suppose the government is particularly worried about the negative multiplier effect on employment in the economy as a whole – it wishes to avoid any short-term rise in the unemployment figures – and so decides to remove current restrictions on hire-purchase agreements. In addition to this the banking sector may have relaxed repayment terms while the retail sector would be competing fiercely for the attentions of consumers. These would have the combined effect of enabling or persuading more consumers, even at the higher interest rates, to borrow more and so consumption would rise again. This is represented now by the upward move of the consumption line to c_2 and the sharp rise in consumer spending to c between period t_2 and t_3. This, however, is a much larger effect than the government may have wished for since it could put upward pressure on prices and as a result the hire-purchase restrictions are quickly reintroduced. In graph (A) this is observed in the consumption line moving back to its original equilibrium, that is, it is line c_0 once again, and retail sales fall back to their original level at point D by the start of period t_4. Note that the original levels being restored is just a consequence of the way we have drawn the consumption lines. There is no particular reason why they should be restored. All of this time the wholesale and manufacturing sectors are experiencing the same fluctuations in terms of retail sector demand for stock and we could easily observe this in a similar graphs to graph (B), the only difference being that the wholesale graph and the manufacturing graph would be shifted to the right in terms of time. This is a key issue for supply chain management, that is, how to plan for and meet fluctuations in consumer spending. The main point about the above analysis is that it reveals how fluctuations in retail sales can occur and why they are related to changes in certain economic variables such as consumption and interest rates.

We have completed our economic framework, found the factors which relate one part to another and used our resulting (although simplified) model of the economic environment to better understand how the system works as a whole and how and why it will have significant effects on the business sector. In Chapter 3 you will study how the key variables within the economic model above can be measured to analyse economic performance and its relationship to business performance.

❑ ❑ ❑ End of Chapter SUMMARY ❑ ❑ ❑ ❑ ❑ ❑ ❑ ❑ ❑ ❑

In this chapter there are a number of key concepts and relationships you should now be familiar with. In particular:

■ The nature of an economic model

■ Functional relationships

■ Aggregate demand

■ The consumption function

■ Marginal propensity to consume

■ The multiplier

■ Autonomous components of aggregate demand

■ National Income

In addition you should be able to relate the behaviour of the above to their impacts on business and to use the theoretical concepts learned to critically analyse the implications for firms in the economy of significant changes in economic policy as they operate through these variables. Further, you should also be in a position to critically assess such impacts given the implicit (and explicit) assumptions which are themselves a key element in the models studied in the chapter.

■ ■ ■ ANSWERS to Self-Assessment Questions ■ ■ ■ ■ ■ ■

In some cases the answers given below are detailed while others are general outlines. Do not worry if your answer does not appear as detailed as some of those below. You should consider the answers below as an integral part of your study of the text. It is very important that you take time to think about the answers given below.

Q1   People save and firms invest in order to raise their future consumption levels. This can only be achieved where interest is accruable on the amount saved or a return is expected on the amount invested. Thus, saving will be dependent on the rate of interest available. Similarly, investment will only proceed if a return is expected. Since firms often borrow for investment purposes it follows that the return on the investment must at least equal the cost of borrowing, that is, the interest rate. Even where investment funds come from retained profit the interest rate is still important, since firms will not invest in projects which do not give a return which is at least equal to the rate of interest. So, investment also depends on the rate of interest. Thus,

$$S = f(r) \quad \text{[as } r \text{ rises } S \text{ rises]} \qquad \text{[Eq. 2.4]}$$
$$I = f(r) \quad \text{[as } r \text{ rises } I \text{ falls]} \qquad \text{[Eq. 2.5]}$$

Q2   Yes, since saving equals the amount left after consumption and all saving must be invested (if interest is to be accrued), it follows that the amount saved will, by definition, always equal the amount invested. That is, $S = I$.

Q3   The obvious weakness is that since UK imports are deemed in the model to be a function of UK income it follows that UK exports will be a function of the income of the countries the UK exports to. That is, UK exports represent part of other countries' imports. This, however, is not the main weakness in the statement since we do not include other countries' income in the model. The main weakness is simply that the statement itself is a gross simplification of reality, even in terms of our simplified model.

Q4   UK domestic price levels and the supply of labour to exporters in the UK will clearly affect the level of exports the UK can supply. This is because higher domestic prices feed into export prices, while if the price of labour is too 'low' labour supply to all sectors, including the export sector, will be reduced. Additionally, if demand in the domestic economy grows rapidly, exporters may direct their output at the domestic economy because it is easier to deal with. So domestic price levels, labour supply and domestic income levels will influence the level of exports achieved. Other factors not in Figure 2.1 include: the sterling exchange rate with the UK's main trading partners, the perceived 'quality' of UK goods and the effectiveness of export marketing.

Q5   When the MPC = 1 this means every penny of every extra £ of income will be consumed. Thus there will be zero saving out of extra income. When the MPC = 0.1 only 10 pence in every extra £ of income will be consumed, while the remaining 90 pence is saved. This degree of saving is highly unusual, even among very rich consumers!

Q6   (a) Even at zero income the desired level of consumption is positive since consumers require some 'minimum' level of consumption. This is usually financed out of prior saving (that is, consumption via dissaving) and/or via social welfare funding.

(b) The MPC is always less than 1 simply because in the economy as a whole the number of people who do not need to or wish to spend all extra income outnumber those who do. Hence, the MPC for the economy as a whole is just the average of the MPC for each individual.

(c) The marginal propensity to save.

(d) The MPC.

Q7

(a) National income will rise.

(b) National income will fall.

(c) National income will fall.

(d) National income will fall.

(e) The outcome for national income in this case depends on two things – first the magnitude of the increase in investment spending as compared with the fall in export demand and second, the proportionate share of investment demand relative to export demand in aggregate demand.

(f) If interest rates rise then the demand for saving will rise so consumption will fall. But the level of planned investment also falls since the cost of borrowing has risen. The final effect on national income will definitely be a negative one. The extent to which national income will fall in such circumstances depends crucially on the strength of reaction by consumers and firms alike to the rise in interest rates.

Q8

(a) $204.06/0.5408 = 377.33B$

(b) $205.68/0.6248 = 329.19B$

(c) $205.68/0.648 = 317.41B$

Q9

(a) Real national income rises to 372.22B.

(b) It now falls to 320.92B.

(c) It now rises to 338B.

(d) Now it rises to 341.42B.

3 Measuring economic performance

■ 3.1   Introduction

This chapter aims to provide you with an understanding of how the general economic perfor-mance of an economy can be measured and analysed and how such performance is directly linked to business performance. The main topics addressed in the chapter are as follows:

Section 3.2   Measurement of Economic Variables
Section 3.3   Macroeconomic Performance Indicators
Section 3.4   Business and Macroeconomic Performance

At appropriate junctures the key relationships which exist between economic performance and business will be pointed out and explained in some detail.

In addition you will be asked to provide an analysis of some of the key performance indicators yourself and to assess the relevance of these to your own organisation. This will help you to better understand the particular role of your own organisation and the many day-to-day and year-to-year problems it faces as part of a much larger economic process.

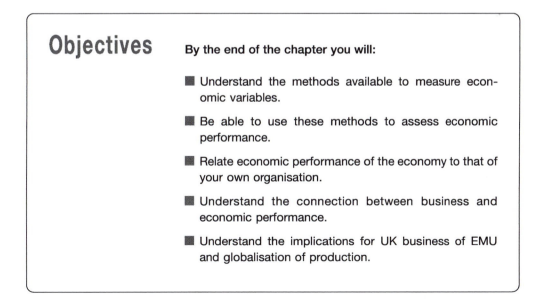

Objectives

By the end of the chapter you will:

■ Understand the methods available to measure econ-omic variables.

■ Be able to use these methods to assess economic performance.

■ Relate economic performance of the economy to that of your own organisation.

■ Understand the connection between business and economic performance.

■ Understand the implications for UK business of EMU and globalisation of production.

■ 3.2 Measurement of Economic Variables

We now know that changes in the level of any of the components of aggregate demand will lead to changes in national income as explained in Chapter 2. It is clearly important that any such change is measurable in a reliable and consistent way since information of this type can be used to inform decision makers in both business and government.

Changes in the main macroeconomic variables such as imports, exports, employment and national income are usually measured in percentage terms per period of time – normally over a quarter or a full year. When measured this way it is possible (to some extent) to infer whether a new trend is beginning or recent trends are continuing. From such inference it is then possible to make informed estimates of the economy's future prospects and that of many sectors of business. For this reason economic and business forecasting is itself a big business!

You will be concerning yourself with statistical analysis and forecasting in later parts of the text, but for now we want to concentrate on one of the more important ways by which economic variables are measured. Economic data are usually presented in one of three forms (and sometimes in all three):

■ Absolute numbers

■ Percentage changes

■ Index numbers

We want to concentrate on the last one since an absolute number and a percentage change do not need much explaining. In many instances an economic quantity (for example national income) is of such a magnitude that writing it as an absolute number is not always the best way to engage the reader! But there is another reason why economic quantities are not always expressed as absolute numbers.

The movement in many economic variables needs to be considered over time, and since many such variables are expressed in monetary terms it is often the case that they can grow substantially because prices rise over time.

This makes it very difficult to effectively express what is happening to a variable over a long period of time without getting into percentage changes of the order of thousands and/or graphs which simply look ridiculous and do not properly reflect the true change which has been occurring.

This is mainly due to the fact that many economic variables can be expressed in *nominal* or *real* terms. You will remember that we have already made this distinction in discussing national income – in fact it can be made of any economic variable which is measured using money as the mode of measurement.

More specifically we can define what is meant by nominal and real:

■ The nominal measurement of an economic variable is where the variable is expressed in terms of its price at the time the variable is measured.

■ The real measurement of an economic variable is where the variable is expressed in terms of *constant* prices, that is, its nominal magnitude has been adjusted to remove price inflation relative to a specific date.

As an example consider the data in Figure 3.1 which describes the value of exports to the UK economy over a number of years.

Clearly there is major disagreement between the two sets of trends yet they are measuring the same variable – the value of UK exports. There are two ways we can consider these data: have these exports risen or fallen between 1972 and 1997 in nominal terms or in real terms? As you can see, if we were only to concern ourselves with the nominal measurement the answer is that they have risen substantially – in fact by over 1200 per cent!

Such a rise would obviously cause the UK-based producers to be jubilant since it appears to indicate that home-produced goods for export have been providing and winning the competition in the UK's major export markets. In fact these nominal data tell no such story! Quite the opposite in fact – if we deduct UK inflation from the nominal data we get a true picture of the economy's export performance over 25 years and it is not a particularly good one. At best the UK has only managed to 'hold on' to a very average export growth performance during this period.

Over the 25-year period, measured in real terms, the UK has only managed to expand exports by an average of 1.12 per cent per annum. This compares,

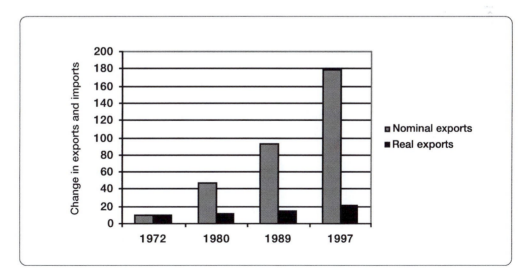

Figure 3.1   Nominal and real exports
Source: Economic Review (various years)

over the same 25 years, with an average per annum growth in the value of real imports to the UK of 1.62 per cent – that is, an extra growth factor of half a percentage point every year!

So, in this case the nominal indicator reveals a trend which is nothing like the real indicator!

■ ■ ■ Self-Assessment Question ■ ■ ■ ■ ■ ■ ■ ■ ■ ■ ■ ■

Q1 Explain in your own words what is meant by the term 'real' in economics.

■■■

As identified above, the difference between the two is entirely accounted for by the price inflation which occurred between 1972 and 1997. By removing the price inflation from the nominal data we get an indicator of the change in the physical volume of these exports – that is, the actual quantity of these exports has definitely risen over the period although not in any substantial manner.

The question now is this: how did we arrive at the real data? We used an index of the average price level in the economy taking the year 1972 as our reference or base year. That is, we expressed the value of exports between 1972 and 1997 in terms of the average price level which existed in 1972.

You will have come across this index before – it is called the *retail price index* (RPI) – and it measures price inflation in the economy as a whole over specified periods of time using a chosen base year. Strictly speaking, we should have used another index number known as the GDP deflator; however, this is so close to the RPI that, for measurement purposes, it does not make much difference at all.

The RPI is the key inflation indicator for any economy so it is best to use that in such calculations. The RPI (base year = 1987) in each of the years is shown in Table 3.1.

Table 3.1   Retail price index

Year	RPI	Year	RPI
1988	104.9	1993	138.2
1989	113.1	1994	141.6
1990	123.8	1995	146.0
1991	131.1	1996	150.3
1992	136.0	1997	155.8

What the RPI is saying is that you could buy goods in 1987 to the value of £1 which would cost £1.56 in 1997. That is, the pound has lost 36 pence of its purchasing power over that period. This is calculated as follows:

£1 * (100/155.8) = 0.64

This simply means that £1 in 1997 is only worth 64 pence in 1997 compared with 1987. Another way of interpreting this is that 64 pence in 1997 would buy £1 worth of goods in 1987.

In order to convert a nominal variable to a real one all we do is use a very simple formula known as the constant price equation:

$$\text{Nominal value in year } t * \left(\frac{\text{RPI base year}}{\text{RPI current year}} \right) = \text{real value in year } t$$

The RPI in any base year chosen is always given the number 100 – not 100 pence or 100 anything – just the pure number. This means we can substitute values for imports, exports, wages, profits and numerous economic variables into the constant price equation above and convert all the nominal values to real ones. That is, we can get a true picture of the performance of a whole economy, individual sectors and also companies in terms of economic value produced relative to any selected period of time.

To highlight the importance of removing price inflation we have provided Table 3.2 which you can think about. It describes the purchasing power of the pound in relation to various base years where the value of the pound is equivalent to 100 pence.

From the table: compared to 1900, the purchasing power of the pound in 1998 was only 1.6 pence but compared to 1978 it was 38.9 pence. You can use this table to find out what your wages are worth today, or what your holiday costs or your living room carpet (!) compared to previous years. It can be fun but also sometimes depressing!

Table 3.2   Purchasing power of the pound relative to various years

	1900	1938	1958	1978	1988	1998
1900	100					
1938	58.6	100				
1958	20.9	35.7	100			
1978	5.2	8.8	24.6	100		
1988	2.4	4.1	11.6	46.7	100	
1998	1.6	3.4	9.7	38.9	65.3	100

The RPI is therefore very important in establishing whether an economic variable measured in terms of money is rising, falling or staying constant.

The RPI is constructed from the average household's expenditure pattern in a typical week of the year. The cost of the 'basket of goods and services' bought by the average household is recorded and compared with the cost one month or one year later of the same basket of goods. If the cost has risen, then inflation has occurred in the intervening period.

Now, as we said above, some goods and services take a much higher proportion of total weekly expenditure than others, so price rises in these will affect consumption more and also have a greater effect on the RPI. The proportion which an item takes of total expenditure is referred to as a weight and in the UK in 1997 the weights for the main items were as follows:

Items

Food	0.192	Transport	0.158
Housing	0.152	Clothing and footwear	0.076
Services	0.064	Durable household goods	0.066

Not all the things that a household buys are included in the above table (for reasons of space), but once everything is included the weights will add up to 1 – that is, 100 per cent. Now, suppose on 1 January 1997 the average household spent £144 per week on goods and services (including rent and so on), and that the following price rises occurred between then and 31 December 1997:

| Food | 15% | Housing | 10% |
| Services | 22% | Transport | 12% |

Assume everything else has not risen in price at all during the period. By how much has the cost of living risen for the average household overall? All we need do is multiply the percentage price rise by the relevant weights and we will find out. Thus:

$$[\text{Food: } 0.192 * 0.15 + \text{Housing: } 0.152 * 0.1 + \text{Services: } 0.064 * 0.22$$
$$+ \text{Transport: } 0.158 * 0.12] = 7.7 \text{ per cent}$$

and the total increase in the cost of living is 7.7 per cent and the weekly expenditure on the same basket of goods is now £155.09. Notice that if you were simply to take the average of all the price rises this would give a total increase of 14.75 per cent! Hence the importance of the weights in constructing the RPI. Now, how do we get our pure index numbers?

We know that the expenditure per week on 1 January 1997 was £144 so, since we want 1997 as our base year, we simply let £144 equal 100 – not £100, just 100 as a number. The total rise in the cost of living is 7.7 per cent so if we multiply 100 by this percentage we get the index for 31 December 1997 as 107.7. To check this we can use the constant price formula:

155.09 * (100/107.7) = 144

and sure enough, the same basket of goods and services one year earlier would have been 7.7 per cent cheaper to buy. Thus, retail price inflation during the year has been 7.7 per cent, resulting in a reduction in the purchasing power of the pound. Quite clearly if this is how inflation affects households then it must also affect business in exactly the same way. That is, the operating costs for firms will change substantially/minimally if an input price rises, but that input represents a *high/minimal* proportion of total costs.

Since total costs are just the sum of all input costs it follows that the actual change in total costs as a result of a change in some of the inputs will be a weighted sum of those input cost changes. Mathematically this can be written as:

$$\Delta\% \, C = \sum_{i=1}^{N} \% \, \Delta p_i * S_{c,i}$$

The equation states that the total percentage change in total costs is equal to the addition of any percentage change in the price of input i ($-p_i$) multiplied by input i's current share ($S_{c,i}$) of total costs. If a firm has 10 main inputs to production and three of these experience an increase in cost then the calculation would be:

Input i_1: current share = 15% and change in price = +10%
Input i_2: current share = 30% and change in price = +7%
Input i_3: current share = 12% and change in price = −5%

and inputs 4 to 10 remain unchanged.

% ΔC = (0.15 * 0.1) + (0.3 * 0.07) − (0.12 * 0.05) = 4.2

If we were simply to average out the input price rises we would get $(10 + 7 - 5)/3$ = 4 per cent. Notice that this is only two percentage points less than the cost allocation equation above. This is a small difference in percentage terms but could be highly significant in monetary terms: for example 4 per cent of a total annual cost of £100,000 is not much less than 4.2 per cent but it is considerably less if the annual costs are £10m. The RPI base year is usually changed every 5 years in the UK to take account of changes in consumption patterns which are occurring all the time as new products and services reach the market and as tastes change.

We have spent considerable time on the difference between nominal and real variables and in explaining the RPI, because the real/nominal distinction and index numbers generally are important concepts and tools for measuring change in the economy and are indispensable in any attempt to measure economic performance of both the economy and individual sectors or of individual businesses.

■ ■ ■ Self-Assessment Question ■ ■ ■ ■ ■ ■ ■ ■ ■ ■ ■ ■

Q2 Why is the use of index numbers necessary in measuring economic variables?

A key question which arises, however, is how performance should be measured – that is, what indicators are relevant and the most useful for a clear analysis of the performance of the economy as a whole or of the business sector in relation to the economy? These can be divided neatly into two broad categories of performance measurement: macroeconomic (the economy) and microeconomic (firms). Clearly these two sets of performance measurement will be interconnected, but it is nevertheless useful to identify key indicators within each. These provide analysts with the type of information needed to form forecasts and 'views' of the likely future performance of the economy as a whole and of individual firms within it. Both types of analysis are very important for policy decisions and act as key information for shareholders and potential investors. For these reasons the business of analysing stock market trends, company prospects and general economic prospects has become an industry in itself. First we can look at indicators relevant to the performance of the economy as a whole.

■ 3.3 Macroeconomic Performance Indicators

What is good and what is bad performance in an economy? This appears a very straightforward question but in fact it begs many other questions. For example, one sector of an economy may be booming in terms of investment, productivity and employment while another is in decline: this was the case in the UK in the early 1990s when the service sector was expanding and manufacturing production contracting. We are sure you can think of many examples for yourself of growth sectors and declining sectors. It is also possible for real national income itself to be growing while unemployment is increasing! Depending very much on your personal perspective, these contrasting situations represent either a 'good' or a 'bad' performance. It is, however, vitally important that when we are concerning ourselves with the question of economic performance at the national economy level it is the national economy and not some part or parts of it which is being assessed. It therefore seems reasonable that at least one performance indicator to be used at this level is real national income itself. But another issue arises: what timescale should we be concerned with? There is no particular advantage in choosing a timescale which goes back too far since the very nature of the economy will have changed, that is, in terms of labour skills, technology, products and production techniques. So much so in fact that we would not be directly comparing like with like. At the same time we could choose a timescale which is politically reasonable – the lifetime of a government. But in economic terms this is rather short since it does not even cover the typical length of a business cycle (about 8 years). So, in the absence of any obvious criterion the answer to the question is simply this: it depends on why you are measuring performance and what is being measured. As to why, there are really three types of analysis which call for economic performance measurement:

1. How has the economy been performing in the short run and what does its recent performance herald for the near future?

2. How has the economy been performing over the long run and what does this indicate about its likely structure in the future?

3. How has the economy been performing relative to its main competitor economies in the long run?

Which macroeconomic variables are relevant to each of these types of performance analysis? In general there are eight variables which tend to be used (either together or a selected number) in all three types of analysis.

Common Indicators of Performance of the National Economy

■ Gross domestic product (GDP) change in real terms

■ Labour productivity

■ Inflation

■ Investment

■ Unemployment

■ Exports

■ Imports

■ International competitiveness

Table 3.3   Economic performance criteria

Performance indicator	'Good' performance	'Bad' performance
Real GDP	If it rises	If it falls
Inflation	If it falls	If it rises
Unemployment	If it falls	If it rises
Real imports	If they fall*	If they rise
Real exports	If they rise+	If they fall
Real investment	If it rises	If it falls
Labour productivity	If it rises#	If it falls
International competitiveness	If it rises	If it falls

Notes: (*) In absolute terms and relative to exports.
            (+) In absolute terms and relative to imports.
            (#) In absolute terms and relative to earnings.

Economists do not all agree that these are necessarily the best indicators of performance, but that is hardly surprising when we consider that there are so many economic variables which could be used. Note that three of the indicators listed are components of national income, that is, they are explicitly included in our simplified model (Chapter 2), while the others are either part of the economic framework or have already been mentioned in Chapter 2 as directly relevant to the macroeconomic environment as a whole. Now we want to use the above variables (or a selection of them) to enable you to assess how the UK economy has performed in terms of the first two types of analysis above (we will summarise the third), but before doing so it will be useful to define what (in general) is good and bad performance for an economy in relation to each of the performance indicators above. Table 3.3 describes the simple criteria which are often applied in assessing a country's economic performance and economic prospects.

These are the criteria upon which we want you to assess whether the UK economy is performing well or poorly. Beginning with the short-run analysis, we have listed the variables in Table 3.4.

■ ■ ■ Application Exercise ■ ■ ■ ■ ■ ■ ■ ■ ■ ■ ■ ■ ■ ■

Write a short report based on the data in Table 3.4 on how the economy has performed between 1994 and 1997. (See Appendix 1 of this chapter for our 'report'.)

Table 3.4   UK economic performance in the short run

Indicator/year	1994	1995	1996	1997
Real GDP growth (%)	4.3	2.76	2.3	3.4
Inflation (1990=100)	144.1	149.1	152.7	156.6
Unemployment level (%)	9.4	8.3	7.6	5.9
Real imports (% change)	8.6	11.7	8.9	−0.2
Real exports (% change)	0.7	4.9	1.8	−4.4
Real investment (1990=100)	99.5	106.4	110.1	111.9
Average earnings (1990=100)	123.3	127.4	132.3	138.1
Labour productivity	119.1	120.7	121.1	122.3
International competitiveness (1990=100)	96	97.6	97.5	98

Sources: Economic Review (various issues) and *Economic Outlook*, London Business School.

In practice many economists working in the Treasury, academic institutions and the City use sophisticated numerical models of the economy to forecast the future short-run prospects for growth, inflation, net exports, investment, unemployment and many other economic indicators. But even these sophisticated models can produce forecasts which turn out to be significantly in error.

This is hardly surprising, of course, if you think back to the nature of the economic framework described in Chapter 2 and to the changeability of the main macroeconomic components of aggregate demand described in our simplified economic model in Chapter 2. What about economic performance in the long run? Again we can use our indicators and the simple performance criteria to assess whether the UK economy has performed well or not so well over a much longer period of time. But this time, because we are considering long-run performance, it is more useful to use only some of the above indicators and we want to introduce another – profitability. Note that we will shortly be considering how the UK's economic performance has compared over the long run with that of other industrialised economies. But for the moment let us concentrate on the following indicators of the UK's own long-run economic performance.

3.3.1   Macroeconomic Performance in the Long Run

Indicators to be used are:

■ Growth of real disposable income and real consumption

■ Profitability

■ Balance of trade

The long-run data on these performance indicators are given in Figures 3.2–3.4.

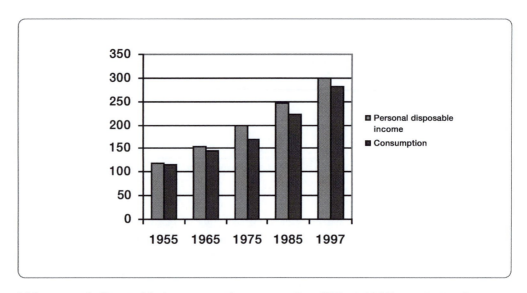

Figure 3.2   UK personal disposable income and consumption (£B) at 1985 constant prices

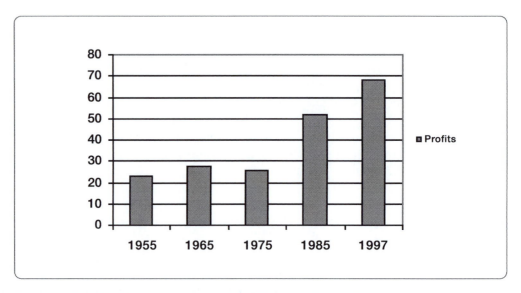

Figure 3.3   Gross trading profits of UK companies (£B) at 1985 constant prices

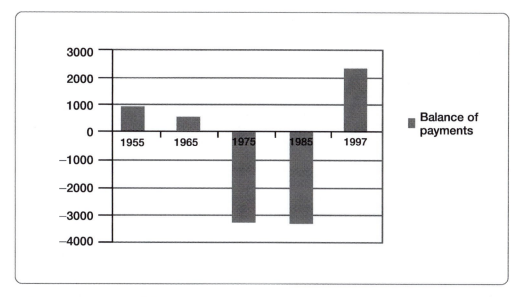

Figure 3.4   UK balance of trade (£B) at 1985 constant prices

■ ■ ■ Application Exercise ■ ■ ■ ■ ■ ■ ■ ■ ■ ■ ■ ■

Consider Figures 3.2, 3.3 and 3.4. Write a brief report of how you think the economy has performed over the long run in terms of the three indicators. Compare your assessment with the one provided at the end of this chapter. For a more refined picture of how the UK economy has been doing it is useful to consider its performance compared to other industrialised economies.

Here, the indicators of performance are as follows:

■ Comparative real GDP growth

■ Share of manufactured exports

■ Innovation indicators

The data for this analysis are presented in Tables 3.5–3.7. However, it is the case that since the 1950s a larger part of the change can be attributed to comparatively poor productivity growth, high import penetration (as discussed above), a significant loss of UK export markets, lagging behind in new investment, a serious deterioration in innovative activities and a generally poorer performance in GDP growth as compared with the UK's main competitor economies. You can see this for yourself in the comparative performance indicator tables above.

Table 3.5   Real GDP and inflation (annual averages)

1955–97	UK	USA	Germany	Japan
GDP growth	2.6	3.3	4.1	6.1
Inflation rate	4.7	1.51	2.2	4.2

Table 3.6   Share of world manufactured exports (%)

	UK	USA	Germany	Japan
1955	32.5	21.1	11.9	6.8
1997	9.3	19.4	16.8	24.1

Table 3.7   Indicators of innovation

	UK	USA	Germany	Japan
R&D as % of GDP	2.3 (1964)	2.9 (1964)	1.6 (1964)	1.5 (1964)
	2.2 (1989)	2.8 (1989)	2.9 (1989)	3.0 (1989)
% Share of non-USA patents granted in USA	36.0 (1950)		0.6 (1950)	0.03 (1950)
	8.1 (1988)		17.4 (1988)	41.3 (1988)

Sources for above tables: Mackintosh et al. (1995) and *Economic Trends* (various years).

We will not ask you to provide a summary report of the data this time since it is fairly self-evident in terms of what we just said in the above paragraph. Nevertheless you should consider the tables to aid your own appreciation of the extent of change in the UK's own economic environment.

■ ■ ■ Self-Assessment Question ■ ■ ■ ■ ■ ■ ■ ■ ■ ■ ■ ■ ■

Q3   Why might 'innovation' be an important indicator of comparative performance in the long term?

The short-run, long-run and comparative performance indicators of the UK's economic fortunes are useful, although not perfect, in tracing out the likely future path of the economy and in reminding us that the simple economic environment described in Chapter 2 requires to be considerably improved upon if we are to develop a much deeper understanding of the economy's processes in general. This, however, needs to be left for a future course!

A key issue which arises in assessing the performance of a whole economy, in the short run, long run or in comparative terms, is the extent to which such performance is related to the performance of the business sector itself. That is to say, the modern economy is composed of a significant public sector funded (largely) through taxation and a private (business) sector. Since it is primarily the private sector which acts as the 'engine' of growth and the producer of wealth in a modern economy, we need to ask whether this key feature of the economy is closely linked to the economy's overall performance.

It seems fairly obvious that it ought to be! However, we need to have a clearer idea of *how* that link manifests itself over the longer term. This is considered in the next section.

■ 3.4   Business and Macroeconomic Performance

There are many 'indicators' which can be identified in relation to the 'performance' of firms in the economy such as return on capital, earnings per share, investment profile, capital base, profitability, market share and many others. However, the key indicator most analysts would accept as *the* measure of business performance over the long term is profitability. After all, indicators such as return on capital and earnings per share are essentially just derivatives of profitability. Similarly, profitability is largely a function of changes in market share and of past investment decisions.

Even future investment decisions are dependent on current and expected profits. It seems reasonable therefore to test the extent to which business profits are related to the performance of the wider economy.

We know from Chapter 2 that investment is a function of interest rates. We can also make the reasonable assumption that it will partly be related to current and expected profit levels. In an economy where the business sector primarily funds investment via borrowing, such as Germany and Japan, we would expect interest rates to be the key parameter controlling investment levels.

However, in an economy where investment has historically been and continues to be funded from retained profit we would expect current profit levels to be the key controlling parameter.

This is precisely the case for the UK economy. Most firms in the UK fund investment from retained profit. It therefore follows we should expect to see some form of relationship between the economy as a whole (GDP growth), profit levels and investment behaviour.

This analysis (Turner, 1993) therefore links the key measure of business performance (profits) to two fundamental variables we observe in the national economy – GDP and investment movements.

Consider the chart in Figure 3.5. A visual inspection of these data clearly reveals a definite pattern: as profits fall from the previous year the strong tendency is for investment to fall shortly after. Thus, there appears to be a

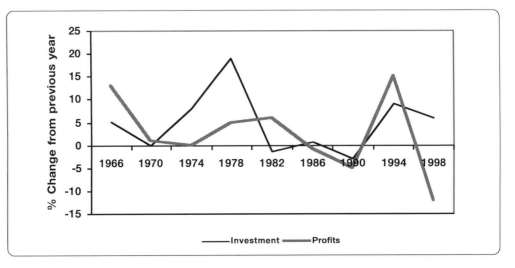

Figure 3.5   Percentage change in profits and investment from previous year (1966–98)

lagged relationship between the change in profits and the subsequent change in investment behaviour. It can also be argued that subsequent upswings in profits may well be associated with previous upswings in investment. However, the data are not detailed enough to test that hypothesis.

There is nevertheless a familiar 'look' to Figure 3.5 – it is very similar to the pattern we expect to see in the business cycle. Such cyclical behaviour in investment and profit levels is typical of many industrialised economies and can also be linked directly to the business cycle itself, as is clear from Figure 3.6.

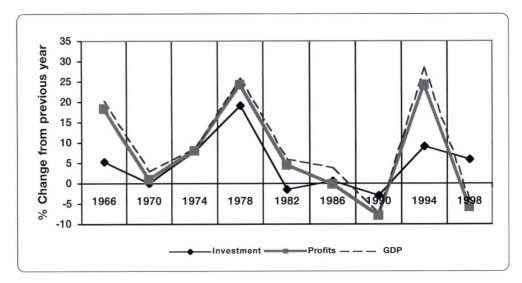

Figure 3.6   Change in investment, profits and GDP

3.4.1   The UK Business Cycle – Investments and Profits

As is patently clear from Figure 3.6, there is a very close relationship between profits and the fluctuations in the national economy. The quantitative relationship between profits, as a dependent variable, and GDP as the independent variable, can be written as follows (using the above data):

$$\% \ \Delta \text{Profit} = -3.12 + 2.63 \Delta \text{GDP}$$

This regression equation simply says that a 1% fall in GDP in the UK will generate a fall of 2.63 per cent in profits. If we now relate changes in investment to changes in profits we get:

$$\% \ \Delta \text{Investment} = 1.94 + 0.73 \Delta \text{Profits}$$

That is, if profits rise by 1 per cent then business investment will subsequently rise by 0.73 per cent. If we now combine the two coefficients in the above equations we get the following:

$$(0.73 * 2.63) = 1.92$$

This means that a 1 per cent fall in GDP will reduce business profits by 2.63 per cent, which subsequently will reduce business investment by about 2 per cent. In other words, the relationship between business performance, as measured by profit changes, and the wider economy is very close indeed. It thus follows that upswings and downswings in the national economy, through their impact on aggregate demand, will directly affect business performance.

However, it is also the case that the UK business cycle is itself dependent on what is happening in the global economy. By default the performance of many UK firms is also dependent on trends and cycles in the global economy. This was a key feature of economic development and the economic constraints facing both national economies and individual firms discussed in Chapter 1.

Measurement of these relationships is important so that we can better understand how the international economic situation will impact on UK business. There are many aspects to this topic, but we wish to focus on two which are crucial to the future of UK business and therefore to the future of the UK economy. These are globalisation of production and EMU.

❏ ❏ ❏ End of Chapter SUMMARY ❏ ❏ ❏ ❏ ❏ ❏ ❏ ❏ ❏ ❏ ❏

There are a number of key concepts covered in this chapter and which you should be clear that you understand:

■ Real and nominal values

■ Constant price equation

■ Weighted average cost change equation

■ Short- and long-run performance indicators

■ Comparative performance indicators

■ Business cycle

These are not an exhaustive list of the key elements in the chapter but if you are confident with how they have been used in the chapter and of your understanding of them you should already have achieved the learning outcomes set out at the beginning of the chapter.

APPENDIX 1

Analysis of the UK's Economic Performance in the Short Run

We hope you remembered to use the criteria set out above in constructing your report. If you did then we are sure it is very similar to our assessment below.

All of the data are expressed in real terms so it is not necessary to directly compare these data with the inflation rate. Real GDP has been rising consistently over the period, indicating that the economy is growing at a respectable pace. However the growth rate has been slowing, an indication that aggregate demand is cooling off towards the end of the decade. The inflation rate showed signs of slowing down but has picked up again. This may be a lagged response to the expansion in demand, and while the growth in demand is slowing this has not weakened the consistent fall in unemployment over the period. In fact unemployment is falling at an increasing rate.

This is clearly related to significant growth in real investment in the economy over the period although the investment growth could face a threat from higher inflation in 1997 if the relatively sluggish labour productivity growth fails to improve. This problem could be further exacerbated if productivity fails to keep pace with increases in real average earnings as has been the case in several years over the period.

Despite the relatively good performance in GDP growth, unemployment and investment a worrying trend has appeared in net export growth which became negative in 1997 and looks set to continue on that trend. This is because the value of the pound relative to most European currencies has been rising since 1996.

Although the UK's international competitiveness has improved slightly in the four-year period this is also going to be put at risk if inflation is not dampened and if labour productivity does not catch up with earnings growth. This does not augur well for the UK balance of payments in the future unless these trends can be reversed.

As you have probably discovered from constructing your own assessment and from reading ours above, it is not particularly easy to arrive at a definite and unambiguous statement on short-run economic prospects – all that is possible from this type of analysis is a reasonably informed assessment using the limited criteria set out above.

APPENDIX 2

Analysis of the UK's Economic Performance in the Long Run

Taking real disposable income and consumption first it is quite obvious that both have consistently followed an upward trend since the 1950s. This indicates that standards of living in the economy have improved in real terms over the period. However the improvement is more respectable than substantial, representing as it does an average growth rate of just under 4 per cent average per year. It is also noteworthy that the gap between income and consumption (that is, savings) has not consistently widened, perhaps reflecting greater interest in consumer goods acquisition than saving on the part of the majority of UK consumers.

The performance on profitability was very poor up to the mid-1970s but thereafter has improved substantially. The bottom of the profits slump in the mid-1970s reflects the impact of higher inflation and reduced demand resulting from the oil crises of 1973 and 1975. But even so UK firms were already suffering declining profits from the 1960s onwards.

Alternative explanations include a rise in real earnings thus cutting the profit share (consistent with the rise in real disposable incomes), loss of home and export markets and low productivity growth compared with earnings growth. The actual explanation is likely to be a combination of all of these factors.

This seems to be borne out in the import penetration data. UK firms clearly lost ground to imports from the 1950s onwards, reflecting either poor price competition on their part and/or poor quality in consumer goods. Whatever the reason, this trend will certainly have helped to change the structure of GDP in the UK since manufacturing employment will have declined as a result of the increased import penetration.

There is no doubt that the profit decline and the increased import penetration will have been strongly aided by the relatively poor growth in labour productivity over the 1960 to 1990 period – averaging a mere 2 per cent per annum average. Compared with the 4 per cent growth in real disposable income it is not surprising that import penetration has increased since domestic demand for consumer goods would not have been satisfied, particularly in the period 1950 to 1980.

In summary, living standards have definitely risen over the long run but the degree of import penetration into the economy by the 1990s is worrying. It suggests UK manufacturing industry has not been capable of competing on the global scale and this may well continue in the absence of better productivity growth in the future. So, not a particularly dazzling economic performance over the long run but on the other hand not disastrous either.

References

Mackintosh, M., Brown, V., Costello, N. et al. (1995) *Economics and Changing Economies*, The Open University.

Turner, P. (1993) 'Investment, Profits and the Business Cycle', *The Economic Review*, **10**(4): 18–21.

■ ■ ■ ANSWERS to Self-Assessment Questions ■ ■ ■ ■ ■ ■

Q1   Your answer should be along the following lines:

A real variable is one which measures a nominal variable after the effect of price inflation is removed. In other words, when a variable is measured in real terms it simply means we are measuring the change in volume (magnitude) of that variable as opposed to its (nominal) monetary magnitude.

Q2   Index numbers enable change in an economic variable to be measured relative to a scale which is based upon a particular start point of the data. Given that many economic variables are measured in terms of money and that many can be very large numbers, then it is sensible to convert these numbers to index numbers which are more easily graphed, listed and understood. In addition, since the nature of an economy's output can change considerably over time it is important that the measurement of economic variables relates to a reasonable time period, as opposed to say, 100 years, which would not make much sense. Index numbers allow us to 'rebase' a series of economic data in this way.

Q3   Innovation rates as measured in terms of patents enable us to check whether an economy's industry is continuing on a dynamic path of development as compared with other economies. We know that labour productivity trends are closely related to changes in technology and therefore changes in technology must be linked to innovation activity. A slowdown in the rate of innovation is likely to be a major cause in the development of a technological 'gap' between highly innovating economies and those which spend less per capita on research and development.

Part II

The Theory of the Firm and Competitive Strategy

Part I examined the external environment of the firm in terms of its role within the global and national economy. Part II concentrates on the internal environment of the firm, that is it explores in more detail the ways in which the firm will make its strategic and operational business decisions. Chapter 4 examines the alternative business objectives which a firm may choose to pursue. The firm's choice of objective will be determined by both market conditions and the actions of its competitors. This in turn will have implications for its day-to-day activities. In order to make the most appropriate choice, it is necessary for the firm to have as much information as possible about both prevailing market trends and its own activities. Chapter 5 examines the tools which the firm can use to estimate the demand for its product(s). Chapter 6 focuses on the firm's ability to supply the market in terms of its production capability and costs. Chapter 7 then examines the alternative pricing strategies which the firm may pursue. Chapter 8 concentrates on the firm's advertising, product policy and location decisions which when combined form the firm's non-price competition strategy. Finally in Part II, Chapter 9 combines the material contained in Chapters 4 to 8 within the context of the firm's overall competitive strategy.

4 Business objectives

■ 4.1   Introduction

This chapter examines the alternative business objectives which the firm may pursue and considers their implications for a range of decisions made by the firm. These decisions are then considered in more detail in terms of the specific policy options available to the firm in later chapters. The firm's choice of objective will of course make certain courses of action more (or less) desirable in terms of whether or not these actions will help the firm to achieve its desired goal. For example, if the firm chooses objective X then although it may have a choice between, say, pricing decisions A, B or C, the fact that it has chosen X means that B is the right pricing decision to take given this objective. Consequently, the firm has no real choice, it must choose B as a consequence of its earlier decision to target objective X. (Note: it could of course in practice choose either A or C but this might either prevent it from achieving X or indicate that the firm is about to change its objective to, say, Y.) This is known as 'contingent decision making', that is, the right option to pursue in a given situation will be either influenced or constrained by decisions which have already been taken.

Some of the possible ways in which the choice of objective will define the firm's subsequent courses of action are covered in the relevant sections of this chapter. Specifically, these sections cover the following models – profit maximisation; sales revenue maximisation; sales volume or output maximisation; managerial utility maximisation; wealth or value maximisation; growth maximisation, including the Marris growth model and the profit-maximising rate of sales growth model; and the behavioural models of business objectives, satisficing and the Cyert/March model. The underlying rationale for many of these models is that while firms will always need to make a profit in order to survive, they may be prepared to sacrifice some of their (potential) current profits in order to obtain higher profits in future. Consequently, a number of these models consider the activities of the firm over a relatively long time horizon, but it is of course always possible for the firm to shift from targeting one objective to another if its circumstances change and an alternative course of action appears to be either more desirable or more feasible.

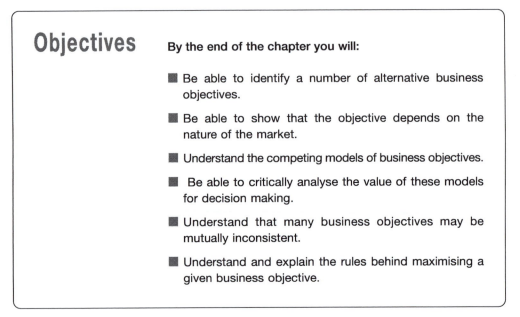

Objectives

By the end of the chapter you will:

■ Be able to identify a number of alternative business objectives.

■ Be able to show that the objective depends on the nature of the market.

■ Understand the competing models of business objectives.

■ Be able to critically analyse the value of these models for decision making.

■ Understand that many business objectives may be mutually inconsistent.

■ Understand and explain the rules behind maximising a given business objective.

■ ■ ■ Self-Assessment Question ■ ■ ■ ■ ■ ■ ■ ■ ■ ■ ■ ■ ■

Q1 What is meant by the term 'contingent decision making'?

CASE STUDY *ConsFirm*

The fortunes of the UK construction industry are very closely linked to the stages of the business cycle. Consequently, the industry is sensitive to changes in the overall state of the economy which in turn may affect what firms within it wish to do, or indeed can do, in terms of setting their business objectives. This case study, which runs in stages throughout the chapter, looks at a hypothetical construction company 'ConsFirm' and how it may pursue different business objectives at different points in time in order to take changes in the business environment into account. Thus

'ConsFirm' and the decisions which it takes are illustrative of those which may be made by individual firms within the construction industry in response to a particular set of market conditions. Given that in practice different firms within the industry make different decisions based upon both their perception (which may be more or less accurate) of the business environment and their knowledge (which may be limited) of the alternative courses of action available, this approach enables us to consider a wider range of possibilities than would be the case if we were looking at one

CASE STUDY *continued*

specific, 'real-life' construction company.

'ConsFirm' is a medium-sized company which employs 250 staff with a range of construction orientated skills. Its core business is house building, but it also undertakes subcontracting work for larger firms in relation to the 'fitting out' of office blocks, that is, it hires out its electricians, carpenters and plumbers to other firms at times when they are not needed on the firm's own construction sites in order to generate additional revenue for the business. The company is based in the north of England and has been making a reasonably healthy level of profit for the last 3 years. The company's management have now decided, however, to increase its profit level in order to finance an expansion of the company. We begin, therefore, with the assumption that profit will be a dominant motivating force for our company at this particular point in time.

■ 4.2   Profit Maximisation

4.2.1   Definition

This is the oldest of the models of business objectives dating from a time when the vast majority of firms were managed by the people who owned them. Thus the higher the profit obtained, the greater the level of income the owner-manager could enjoy. The objective of the firm, therefore, was to 'achieve the highest possible level of profit'. This is what we mean by profit maximisation.

Many firms still have this as their primary objective today but, as we shall see later, as firms have become larger and more complex profit maximisation has either become more difficult to achieve or has started to take second place to other objectives. For now, however, let us concentrate on how the firm can achieve profit maximisation.

4.2.2   Rules for Profit Maximisation

In order to profit maximise, the firm needs to obey three basic rules:

1. The firm should only produce the product if total revenue (TR) is greater than or equal to total variable cost (TVC).

2. Marginal revenue (MR) from the last unit of output produced must equal the marginal cost (MC) of that unit.

3. MC is less than MR at lower output levels and MC is greater than MR at higher output levels.

In the case of the first rule, what we are saying is that the firm should only begin production if it is sure that the total amount of money it will obtain from selling the good (TR) will exceed the cost of making it (TVC). If the firm produces nothing at all, it will make a loss equivalent to its fixed costs (the rent on its factory/office space and machinery). By beginning production, it is attempting to reduce the size of this loss initially before going on to make a profit. It will be able to do this as long as the total revenue obtained from selling the good is equal to or greater than the cost of the labour, materials and so on which are needed to produce it (TVC). If, on the other hand, total revenue is less than total variable cost, then all the firm will achieve by going into production is an increase in the size of its losses and so the best decision to take is to stop producing the product until market conditions improve.

In the case where the firm wishes to begin production as it believes it will be profitable to do so, the next question to be asked is, what level of output is consistent with profit maximisation? Figure 4.1 is a simplified graph for single period profit maximisation drawn in terms of marginal cost and marginal revenue. It assumes that the firm faces a constant, stable price for the product so that the marginal revenue curve is a horizontal straight line, that is, each unit of the product produced is sold for the same price so the revenue generated by each sale is the same as for the one before. The marginal cost curve is U-shaped as costs at first fall, due to the firm operating more efficiently, and then rise again as production increases as more workers need to be brought in to produce this higher level of output.

We can see from Figure 4.1 that there are two points which fulfil the second of our rules – that MR from the last unit of output produced must equal MC – output levels Q_1 and Q_3. Only one of these, however, Q_3, satisfies the third of

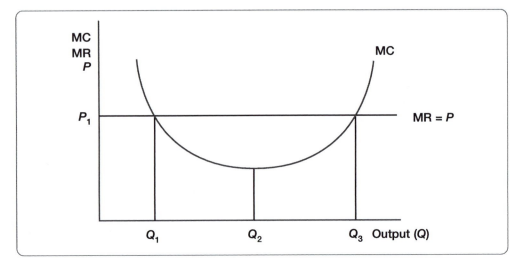

Figure 4.1   The profit-maximising level of output

our rules – that MC is less than MR at lower and MC is greater than MR at higher output levels.

It follows from this that Q_3 is the profit-maximising level of output. In contrast, Q_1 represents the level of output where the firm is just starting to make a profit on each unit sold.

Prior to Q_1, marginal cost exceeds marginal revenue so that the firm is making a loss on each unit of output sold until this threshold level of output is reached. Once the level of output has expanded beyond this point, marginal revenue is greater than marginal cost so that the firm makes a profit on each additional unit of output sold. The amount of profit made per unit continues to rise as the gap between the MR and MC curves increases up until point Q_2. After Q_2, the gap between the two curves starts to narrow again. Q_2 is therefore the point where the profit margin per unit of output is greatest. The firm can still, however, increase its total profit by increasing its level of production beyond Q_2. The additional contribution which each extra unit of output makes to the firm's profits is smaller than that for the previous unit after this point, but it still represents an increase in the total amount of profit made by the firm. Thus the firm should continue to expand production until it reaches Q_3 at which point the marginal revenue obtained from the last unit of output is equal to its marginal cost, that is the firm obtains no additional profit from this unit of output. This is reinforced by the fact that after Q_3 the marginal cost of each extra unit of output produced exceeds the marginal revenue obtained from it so that profits are reduced rather than increased after this point. Consequently, Q_3 is the profit-maximising level of output.

We have assumed for the sake of simplicity in Figure 4.1 that the firm faces a constant market-determined price for its product, but the same conditions for profit maximisation can also be applied in markets where price is variable. In fact, as we shall see in Chapter 7, if the firm chooses profit maximisation as its objective and has the ability to set the price of its product rather than accept a market-determined one, then the firm can use these rules to identify the price at which it should sell the product in order to maximise its profits. This way of choosing its price is known as 'marginal cost pricing'.

4.2.3 Reasons why a Firm May Not Attempt to or May Be Unable to Maximise Profit

Given that firms must make a profit in order to survive, it can be argued that the more profit a firm makes, the more successful it is and the better its prospects for the future. While this may well be true, it is not the same as saying that the firm must maximise its profits all of the time. In highly competitive markets where margins are slim, this may be its only option. In reality, however, there are a significant number of markets in which competition is not this intense and so the firm has a wider range of options available to it. In addition, the adoption of this objective assumes that the firm not only wants to maximise profits but that it also has the ability to do so. As we shall see below, this may not always be the case in practice.

We can identify four main reasons why the firm may not actually achieve, or even pursue, the objective of profit maximisation:

1. The 'principal–agent problem'

2. Data or time constraints

3. The existence of non-perfect competition

4. The need to avoid government regulation

Most of these issues arise as a result of the increased complexity of modern business organisations. Profit maximisation is likely to be the main objective of a firm's owners as this is the way in which they can obtain the highest level of income. For an increasing number of businesses, however, the owners of the firm – the shareholders or 'principals' – are not the people who are actually in charge of the day-to-day running of the firm – the managers or 'agents'. The extent to which profit maximisation will be important to the firm as a whole will therefore depend upon the extent to which the managers agree with the views of the shareholders. While it may be possible to encourage managers to profit maximise, for example via the use of profit-related pay, the managers may have other goals such as entering new markets or increasing the size of the firm. As we shall see later on in this chapter, these goals may be incompatible with profit maximisation, at least in the short term.

In addition to this, data or time constraints may affect the firm's ability to profit maximise even if it wishes to do so. The model outlined above assumes that the firm can accurately calculate its marginal costs and marginal revenues. While this may be true for a small single product firm which faces a relatively stable market and known costs, this model is more difficult to apply to a multi-product firm which operates in several markets simultaneously. In this case, for example, should the firm calculate a separate profit-maximising level of output for each product or try to identify the optimal product mix for the firm as a whole?

At a time when some or all of the firm's product markets are volatile, with, say, rapidly changing prices, it may be difficult to calculate marginal revenue accurately. Likewise if the prices of the inputs needed to produce the products, such as raw materials, are fluctuating significantly, marginal cost may need to be recalculated relatively frequently. Thus there may be a data constraint in terms of the availability of accurate information regarding both product and input prices and a time constraint in terms of whether the manager has the time to do the necessary recalculations on a regular basis. The introduction of computers has of course reduced the burden of the latter, but the gathering of accurate data may still be problematic. It may be the case, therefore, that the firm will think that it is profit maximising given the data that it has at its disposal but that it is not actually doing so in practice due to data inaccuracy.

Even if this is not a problem for the firm, situations may arise in which it is not in its interests to attempt to maximise profits, for example where there is non-perfect competition or the threat of government regulation. If attempting to maximise profits in the short run means that the firm needs to cut the price of the product in order to sell more, this might result in similar price cuts by rival firms. The net result of this could be lower profits for every firm as each one may end up selling only slightly more of the product than before but at a lower price. Thus short-run profit maximisation may be incompatible with the long-run interests of the firm. In this case, both managers and shareholders may wish to pursue an alternative objective.

Similarly, if a company is either the dominant firm or a monopolist in a particular market, exploiting this position in order to maximise profits may prove to be detrimental to the firm's longer-term performance if it forces government to regulate the industry in order to bring profits and/or prices down. In this case, it may be in the firm's interests not to maximise profits in the short term in order to avoid regulation altogether. Another slightly different case where profit maximisation is not possible, or even desirable, as an objective occurs within the 'not-for-profit' part of the service sector. This includes both public sector organisations which are directly controlled by government and private sector charities which may be subject to specific rules which prohibit profit-making as it is contrary to their social obligations. Thus in summary we can say that pursuing an objective of (short-run) profit maximisation may not always be in the best interests of the firm even if it is possible to achieve.

■ ■ ■ Self-Assessment Question ■ ■ ■ ■ ■ ■ ■ ■ ■ ■ ■ ■ ■

Q2 What are the three rules which the firm should follow in order to profit maximise? Which point in Figure 4.1 represents the profit-maximising level of output?

CASE STUDY *ConsFirm*

As 'ConsFirm' is seeking to increase its profitability, what are the issues that it would have to consider in deciding whether or not to adopt profit maximisation as its objective? Firstly, there is the state of the economy and the housing market to be considered. The firm's management believe that the economy and the housing market are both sufficiently strong that selling any additional houses that the firm would need to build in order to increase its revenue and profits would be relatively easy. They also believe, however, that any attempt to raise their house prices beyond their current level would result in a loss of

continued

customers to their competitors. In addition, in order to increase the number of houses being built the firm would need to employ additional staff which would raise its costs at a time when the price of construction materials is also rising. The combined effect of these factors would be to reduce the profit margin on each house that the company sells. Thus in terms of Figure 4.1, the firm will be moving away from a position similar to Q_2 and towards Q_3. This will increase its overall profitability, even though the profit margin per house will be reduced. Thus the company will obtain the increase in profitability it requires but the question then is, how far along this route should it go in trying to reach Q_3 and so profit maximise?

The answer to this will depend upon the further assumptions that the management make about the current and future state of the housing market and whether or not their current assumptions are correct. For example, how long will market conditions remain favourable? Will the firm have to reduce the price of its houses in order to sell more of them at some point? Will the firm have to pay its staff more than expected in order to hire and retain them given that when demand for construction staff is high, skills shortages tend to emerge? Will the cost of construction materials rise significantly? All of these 'what ifs?' will operate as data and time constraints on the ability of the firm to profit maximise and if there is sufficient fluctuation, for example rising marginal costs combined with falling marginal revenue, the firm may 'overshoot' point Q_3 and find itself in a situation where it needs to cut back on its activities in order to get back to the profit-maximising position. What this illustrates, therefore, is that although a firm may wish to maximise its profits, this is not necessarily an easy thing to achieve.

■ 4.3   Sales Revenue Maximisation

4.3.1   Definition

In this case, rather than maximising profit, the firm wishes to maximise the amount of money (revenue) which it obtains from the sale of the product. Thus it will be less immediately concerned about minimising costs than a profit-maximising firm but correspondingly more concerned about raising revenue (Baumol, 1967). Why would the firm wish to pursue such an objective?

There are two basic reasons why a firm may want to do so – to alleviate a cash flow problem or to raise money for new investment/product development. In the first case, if the firm is very short of money, for example because of lower than expected sales during a recession, it may be in the firm's interests to cut the price of the product in order to increase sales and so generate revenue for the firm, even though this may in extreme cases mean it is selling the product for less than it costs to produce. This may enable the firm to raise sufficient money to service its debts, pay wages and so on, while at the same time reducing the costs of storing either the product or raw materials. Consequently, this approach is sometimes used in order to keep the business 'ticking over' by generating cash flow until the market improves. The short-run sacrifice it involves is a way of ensuring the long-run survival of the business.

Alternatively, if the firm needs to restructure in order to make its production more efficient, it will need money to finance the necessary investment or, if it is in a declining market, it will need to invest in new product development, again in order to survive. The safest way of raising funds in either case will often be to generate the money within the firm as this avoids the risks associated with borrowing, such as rising interest rates. In such circumstances, therefore, the sales revenue maximisation may be the appropriate objective to pursue.

4.3.2   Rules for Sales Revenue Maximisation

In order to maximise sales revenue, the firm should:

1. Choose the output level and price at which total revenue (TR) is highest, that is where marginal revenue (MR) equals zero.

2. Determine the constraint level of profit which is necessary to satisfy the shareholders.

What we have here, therefore, is what is known as a 'constrained maximisation' model. In the case of profit maximisation, managers and shareholders (if any) were pursuing the same objective. In this case, however, shareholders continue to be focused on profit while the firm's management are more immediately concerned with sales revenue. Thus the managers can only truly maximise sales revenue if the shareholders agree that this should be the firm's objective (which of course they may do if the firm is facing a serious threat to its survival as it is not in their interests for the firm to go into receivership). If they do not agree, however, then sales revenue maximisation may not actually be possible. The result of this is likely to be a compromise which involves some sacrifice of profit by the shareholders in order to allow the managers to increase sales revenue but not to the maximum possible level. The final outcome of the model will therefore depend upon the relative strengths of the two sides. If the firm has a strong management but there are many shareholders who are divided in their views with respect to what is best for the firm, then the managers will be in a much stronger position to target this objective than in the case of a weak management team in a company which has a small number of powerful and united shareholders. This potential conflict is illustrated in Figure 4.2.

According to this model, if the shareholders (or the firm as a whole) wish to pursue a profit maximisation strategy then the optimal level of output is Q_1, that is the point at which the total profit curve peaks (and, by definition, the point where the difference between the total revenue and total cost curves is

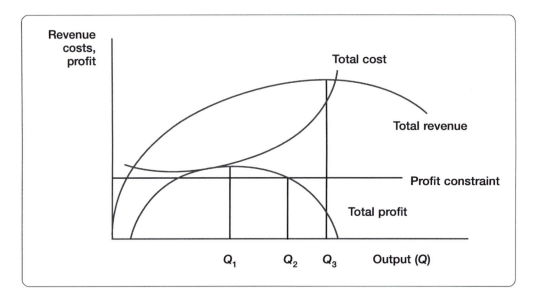

Figure 4.2   The sales revenue maximisation model

greatest). In contrast, if the managers wish, and are able, to fully pursue the objective of sales revenue maximisation, then in accordance with the two rules which we identified earlier, the optimal level of output for the firm is Q_3. At this level of output, the total revenue curve is at its highest point so that its slope, which equates to marginal revenue, is zero. This complies with the first of the model's two rules.

The second rule assumes that, in practice, neither side will be able to fully pursue their preferred objective so that a compromise will be reached between the shareholders' wish to profit maximise and the managers' desire to maximise sales revenue. Thus in the longer term interests of the firm, the shareholders will be prepared to forgo some profit now in order to ensure the firm's survival (and hence its future profitability), while the managers will accept that the share-holders require an adequate return on their investment. Consequently, the firm will maximise sales revenue subject to a profit constraint as shown in Figure 4.2.

The actual level of output produced will therefore always lie somewhere between Q_1 and Q_3,depending on how much profit the shareholders require. In Figure 4.2, this compromise level of output is Q_2 where the profit constraint intersects the total profit curve. Thus the shareholders are prepared to sacrifice the amount of profit shown by the move from Q_1 to Q_2 while the managers are prepared to accept this level (Q_2) as an improvement on the profit-maximising level Q_1, although this is still lower than the level which they would ideally like to achieve (Q_3). This outcome can be maintained as long as neither side wishes to change it. For example, if at a later date the shareholders increased their profit requirements (and hence the profit constraint moved upwards on the graph) then the managers would be faced with a choice between either meeting this demand by cutting the level of output to a point to the left of Q_2 or refusing to do so. The ease with which they could take the latter course of action would again depend on the relative strengths of the two groups so that there is potential for conflict within the model.

■ ■ ■ Self-Assessment Question ■ ■ ■ ■ ■ ■ ■ ■ ■ ■ ■

Q3 What, according to Figure 4.2, would be the effect on the firm's profits if the firm's managers were to ignore the shareholders' profit constraint and fully pursue the objective of sales revenue maximisation? What might the implications of this be for the firm?

CASE STUDY *ConsFirm*

We left 'ConsFirm's' management in a position of wanting to increase the company's profitability and debating whether or not they could actually profit maximise in practice given their expectations about current and future market conditions. Unfortunately for the company, their optimism about the healthy state of the economy and the housing market proved to be unfounded. Concerns about an over-heating economy with rising inflation resulted in the government substantially increasing interest rates. The effect of this was to deflate the economy as had been intended, but the time lag between each individual rise in interest rates and its actual effect on the economy was such that interest rates were raised to a higher level than proved to be necessary in order to tackle the problem. The consequence of this was that the economy moved from a boom into a downturn and then into recession and the construction industry followed suit. (You may recognise this as a very simplified version of what actually happened to the UK economy and construction industry in 1989–92.)

The impact of this on 'ConsFirm' was to substantially reduce the demand for houses, while at the same time the revenue which they had been obtaining from hiring out their staff to other companies in the office building sector also fell substantially. In addition, the firm's costs were higher than they had been previously due to its decision to hire more staff in order to enable it to build more houses and so increase (maximise) its profits. The net result of this, therefore was that the firm very quickly moved from profit into loss. The firm's management now needed to find a way to deal with this situation. After an inspection of the company's books it also became apparent that the firm had bought a lot of its materials on credit and that payment for them would fall due within the next 3–6 months with failure to pay resulting in the company being declared bankrupt. So what then was the company to do?

The management team decided that as it was likely to take more than 6 months to move the company from loss into profit given the current state

CASE STUDY *continued*

of the economy and industry, it had to concentrate on getting enough cash into the business to pay its immediate debts in order to buy the time to turn the company around. Consequently sales revenue rather than profit was now the priority, although it was also decided that the firm would embark on a cost-cutting programme to make it more competitive and improve its chance of long-term survival. As a result of the former decision, the managers decided to pursue a strategy designed to maximise sales revenue even where this was at the expense of profitability.

The first stage of this process was to decrease the price of its completed houses in order to try to increase demand. Within the first two months of doing so, however, it became apparent that although this generated a few extra sales on all of which it made a small profit, in order to increase sales any further it would have to be prepared to take a loss on some of its properties. A final demand, accompanied by a threat of legal action, from a major creditor forced the issue a month later and in order to pay them 'ConsFirm' sold a number of its partly completed houses at a loss to a rival company in order to raise the

necessary cash. At the same time, 'ConsFirm' started to compete more aggressively for subcontracting work by putting in low priced, but not necessarily profitable, tenders and began to target the housing repair and maintenance market within the industry which it had previously avoided.

The dual rationale for this approach was that, on the one hand, it would enable it to reduce the size of its losses by covering at least some of its costs until further restructuring could take place and, on the other hand, it needed to retain a proportion of its skilled staff in preparation for the upturn in the market if it was to succeed in the future, as once they left the company it would be difficult to persuade them to return. Fortunately for the company, this plan of action proved to be successful and the business survived. Finally, it should be noted that the potential shareholder–manager conflict which might have arisen as a result of the decision to focus on increasing sales revenue did not in fact occur in this case as the shareholders accepted that the company was in such severe difficulties that without this recovery plan they would lose their investment.

■ 4.4 Sales Volume or Output Maximisation

4.4.1 Definition

In this model, the firm's objective is to produce and sell as much of the good as possible. Thus the focus is on the total amount of the good being sold by volume rather than the amount of money that this generates for the firm as was the case for the sales revenue maximisation model. There are two separate but related reasons why the firm may wish to pursue this objective – to gain entry into a market and to increase market share. If a firm is entering a market for the first time, it needs to ensure that there is a sufficient supply of the product so that potential customers do not experience delays in obtaining it which will discourage them from making repeat purchases at a later date. Alternatively, where there is an existing product which is a market leader with a strong brand identity, the entrant firm may wish to undercut this brand on price in order to weaken customer loyalty to it. Once this has been achieved and the entrant has penetrated the market, supply can be reduced and/or the price raised in order to increase profits.

Similarly, in the case where the firm is pursuing this objective in order to increase market share, supplying enough output at a low enough price may be the key to expansion, particularly if the higher level of output being produced means that the firm can reap previously unobtainable economies of scale. It can then use these lower costs per unit of output either to cut the price and increase the volume of sales even further or to increase its profit margin by maintaining a constant price.

4.4.2   Rules for Sales Volume (Output) Maximisation

In this case, there is only one decision rule which the firm needs to follow. It should choose the level of output where average total cost (ATC) is equal to average revenue (AR). By doing so, it will ensure that the firm will produce the maximum amount of output possible without making a loss. The firm will break even at this point as the amount of revenue coming into the firm will exactly cover the firm's costs. This also has implications for the firm's pricing strategy. As average revenue is equal to total revenue divided by the quantity of output, and total revenue is equal to price times quantity, the firm should set its price equal to average revenue, that is:

$$AR = \frac{TR}{Q} = \frac{P \times Q}{Q} = P$$

This means in turn that the firm should set average total costs equal to price, that is, $ATC = TC/Q = AR = P$. The resulting outcome for the firm is shown in Figure 4.3. The average total cost curve is U-shaped as costs at first fall as output rises and then start to increase again, while the average revenue curve is a horizontal straight line at price level P_1 reflecting the firm's breakeven strategy in this case. The only point on the graph which satisfies the decision rule, that the firm should set $ATC = AR$, is Q_1, which is therefore the sales volume maximisation level of output.

Thus in a similar way to the case of sales revenue maximisation, the firm has traded short-run profitability in return for an alternative, in this case an increased volume of sales. In the short run this is designed to improve its market position and, if it is done correctly, this may enable it to improve its

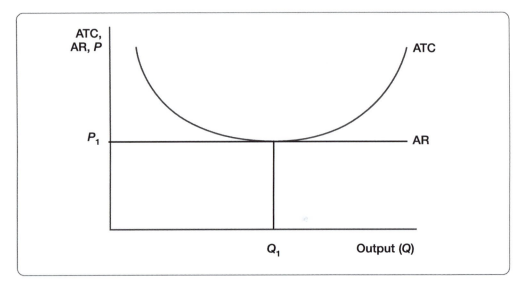

Figure 4.3   The sales volume maximisation model

long-run profitability as well. One particular difference between the sales volume and the sales revenue maximisation models is that the former does not explicitly include the possibility of conflict within the firm between the shareholders and managers regarding the firm's objective.

This does not mean, however, that such a conflict will not exist. Again, the firm's managers may only be able to pursue such a strategy if they have at least some minimum level of shareholder support, that is, they are prepared to sacrifice profitability now for greater profitability later.

■ ■ ■ Self-Assessment Question ■ ■ ■ ■ ■ ■ ■ ■ ■ ■ ■ ■ ■

Q4   Why may the firm pursue the sales volume maximisation objective and how should it set the price of the product according to this model? To what types of product might this model be most easily applied?

■ 4.5   Managerial Utility Maximisation

Up until this point we have assumed that while the shareholders are in constant pursuit of profit they may be flexible enough to allow the firm's management to sacrifice short-run profitability in return for the chance that long-run profits can be increased, either by raising money for new product development or investment (sales revenue maximisation) or by trying to enter new, or expand existing, markets (sales volume maximisation). We have also assumed, at least implicitly, that managers will act in the best interests of the firm. What we have not really considered so far, however, is that managers may have their own agendas in terms of what they themselves want from the firm. The managerial utility maximisation model specifically incorporates this possibility.

4.5.1   Definition

According to this model (Williamson, 1963), the objective of the firm's managers is to maximise their own utility (or satisfaction), that is, they take decisions in the light of what will be most beneficial to them rather than necessarily to the firm as a whole. The interests of the firm and of the managers may of course coincide but sometimes they will not. The managers' ability to pursue their own interests will therefore depend upon the degree of freedom of action that they have within the firm which in turn depends upon the type of market in which the firm operates. The more able they are to act independently, the more of the firm's (potential) profit will be spent on things which give the managers utility, at least in the short run.

4.5.2   Rules for Managerial Utility Maximisation

In order to achieve managerial utility maximisation it is assumed that :

1. Managers can act independently.

2. The firm's market is not highly competitive, that is, the firm can obtain large (supernormal) profits.

3. Managerial utility (U) is obtained from a combination of additional expenditure on staffing (S), managers' salaries and benefits (M) and discretionary investment (I_D).

We have already discussed the first of these rules which states that managers must be able to pursue their own interests within the firm independently of other considerations. The second rule enables them to do so by allowing for a reasonable return on investment for the shareholders while using any additional profits to 'buy' the managers the things they want from the firm. If profits are high enough, shareholders will be prepared to allow the managers to do this as a reward for the good performance of the firm and to keep together a managerial team which is beneficial to the company. In a very competitive market, however, this might not be an option as the firm would need to place a much greater emphasis on profit maximisation in order to survive. In the case where profits are high as a result of a relative lack of competition, it matters less if some of the company's income is diverted into providing managers with higher salaries and benefits than they might otherwise obtain. These obviously constitute a direct financial benefit to the individuals running the firm – the inclusion of staffing expenditure and discretionary investment within the model perhaps needs a little more explanation.

Additional staffing expenditure is seen as being of benefit to managers as it is a measure of their power within the organisation. The more staff a manager controls, the greater their status within the firm. In purely economic terms this may involve a misuse of resources, for example if the firm is overstaffed, as labour is not being used efficiently. As long as the firm can afford it, and the manager desires it, however, this source of inefficiency may be tolerated or even encouraged. In any case, it is argued, if market conditions worsen, the firm can always make the surplus staff redundant in order to maintain its profitability.

Discretionary investment also gives the manager utility in a similar way. What we mean by discretionary investment is that managers have money to spend on 'pet projects' in which they are interested but which may not be necessary to the firm's survival. This allows them, for example, to experiment in relation to new product development or to diversify the firm into non-core areas of the business. It may be that some of these projects will in fact be beneficial to the firm in the long run, but this cannot be guaranteed. Having looked at the assumptions underlying the model, let us now examine the model itself.

Again, as in the case of sales revenue maximisation, the model is constrained by the need to make a minimum level of profit in order to satisfy the shareholders. Specifically the firm will:

Maximise $U = f(S, M, I_D)$

subject to $P_R > P_{MIN} + T$

where U is utility, f means is a function of, S is staffing expenditure, M is managers' salaries and benefits, I_D is discretionary investment, P_R is reported profits, P_{MIN} is the minimum level of profits required by shareholders and $T =$ corporation tax.

Thus the first equation writes the third of the model's underlying assumptions in a different form while the second introduces a profit constraint on the managers' ability to pursue their own objectives. The overall reported profit made by the firm must be greater than the minimum amount of profit required by the shareholders if they are to continue supporting the managers and it must also be sufficient to pay the firm's tax bill. Once these two prior commitments have been paid, the rest of the firm's reported profits are the managers' to do with as they wish. Figure 4.4 demonstrates the outcome arising from this, which is that staffing expenditure (or managerial salaries or discretionary investment levels or any combination of the three) will be higher than for other similar firms for whom profit alone is the primary objective.

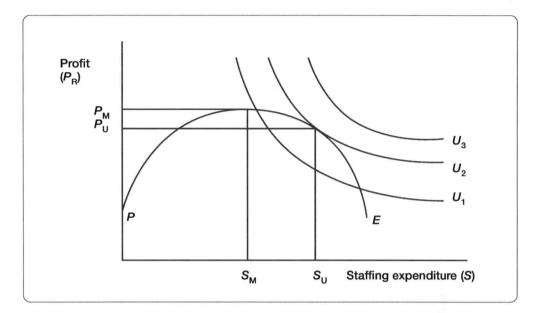

Figure 4.4 Managerial utility maximisation

In Figure 4.4, the curve *PE* shows the trade-off between profit and staffing expenditure. Initially, as we move from left to right along the curve, both the level of profit and the level of staffing expenditure increase. After point $P_M S_M$, however, any further increase in staffing expenditure is associated with a decrease in profit as the *PE* curve turns downwards. This is because the firm is now spending more on staff than is compatible with maximising profit. Consequently, $P_M S_M$ is the profit maximisation point for the firm. If all of the firm's reported profits were taken up by the shareholders' requirements and/or taxes then this would be the optimal point for the firm. The model assumes, however, that this is not the case and that the managers will increase the amount of money spent on staff beyond this point in order to generate increased utility for themselves. The question is, how will they maximise that utility?

U_1, U_2 and U_3 are indifference curves. Along any of these curves, for example U_1, the managers gain equal amounts of utility but the further to the right of the graph the utility curve is, the greater the total amount of utility which they obtain. Thus U_2 is preferred to U_1 as it yields a higher level of utility and similarly U_3 is preferred to U_2. The managers' ability to obtain a particular level of utility is, however, constrained by what the firm can afford. In Figure 4.4, U_3 is out of reach of the managers as the profit–expenditure trade-off curve lies too far to the left of it. The managers can, however, achieve either U_1 or U_2 as both of these are possible given the position of the *PE* curve. Given what we said earlier, however, the managers will always prefer U_2 to U_1. Consequently, the managers will choose the point $P_U S_U$ on the graph where the *PE* curve is tangential to U_2 which is the highest level of utility obtainable given the relative position of the curves. $P_U S_U$ is therefore the managerial utility maximisation point on the graph. At this point, staffing expenditure is higher, and profit lower, than if the firm were pursuing a profit maximisation strategy. (Alternatively, of course, as was the case for sales revenue maximisation, the firm may adopt a compromise between profit maximisation at $P_M S_M$ and managerial utility maximisation at $P_U S_U$ by locating somewhere on the profit–expenditure curve between these two points if circumstances, for example a conflict between managers and shareholders, dictate that this is a more sustainable position to adopt over the longer term.)

■ ■ ■ Self-Assessment Question ■ ■ ■ ■ ■ ■ ■ ■ ■ ■ ■ ■

Q5 What are the three assumptions on which the managerial utility maximisation model is based and what is the outcome of the model?

CASE STUDY *ConsFirm*

Having survived the recession, 'ConsFirm' has regained its profitability as a result of the upturn in the housing market. Consequently, the management team have decided to abandon the company's sales revenue maximisation strategy as they no longer deem it to be necessary. They do not, however, wish to return to the previous strategy of profit maximisation as they found that it was too difficult to determine in practice whether the firm was actually maximising profits at all. In addition, having steered the company out of recession successfully, the managers feel that they should now be rewarded for their efforts.

Consequently, given the improved profitability of the company, they are now seeking to increase their level of utility by obtaining substantially higher salaries and benefits than before. (Within the context of Figure 4.4, this can be represented by replacing staffing expenditure with managerial salaries and benefits on the horizontal axis.) Their ability to improve their pay and benefits packages will, however, at least partly depend upon the shareholders' willingness to allow this to happen (the trade-off along the PE curve in Figure 4.4). The initial problem here is that any money spent on these items is money which is no longer available for distribution among the shareholders. Consequently, the managers will seek to calculate the minimum rate of return on their investment that shareholders will be prepared to accept before using the remainder to improve their pay and benefits levels. Two particular factors may be especially important in making this calculation. Firstly, after several lean years, the shareholders themselves will be keen to make up lost ground in terms of their income from dividends and so will

CASE STUDY *continued*

expect a larger share of the profits to be distributed to them. Secondly, if the shareholders are not satisfied with the returns they are receiving they may decide instead to substitute capital gain for dividends by selling their shares in what will now be a rising market for them. In this situation there is a risk to the managers that if enough of the shareholders decide to do this, and particularly to a single buyer, then the firm could be threatened by a takeover. If so, one result of this could be the loss of the managers' jobs. The final outcome is, therefore, a question of balance between the competing needs of the managers and shareholders with regard to this year's profits. Profitability in future years will, however, also be affected by the decision made now as it is comparatively difficult to cut managers' pay once an increase has been granted. Consequently, a large increase in their pay and benefits packages now will erode the future profits of the firm.

■ 4.6   Wealth or Value Maximisation

According to this model (Pappas et al., 1983), the objective is to increase the total (current and future) wealth of the firm. Managers will therefore try to 'maximise the economic value of the net assets of the firm under their control', that is they will attempt to ensure that there is the greatest possible margin between the value of the assets of the firm, such as property and cash reserves, and its liabilities, for example outstanding suppliers' bills and interest payments on loans.

The firm may pursue this objective if it wishes to improve its standing in the financial markets, for example in order to obtain a higher share value or credit rating. Consequently, it may be the best objective to pursue at a time when there is a surge in takeover activity (as a higher share price will potentially safeguard the firm by making it more expensive to acquire) or when the firm knows it will have to borrow large sums of money in the future in order to pay for restructuring or new product development.

As it is comparatively difficult to value assets and liabilities over a long period of time, the model uses profit as a proxy variable for the value of the net assets of the firm. In order to find its value, therefore, the firm will use the following equation:

Value of the firm = present value of expected future profits

$$= \frac{\text{profit 1}}{(1+i)} + \frac{\text{profit 2}}{(1+i)^2} + \frac{\text{profit 3}}{(1+i)^3} + \ldots\ldots + \frac{\text{profit } n}{(1+i)^n}$$

where profit 1, profit 2 ... are the levels of profit expected in years 1 and 2 and so on and *i* is the interest (or discount) rate. The power terms 1 to *n* on the bottom part of the equation represent the fact that current profits are worth more to the firm than projected future profits as the former are considerably more certain than the latter. Thus over time, for any given interest rate, the firm will need a higher level of profit in the future in order to maintain its value. In addition, as interest rates rise, the firm will need to become more profitable in order to maintain its value as the same sum in expected future profits is divided through by a bigger number each time. Thus the firm's value may change if the interest rate changes even if its projected profit levels remain constant.

■ ■ ■ Self-Assessment Question ■ ■ ■ ■ ■ ■ ■ ■ ■ ■ ■ ■

Using the data below, calculate the value of the firm over a four-year period.

Year	1	2	3	4
Profit (£)	20,000	25,000	22,000	25,000

Interest rate (*i*) = 10%

Recalculate the value of the firm using a 5% interest rate. What does this demonstrate about the importance of the interest rate to the firm? What is the main difficulty which arises in using this model?

■ 4.7 Growth Maximisation Models

This section looks at two specific models – the Marris growth maximisation model (Marris, 1964) and the profit-maximising rate of sales growth model (Baumol, 1967). To begin with, however, we need to define what is meant by the term 'growth maximisation' and to examine the general principles upon which such models are based.

4.7.1 Definition and General Principles

Growth maximisation is defined as 'an attempt to increase the size of the firm as far as possible and/or at as fast a rate as possible'. The firm may try to do this in order to control its production or market environment (or both) and so reduce the level of risk to which it is exposed. The underlying assumption behind this approach is that the larger the firm is, the less vulnerable it will be to adverse changes in market conditions. For example, if the firm is operating in several markets simultaneously, then if demand in one market collapses it still has its other markets to fall back on. Consequently, this fall in demand will be less damaging to the firm than if it was operating in only one market. As far as the rate of growth is concerned, fast growth may be desirable if the firm is to keep ahead of the competition, particularly in an expanding market. There may come a time, however, when an excessive rate of growth places too much strain on the firm and so begins to have negative consequences, for example a loss of managerial control. The next question is how can the firm achieve growth?

Growth may take the form of either external growth or internal growth. External growth may occur via merger, that is by two firms agreeing to join together in order to become one larger company, or acquisition, in which case the firm expands by buying another firm. In either case, this type of growth may take place through the joining together of similar firms in the same industry (horizontal integration) or through a movement up or down the firm's supply chain by taking over an input supplier (backward vertical integration) or a retailer (forward vertical integration). Alternatively the firm may take over an unrelated business in order to increase the number of markets in which it operates. All of these options share the advantage that they enable the firm to expand fairly rapidly by 'buying in' additional expertise to complement their existing activities. Horizontal integration increases the firm's market share within its existing market(s) while potentially allowing it to operate at lower cost, for example as a result of economies of scale. Backward vertical integration enables it to ensure that it has the inputs it needs at the time that it needs them and forward vertical integration allows it to secure its distribution network. Unrelated business acquisition lets it diversify its product range. All of these strategies, if carried out successfully, enable the firm to strengthen its market position.

Alternatively the firm may choose the internal growth option. In this case the firm 'grows from within' by expanding its established markets or entering new ones, for example overseas, with its existing products. Another part of this strategy may be to develop new products for future use. These may either be related to the firm's current products, for example different brands of the same core product, or be completely new if the firm is seeking to extend its product range. Thus there are certain similarities with the types of external growth discussed above – it is the methods by which such growth is achieved that are different. The firm's ability to grow by any of these means is subject to four interrelated constraints:

1. Demand

2. Financial

3. Managerial

4. Security

The demand constraint arises from the fact that there may be insufficient demand for its existing products to enable the firm to grow. The solution to this is to diversify the firm's product base. There are, however, a number of issues which the firm will have to consider in deciding how this should be done. These include whether it should pursue a path of internal or external growth; how much risk it is prepared to take; and how many new products should be introduced in order to ensure success.

The growth process which the firm chooses to adopt will obviously depend upon the speed with which it wishes to grow and the resources that it has at its disposal. Some of its potential choices will be riskier than others, and this in turn is related to the issue of whether the firm has sufficient market knowledge. The more the firm knows about the market(s) into which it is expanding, the less likely it is that the firm will make a serious mistake. If it knows relatively little, then an external growth strategy, for example a merger with a firm which is already operating in the relevant market, may be the best option to pursue as it reduces the element of risk involved. Regardless of which approach to growth it adopts, however, the firm will need to know how many products it should be introducing in order to ensure that at least one is successful and what the appropriate pricing and advertising strategies and so on for each of them are in the markets in question. Getting these decisions right will be the key to the success of the firm's growth strategy and the costs of getting them wrong are potentially high. In any case, whether it is successful or not, the firm may need to sacrifice some of its current profits in order to 'buy' future growth and profitability.

This brings us to the second of the constraints identified above – the financial constraint. The problem here is that the greater the amount of growth required, and the more rapidly it needs to be achieved, the more difficult it will be to find sufficient affordable finance in order to pay for it. The easiest option for the firm is to finance this growth out of retained profits, that is by reducing the amount of profit which is given back to the shareholders in the form of dividends. This assumes, however, that the shareholders will be willing to accept this arrangement. If they are not, then this may create tensions within the firm, possibly resulting in a vote of no confidence in the management, or a fall in the firm's share price as disaffected shareholders sell their shares in order to purchase more profitable investments.

An alternative means of raising finance, particularly for a major investment programme, is to issue new shares in the company. This can only be done occasionally, however, and does carry some risk, for example a falling share price if the issue fails. A third option is to borrow the money from a bank or some other financial institution. The firm's ability to do so will depend upon its credit rating and the strength of its business plan. Normally, the higher the risk associated with the investment, the more safeguards the lender will want in terms of security for the loan. In addition, the greater the risk, the higher the interest rate the firm may have to pay which may create problems for it in terms of servicing the debt. Thus none of these methods of finance are risk free and it is up to the firm to find the right balance between the amount of finance needed for growth and the associated risks of each of the options available.

The third constraint on the firm's growth, the managerial constraint, is concerned with the ability of its managers to adapt to change. As the firm grows, either the existing managers will have to take on additional work or more managers will need to be appointed. The faster the firm is growing, the greater will be the strain that this imposes on the management team. Job specifications may need to be rewritten, and each time the management team expands there will be a need for greater co-ordination of its activities. If this is done badly, for example if managers in different parts of the firm are issuing contradictory instructions, then the firm may suffer as a result. Thus the firm's ability to grow effectively may depend on the flexibility and responsiveness to change of its managers. Related to this, the firm may be subject to the fourth of the constraints listed above – the security constraint. Excessive growth may cause severe problems within the firm which in turn may lead either to bankruptcy or to the firm being taken over, particularly if these problems result in a falling share price. If this happens, then managers' jobs are at risk, especially if these problems can be attributed directly to poor management. Thus there may be an incentive for the managers to put their own job security ahead of the (potential) benefits to the firm of expansion in order to ensure that any such associated costs are avoided.

In summary, therefore, the firm's management will need to carefully consider the possible impact of these four constraints upon the business if the firm is to expand. If the company is already highly profitable and has a lot of money to spend on expansion, then the financial constraint may not be of particular importance. Similarly, if the management team is dynamic, flexible and prepared to take risks in the pursuit of growth, then the managerial and security constraints may not apply and so on. Consequently we can say that the firm will 'maximise growth subject to the four constraints depending upon their relative importance to the firm's management'. Thus two firms in a similar position may make different decisions regarding future growth because of the differing priorities of the two management teams involved. Having looked at the general principles underlying growth maximisation models, the next step is to undertake a closer examination of the Marris growth maximisation model.

■ ■ ■ **Self-Assessment Question** ■ ■ ■ ■ ■ ■ ■ ■ ■ ■ ■ ■ ■

Q7 What is the definition of growth maximisation? What is the difference between horizontal integration and vertical integration as a source of growth for the firm? What are the four constraints on growth? Give an example of each of these four constraints.

4.7.2   The Marris Growth Maximisation Model

There are three basic assumptions which underpin this model:

1. Managers try to maximise their own utility which is a function of the rate of growth of the firm.

2. Shareholders try to maximise their wealth.

3. Growth occurs via diversification into new products and occurs in the form of either supply growth or demand growth.

Thus the model combines elements of both the managerial utility maximisation model and the wealth maximisation model which were covered earlier on in this chapter in terms of the motivations of managers and shareholders. The latter are still primarily interested in profit but they are also prepared to take a longer term view and to sacrifice profit in the current period in order to 'buy' growth in the expectation that this will strengthen the position of the firm and lead to higher profits later on. The managers also have the same underlying motive in terms of their own utility as was the case before, but the source of this utility is different. In the managerial utility maximisation model they obtained utility from a combination of staffing expenditure, managers' benefits and salaries and discretionary investment. According to the Marris model, they obtain utility from the rate of growth of the firm. These two approaches are not incompatible, however, as large and growing firms will hire more staff, the managers are likely to be more highly paid and new (discretionary) investment will be necessary in order for growth to take place. Within the model, supply growth arises from the fact that if the firm is successful, and so is making high profits, then money is readily available for reinvestment in the business. Providing this is done correctly, this will in turn result in even higher profits and enable the firm to invest more in the future. Conversely, if the wrong investments are made, this will damage the firm's profitability and less money will be available for future investment. This will result in lower future growth unless money can be obtained from another source, that is, the financial constraint will be a significant factor in this case.

While there is this strong direct relationship between high levels of growth and high levels of profit in the case of supply growth, the relationships between the factors which lead to demand growth are more complex. To begin with, when the rate of growth of the firm is relatively low, any increase in the growth rate increases profitability significantly as the best of the firm's new products are introduced. At the same time, there is also an incentive for managers to make the firm more efficient in order to widen profit margins and so obtain more money to invest in achieving further growth. This process cannot continue indefinitely, however, as at some point the potential for further growth will become more limited. Specifically, at relatively high rates of

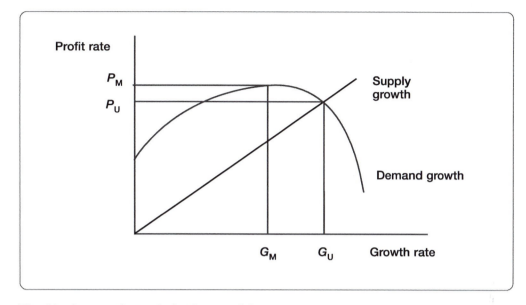

Figure 4.5   The Marris growth maximisation model

growth, increased growth can only be achieved through higher levels of expenditure on advertising and product development which, combined with the increasing stresses on the management team, results in a fall in profitability. Thus the demand, financial and managerial constraints begin to make an impact at this point. If the fall in profitability is very steep, the security constraint may also come into play in terms of the managers' future decision making. The effects of supply growth and demand growth within the firm are shown in Figure 4.5.

The direct relationship between profitability and the growth rate in the case of supply growth is clearly demonstrated in Figure 4.5. The slope of the supply-growth line may vary, however, depending upon the precise nature of this relationship. If a high rate of growth results in a lower or higher profit rate than that shown in Figure 4.5, the supply-growth line will be relatively flatter or steeper respectively. This will mean that the supply-growth and demand-growth curves will intersect at a different point on the graph, further to the right or further to the left respectively than the point shown in Figure 4.5 .

As far as the demand-growth curve is concerned, Figure 4.5 again shows quite clearly the fact that after a certain point, $P_M G_M$, (which is the profit-maximising rate of growth as it is at the peak of the demand-growth curve) a higher growth rate can only be acquired at the expense of a reduction in the rate of profit. Thus while initially an increase in the rate of growth has a positive effect on the firm's profit rate, this will not continue indefinitely. If the shareholders are solely interested in maximising profits, then $G_M P_M$ will be their preferred position.

In Figure 4.5 the optimal position for the managers is $P_U G_U$, the growth (utility) maximisation point. Both the supply-growth and the demand-growth constraints are satisfied at this point as the two curves intersect. It is apparent from the graph, however, that at this point the rate of growth is faster than that which is consistent with profit maximisation. Thus, as was the case for some of the previous models, there is the potential for shareholder–manager conflict as the rate of growth which yields the highest level of managerial utility is greater than that which the shareholders would normally prefer. A compromise may, therefore, have to be reached with a rate of growth between G_M and G_U. This will not completely satisfy either side, but the managers will gain a higher rate of growth than would be the case for a profit-maximising firm while the share-holders will obtain a higher level of profit than that which is consistent with a firm trying to maximise its rate of growth. What factors then will this compro-mise be based on?

The key element here is the security constraint. By pushing the share-holders too far in terms of the loss of profits associated with a higher growth rate and/or exposing the firm to the risk of takeover from another firm which is more profit orientated as a result of a falling share price (which reflects the lower dividends being paid to shareholders as more of the firm's profits are being retained to finance further expansion), there may be a risk of managers losing their jobs. If the managers wish to avoid this then they may have to return a higher proportion of the firm's profits to the shareholders than they would ideally like to do. This of course limits the amount of money available to finance future growth and so results in a steeper supply-growth curve with the result that the optimum point for the firm lies further to the left than that shown in Figure 4.5. In fact, if job loss is a very real threat, then the managers may reduce the rate of growth back to that compatible with profit maximisa-tion, G_M. They obtain significantly less growth-based utility at this point but in exchange they achieve greater job security. Thus a risk-averse management team may be more willing to make this kind of compromise than one which is risk loving and keen to pursue a faster rate of growth. It is apparent from this, therefore, that there is no one single outcome of this model for the firm as the final result depends once again on the relative strengths and attitudes of the shareholders and managers. This is less true, however, of the profit-maximising rate of sales growth model.

■ ■ ■ Self-Assessment Question ■ ■ ■ ■ ■ ■ ■ ■ ■ ■ ■ ■

Q8 What is the difference between supply growth and demand growth in the Marris model? How is the growth maximisation point for the firm determined in this model?

4.7.3 The Profit-maximising Rate of Sales Growth Model

In the profit-maximising rate of sales growth model, the firm's objective is to identify the rate of growth at which the firm will maximise the present value of expected future profits. How the firm can do this is demonstrated in Figure 4.6.

The present value of profit (PVP) is the difference between the present value of revenues (PVR) and the present value of costs (PVC). Thus the rate of growth at which the difference between the PVR and PVC curves is greatest is the one which gives the maximum profit, g^* in Figure 4.6. (Note: the present value of the firm's profits is calculated in the same way as in Section 4.6. In order to calculate PVR and PVC the relevant figures for revenue and costs are included in the top part of the equation instead of profits.)

In this model, the PVC curve includes both the total costs of production and the costs of expansion associated with the managerial and financial constraints. The latter elements account for the steeper slope of the PVC curve beyond g^* as these costs will increase significantly as the rate of growth increases, whereas production costs will increase at a fairly steady rate as the level of output expands. Thus expansion beyond g^* is not really in the firm's interests as it brings with it much higher costs.

The PVR curve increases in slope after g^* for a different reason – that as the volume of sales increases at higher rates of growth, the present value of future revenues will also be higher as the sums of money accruing from additional sales will be greater. Even when the absolute values for sales revenue are discounted to give net present values, these will still be larger at higher rates of growth.

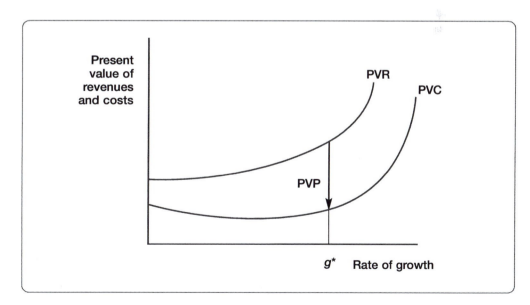

Figure 4.6   The profit-maximising rate of sales growth model

Thus it is the relative positions of the PVC and PVR curves which give us the optimal rate of growth for this model, g^*, where the difference between the two curves is at its greatest and where the present value of future profits will be maximised. Anywhere to the left (right) of this point, profits could be increased by moving to the right (left) on the graph until g^* is reached, that is, either a lower or a faster rate of growth than g^* will yield less profit and therefore be suboptimal.

■ ■ ■ Self-Assessment Question ■ ■ ■ ■ ■ ■ ■ ■ ■ ■ ■

Q9 How are the managerial and financial constraints included in the profit-maximising rate of sales growth model?

CASE STUDY *ConsFirm*

In its attempts to obtain an increase in the salaries and benefits being paid to its members, the management team soon realised that there was a limit to the extent to which this could be done given the current size of the company. Consequently, they returned to their original idea (Section 4.1) of using the firm's increased profitability to finance an expansion programme. As the economy was still in the upturn phase of the business cycle, it was reasonable to expect that the firm would continue to be profitable during the next few years and consequently such a strategy would be feasible. Within the team, however, there were concerns about the level of risk that would be acceptable and the way in which growth could be achieved. After some discussion it was decided that the firm should build on its existing base and expand via internal growth. Specifically, the firm would expand its core business of house building by setting up a separate subsidiary company in the south of England while also increasing the amount of housing repair and

maintenance work that it undertook in its existing area as this diversification had proved successful during the recession. In addition, it would continue to subcontract its staff to other companies to fit out office buildings but would also tender for shop-fitting contracts as well. This would give it the demand growth which it required, while the rising profits resulting from this expansion would also enable supply growth to occur. Thus the utility focus of the management team had now shifted from salaries and benefits per se to a high rate of company growth which would enable them to obtain these benefits anyway. What then would be the result of this?

The first problem which emerged was one of co-ordination. The existing management team could not adequately control both the north and south of England subsidiaries so that a new team had to be brought in to run the latter (the managerial constraint). In addition, its lack of expertise in shop-fitting work led the company to underprice a

continued

number of its tenders resulting in losses on this part of its business. The firm's financial situation then deteriorated further as a result of a 10 per cent rise in the price of house-building materials at a time when the company had budgeted for a rise of just 5 per cent. This combination of losses and increased costs in turn reduced the amount of internally sourced finance available to fund its expansion (the financial constraint). Unwilling to borrow any more money as interest rates had begun to rise, the management team then decided to reduce the dividend paid to shareholders by 50 per cent in order both to retain sufficient funds to continue the company's programme of growth and to award themselves a substantial pay increase. After narrowly surviving the resulting vote of no confidence which was proposed by some of the shareholders at the annual general meeting (the

security constraint), the management team decided to reverse this decision and to cut back the firm's expansion programme significantly. In the light of further co-ordination problems between the north and south of England branches, 'ConsFirm' decided to dispose of its southern subsidiary via a management buy-out. The experience, although initially negative, which it had gained in tendering for shop-fitting work enabled it to expand this side of the business considerably over the next few years. At the same time the firm went from strength to strength in its northern house building and repair and maintenance business while continuing to attract a steady amount of subcontracted office fitting work from other companies. In summary, therefore, the company has now consolidated its business and is achieving a slow but steady rate of growth in its turnover and its profits.

■ 4.8 Behavioural Models of Business Objectives

The behavioural models examined in this section – satisficing (Simon, 1959) and the Cyert/March model (Cyert and March, 1963) – share the assumption that many of the alternative models of business objectives are oversimplifications of the way in which firms really behave. They argue that in practice such optimising models do not truly represent how a firm makes decisions. Consequently they conclude that there may be no one definitive outcome for the firm but a series of possibilities based on the availability of information and/or the bargaining strengths or attitudes of groups within the firm. The satisficing model largely concentrates on the former, that is, the problem of imperfect information. The Cyert/March model, on the other hand, emphasises the potential for organisational conflict between different groups within the firm.

4.8.1 The Satisficing Model

This model is based on three assumptions:

1. Managers have imperfect knowledge.

2. Decision-making calculations are too complex to undertake frequently.

3. Managers can never really know if they are maximising profits, sales or growth or not.

Thus the model questions whether the firm ever really has sufficient information about the market in which it operates and its own activities in terms of its costs of production and so on to enable it to make any optimising (maximising) decisions at all. In addition, even if the firm does have access to good, reliable information, the changing nature of markets and the firm's operations makes it difficult to use effectively as by the time any decision is taken at least one of the factors in question will have changed. Consequently the firm's managers will be unable or unwilling to carry out the necessary calculations frequently enough to ensure their accuracy. As a result of this, the firm may think that it is maximising, for example profits, sales revenue or growth, while in reality it is not. Moreover, the managers will never know that this is the case and so may be pursuing the 'wrong' strategy for the firm.

The outcome of the model, therefore, is that the firm's managers will 'satisfice', that is, they will aim for satisfactory rather than maximum levels of profit, sales revenue or growth. Specifically, in the case of profit, for which this model was originally designed, this satisfactory level will depend upon the amount of money needed to finance the firm's existing operations or future expansion; the shareholders' requirements; and the degree of risk involved in the firm's activities, all of which we have discussed earlier in this chapter. Thus the model again results in compromise and so has no definitive outcome. The precise strategy which the firm decides to pursue will depend upon the information at its disposal, its resources and the need to satisfy the various groups within the firm such as the managers and shareholders. This was also true of some of the models described earlier. The last of the models of business objectives – the Cyert/March model – takes this scenario a stage further by including other groups which have an interest in the firm's activities.

4.8.2 The Cyert/March Model

The basic assumption which underlies this model is that the manager–shareholder split within the firm is an over-simplification of the true position. The model states that in practice the firm consists of an 'organisational coalition' of managers, workers, shareholders and customers. Each of these groups either will have different objectives or will have different views regarding the relative importance of various parts of the firm's activities. In addition, the firm itself has five competing goals – production, inventory, sales, market share and profits – which will be of greater or lesser importance to each of the four groups. Consequently the goal which the firm will actually pursue depends upon the relative bargaining powers of the groups and any alliances between them which are formed at particular points in time.

Production, for example, will be of particular importance to the workers as if the firm is not producing very much of the good, one consequence of this may be job losses. In this case, it is in the workers' interests to expand production in order to obtain greater job security. At the same time, however, this may also be in the customers' interests as restricted supply relative to demand will have the effect of driving up the price of the firm's product which is obviously not in their interests.

Thus a strategic alliance may be, at least implicitly, formed between the workers and customers but this in turn may be opposed by the managers and shareholders if they see restricted production as a way of reducing costs and increasing prices and/or profits. In this particular situation, it would be reasonable to expect the manager–shareholder alliance to prevail as they are generally the most powerful groups within the firm.

An alternative set of alliances may arise in the case of profit. If the shareholders are collectively short-run profit maximisers then this will be the most important goal to them. This may not, however, be true for the other groups. The managers, for example, may be prepared to sacrifice short-run profits for long-run gain in the form of increased market share. Likewise, the workers may be interested in the long-run job security which an increase in market share would bring and in this case would ally with the managers, especially if higher short-run profits meant cutting the firm's labour costs. As far as the customers are concerned, they may be relatively indifferent in this scenario, unless they viewed the firm's profits to be excessive, in which case they in turn might ally with the managers and workers against the shareholders. In this situation, therefore, the ability of the shareholders to push through their goal of higher short-run profits would be constrained by the opposition which they face from the other groups. Only a very powerful group of shareholders could insist on the firm targeting the profit goal in this case.

Similar scenarios can be constructed for each of the goals in turn, but in each case the final outcome will depend on the relative strengths of either the individual groups or the alliances which they form. The result of this model will therefore be a compromise between the groups within the firm. Thus, for example, some profit may be sacrificed in the short run in order to achieve an increase in market share or the firm may hold a smaller inventory or stock of goods in order to keep costs down, even though customers would prefer shorter waiting times for the delivery of their goods.

This need to compromise between the groups will reduce the overall efficiency of the firm as it, and its resources, will be less focused on one particular target. This particular phenomenon is known as 'organisational slack' and is detrimental to the firm as it will be operating in a suboptimal way because of the need for 'give and take' between the various parts of the organisational coalition.

■ ■ ■ Self-Assessment Question ■ ■ ■ ■ ■ ■ ■ ■ ■ ■ ■ ■

Q10 The two behavioural models of business objectives – satisficing and the Cyert/March model – are both critical of optimisation models but from a different perspective. On what particular basis does each of them question the applicability of the economic models of business objectives to firms?

❑ ❑ ❑ End of Chapter SUMMARY ❑ ❑ ❑ ❑ ❑ ❑ ❑ ❑ ❑ ❑ ❑

In this chapter we have looked at a number of models of business objectives. Most of these are optimising models, that is they seek to maximise something be it profit, sales or growth. Some involve compromises between the different groups within the firm, principally, although not solely, between managers and shareholders. In summary, therefore, what this chapter demonstrates is that the firm has a range of possible options to choose from in setting the overall objective or policy which will determine the future direction of the business. There is no right or wrong answer to the question of which of the business objectives a firm should adopt, as the choice of objective will depend upon the firm's individual circumstances, including the preferences of its management team and the type of market in which it operates. There is, therefore, an element of subjectivity in the decision-making process.

The choice of objective will, however, determine what the firm should do next in terms of the various elements of its overall corporate strategy. Thus the decisions which it takes regarding, for example, its pricing, advertising and investment strategies, will be influenced by its choice of objective. Any subsequent change in this objective may necessitate a new approach to any or all of these decisions.

References

Baumol, W. (1967) *Business Behaviour, Value and Growth*, Harcourt Brace, New York.

Cyert, R.M. and March, J.G. (1963) *Behavioural Theory of the Firm*, Prentice Hall, Hemel Hempstead.

Marris, R. (1964) *The Economic Theory of Managerial Capitalism*, Macmillan – now Palgrave Macmillan, Basingstoke.

Pappas, J.L., Brigham, E.F. and Shipley, B. (1983) *Managerial Economics*. UK edition, Cassell Education, London.

Simon, H. (1959) 'Theories of Decision Making in Economics and Behavioral Science', *American Economic Review,* **49**: 253–83.

Williamson, O. (1963) 'Managerial Discretion and Business Behavior', *American Economic Review,* **53**: 147–62.

■ ■ ■ ANSWERS to Self-Assessment Questions ■ ■ ■ ■ ■ ■

Q1

The term 'contingent decision making' means that the firm's choice of, for example, pricing strategy will depend upon which of the models of business objectives it chooses, that is its decision about pricing is contingent on (or constrained by) its original decision regarding which objective to pursue.

Q2

The three rules for profit maximisation are: the firm should only produce the good at all if total revenue is greater than or equal to total variable cost; the marginal revenue obtained from the last unit of output produced must equal the marginal cost of producing that unit; and marginal cost is less (greater) than marginal revenue at lower (higher) output levels. The point on Figure 4.1 which represents the profit-maximising level of output is Q_3, as it is the only one which satisfies all three of these conditions.

Q3

If the firm's managers were to ignore the shareholders' profit constraint and fully pursue the objective of sales revenue maximisation, then profits would be reduced significantly as output was expanded in order to generate additional sales. The implications of this for the firm might include a falling share price as shareholders sell their shares and transfer their money into more profitable investments. This could put the firm at risk of takeover due to the associated fall in the value of the company. Alternatively, there could be a positive effect on the firm if pursuing this strategy ensured its long-term survival by increasing its cash flow or providing the necessary funds for future investment in the company.

Q4

The firm may pursue the sales volume maximisation objective in order to gain entry into a market or to increase its market share. It should set its price equal to average revenue under this model. The types of product to which this model might most easily be applied are consumer goods and services, such as cars or insurance, which can be produced or supplied on a large scale and for which economies of scale can consequently be reaped. (Note: as this is of limited applicability to house building, the case study of 'ConsFirm' has not been used to illustrate the outcomes of this model.)

Q5

The three assumptions on which the managerial utility maximisation model are based are: that managers can act independently; that the firm is not in a highly competitive market and so can earn supernormal profits; and that managerial utility is a function of staffing expenditure, managers' salaries and benefits and discretionary investment. The outcome of the model is that profits will be reduced as more money is spent on the three things which give the managers utility at the expense of higher profit levels.

Q6

With an interest rate of 10 per cent, the value of the firm will be:

$$\text{Value} = \frac{20{,}000}{(1 + 0.1)} + \frac{25{,}000}{(1 + 0.1)^2} + \frac{22{,}000}{(1 + 0.1)^3} + \frac{25{,}000}{(1 + 0.1)^4}$$

$$= 18{,}182 + 20{,}662 + 16{,}539 + 17{,}075 = £72{,}458$$

With an interest rate of 5 per cent, the 0.1 in the bottom part of the equation is replaced by 0.05 to give: Value = 19,048 + 22,676 + 19,004 + 20,568 = £81,296. This demonstrates that the higher the interest rate, the smaller will be the firm's value for any given profit level. Thus a rise in interest rates will reduce the value of the firm and vice versa. The main difficulty in using this model is that both interest rates and profit levels fluctuate and so are inherently difficult to forecast. This obviously affects the accuracy of the wealth (value) maximisation calculation, and in the case of a company whose fortunes are comparatively volatile such as 'ConsFirm' the usefulness of this model is limited unless a series of alternative possible combinations of interest rate and profit levels are considered.

Q7

Growth maximisation is defined as 'an attempt to increase the size of the firm as far as possible and/or at as fast a rate as possible'. The difference between horizontal and vertical integration is that the former involves the company merging with or taking over a similar firm in the same industry, while the latter involves it either taking over one of its suppliers (backward vertical integration) or one of its retailers (forward vertical integration). The four constraints on growth are: demand, for example insufficient demand for existing products; financial, for example an inability to raise money quickly enough to finance future expansion; managerial, for example the managers' inability to mange rapid growth which results in them becoming overstretched and overstressed; and the security constraint, for example the threat of job losses or a takeover of the company.

Q8   The difference between supply growth and demand growth is that the former results directly from the firm making high profits which it can then reinvest in the business, while the latter, although still related to profit, operates in a different way. Specifically, at low rates of growth, further growth increases profitability as the firm expands its sales and/or product line. Later on, however, any further increase in the rate of growth damages the firm's profitability as greater expenditure on things like product development is necessary in order to secure any additional growth. Thus whereas the supply-growth function is an upward-sloping straight line, the demand-growth function is an inverted U-shape (see Figure 4.5). The growth-maximising point in this model is determined by the intersection of the supply-growth and the demand-growth curves (point $P_U G_U$ in Figure 4.5).

Q9   The managerial and financial constraints are incorporated into the profit-maximising rate of sales growth model via the inclusion of the associated costs of expansion in the present value of costs curve. These two constraints combined account for the steep slope of the PVC curve beyond the optimal growth rate g^*, as any additional growth beyond this point is associated with both the increased difficulty of financing such growth and the increased stresses on the management team which result from growth.

Q10   The satisficing model criticises optimisation models on the grounds that in the presence of imperfect market information (and due to the complexity of the associated calculations) it is impossible for the firm to know whether it is maximising any of the decision variables at all. The Cyert/March model, on the other hand, takes the view that the optimisation models are oversimplified in that they do not take sufficient account of the tensions between the different groups within the firm. Consequently, according to this model, compromise between these groups is a more likely outcome than maximisation.

Demand estimation and forecasting

■ 5.1 Introduction

This chapter examines the ways in which the firm can estimate the current demand for its product and forecast likely values for future demand. The need to do this is not confined to private sector organisations. It is equally necessary for many public sector organsations – for example we need to be able to predict the future demand for primary school places, health care and public housing. The principles of demand forecasting for public sector organisations are not significantly different from those applied in the private sector. However, this chapter very much focuses on the range of demand forecasting techniques often used in the private sector.

Accurate information on prospective demand is important to the firm for a number of reasons. Firstly, the level of demand for a product will determine the amount of it that the firm will wish to produce. If demand is low, then the firm will want to reduce production in order to avoid excessive stockpiles of the good and the storage costs associated with them. On the other hand, if demand is high and the firm is producing at less than full capacity, it is losing potential sales and profits.

Secondly, the level and method of production will determine the firm's cost structure. If, for example, demand for the firm's product is expected to fall, then advance warning of this decline in demand will enable the firm to reduce its costs in order to minimise the effect on profitability. Without this knowledge, the firm would be exposed to a higher level of risk. Thus accurate predictions of future demand allow it to minimise the effects of uncertainty in the market on the firm.

Thirdly, the firm needs to have information about likely future demand in order to pursue an optimal pricing strategy. It can only charge a price which the market will bear if it is to sell the product. On the one hand, over-optimistic estimates of demand may lead to an excessively high price and lost sales. On the other hand, over-pessimistic estimates of demand may lead to a price which is set too low resulting in lost profits. Again the more, and the more accurate, information the firm has, the less likely it is to take a decision which will have a negative impact on its operations and profitability.

Fourthly, the level of demand for a product will influence the decisions which the firm will take regarding the non-price factors which form part of its overall competitive strategy. For example, the level of advertising it carries out will be determined by the perceived need to stimulate demand for the product. As advertising expenditure represents an additional cost to the firm, unnecessary spending in this area needs to be avoided. If the firm's expectations about demand are too low it may try to compensate by spending large sums on advertising, money which in this instance may be at least partly wasted. Alternatively it may decide to redesign the product in response to this, thus incurring unnecessary additional costs in the form of research and development expenditure. Thus insufficient or inaccurate knowledge of prevailing demand conditions in a particular market may have detrimental effects on the firm in these areas as well.

It is important to remember that any decisions taken within the firm will have knock-on effects on other factors affecting the firm including demand. For example, the price of the good will determine the demand for it, but in turn the firm's expectations about demand will influence the price it sets. Thus what we have is a series of complex interrelationships between the firm's various decisions and its decision-making processes. One persistent theme, however, is that the firm is seeking to minimise risk. The more knowledge it has, and the greater the control it can exercise over its environment, the less uncertainty it will be exposed to. This can only be beneficial to the firm.

Having considered some of the reasons why the firm would wish to know the likely level of demand for its product, let us now go on to look specifically at the issues involved in predicting demand. We begin with a brief summary of the basic theory of demand which should already be familiar to you, before going on to examine the various estimation and forecasting techniques.

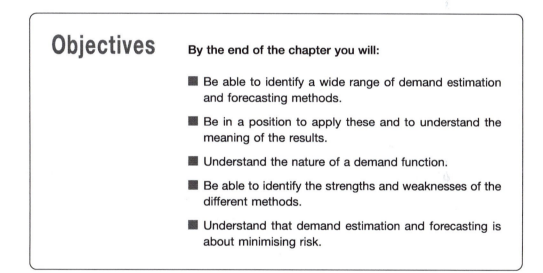

Objectives

By the end of the chapter you will:

■ Be able to identify a wide range of demand estimation and forecasting methods.

■ Be in a position to apply these and to understand the meaning of the results.

■ Understand the nature of a demand function.

■ Be able to identify the strengths and weaknesses of the different methods.

■ Understand that demand estimation and forecasting is about minimising risk.

■ ■ ■ Self-Assessment Question ■ ■ ■ ■ ■ ■ ■ ■ ■ ■ ■ ■ ■ ■

Q1
Give three reasons why the firm might need accurate demand information.

■ 5.2 Demand Theory

This section reviews the theory of demand. It covers the demand function, the demand curve and demand elasticities and assesses their usefulness as tools for the firm in its attempt to predict future demand for its product.

5.2.1 The Demand Function

The demand function sets out the variables which are believed to have an influence on the demand for a particular product. The demand for different products may be determined by a range of factors which are not always the same for each of them. What is presented here is a generic demand function which includes some of the most common variables that affect demand. For any individual product, however, some of these may not apply. Thus, any attempt by the firm to predict demand for a product on the basis of the demand function will require some initial knowledge, or at least informed guesswork, about the likely influences on it.

The demand function can be written as:

$$Q_D = f (P_O, P_C, P_S, Y_D, T, A_O, A_S, A_C, C_R, R, E, N, O)$$

The first three variables in the function relate to price. They are the own price of the product (P_O), the price of complements (P_C) and the price of substitutes (P_O) respectively. In the case of the own price of a good, the expected relationship would be, the higher the price the lower the demand, and the lower the price the higher the demand. This is the law of demand on which the demand curve (Figure 5.1) is based. In the case of complements, if the price of a complementary good increases, we would expect demand to fall both for it and for the good which it is complementary to. This is the case as fewer people would now wish to buy either good given that the complementary good is now more expensive, and this has a knock-on effect of reducing demand for the other good as well. In contrast, if the price of a substitute good rises, then demand for the good which it is a substitute for would be expected to rise as people switched to buying the latter rather than its now more expensive substitute.

The fourth variable in the demand function, Y_D, stands for disposable income, that is, the amount of money people have available to spend. The greater the level of disposable income, the more people can afford to buy and hence the higher the level of demand for most products will be. This assumes of course that they are 'normal' goods, purchases of which increase with rising levels of income, as opposed to 'inferior' goods which are purchased less frequently as income rises. The use of disposable income rather than just income is justified on the grounds that people do not have total control over their gross incomes. There will, for example, be deductions to be made in the form of taxes. Even after such factors have been accounted for, part of most people's incomes is 'pre-spent' in the form of existing commitments such as mortgages and so is not available for alternative purchases. Thus the level of disposable income can change over time, for example as mortgage rates change. Higher mortgage rates leave less left over for additional spending whereas lower ones release additional funds. On a national level, of course, this will to some extent be counterbalanced by the associated loss of income to savers. It is the overall effect that is important.

The effect of changes in disposable income on the demand for individual products will of course be determined by the ways in which it is spent. This is where the fifth variable, tastes (T), needs to be taken into account. Over time, tastes may change significantly, but this may incorporate a wide range of factors. For example, in the case of food, greater availability of alternatives may have a significant effect in changing the national diet. Thus, in the UK for instance, the demand for potatoes has fallen over the past 20 years as people have switched to eating rice and pasta instead. Social pressures may also act to alter tastes and hence demand. For example, tobacco companies have been forced to seek new markets as smoking has become less socially acceptable in the USA and western Europe, thus reducing demand in these areas. Changes in technology may also have an impact. For example, as the demand for colour televisions increased, the demand for black and white televisions fell as tastes changed and the latter were deemed to be inferior goods. Thus there are a number of ways in which tastes may change over time.

The next set of variables, the A variables, relate to levels of advertising, representing the level of own product advertising, the advertising of substitutes and the advertising of complements respectively. The relationships here are as follows. In general, the higher the level of own advertising for a good, the higher demand for that good would be expected to be, other things being equal. Likewise, the higher the level of advertising of a complementary good, the higher the demand for it and the good(s) which it is complementary to will be, given their symbiotic relationship. Conversely, however, the higher the level of advertising of a substitute good, the lower the demand for the good for which it is an alternative will be as people buy the more heavily promoted good. The overall effect of advertising will depend on the extent to which each of these forms of advertising is used at any given point in time as they may, at least in part, cancel each other out. This is something the firm will also need to know in order to determine its optimal advertising strategy.

The variables C_R and R are also related. The former represents the availability of credit while the latter represents the rate of interest, that is the price of credit. These variables will be most important for purchases of consumer durable goods, for example cars. Someone's ability to buy a car will depend on their ability to raise money to pay for it. This means that the easier credit is to obtain, the more likely they are to be able to make the purchase. At the same time credit must be affordable, that is the rate of interest must be one which they have the money to pay. These two variables have traditionally been regarded as exogenous to the firm, that is they cannot be controlled by it. In recent years, however, major car manufacturers have increasingly sought to bring them under their control through the provision of finance packages.

The letter E in the demand function stands for expectations. This may include expectations about price and income changes for example. If consumers expect the price of a good to rise in future then they may well bring forward their purchases of it in order to avoid paying the higher price. This creates an increase in demand in the short term, but over the medium term demand may fall in response to the higher price charged. The firm will need to adjust its production accordingly. An example of this might be when increased taxes are expected to be levied on particular goods, for example an increase in excise duties on spirits or tobacco. Consumers of these products may buy more of them prior to the implementation of the duty increases in order to avoid paying the higher prices arising from the higher level of duties. Alternatively, expectations about incomes may be important. For example, people who expect their incomes to rise may buy more goods as a result, whereas those who expect their incomes to fall will buy less. At the level of the individual consumer this may not be significant but when aggregated across a country's population it can be. Thus during a boom in the economy the additional expected purchasing power of consumers will lead to increases in demand for a significant number of products. Conversely, the expectation that incomes will fall, perhaps as a result of redundancy during a recession, will reduce demand as consumers become more cautious.

The variable N stands for the number of potential customers. Each product is likely to have a target market, the size of which will vary. The number of potential customers may be a function of age or location. For example, the number and type of toys sold in a particular country will be related to its demographic spread, in this case the number of children within it and their ages.

Finally, we come to O which represents any other miscellaneous factors which may influence the demand for a particular product. For example, it could be used to represent seasonal changes in demand for a particular product if demand is subject to such fluctuations rather than evenly spread throughout the year. Examples of such products might include things such as umbrellas, ice cream and holidays. In sum, this is a 'catch all' variable which can be used to represent anything else which the decision maker believes to have an effect on the demand for a particular product.

Thus each product will have its own particular demand function depending on which of the above variables influence the demand for it. The ways in which the level of demand can be estimated on the basis of this demand function will be discussed later in the chapter.

■ ■ ■ Self-Assessment Question ■ ■ ■ ■ ■ ■ ■ ■ ■ ■ ■ ■

Q2 Name any five variables which may be included in the demand function.

■■■

5.2.2   The Demand Curve

The demand curve shows the relationship between the own price of a good and the quantity demanded of it. Any change in own price causes a movement along the curve as shown in Figure 5.1. In this case, a rise in price from P_1 to P_2 results in a fall in quantity demanded from Q_2 to Q_1.

A change in any of the other variables in the demand function will shift the demand curve. It will shift upwards to the right if the effect is to increase the amount of the good demanded at every price. It will shift downwards to the left if the effect is to decrease the amount of the good demanded at every price. Figures 5.2 and 5.3 show examples of these two changes.

Figure 5.2 shows a rightward shift in the demand curve from D_1D_1 to D_2D_2, which means that for any given price, such as P_1, more of the good is demanded, Q_2 instead of Q_1. Figure 5.3 shows the converse case where the result of the change in the demand function variable is to reduce the quantity demanded at every price, for example at price P_2 the quantity demand of the good falls from Q_2 to Q_1. This time the demand curve shifts leftwards from D_1D_1 to D_2D_2.

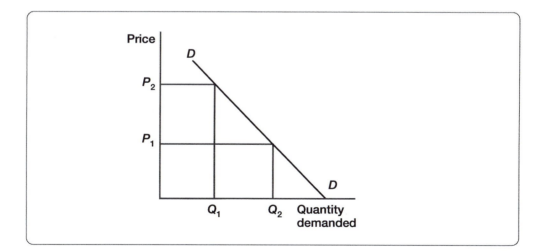

Figure 5.1   The demand curve

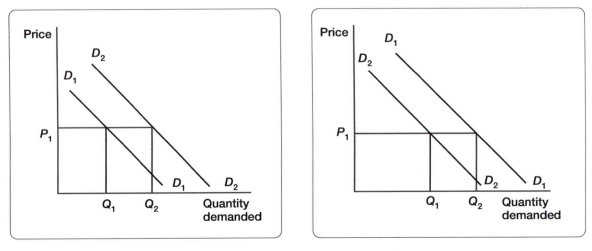

Figure 5.2   Increased demand   **Figure 5.3**   Decreased demand

What changes in the variables might cause these effects? In the case of the rightward shift in the demand curve, this could result, among other things, from increased advertising by the firm of its own product, a rise in disposable incomes or a change in tastes in favour of the good. The leftward shift in the demand curve could be caused by an increase in the advertising of substitute goods, a fall in the number of potential customers or a rise in the rate of interest. In fact, a change in any of the variables affecting demand, except the own price of the good, will have the effect of shifting the demand curve. The main problem arises in assessing the actual size of the effect of these changes, particularly when more than one variable is involved at any given time. One way of quantifying their effect is through the use of demand elasticity calculations.

■ ■ ■ **Self-Assessment Question** ■ ■ ■ ■ ■ ■ ■ ■ ■ ■ ■ ■

Q3   What causes a movement along the demand curve and what causes shifts in the demand curve?

5.2.3   The Calculation of Elasticities of Demand

When suitable quantitative data are available, elasticities of demand can be calculated for a number of the variables within the demand function. This can be done by adapting the generic elasticity of demand equation to include the relevant variable. The generic equation is written as follows:

$$\text{Elasticity } (E) \;=\; \frac{Q_2 - Q_1}{X_2 - X_1} \cdot \frac{X_1}{Q_1}$$

In this equation, the term $Q_2 - Q_1$ represents the change in quantity demanded arising from the change in the relevant variable, $X_2 - X_1$. The first term in the equation is then multiplied by X_1 / Q_1 in order to give the elasticity value. For example, if we were interested in finding out the effect of a change in the own price of a good on the quantity demanded of it, we would replace X with P_O. Alternatively, if it was the effect of a change in the firm's own advertising expenditure we wished to calculate, X would be replaced by A_O and so on. Using this method we could then assess the effectiveness, or otherwise, of the firm's decision to change its price or advertising level.

In order to do this, it is necessary to know the likely values of these calculations and what they mean. The own price elasticity of demand, when we substitute P_O for X in the equation, will take one of three main values in terms of the size of the value obtained – greater than one, equal to one or less than one. (In all three cases, the figure will be preceded by a minus sign which represents the downward slope of the demand curve, but it is the number obtained which is important. The minus sign can be ignored in assessing how elastic demand actually is.) If the own price elasticity of demand is greater than one, this means that demand is elastic with respect to price, that is a relatively small decrease (increase) in price will lead to a proportionately larger increase (decrease) in demand for the product. The higher the value obtained, the more elastic demand is with respect to price. If the own price elasticity of demand is equal to one, then the change in price will generate an equal change in quantity, for example if the price of a good rises by 5 per cent, demand for it will drop by 5 per cent. If the own price elasticity of demand is less than one, then demand is inelastic, that is comparatively unresponsive to changes in price. In this case, an increase in price of 5 per cent would lead to a fall in demand of, say, only 2 per cent. (Note: In terms of the slope of the demand curve, which is what the own price elasticity of demand measures, an elastic demand curve is one which is relatively flat while an inelastic demand curve is one which is relatively steep.)

The value of the own advertising elasticity of demand (E_A) is found by replacing X with A_O in the equation. If the value of the advertising elasticity of demand is zero, then the firm's advertising strategy is having no effect at all on demand. A value greater than zero indicates that the firm's advertising is increasing demand and the larger the figure the greater the increase. A negative value would give cause for concern as the firm's advertising strategy would be related to decreasing demand, perhaps because it was being cancelled out by other stronger forces within the market place.

Another frequently calculated elasticity is the income elasticity of demand. In this case, Y_D is substituted for X. If the income elasticity of demand is greater than zero, then the firm is producing a normal good whose demand will rise as disposable incomes rise and vice versa. On the other hand, if this figure is negative, the firm is producing an inferior good for which demand will fall as income rises.

A fourth, slightly more complex, elasticity calculation is the cross-elasticity of demand which measures the responsiveness of demand for one good to changes in the price of another. In this case the elasticity equation is written as:

$$\text{Elasticity } (E) = \frac{Q_{2A} - Q_{1A}}{P_{2B} - P_{1B}} \cdot \frac{P_B}{Q_A}$$

where A and B are two different goods.

A cross-elasticity of demand equal to zero indicates that the two goods are unrelated so that a change in the price of one has no effect on demand for the other. If the value is greater than zero then the two goods are substitutes for one another, so as the price of one of the goods rises, demand for the other increases as a result. Conversely, if the value is less than zero, the two goods are complements so that a rise in the price of one good will decrease the demand for the other.

These four are all examples of point elasticities of demand, that is, they measure the elasticity of demand at a specific point on the demand curve or function. Another form of elasticity is the arc elasticity of demand which measures the average elasticity over some range of the demand curve or function. This is generally used when there are insufficient data to calculate a series of point elasticities. This means that it is inherently less useful as an accurate predictor of demand in response to a particular change in the independent variable.

The equation for the arc elasticity of demand is:

$$\text{Arc elasticity} = \frac{\text{change in } Q \text{ / average } Q}{\text{change in } X \text{ / average } X} = \frac{Q_2 - Q_1 / 0.5(Q_2 + Q_1)}{X_2 - X_1 / 0.5(X_2 + X_1)}$$

$$= \frac{Q_2 - Q_1}{X_2 - X_1} \cdot \frac{X_2 + X_1}{Q_2 + Q_1}$$

Again, the variables within the demand function can be used to calculate arc elasticities with respect to price, advertising and so on.

Elasticities are a useful way of estimating the likely effect on demand of changes in the independent variables. Problems can arise, however, when more than one of the variables are changing simultaneously as individual elasticities of demand cannot pick up their combined effects. For example, if the price of the good fell at the same time as the firm started an intensive advertising programme, then demand would be expected to rise but how much of this increase would be attributable to each of these two factors? A calculation of price elasticity alone would attribute all of the increase in demand to the change in price, thus making demand for the product appear more responsive to price changes than is actually the case. This could have serious implications for the firm's future pricing strategy. A more sophisticated approach is needed, and for this reason a number of ways of predicting demand have been developed for use in different circumstances. Before going on to review these, however, let us summarise the main implications of demand theory for demand estimation and forecasting.

■ ■ ■ Self-Assessment Question ■ ■ ■ ■ ■ ■ ■ ■ ■ ■ ■ ■

Q4 What is the generic equation used to calculate a point elasticity of demand?

Using this equation calculate the following elasticities:

(a) the own price elasticity of demand for cars when the original price of a car of £8000 is raised to £9000, resulting in a fall in the number of cars sold from 50,000 to 40,000.

(b) the own advertising elasticity of demand when a firm increases its spending on advertising from £10,000 to £15,000, which leads to a rise in the number of chocolate bars sold from 50,000 to 75,000.

5.2.4   Summary

The demand function provides a good starting point for a consideration of the appropriate methods for predicting demand for a particular product as it identifies the main determinants of demand. Not all of these will apply simultaneously in the case of every product, but some, such as the own price of the product, can reasonably be expected to be almost universal. It is up to the decision maker to select those which will influence demand for the firm's product at any particular point in time.

In order to make the best use of demand theory in an applied setting, it is necessary to be able to quantify the variables. This can give rise to problems, particularly with those variables such as tastes and expectations which may be more qualitative than quantitative in nature. For this reason it will be essential for the firm to collect primary information on these variables, that is, to adopt what is known as the 'marketing approach' to demand estimation which is described in the next section. This will also be the case for new products for which little or no secondary data are available.

Where a firm has prior experience of producing and selling a product, it may already have relevant quantitative data which it can use to estimate future demand. It may do so by drawing the demand curve, although it may be difficult to quantify the shifts resulting from changes in the variables other than own price. Alternatively, elasticities of demand may be calculated, but again the calculation of individual elasticities is only really useful when just one of the independent variables is changing at any given time.

Thus demand theory provides us with some relatively simple ways of estimating demand under a restricted set of circumstances, but in order both to gather additional information and to calculate the impact on demand when several variables may be changing simultaneously more effective methods are needed. There are a range of alternatives which the decision maker can use, depending upon what he or she wishes to achieve. These are examined in the remainder of this chapter.

CASE STUDY *Marks & Spencer*

Marks & Spencer (M&S) is a well-known name in UK shopping centres, having established a high quality reputation for both clothing and food retailing. In recent years, however, the company has experienced a drop in demand for its women's clothing range. This case study details the ways in which M&S has tried to reverse this trend by attempting to establish which of the factors influencing demand has changed in this particular market.

For many years M&S traded on its strong brand name in this area which proved to be a successful strategy until the mid to late-1990s when competition in the high street clothing market increased significantly. Firmly positioned in the mid-range of the clothing market in terms of its customer base, the company experienced increased competition from those clothing retailers which were positioned in the same market segment such as Next and Debenhams. Further challenges were also emerging from the expansion of newer clothing retailers such as Gap and New Look who were attracting more and more of the younger female customers within the market (although this

was mainly at the expense of other retailers such as C&A which subsequently closed down).

Market analysis in 1998–99 revealed that M&S was facing several specific problems in relation to its sales of women's clothing. Firstly, some of its clothes were perceived to be overpriced relative to similar items sold by its competitors (the effect of the P_O and P_S variables in the demand function), which had a negative effect on sales even though they were often seen as being of better quality. In the short term this was dealt with by discounting prices in order to clear out-of-season stock, but a longer term pricing strategy was needed and is still being developed. Secondly, the firm appeared to have lost ground as a result of its lack of advertising (the A_O variable), having previously relied on repeat custom and word of mouth to generate sales. The importance placed on the need to start advertising more aggressively can be demonstrated by the fact that in December 1998 the company launched a television advertising campaign, its first for 15 years. Thirdly, there arose the issue of tastes (T). In order to try to widen its market base, M&S had begun to

continued

stock new fashion ranges which were targeted at 18–30-year-olds. Unfortunately for the company, however, this age group continued to prefer to shop elsewhere, while at the same time many of its more traditional, more mature customers were, at least temporarily, lost to the business because, as they perceived it, their tastes were no longer being adequately catered for by M&S. Turning around this situation was deemed to be vital for the long-term survival of M&S. The St Michael brand of clothing was dropped and new fashion lines from top designers were introduced in order to try to get customers back into the stores. Clothing sales continued to fall throughout 1999, however, and contributed significantly to the 7 per cent fall in total sales and reduction in profits from £1168 million in 1998 to £517 million in 1999.

A new chairman of the company, Luc Vandevelde, was appointed in January 2000 with the specific remit of improving Marks & Spencer's fortunes. In relation to the women's clothing part of the business, the process of redesigning the firm's product range and pricing and advertising it more aggressively continued. The fashion lines from top designers which were introduced between 1999 and 2001 under the Autograph label had limited success. Consequently in 2001, in the face of further falls in clothing sales which contributed to a fall in profits to £481 million in 2000, the company announced it would be returning to its own brand clothing with a greater focus on 'classic' clothing lines, which would be sold at more competitive prices, in an attempt to lure its traditional customers back to its stores. This change in policy coincided with the appointment of Yasmin Yusuf, the former head of Warehouse, as creative director of M&S, and Steve Longdon, the former managing director of Top Shop, as head of womenswear to oversee the redevelopment of the company's product lines. Among the product lines introduced (in October 2001) was the 'Per Una' range designed by George Davis who set up clothing retailer Next and was responsible for reviving the clothing part of the ASDA supermarket chain through the creation of the 'George at ASDA' brand. Early indications are that the range has been successful in bringing women back into the M&S stores where they are buying not only from this range but from M&S's new autumn fashion range as well. The new spring/summer 2002 ranges were well received by the fashion press on their launch and there is now speculation that M&S has 'turned the corner' with respect to this part of its business. Given that the company was the stock market's top performer in 2001 with a 90 per cent increase in share value to 375p at the end of 2001 (from a low of 170p in October 2001) this may well be the case. Compared to its highest share value of 664.5p in 1997, however, it still has a long way to go and only time will tell if its new approach will be successful.

■ 5.3   Demand Estimation and Forecasting

The first question which arises is, what is the difference between demand estimation and demand forecasting? The answer is that estimation attempts to quantify the links between the level of demand and the variables which determine it. Forecasting, on the other hand, just attempts to predict the overall level of future demand rather than looking at specific linkages. For this reason the set of techniques used may differ, although there will some overlap between the two. In general, an estimation technique can be used to forecast demand but a forecasting technique cannot be used to estimate demand. A manager who wished to know how high demand was likely to be in two years' time might use a forecasting technique. A manager who wished to know how the firm's pricing policy could be used to generate a given increase in demand would use an estimation technique.

The next section considers the marketing approach to demand measurement. The methods covered within it can be used both as a means of collecting primary data on the demand function variables, and as techniques in their own right for use in those cases where no other market information is available, for example for new products. The subsequent section considers the demand estimation technique of regression analysis. This is then followed by an examination of three forecasting techniques – extrapolation, decomposition analysis and barometric forecasting.

■ 5.4   The Marketing Approach to Demand Measurement

The marketing approach includes a number of techniques designed to give an insight into prevailing market conditions. All of them have their own individual strengths and weaknesses which will be discussed below. The methods are market surveys, expert opinion, sales force opinion and market testing. The last of these can be further subdivided into sales-wave research, simulated store techniques and test marketing.

5.4.1   Market Surveys

The purpose of a market survey is to question would-be purchasers of a product about their future buying intentions. Thus it can be used to predict likely demand for a product, but if done well it can also provide the firm with a great deal of supplementary information. This may include a breakdown of the type of consumers most likely to buy the product on the basis of age, sex and income. Such information could be used, for example, to target the firm's advertising strategy towards the specific groups which are most likely to be influenced by it. Alternatively, market surveys can be used to test buyers' reactions to new products or to changes in established products prior to their launch in order to see if they would be popular with consumers before any final, and potentially expensive, decision is made. Consumers can be asked, for example, whether a rise in the price of the product would lead to them buying it less frequently or not at all; whether they had seen the company's latest product advertisement and how it had affected their purchasing behaviour;

whether a change in the design or packaging of the product would influence them and so on. Thus the firm can potentially gather a significant amount of both quantitative and qualitative information about the factors which influence demand for its product.

How can the firm go about collecting this information? Firstly, there is the postal survey. This type of survey can be carried out on a relatively large scale. Households are sent a questionnaire designed to find out their opinions about a particular product or products. In order to encourage them to complete it, incentives are often offered such as prizes, product samples or coupons. Secondly, telephone surveys may be used where a company telephones people who are potential customers for a product, for example because they live within a certain geographical area. The main difficulty with this approach is that it is often deemed to be intrusive and so can generate significant customer resistance and perhaps negative feelings about the company concerned. Thirdly, there is the face-to-face survey which can operate on several levels. At its most basic it can amount to just stopping people at random in the street and asking them a few broad questions. A more sophisticated form of this type of survey, however, may involve in-depth interviews conducted over a long period of time in order to gauge any longer term changes in tastes. Once the survey has been conducted, the responses obtained are aggregated to give estimates of demand under different market conditions.

Although surveys may yield important information for the firm, a number of issues arise in terms of their suitability. Firstly, there is the issue of questionnaire design. Ideally, a questionnaire should be as short and easy to fill in as possible in order to generate the maximum response rate. Particularly in the case of an on-street survey, people will be unwilling to remain answering questions for long. If a lengthy questionnaire is unavoidable, then a postal survey may be the best approach as people can take their time filling it in. Many questionnaires require respondents to tick the appropriate box out of a list of choices which has the virtue of relative simplicity, although it is comparatively difficult to obtain in-depth information this way. Secondly, as already mentioned above, there is the problem of obtaining a satisfactory response rate. Although good questionnaire design can help, the firm needs to make sure that enough people are questioned to provide it with widely applicable information on which to base its decisions. This is related to the third issue, that of the need for a representative sample. If a firm is, say, seeking to identify the type of person who is most likely to buy the product, then it will need to ensure that the sample of responses obtained through the survey is representative of the total population. If not, any demand predictions made from the data obtained may be inaccurate. For example, if everyone who completed the questionnaire was aged between 20 and 30, then the firm would find out nothing about the demand for the product from people of other ages. Thus unless it was absolutely sure that this was the only age group that would be interested in the product, and hence the only one which would be influenced by any changes in the product's characteristics, it would have obtained biased information. This would almost certainly lead it to draw inaccurate conclusions about the demand for its product. The question of bias can therefore be identified as a fourth issue which arises in the administration of a market survey. Additionally, the presence of an interviewer can result in another form of bias. In this case, the interviewee may tell the interviewer what they think the interviewer wants to hear rather than what the interviewee would really do in particular circumstances. This judgement may, for example, be based on how the questions are asked in terms of voice intonation or whether the consumer can identify the company or companies responsible for the questionnaire. Fifthly, and relatedly, there is the problem of misinterpretation. This can arise either from the interviewee not understanding the question or the interviewer misinterpreting their response. In practice, there is little or nothing which can be done to remedy this problem. Finally, there is the possibility of a gap between the consumer's intentions and their actions. For example, when questioned the consumer may really intend to buy a new car next year but when the time comes can no longer afford to do so. This of course means that the shorter the time period between the survey and the actual purchase, the more accurate the survey is likely to be as there is less time for the consumer's circumstances to change.

Overall, therefore, a market survey, of whatever type, can provide the firm with good information about the demand, and the factors which affect demand, for a particular product. The use of this method may be especially necessary when existing information is limited, for example in the case of a change to an existing product. Advance indications of how this change will be received by the consumers will be extremely important. It must always be remembered, however, that the figures obtained are just estimates. Their accuracy will depend on how well, or how badly, the survey was carried out.

5.4.2   Sales Force Opinion

In this case, rather than asking the customer, the firm questions the people actually selling the product. The basic idea behind this approach is that the sales force will be in tune with their customers and what they think about various aspects of the product. This should enable the firm to estimate demand for the product under different market conditions, for example, how many more units of the product are likely to be sold when it is on 'special offer' at a reduced price.

The main reason why the firm may use this approach is that the sales force are relatively close to the customer compared to the management of the firm itself. This being the case, they may be the first to spot any changes in demand arising from changes in tastes or the introduction by another firm of a competing product. Thus the firm can use this specialist knowledge in its decision-making process. Again, as was the case for market surveys, the greater the amount of accurate data, the better the firm's demand predictions will be.

As this appears to be a relatively simple approach to demand estimation, why is it not relied on more heavily by firms than it actually is in practice? There are two main reasons. Firstly, although the sales force may have good local information, they may be unaware of wider national trends and their likely effect on future demand. For example, while a sales person may have an in-depth knowledge of the purchasing behaviour of their own particular customers, they may not be aware of broader, more general issues such as future changes in the economy which will affect demand. Thus, for example, if demand for a good was currently low, the sales person might predict that this trend would continue even though perhaps an upturn in the economy was imminent which would result in increased sales. Multiplying this effect throughout the country could result in the firm significantly underestimating future demand and losing out on future sales and profits as a result. For this reason, where the sales force opinion method is used, it is rarely used in isolation. The second problem which arises with the use of this technique is that of biased estimates. The emphasis here is on deliberate bias rather than the sort of accidental bias which arises from the lack of knowledge described previously. It may be the case that the sales force have an incentive to provide biased estimates. These will often take the form of deliberate underestimates of likely sales in order to ensure that they will be set easy to achieve sales targets. This is a particular problem when a significant part of the sales person's salary is linked to performance. In this case, it is obviously in their interests to ensure that their sales targets are met if they are to receive the highest possible wages. Alternatively, but probably more rarely, the sales force may deliberately over-estimate sales in order to ensure their continued employment if low sales would lead to a reduction in the number of sales staff. This is most likely to be the case when staff are paid a salary which is not linked to the level of sales. Thus this approach also has both advantages and disadvantages.

5.4.3   Expert Opinion

One of the problems associated with the sales force opinion technique was its inability to provide a wide overview of trends occurring both within and outside of the market for a particular product. The expert opinion technique, on the other hand, can be used to obtain this broader picture at the expense of a more detailed knowledge of local market conditions. Thus in some ways the two techniques are complementary. The experts in question may be stockbrokers' industry analysts, management or economic consultants, or relevant trade associations. These groups can reasonably be expected to have relatively detailed knowledge of the product markets in which they specialise.

There are two main ways in which this technique can be carried out. Firstly, each expert can be asked independently to produce a confidential estimate of likely future demand for the product and/or the factors which are most likely to affect demand over a given period. The results are then averaged to give a final forecast. The success of this method may depend on how similar the forecasts of the experts are – if they are very similar then this average will be more reliable than if they are very different from one another. The latter may be the case if some of the experts have access to information which the others do not. In this instance, the second method which can be used to take advantage of expert opinion may be more appropriate. This is known as the 'Delphi technique'. The first stage of the Delphi technique is the collection of individual experts' reports as before. Next, however, instead of averaging the results, each of the experts is allowed to see the reports produced by the others, although anonymity is usually guaranteed so that the reports' authors cannot be identified. Each of the experts is then asked to produce a second report which either reconfirms their original view or presents a revised view based on the new information they now have at their disposal. This process will be continued until a consensus is reached which can form the basis of the firm's product demand forecast. The main problem with this version of the technique is, of course, that the experts may fail to agree in which case the firm is no better off than before.

All of the methods examined so far involve the collection of opinions from different groups – the consumer, the sales force and market experts respectively. The remaining techniques which fall under the heading of the marketing approach to demand measurement all involve observing actual purchasing behaviour. These are sales-wave research, the simulated store technique and direct market experiments.

5.4.4   Sales-wave Research

This is most often used to assess potential demand for relatively inexpensive, frequently purchased products such as new types of chocolate bars, washing powders and other non-durable goods. A number of groups of consumers are selected who are given free samples of the good to try out. Each group is then given the chance to buy the product at, for example, different prices and the amount of the product they buy at each price is noted. This allows the observer to assess the effect of price on the amount demanded. An extension of this might be to give groups a choice between the firm's own good and competing goods to see which they prefer at any given price. Alternatively, the firm may offer the different groups the same product in different types of packaging, expose them to different forms of product advertising and so on in order to assess the effects of these variables and to help develop the best possible overall product strategy. Research of this type prior to the launch of a product can also identify any perceived problems with it and reduce the chances of an unsuccessful product launch.

5.4.5   Simulated Store Techniques

These are similar in form to sales-wave research but usually operate on a larger scale with multiple products. They are often carried out by independent market research organisations on behalf of several companies at a time. Again, a group of consumers is selected, but this time their behaviour in an artificially constructed market is observed. This market contains a range of products of different types and brands. The members of the group are then given a sum of money to spend on these goods and their purchases are recorded. Depending upon what the researcher is trying to ascertain, they may either be told to purchase whatever they want to or to purchase a certain number of generic items. In the case of the latter, it is the brand they buy which is recorded. The next stage of the process is to alter one or more of the relevant variables in order to assess their effect on purchasing behaviour. For example, while the purchases already made are being noted by the researcher, the group may be asked to watch a series of advertisements for a range of product brands or perhaps even a new product which was not available to them originally. The consumers are then sent back into the artificial market (simulated store) with same amount of money as before. Their subsequent purchases would then be examined in order to assess the effect the advertisements had had on their behaviour. For example, if a new product had been introduced, how many of them had bought it? Or had advertising of a particular brand of a good led more people to buy it than before? This would allow the effectiveness of various forms of advertisement to be gauged. Alternatively, the prices of certain brands could have been changed between the first and second round of buying in order to assess the effect of charging more or less for a particular brand of, say, coffee. There are all sorts of possibilities, including changes in packaging or product displays, and the process may be repeated a number of times.

This technique has the advantage of being controllable in the sense that the consumers are exposed to specific changes in the variables without coming under the influence of external factors which might distort the results. This method also allows the researchers to discuss with the consumers their reasons for buying particular products and the extent to which they were influenced by the changes made during the intervals between buying rounds. This can give them useful insights into the consumers' behaviour and the effectiveness of particular courses of action. The participants may also be contacted at a later date in order to see if they are still buying particular brands of a product.

There are, however, a number of problems associated with this technique. Firstly, as in the case of market surveys, there is the problem of obtaining a representative sample of consumers, this time in terms of both being able to contact them initially and then finding a time and place to suit them. Those who are most likely to volunteer to participate in this process are those with the time to spare such as unemployed and retired people whose behaviour may not be truly representative of the entire population. Secondly, the relatively high cost of setting up and running this type of operation means that the size of the sample group will be limited. As well as paying the market research company, the participants will have to be rewarded with either money or goods. There may also be additional expenses such as the hiring of suitable premises, for example a shop or supermarket, and the cost of preparing advertisements and displays. It is for this reason that firms producing different goods may co-operate in order to share the expense of market research. Thirdly, there is the problem of distorted behaviour. One of the reasons why independent market research organisations are used is that it makes it more difficult for the participants to identify the purpose of the exercise. This means that they are less likely to behave in the way that is 'expected' of them than would be the case if they could identify the firm whose product(s) were under examination. Even so, it may be the case that the mere fact that they are participating in an artificial situation will result in them behaving differently from normal. They may, for example, be more price conscious or more responsive to advertising than they would usually be. Thus this technique also has a number of advantages and disadvantages of its own compared to the others we have looked at so far.

5.4.6 Direct Market Experiments

In this case, consumer behaviour in actual rather than simulated markets is examined. The firm selects individual shops, cities or regions which share similar characteristics as 'test markets' for the product. It then sets different values of the variables under its control, such as own price and advertising levels, in order to assess the effect on the consumers within each test market. By doing this it can, for example, experiment to find out the highest possible price it can charge for a product without experiencing too great a drop in demand. It can then use this information to develop an overall strategy for selling the product at national level. Another advantage of using this approach is that it can give the firm important information prior to the national product launch. Thus as well as helping it to determine the best price and advertising strategy for the product, it can also identify any problems with it. It can also be used to assess whether there are any particular improvements in the product's design which would make it more attractive to the consumer, or if an alternative form of packaging would attract more attention to it. A great deal of information can be obtained in this way.

As with all of the other methods looked at so far, there are a range of issues associated with direct market experiments. Firstly, there is the problem of selecting comparable areas. Ideally, the firm needs to use areas which are representative of the market as a whole and these may not be easy to find. In any event, there will be search costs involved in locating them which will increase the overall cost of the exercise, which may be significant in any case. Secondly, due to the costs involved, such experiments are often only used for short periods. This may not be long enough to identify longer term trends, for example what happens to demand once the product's 'novelty value' wears off. Alternatively, demand estimates obtained at a time when the economy is booming will tell the firm nothing about the likely effect on demand when the economy begins to slump. Thirdly, there is the problem that uncontrollable variables may distort the results. A change in economic conditions would fall into this category as would a rise in the area's unemployment rate or a change in the behaviour of a competitor. The latter represents the fourth problem with this type of experiment. By operating in an actual market, the firm reveals its intentions to its competitors who then can adapt their behaviour accordingly. This may invalidate the results of the test if between the time of its operation and the national launch of the product a rival firm, for example, cuts the price of its product significantly in response to this perceived threat. Given the level of uncertainty which exists in most, if not all, markets it is usually impossible to eliminate these distorting factors completely.

5.4.7   Summary: Choosing the 'Right' Technique

To summarise, all of the marketing approaches to demand measurement have a number of strengths and weaknesses. It is up to the decision maker to decide which is most suitable for the company's needs. How will they make this choice? Their decision will depend in part on what the firm can afford. If the firm only has a small budget, it might choose to use, say, the sales force opinion approach as the costs of data collection are minimal. This approach would be of little use, however, in the case of a totally new product as the sales force would not have the necessary knowledge to accurately forecast future demand. In this case, a direct market experiment would be more useful, if of course the firm could afford it. This raises another point, what can be called the risk–expenditure trade-off. What are the costs of market research compared to the costs of lack of market research? In general, the higher the cost to the firm of the failure of a product, the more likely it is to conduct market research, and more of it, prior to its launch. For example, if the firm has invested substantial sums of money in product development, it needs to be sure that the final product is one that consumers will be happy to buy. The costs to the firm of finding a defect in a product after its launch can be substantial both in terms of loss of sales for that product and the loss of the firm's reputation. Thus the greater the risk, the more the firm will spend on market research. In this case, more than one of the above techniques may be used in order to generate as much information as possible.

In the case of an established product, that is one which has been on the market for some time, the firm is perhaps more likely to use market surveys. This will keep them in touch with what consumers think about the product. Sales force opinion may also be used for a similar reason. It is also, of course, easier to use the expert opinion technique in a known market, so that this method may be used to give a broader overview of market trends. Thus, precisely what methods will be used by a firm depends very much on its current circumstances and what it is trying to achieve.

In every case, however, the firm is interested in data collection and using those data to predict the future demand for its product. In order to do so, it will need to adopt statistical techniques in order to quantify the information obtained. While simple frequency tables and cross-tabulations may be adequate for some purposes, there will come a time when the firm needs to use a more sophisticated form of analysis. This is when the next type of demand estimation technique, regression analysis, becomes a useful tool in the managerial decision-making process.

■ ■ ■ Self-Assessment Question ■ ■ ■ ■ ■ ■ ■ ■ ■ ■ ■ ■

Q5 What are the six marketing approaches to demand measurement?

■ 5.5 Regression Analysis

Regression analysis can clearly be classified as a demand estimation technique given that it involves identifying and calculating specific relationships between the independent variables and the level of product demand. It involves a number of stages which will be described below.

5.5.1 Stage 1: Specifying the Variables

The first thing that the organisation carrying out the regression analysis needs to do is to determine the range of variables which may affect demand for the product concerned. The demand function provides a good basis for this. For example, the own price of a good might reasonably be expected to be a determinant of demand for most products, as would any advertising being done by the firm. The question of whether there are any substitute or complementary goods which need to be taken into account could then be raised. In the case of an expensive consumer durable good the cost and availability of credit might be a consideration. Any special 'other' factors affecting demand could then be identified and so on. This choice of variables has to be made before it is possible to progress to the next stage.

5.5.2   Stage 2: Data Collection

Once the relevant variables have been identified, quantitative data need to be assembled for each of them. This will be easier for some of the variables than for others. In dealing with an established product, for example, the firm might reasonably be expected to have access to a range of information regarding the variables which it controls such as own price and advertising. What may be more difficult to obtain, however, is information about competitors' products. On this front, price data can be obtained through observing retail prices, as this information by definition is in the public domain and cannot be hidden. This requires continued market observation, perhaps over a long period of time. Likewise, information about product design changes can be obtained by buying the competitors' product(s), but this may be expensive if there are many on the market. Confidential, commercially sensitive information such as actual advertising expenditure by competitors and their proposed new products present much more difficult problems in terms of access and may have to be left out of the process altogether. Data on levels of disposable income, population variables, interest rates and credit availability are easier to obtain, for example from government statistics, but other variables are more problematic. How can things like expectations and tastes be measured for instance? In these cases the available data, perhaps resulting from market surveys, may be qualitative rather than quantitative. Some means of conversion need to be found if they are to be included in the regression analysis at all. These are all things which the decision maker needs to keep in mind while collecting and selecting data on the relevant variables.

5.5.3   Stage 3: Specifying the Regression Equation

Once the first two steps have been completed, the next stage is to specify the likely form of the regression equation. There are two main forms which are used in practice – the linear demand function and the exponential or power function. Both treat the demand for the product as the dependent variable, while the independent variables are those which have previously been identified as having an effect on demand. If, for example, the firm had decided that the only variables affecting demand for a particular product were its own price and advertising levels then the linear demand function would be written as:

$$Q_D = a + bP_O + cA_O$$

Alternatively, under these conditions the exponential (power) function would be written as:

$$Q_D = a \, P_O^b \, A_O^c$$

In each case, the a term represents the intercept of the line drawn from the equation with the vertical axis. The b and c terms represent the regression coefficients with respect to own price and advertising respectively. These show the impact of each of these variables on product demand. Once they have been estimated it is possible to predict the level of demand for any set of values of the independent variables simply by substituting them into the equation.

The exponential form of the equation has the advantage that it can be rewritten to give direct estimates of the respective elasticities of demand for the independent variables. This is done by taking the log-linear form of the equation which in this case would be:

$$\log Q_D = \log a + b \log P_O + c \log A_O$$

where b and c are the own price and advertising elasticities of demand respectively. This is a much easier approach than calculating elasticities through use of the linear form which involves using the equation:

$$E_D = b \cdot \frac{P_O}{Q_D}$$

to calculate the elasticities in each case. (To calculate the own advertising elasticity of demand P_O would be replaced with A_O and so on.)

Which of the two forms of equation is chosen depends upon the expected relationship between the variables being included. In practice, however, the actual relationship between them may not be known in advance. In this case, the decision maker may experiment with both forms of equation in order to find the one which most closely fits the data.

5.5.4   Stage 4: Estimating and Interpreting the Regression Equation

Both the linear and log-linear forms of the regression equation can be estimated in the same way, by a technique known as ordinary least squares (OLS). A number of statistical computer packages are available that use this technique which selects the values of a, b and c which best fit the data on own price and advertising levels which the firm has collected. The validity of the equation can then be assessed by examining the extent to which the variables in it do in fact explain the demand for the product. This is done via the analysis of a series of statistical tests which are produced as part of the process.

Suppose, for example, that the estimation process had given the following figures for the coefficients:

$$\log Q_D = \log 200 - 1.5 \log P_O + 2.4 \log A_O$$

What can we deduce from this?

Firstly, a, the intercept term, in this case 200, cannot be interpreted as the level of demand which would occur when the product was being given away without advertising, that is, the values of P_O and A_O were both zero. The only exception to this would be when this state of affairs had actually existed within the time period covered by the data which is unlikely. Thus it is important to note that care must be taken when interpreting points outside of the observed data range. These are less likely to be accurate than is the case for those within the range.

Secondly, as this is a log-linear equation, the b and c coefficients are the own price and own advertising elasticities of demand respectively. From these it is apparent that demand is elastic with respect to both of these variables. Consequently, both a price cut and increased advertising might be expected to increase demand for the product significantly. This only takes us so far, however, in our analysis of the effects of changes in the independent variables on demand. In order to go further we need to assess the accuracy of the equation itself.

5.5.5   Stage 5: Evaluating the Accuracy of the Regression Equation – Regression Statistics

There are five main regression statistics which are produced by most computer packages – the coefficient of determination (R^2), the F-test, the standard error of the equation (SE_E), the standard error of the coefficient and the t-test. The first three of these measure the accuracy of the whole equation while the last two measure the accuracy of the individual coefficients.

The R^2 statistic gives an indication of how well the equation explains the changes in the dependent variable, demand. It takes a range of values between 0 and 1. A value of 0 indicates that the equation does not explain the changes taking place in demand at all while a value of 1 indicates that they are fully explained. Thus the closer the value is to 1, the better the fit of the equation is to the data, while a small value of R^2 on the other hand might indicate that an important explanatory variable was missing from the equation. The main problem with the R^2 statistic is that its value can be increased simply by including more variables. For this reason, most packages also calculate the adjusted coefficient of determination (adjusted R^2) which eliminates the effects of this additive influence. It also takes the values 0 to 1. Thus a value of R^2 which is significantly higher than the adjusted R^2 value indicates that the accuracy of the equation could be improved by taking out the extra variable(s).

The *F*-test is calculated using the coefficient of determination:

$$F = \frac{R^2 \ / \ (m)}{(1 - R^2) \ / \ (n - m - 1)}$$

where *m* is the number of independent variables in the regression equation and *n* the number of data observations. A value of *F* equal to zero indicates that the equation has no explanatory power. As the value of *F* increases, however, the more likely it is that the independent variables are significant factors in determining the variations in the dependent variable. Exactly how significant they are in this respect depends upon the values of *F*, *m* and *n*. Statistical tables for the *F*-distribution are used to determine this.

The standard error of the equation is used to determine the likely accuracy with which we can predict the value of the dependent variable associated with particular values of the independent variables. As a general principle, the smaller the value of the standard error of the equation, the more accurate the equation is and hence the more accurate any predictions made from it will be. To put this another way, the standard error represents the standard deviation of the dependent variable about the regression line. Thus the smaller the value, the better the fit of the equation to the data and the closer the estimate will be to the true regression line. Conversely, the larger the standard error, the bigger the deviation from the regression line and the less confidence that can be put in any prediction arising from it. The standard error of the coefficient works along similar lines. It gives an indication of the amount of confidence that can be placed in the estimated regression coefficient for each independent variable. Again, the smaller the value, the greater the confidence that can be placed in the estimated coefficient and vice versa. Finally, the *t*-test provides a further measurement of the accuracy of the regression coefficient for each of the independent variables. It is calculated as follows:

$$t = \frac{\text{regression coefficient}}{\text{standard error of coefficient}}$$

A value of *t* greater than or equal to 2 generally indicates that the calculated coefficient is a reliable estimate, while a value of less than 2 indicates that the coefficient is unreliable. (Note: This also partly depends, however, on the number of data observations on which the equation is based so that *t*-test tables need to be used in order to ensure an accurate interpretation of this statistic.) Having described the statistics let us now consider how they may be used in practice. To do this, we can add example regression statistics to the previously estimated regression equation:

$$\log Q_D = \log 200 - 1.5 \log P_O + 2.4 \log A_O$$
$$\qquad\qquad (0.3) \qquad\quad (0.4)$$

$R^2 = 0.95$, adjusted $R^2 = 0.93$ $SE_E = 1.25$
$m = 2$ and $n = 20$

What does this tell us? The R^2 and adjusted R^2 statistics indicate that the equation is a good fit to the data and so explains most of the variation in quantity demanded arising from changes in the independent variables. In addition, as the two figures are close together, this result has not merely been obtained as a result of the inclusion of additional independent variables. This is supported by the low value of the standard error of the equation, SE_E. Calculation of the F-test gives a similar result:

$$F = \frac{(0.95)^2/(2)}{(0.05)^2/(20-2-1)} = \frac{0.45125}{0.00015} = 3008.3$$

The size of this figure clearly indicates good explanatory power.

In terms of the coefficients, both of the standard errors, which are given in the brackets below their respective coefficients, are comparatively small. Thus it is reasonable to say that the values of the two coefficients are reliable. This is borne out by a calculation of their respective t-test values. For own price, $t = 1.5/0.3 = 5$ and for own advertising, $t = 2.4/0.4 = 6$. Thus both of the coefficients pass the t-test in terms of their reliability. Overall, therefore, this equation appears to provide a good explanation of the factors which affect demand for this particular product. If, on the other hand, the statistics indicated that the regression equation was not a good fit to the data, and hence did not adequately explain the demand for the firm's product, then there would be a need to revisit the earlier stages of the process. A different set of variables might be selected, for example, in order to obtain a better result. This process has the advantages that it can be repeated relatively quickly and cheaply, and that when it is done well it can be an important tool in the firm's decision-making process. It can also, however, be a bit 'hit and miss' if applied incorrectly, for example if inadequate or inaccurate data are used.

■ ■ ■ Self-Assessment Question ■ ■ ■ ■ ■ ■ ■ ■ ■ ■ ■ ■ ■

Q6 A firm has estimated the following demand equation for its product:

$$Q_{dt} = 1.76 - 0.5 \log P_{ot} + 1.2 \log A_{ot} + 2.25 \log Y_{ot}$$
$$\qquad\quad (0.02) \qquad\quad (0.6) \qquad\qquad (1.75)$$

$R^2 = 0.91$, adjusted $R^2 = 0.83$ $SE_E = 1.83$

(a) What do the signs and sizes of the coefficients tell us about the effect of each of the three independent variables on demand?

(b) Calculate the *t*-test value for each of the coefficients and identify which of the estimates of the coefficient are reliable.

(c) What do the R^2 and adjusted R^2 statistics tell us about the equation?

■■

CASE STUDY | *Motorola in Scotland*

In 1999 Motorola, the world's second largest mobile phone maker, announced a £50 million expansion programme to create 1000 new jobs at its mobile phone factory in Bathgate, Scotland which had opened in 1992. This expansion was the result of a rise in demand for the company's new V-series mobile phones at a time when the mobile phone market was estimated to be growing by around 40 per cent a year. Motorola already employed 3400 staff at Bathgate, with another 3700 staff at East Kilbride and 500 at South Queensferry being employed in its Scottish semiconductor plants. In 2000, Motorola announced further expansion plans following its acquisition of the Hyundai plant near Dunfermline where it planned to create an additional 1350 jobs together with a further 550 at a £20 million semiconductor research and development centre in Livingston. The company's future within Scotland seemed to be assured in the face of increasing current demand for its products and strong forecasts in relation to the growth in sales of mobile phones over the next few years.

In 2001, however, the situation began to change. The company reported a first quarter loss of $206 million compared to a profit of $481 million for the same period in 2000. This, combined with downward revisions in global sales estimates for mobile phones and increased competition in the

market from Nokia and Ericsson, led Motorola to announce the closure of the Bathgate factory in April 2001 as part of a wider closure plan, resulting in the loss of almost 40,000 jobs or a quarter of the firm's workforce worldwide over two years. The firm's losses continued over the next two quarters and were accompanied by further downward revisions in demand forecasts. By the end of the third quarter, Motorola was forecasting a 25 per cent drop in chip sales across the industry for 2001 with relatively small future increases of 5 per cent in 2002 and 10 per cent in 2003. The company also forecast that the industry's worldwide mobile phone sales, which analysts had previously estimated would reach 600 million per annum, would be nearer 380–400 million in 2001 – a fall of a third relative to the industry's current expectations. The principal reasons cited for this fall were economic uncertainty and the delayed introduction of new mobile phone technology. This had reduced the number of both new and replacement phone sales being made, particularly in Europe, at a time when the Asian markets for mobile phones had not expanded as fast as had been expected. Further closures of Motorola's factories across the world followed and at the end of 2001 the firm's South Queensferry plant was closed and its workforce transferred to East Kilbride. This coincided with

continued

Motorola's reporting a further loss for the fourth quarter of 2001 of $90 million on sales of $7.3 billion, compared to a profit of $362 million on sales of $9.8 billion a year earlier. The company's final figures for 2001 subsequently revealed that its sales had fallen by 20 per cent to $30 billion, on which it had made a net loss of $3.9 billion compared to a $1.3 billion profit in 2000, although this partly resulted from the non-recurring costs of its international restructuring. The company, like the rest of the industry, is now pinning its hopes on the new generation of more sophisticated, and more expensive, mobile phones combined with economic recovery in the US and Europe to raise both sales and profits in 2002 and beyond.

■ 5.6   Demand Forecasting Techniques

Three techniques will be considered in this section – extrapolation, decomposition analysis and barometric forecasting – each of which is concerned primarily with the direction or absolute size of changes in demand rather than the specific variables which explain them.

5.6.1   Extrapolation

The basic assumption underlying the extrapolation method is that past demand patterns can be used to predict future demand. While regression analysis can be used to perform this function, time series data plots and other statistical methods can also be used. Time series data plots involve simply drawing a graph that plots the level of demand against time and drawing a 'line of best fit' through the data. This line can then be extended to forecast the level of demand in future periods. This is shown in Figure 5.4.

In Figure 5.4 the x values represent the actual observed levels of demand as measured by sales volume over time. The line drawn through them is the line of best fit. Future levels of demand can then be read off this line. This assumes that demand will (on average) be continuously rising, although it is apparent from the data that there is some variance around the trend line. This method cannot, for example, take into account any factor which might have a significant, unexpected impact on demand as, unlike in the case of regression analysis, causality is not taken into account. In order to reduce the effect of this problem, a more sophisticated approach known as decomposition analysis may be used.

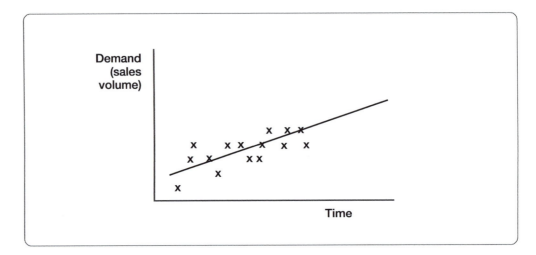

Figure 5.4   Extrapolating demand

5.6.2   Decomposition Analysis

In this case, demand is divided into four parts – the trend (*T*), seasonal movement (*S*), irregular movement (*I*) and cyclical movement (*C*). The trend element
shows the long-run changes in demand, for example the fact that on average
demand is increasing or decreasing over time. The seasonal movement shows
any regular changes in demand that occur during, say, a year. For example, the
demand for umbrellas might be expected to be higher than average in the
months with the highest rainfall. The irregular movement term is designed to
pick up the effects of any unexpected changes in demand which may arise, for
example, due to the destabilising effects of a change in government or a significant change in economic conditions. By definition, because this event is unexpected it can only be incorporated in the analysis once it has occurred,
although the firm may of course produce a series of 'best-case' and 'worst-case'
scenarios to take account of this. The cyclical component of demand is made
up of the regular changes which occur in national economies such as booms
and recessions. The extent to which this affects individual products and industries may vary considerably. For this reason, its impact is also difficult to
measure accurately.

Each individual piece of demand information, for example sales volume per
month, is assumed to be made up of these components. The relationship
between them can then be expressed either additively, that is

$$X_t = T_t + C_t + S_t + I_t$$

or multiplicatively, that is

$$X_t = T_t \, C_t \, S_t \, I_t$$

where t is time. The individual parts of this then need to be identified.

The trend factor can be found by drawing a straight line through the raw data in the same way as was done in Figure 5.4. By reading off the observations obtained from drawing this trend line and subtracting them from the actual observations for each period, the firm can estimate how much of the actual changes in demand are related to the remaining components. The difficulty then is to identify the precise role of each of them. The cyclical component presents a particular problem in this respect. While the firm may be aware of the overall economic cycle and be able to identify the periods when the economy was in recession and so on, there is no way of knowing for sure whether the market for a particular good precisely mirrors this cycle. For example, in the case of a consumer good, there may be a lag behind the time the economy starts its descent into recession and the time this impact is felt by the consumers, thus affecting their purchasing decisions. If so, to be accurate the firm would need to know how long this time lag was. Moreover, it does not follow that the time lag would always be the same within and between economic cycles. It is quite common practice, therefore, for this component to be omitted from the analysis.

Fortunately, identifying the seasonal and irregular components is slightly easier. In order to separate out the seasonal component from the data, an average figure is calculated for the 'seasonal plus irregular' components for each season of the year across the whole period for which the data are available. This has the effect of averaging out the irregular component for each season. What remains is the seasonal component.

Once the trend and seasonal components have been found in this way, the results are fed into a regression equation to calculate the trend value for future periods. The seasonal component can then be added to this for the relevant time periods. The usefulness of the method can be checked by 'back fore-casting' which involves using the equation to forecast known demand in order to assess the accuracy of the model in practice.

Decomposition analysis can be quite complicated to perform so firms may instead choose to carry out a more 'rough and ready' analysis. For example, it might be assumed that the trend in demand is secular with no identifiable distorting factors, that is it is continuously rising (or falling) over time. In this case, the firm can use a relatively simple means of calculating future demand. On the basis of past data, the firm could estimate the average rate of increase in demand, say for example 5 per cent per year. It could then use this know-ledge to forecast future demand on the basis of current sales:

$$
\begin{aligned}
2002 \text{ sales} &= \text{current (2000) sales} \times (1 + \text{growth})^2 \\
&= 100{,}000 \times (1 + 0.05)^2 \\
&= 110{,}250
\end{aligned}
$$

Thus given that the firm knows its year 2000 sales to be 100,000 units of output it can calculate that in two years' time (2002) its sales will have risen to 110,250 units of output. The figure of 0.05 represents the 5 per cent growth rate and the term in brackets is squared because we are predicting two years ahead. If we were predicting three years ahead this term would be cubed, four years ahead to the power 4 and so on. It is worth noting that the power is positive as sales are increasing; if they were falling the power would be negative, that is –2 instead of 2.

Seasonal influences can also be calculated in a simplified way, again assuming that they are the principal source of variations in demand over the course of a year. In this case, monthly average sales are calculated and this figure adjusted to take account of how far above or below this figure they are in any given month on the basis of seasonal trends. For example, if the firm had annual sales of 120,000 units of output, this would give us a monthly average of 10,000 units. If it were known that sales were generally 20 per cent higher in December than at any other time of the year, actual sales in December would be:

$$December\ sales = average\ monthly\ sales \times adjustment$$
$$= 10,000 \times 1.20$$
$$= 12,000$$

Thus the firm could increase production at this time of year in order to meet demand.

Although this technique is relatively unsophisticated it can give the manager an idea of likely demand for the product at different times of year. The same is true of the final method considered here, barometric forecasting.

5.6.3   Barometric Forecasting

Barometric forecasting is based on the observed relationships between different economic indicators. It is used to give the decision maker an insight into the direction of likely future demand changes, although it cannot usually be used to quantify them.

Five different types of indicator may be used. Firstly, there are leading indicators which run in advance of changes in demand for a particular product. An example of these might be an increase in the number of building permits granted which would lead to an increase in demand for building-related products such as wood, concrete and so on. Secondly, there are coincident indicators which occur alongside changes in demand. Retail sales would fall into this category, as an increase in sales would generate an increase in demand for the manufacturers of the goods concerned. Thirdly, there are lagging indicators which run behind changes in demand. New industrial investment by firms is often said to fall into this category. In this case it is argued that firms will only invest in new production facilities when demand is already firmly established. Thus increased investment is a sign, or confirmation, that an initial increase in demand has already taken place. This may well indicate that the economy is improving, for example, so that further changes in the level of demand can be expected in the near future.

One particular problem with each of these three types of indicator is that single indicators do not always prove to be accurate in predicting changes in demand. For this reason, groups of indicators may be used instead. The fourth and fifth types of indicator fall into this category. These are composite indices and diffusion indices respectively. Composite indices are made up of weighted averages of several leading indicators which demonstrate an overall trend. Diffusion indices are groups of leading indicators whose directional shifts are analysed separately. If more than half of the leading indicators included within them are rising, demand is forecast to rise and vice versa. Again, it is important to note that it is the direction of change that is the basis of the prediction, the actual size of the change cannot be measured. In addition, the situation is complicated by the fact that there may be variations in the length of the lead time between the various indicators. This means that the accuracy of predictions may be reduced.

■ ■ ■ Self-Assessment Question ■ ■ ■ ■ ■ ■ ■ ■ ■ ■ ■ ■

Q7 What are the three demand forecasting techniques which were discussed in this section?

❏ ❏ ❏ End of Chapter SUMMARY ❏ ❏ ❏ ❏ ❏ ❏ ❏ ❏ ❏ ❏ ❏

In this chapter we have looked at a range of demand estimation and forecasting techniques which can be used by the firm either singly or in combination in order to predict the level of demand for their product(s). The choice of technique will depend upon the resources at the firm's disposal, the cost to the firm of insufficient knowledge of the market(s) in which it operates and the ease with which information can be obtained. Each of the methods we have considered has its own advantages and disadvantages in its use and there is no 'right' or 'wrong' approach in any given situation. It is for the decision maker to choose the technique(s) which are most appropriate to the firm's needs. As a general principle, however, the more, and the more accurate, information the firm has the better able it will be to take the best decisions possible for the firm's efficient operation. Thus the firm can substantially reduce the risk to which it will be exposed, particularly in rapidly changing markets.

■ ■ ■ ANSWERS to Self-Assessment Questions ■ ■ ■ ■ ■ ■

Q1

Any three of the following reasons why the firm needs accurate demand information: so that it knows how much to produce; so it can control its costs; so that it can set the right price; and so that it can take the best possible decisions for its business.

Q2

Any five variables from: own price of the product; price of complementary products; price of substitute products; disposable income; tastes; own advertising of the product; advertising of substitute products; advertising of complementary products; credit availability; interest rates; expectations; the number of potential customers; other miscellaneous factors, for example seasonality.

Q3

A movement along the demand curve is caused by a change in the own price of the product. A shift in the demand curve is caused by a change in any of the other variables in the demand function.

Q4

The generic equation used to calculate a point elasticity of demand is:

$$\text{Elasticity } (E) = \frac{Q_2 - Q_1}{X_2 - X_1} \cdot \frac{X_1}{Q_1}$$

(a) Substituting the figures given for price for X in the above equation:

$$E = \frac{40,000 - 50,000}{9,000 - 8,000} \cdot \frac{8,000}{50,000} = \frac{-10}{1} \cdot \frac{-8}{5} = -1.6$$

This shows that the demand for cars is elastic, as the rise in price has caused a greater fall in demand. Specifically, we can see from the figures that price has risen by 12.5 per cent but the number of cars sold has fallen by 20 per cent.

(b) This time we substitute the own advertising levels for X in the equation:

$$E = \frac{75,000 - 50,000}{15,000 - 10,000} \cdot \frac{10,000}{50,000} = \frac{25,000}{5,000} \cdot \frac{10,000}{50,000} = \frac{25}{5} \cdot \frac{1}{5} = \frac{25}{25} = 1$$

This shows that the percentage increase in demand yielded by the change in own advertising expenditure will be equal to the percentage change in the advertising expenditure itself. In this case, that is a 50 per cent rise in own advertising expenditure has led to a 50 per cent rise in the demand for the firm's chocolate bars.

Q5   The six approaches are: market surveys, expert opinion, sales force opinion, sales-wave research, simulated store techniques and direct market experiments.

Q6   (a) The value of – 0.5 for P_{ot} tells us that a rise in price will lead to a fall in demand and vice versa (the – sign) but that demand is inelastic with respect to price (the value of 0.5). Specifically, a one unit increase in price would lead to a fall in demand of half a unit. The value of + 1.2 for A_{ot} tells us that a rise in own advertising will increase demand (the + sign) and that demand is elastic with respect to this variable (the value of 1.2). The value of + 2.25 for Y_{ot} tells us that as disposable income rises people will buy more of the product, that is a normal good, and also that demand for the good is elastic with respect to income.

(b) The *t*-test is calculated by using the equation:

$$t = \frac{\text{size of the coefficient}}{\text{standard error of the coefficient}}$$

where the standard errors of the coefficients are given in brackets for the equation.

Using these values the *t* statistics are:

$$t_P = \frac{0.5}{0.02} = 25 \quad t_A = \frac{1.2}{0.6} = 2 \quad t_Y = \frac{2.25}{1.75} = 1.29$$

The *t*-test for price shows that the coefficient value is clearly reliable as it is well in excess of the required value of 2. The coefficient for advertising only just meets the required value and that for income is unreliable as it is less than 2.

c) R^2 indicates that the equation is a good fit to the data, but the adjusted R^2 suggests that there may be an additive influence resulting from the inclusion of too many independent variables. Given the results of the *t*-statistics, the decision maker may now decide to re-estimate the equation by removing income as an independent variable to see if a better fit to the data can be achieved.

Q7   The three demand forecasting techniques we discussed were extrapolation, decomposition analysis and barometric forecasting.

Production and cost estimation

■ 6.1   Introduction

Once the firm knows that there is a demand for its product, it needs to turn its attention to how to produce it and how much this will cost. Given that the firm will wish to make a profit, it will want to keep its production as streamlined and its costs as low as possible. There is little point in producing a product which is so expensive to make that the firm has to charge a higher price than the market will bear or which it has to sell at a loss. This chapter looks at the issues that arise in relation to the firm's decision to supply the product, its production techniques and its costs. The methods which the firm can use to establish the optimal way to produce its product and to estimate its likely future costs are also examined. Again, as in the case of demand, the emphasis is on reducing the level of risk and uncertainty to which the firm is exposed in the course of its operations.

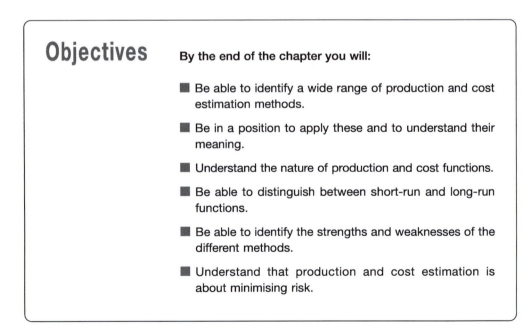

Objectives

By the end of the chapter you will:

- ■ Be able to identify a wide range of production and cost estimation methods.

- ■ Be in a position to apply these and to understand their meaning.

- ■ Understand the nature of production and cost functions.

- ■ Be able to distinguish between short-run and long-run functions.

- ■ Be able to identify the strengths and weaknesses of the different methods.

- ■ Understand that production and cost estimation is about minimising risk.

■ 6.2 Supply Theory

6.2.1 Factors Influencing the Supply of a Product

The supply of a product is defined as 'the amount that producers are willing to sell at a particular price'. Consequently, the first factor influencing the supply of a product is its price. Taking this a stage further, the variables which influence supply can be incorporated into the supply function:

$$Q_S = f(P_O, P_S, P_C, C, E, G_O, T_y, O)$$

where the P variables are the own price of the product (P_O), the price of substitute (P_S) and complementary products (P_C); C represents the cost of producing the product; E is expectations; G_O represents the goals of the firm; T_y is the state of technology and O represents any other miscellaneous factors which may influence the supply of a particular product.

Own Price (P_O)

The relationship between the price of a product and the amount of it that firms will supply is explained by the 'law of supply'. This law states that 'the higher the price of the product, the higher the quantity of it that will be supplied while, conversely, the lower the price of the product, the less of it will be supplied'. This is the reverse of what happens in the case of demand. Why?

Basically, the producer of a good wants to sell it for as high a price as possible in order to obtain the maximum profit which they can from supplying it. Thus a high price acts as an incentive for the producer to supply more of the product in order to gain more profit from selling it. On the other hand, there may be relatively little profit to be made on a product which carries a low price, and so the supply of this product will also be low as it is less profitable to produce. In this case, as the price of the product falls some firms will divert their resources into the production of an alternative product on which they can make more profit. This brings us to the second of the factors which will affect the amount of a product supplied, relative price.

Price of Substitutes (P_S)

In the case of substitutes, if the price of product A falls then the demand for product B also falls as customers switch to the cheaper substitute product (A). As the firm producing product B is now selling less of it than before (or can only sell more of it at a lower price), it has become less profitable to produce. As a result there is an incentive for the firm to switch its production from product B to a more profitable alternative product and so the supply of product B is reduced.

A similar effect would occur if the cost of producing product C fell at a given price so that it was more profitable to produce relative to D. This would encourage firms to switch from supplying product C to supplying product D which is now more profitable for them. In this case products C and D are what is known as 'substitutes in supply'.

Price of Complements (P_C)

In the case of complementary products, a high price for one product (E) leads to a low supply of its complement (F). Alternatively, a low price for product E leads to a high supply of product F. This can be explained as follows. If the price of product E is high then the demand for it will be low and consequently the demand for product F will also be low. Thus there will be little incentive for the firm to produce product E as it is difficult to sell except at a comparatively low price. As a result of this, F is less profitable for the firm to produce compared to alternative products.

In addition to the case cited above, some products can be said to be complementary in that they are 'goods in joint supply'. This situation arises when one good is a by-product of the production of another good. For example, take the case of crude oil. Crude oil can be refined into a number of products such as petrol, diesel and paraffin. Thus if the demand for petrol rises then more crude oil will be refined in order to supply it. As well as the increase in the supply of petrol, however, the supply of diesel and paraffin will also increase as a side-effect of this process.

Costs (C)

The firm's willingness to supply a product depends upon both its price and the amount of profit which it generates for the firm. This in turn depends upon how much the product costs to produce. The bigger the difference between price and costs, the more profit there is to be made and so the more of the product the firm will supply. Thus at a time of falling (rising) costs in an industry, the quantity of the product supplied will increase (decrease). The level of, and the changes in, firms' costs will therefore determine how much of a product they are willing to supply.

Expectations (E)

The firm's expectations regarding the price and costs associated with a product will also determine the level of supply. If, for example, the firm expects the price of the product to rise then it will increase production in order to take advantage of this, while if it expects the price to fall it will do the opposite. Alternatively, if it expects the price to remain the same but its costs to rise, then the firm will reduce its supply of the product as it believes that the product will become less profitable to produce.

The Goals of the Firm (G_O)

So far it has been assumed that the firm will choose its level of supply in such a way as to ensure that it makes the maximum possible profit. Sometimes, however, there may be an incentive for the firm to sacrifice short-term profits in order to try to obtain higher profits over the longer term. The most obvious case of this arises when the goal of the firm is to break into a new market, either in terms of a new geographical area or a new product which it has not previously produced. In order to do this the firm may 'swamp' the market with a large supply of a relatively low-priced product in order to attract customers and to get its name known in that particular market. Once this has been achieved it can then raise its price and obtain additional profits as it has some element of both product recognition and customer loyalty. This technique is most commonly used in consumer goods markets, for example by a company trying to get a foothold in an overseas market. In the short term this could have a negative effect on its profitability, but in the longer term it could generate higher levels of profits and sales.

Technology (T_y)

The level of supply will also depend upon the nature of the technology available to the firm. For example, in some industries the move towards computer-aided manufacture has also changed the nature of production by reducing the number of workers who need to be employed. The effect of the introduction of new technology is to reduce costs which makes the supply of the product more profitable and so encourages the firm to increase its production levels.

Other Factors (O)

This is a miscellaneous category within the supply function which is included in order to account for things which influence the supply of specific products rather than all or most of them. An example might be adverse weather conditions which result in a fall in the supply of wheat produced in a particular year. What factors are included under this heading will therefore depend upon the nature of the product in question.

Now that the factors which will determine how much of a product will be supplied have been identified, the next step is to look at how changes in these factors will affect the supply curve for a product.

■ ■ ■ Self-Assessment Question ■ ■ ■ ■ ■ ■ ■ ■ ■ ■ ■ ■

Q1 Name the factors which will affect the level of supply of a product. To what extent is the supply of your company's product(s) influenced by each of them?

6.2.2   The Supply Curve

The supply curve (Figure 6.1) shows the relationship between the own price of the product and the quantity of it supplied, which means that it is based on the law of supply. A high price (P_2) indicates that the product is profitable to produce and so there is an incentive to supply a large amount of it (Q_2). A low price (P_1) means that the product is less profitable to produce so that a much lower quantity of it will be supplied (Q_1). Consequently, as the price of the product rises, the firm moves up the supply curve to the right whereas if the price falls, the firm moves down the supply curve to the left. If any of the other variables in the supply function change, however, the effect is to shift the curve as shown in Figures 6.2 and 6.3.

Figure 6.2 demonstrates the case of a leftward shift in the supply curve from S_1S_1 to S_2S_2, for example as a result of an increase in the firm's costs. The result

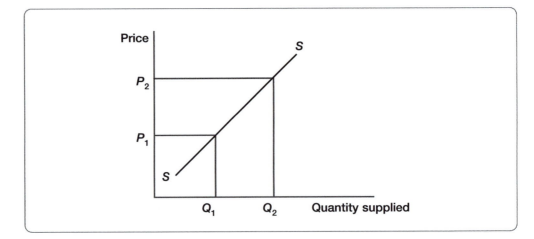

Figure 6.1   The supply curve

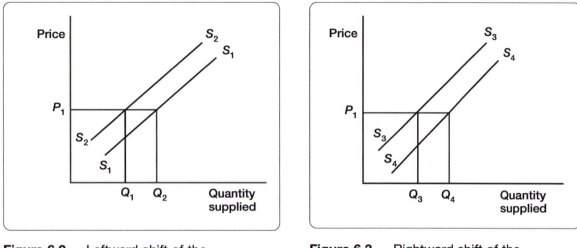

Figure 6.2   Leftward shift of the supply curve

Figure 6.3   Rightward shift of the supply curve

of this is that less of the product is supplied at each price (P_1) than previously, Q_1 instead of Q_2.

Figure 6.3 shows the effect of a rightward shift in the supply curve from S_3S_3 to S_4S_4, for example as a result of the introduction of new technology. This would have the effect of increasing the quantity of output supplied at price P_1, from Q_3 to Q_4.

It is possible, of course, that some of these changes in supply will be occurring simultaneously, so that the firm will be facing some uncertainty regarding the supply conditions prevailing in the market at any given point in time. Once the firm has decided how much of the product to supply, however, the next step is for it to decide how it is going to produce it. This is the subject of production theory.

■ ■ ■ Self-Assessment Question ■ ■ ■ ■ ■ ■ ■ ■ ■ ■ ■ ■ ■

Q2 What is the law of supply? Which of the following would shift the supply curve to the left and which would shift the supply curve to the right?

(a) the introduction of new technology

(b) a rise in wage costs

CASE STUDY | *easyJet*

Following the deregulation of the European airline industry in 1992, which reduced the protection given to existing carriers from the threat of new entrants, a number of new suppliers entered into the airline market (thus shifting the industry supply curve to the right), one of which was easyJet. The high profits being made by the existing airlines combined with rising demand relative to supply meant that the market was very attractive to these new firms, but it was also accepted that this was a comparatively expensive industry to enter. In order to compete successfully, therefore, most of them chose to begin with limited operations in terms of the number of routes flown. Simultaneously,

however, they were also trying to fly at a lower cost, and therefore prices, than the existing airlines. Thus in terms of the supply function, the key variables were own price, the price of substitutes (other airlines) and costs.

From the start, easyJet set out to brand itself as a low-priced provider of flights which in turn required the company to think very carefully about how this could be achieved. Every aspect of the airline business, and in particular the method and cost of production of flights, was reviewed in an attempt to see where economies could be made in order to reduce both costs and prices. How this was done is examined later in the chapter.

■ 6.3 Introduction to Production Theory

In order to produce a product the firm will combine the three factors of production – land, labour and capital – in such a way as to obtain the required level of output. There will be various alternative ways of doing this depending upon the nature of the inputs available to the firm, for example the level of technology, and the relative costs of each of them. Before going on to discuss how the firm will decide which of these options to pursue, it is first of all necessary to define what we mean by land, labour and capital.

6.3.1 The Factors of Production

The way in which the factors of production are combined in order to produce a particular good or service will at least partly depend upon the time period under consideration. In the long run, the way in which the product is produced can be varied to a greater extent than is possible in the short run. Specifically, in this context, we can define the short run as 'the period of time over which at least one factor of production is fixed', that is, the firm has a limited range of options available to it as some factors cannot be changed. In contrast, the long run is defined as 'the period of time which is long enough for all of the factors of production to be varied', that is, there are no fixed factors or constraints on the firm's production at all.

Land is defined in relation to the physical quantity of land used by the firm, for example the land on which its office or factory is built. As it takes time to find new premises and to move into them land is treated as a fixed factor in the short run. Relocation is essentially a long-run phenomenon. Labour is defined in terms of the number of people employed by the firm. It is assumed that it is relatively easy to change the labour input, as the firm can hire and fire workers in response to changes in production levels. Consequently labour is the most flexible of the three factors of production and is deemed to be variable in both the short and the long run. Capital is defined as the total amount of plant and machinery which are needed by the firm in order to produce the required amount of the good or service. Capital is often treated as being fixed in the short run, but the appropriateness of this may depend upon the type of capital which the firm employs. For example, it may take quite a long time to refit an entire factory, but an individual machine which can be hired at short notice can be treated as a variable input so that this element of capital is variable in the short run. In the long run, of course, this is not an issue as land, labour and capital can all be varied.

6.3.2   The Production Function

The ways in which the three factors of production can be combined is shown by the firm's production function:

$$Q = f(K, L, N)$$

where Q is the level of output, f means 'is a function of ', K is capital, L is labour and N is land. Thus the level of output is a function of, or is determined by, the amounts of land, labour and capital employed in its production.

Alternatively, a more complex form of the production function may be specified:

$$Q = AK^a L^b N^c$$

where A is a constant and a, b and c are fractions representing the mix of the three factors used ($a + b + c = 1$). This particular equation is known as the Cobb–Douglas production function.

Production theory can be used to identify the optimal combination of inputs for the firm. In doing so, however, an explicit distinction must be made between production in the short and the long run. This is done in the next two sections which look at production in the short and the long run respectively.

■ ■ ■ Self-Assessment Question ■ ■ ■ ■ ■ ■ ■ ■ ■ ■ ■ ■

Q3
What are the three factors of production? Which one of them is always regarded as fixed and which one is always treated as being variable in the short run?

6.3.3   Production in the Short Run

In order to simplify the analysis, we will assume that both land and capital are fixed in the short run so that labour is the only variable factor. By doing so we can estimate the contribution that each additional unit of labour (worker) will make to the total level of output. Within the context of production theory, the level of output being produced is also known as the 'total physical product' (TPP). This is how we will refer to it for the rest of this section.

Given that labour is the only variable factor, any change in the TPP of the firm can be directly attributed to a change in the amount of labour being used in conjunction with the given amounts of the fixed factors. To begin with, the addition of another unit of labour will be highly productive as the firm is producing below its capacity and so the extra person can increase TPP signif-icantly. As more labour is added, however, at some point each additional worker will produce less additional output than their predecessor, that is TPP will still be increasing but at a diminishing rate. Eventually, the point will be reached where employing an extra person has no effect on output at all, that is their contribution to TPP is zero. Consequently the firm is employing an extra person without getting anything back from them in the form of a return on the money spent on their wages. This is what is known as 'the law of diminishing marginal returns'. Specifically, this economic law states that 'when increasing amounts of a variable factor are used with a given amount of a fixed factor, there will come a point when each extra unit of the variable factor will produce less extra output than the previous unit'. This is shown in Figure 6.4.

From Figure 6.4 it is apparent that employing the first worker only results in a relatively small increase in TPP of 2 units, but the hiring of the second and third workers increases TPP by 4 and 5 units respectively. Worker number four still increases TPP, but only by 1 unit (from 11 units to 12), whereas worker number five does not increase it at all. The employment of worker number six actually reduces TPP by one unit (from 12 to 11) as the TPP curve turns down-wards. Thus when only one person is employed, the firm is operating ineffi-ciently as the fixed inputs are not being fully utilised. The position is improved by hiring the second and third workers so that the firm is operating more effi-ciently. After the third worker is employed, however, diminishing returns set in as shown by the shallower slope of the TPP curve and the smaller amount of

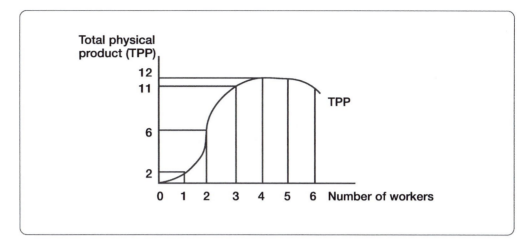

Figure 6.4   The total physical product curve

extra output added by worker number four. By the time worker number five is employed, the firm is producing the maximum possible level of output under these conditions and employing any additional workers actually reduces the level of output as the workplace becomes overcrowded, thus reducing efficiency.

From this analysis, we can also derive the average physical product and marginal physical product of the firm for different numbers of workers. The average physical product (APP) is defined as 'the output produced per worker', that is the total physical product of the firm divided by the number of workers employed (APP = TPP/L). The marginal physical product (MPP) is defined as 'the change in total physical product which arises from the employment of an additional worker', that is, MPP = dTPP/dL (where d stands for 'change in'). The figures for APP and MPP in this example are given in Table 6.1 on which Figure 6.5 is based.

The MPP figures are entered into the spaces between the other figures in Table 6.1 as they represent the difference in output between each level of the input (number of workers) and the next. The MPP points in Figure 6.5 are between 0 and 1, 1 and 2 and so on for the same reason.

Table 6.1   Total, average and marginal physical product

No. of workers	0	1	2	3	4	5	6
TPP	0	2	6	11	12	12	11
APP	0	2	3	3.6	3	2.4	1.8
MPP		2	4	5	1	0	−1

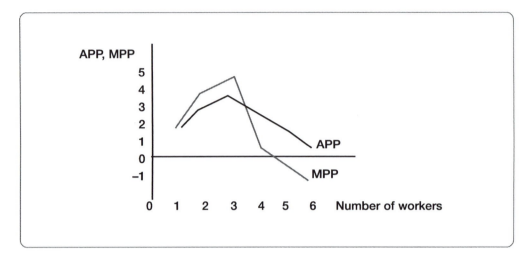

Figure 6.5   Average physical product and marginal physical product curves

Figures 6.4 and 6.5 show three specific relationships between the total, average and marginal physical product curves for a firm:

1. The MPP curve reflects the slope of the TPP curve, for example if employing one more worker increases TPP from 2 to 6 units then MPP = dTPP/dL = 4/1 = 4 which is the slope of the TPP line at that point.

2. As the slope of the TPP curve is rising initially, the MPP curve also rises to reflect this and reaches a maximum when the TPP curve is steepest. As the slope of the TPP curve becomes flatter, however, the MPP curve starts to fall due to the presence of diminishing returns. Eventually, once the TPP curve begins to turn downwards, MPP will become negative.

3. The APP curve rises as long as the MPP from the last worker is greater than the APP calculated for the previous number of workers, but once the MPP is less than the APP, the APP curve begins to turn downwards.

These points merely represent the basic mathematics underlying the curves. What we are essentially saying in this section is that in the short run with only one variable factor of production, labour, the firm's total output (TPP) will increase, although latterly at a diminishing rate, as long as the extra worker(s) employed contribute some additional units of the product. At some point, however, employing more people will become counter-productive as no additional output will be produced, and in the worst-case scenario output will actually decline. The firm can use this analysis in order to identify the optimal number of workers for it to employ. In the above case, this will be five workers, where TPP is at its peak of 12 units of output and MPP = 0. (Note: As a sixth worker would reduce the level of output produced there is obviously no point in employing more than five people. In addition, although the firm could produce the same TPP with four workers, given that the MPP is still positive at this point the firm has no way of knowing that employing the fifth worker would not produce any additional output for the firm until it actually employs them. This is why it will continue employing people until MPP = 0.)

Returning to the Cobb–Douglas production function, the MPP can be identified in a different way by using calculus in order to differentiate the production function with respect to labour. Specifically:

$$\text{MPP} = \frac{dQ}{dL} = \frac{d(AK^aL^bN^c)}{dL} = bAK^aL^{b-1}N^c$$

The slope of the MPP curve is then given by differentiating the equation for MPP:

$$\frac{dMPP}{dL} = (b-1)bAK^aL^{b-2}N^c$$

As the value of b must lie between zero and one (see Section 6.3.2), the slope of the MPP curve is always negative in the case of a Cobb–Douglas production function. This may not always be the case, however, for other forms of the production function. Having considered production in the short run, the next step in the analysis is to consider the more complex case where all of the factors are variable – the long run.

■ ■ ■ Self-Assessment Question ■ ■ ■ ■ ■ ■ ■ ■ ■ ■ ■ ■

Q4 Using the figures given below, fill in the table by calculating the average physical product (APP) and marginal physical product (MPP) for the firm. How many workers will the firm employ in this case?

Number of workers	0	1	2	3	4	5	6	7	8	9
TPP	0	4	10	18	28	40	48	56	56	54
APP										
MPP										

6.3.4   Production in the Long Run

As all of the factors of production are variable in the long run, the firm can change anything it wishes about how, where and what to produce. It can choose different mixes of land, labour and capital with which to make an existing product. It can move its production to another site in order to obtain better or cheaper premises or to reduce its labour costs by moving to a low-wage area. It can also move from one market to another by changing what it produces completely or diversifying into the production of a wider range of products. Thus there are an almost unlimited number of options available to it, although some options may be better or more efficient than others.

For simplicity, we will assume that the firm produces only one product and has already chosen its preferred production site (although this analysis can be extended to a footloose multi-product firm). The remaining decisions it has to take are those regarding how much of the good it should produce and the combination of capital and labour it should use to do so. These issues are discussed below.

How Much Should the Firm Produce?

One answer to this question is that the firm should produce as much of the good as it can sell (at a reasonable price) in order to make as much profit as it can. Its ability to do this will, however, depend upon the demand and supply conditions within the market. On the supply side, one of the determinants of how much the firm will produce is the cost of making the product. This will be explored in more detail later on in this chapter. What can be said at this point, however, is that the costs of production will at least partly depend upon how much of the product the firm chooses to produce and how efficiently it does so. This brings us to an examination of the concepts of returns to scale and economies and diseconomies of scale.

Returns to scale are a way of measuring the amount of extra output which the firm will produce as a result of increasing the amount of inputs that it uses. Some firms will be more efficient in this context than others. Suppose, for example, that a firm decides to double the amount of inputs it uses, that is to increase them by 100 per cent. This may have one of three effects:

1. *Constant returns to scale* – doubling the amount of inputs used leads to double the amount of output being produced, that is a 100 per cent increase in the inputs used results in 100 per cent more output.

2. *Increasing returns to scale* – doubling the amount of inputs used leads to three times as much output being produced, that is a 100 per cent increase in the inputs results in 200 per cent more output.

3. *Decreasing returns to scale* – doubling the amount of inputs used leads to output rising by a half, that is a 100 per cent rise in the inputs used results in a 50 per cent increase in output.

Thus in these three cases, the same change in the amount of inputs used has different effects, depending upon whether the firm is experiencing constant, increasing or decreasing returns to scale. This translates into an assessment of the relative efficiency of the firm in terms of the costs of production which it will incur. In the case of constant returns to scale, the cost per unit of producing the product will remain the same. In the case of increasing returns, the cost per unit of output will fall as more output is being produced for a given rise in costs. If, on the other hand, the firm is experiencing decreasing returns, then the cost of producing each unit of the product will rise as the increase in costs associated with using the additional inputs is proportionately greater than the increase in output.

This brings us to the issue of economies and diseconomies of scale. An economy of scale arises when increasing the scale of production leads to a lower cost per unit of output. Economies of scale can be divided into two types – internal and external. Internal (plant or firm) economies of scale arise because of the large size of a particular production site, for example a factory, or the firm. External economies arise as a result of the size of the industry as a whole. A diseconomy of scale arises when increasing the scale of production leads to a higher cost per unit of output. These can be similarly divided. Internal diseconomies of scale occur as costs per unit of output rise as a result of the increasing size of the production site or firm. External diseconomies of scale occur as a result of factors pertaining to the increasing size of the industry as a whole. Examples of each of these are given below.

Internal economies of scale may result from:

1. *Indivisibilities*. These occur when an input has a minimum size, for example a piece of machinery. For example, suppose that a particular machine produces 500 units of a component part per week, but the firm only needs 300 of these given its current level of production of the final good. It therefore has a choice between installing the machine and getting 200 extra units of the component per week that it does not need or not installing the machine. If it takes the latter course of action it would then have to reduce its production of the final good by 300 units per week as it has insufficient components to maintain its current level of production. Under these circumstances it might pay the firm to increase its production of the final good by 200 units in order to make efficient use of the new piece of machinery. If demand is sufficient to allow the firm to do this, then the firm is benefiting from an economy of scale. The cost per component part is reduced as the total cost of producing the components can be divided by 500 instead of 300 units. This will feed through into lower costs per unit of output for the final good and so make the firm more competitive as well.

2. *Greater efficiency of large machines*. Economies of scale arise from this source when, for example, a machine producing 1000 units of output per day requires the same number of people to operate it as a machine producing just 500 units of output per day. By using the first machine more output can be obtained by using the same amount of labour, which means that this is a more efficient and lower cost method of production.

3. *Specialisation and the division of labour*. In general, the larger the amount of a product that the firm produces, the greater the number of people it will need to employ in order to make it. This means that each of them can become specialised in a particular task or tasks rather than trying to perform a much wider range of functions. Consequently each of them will become more efficient in carrying out their allotted tasks and so will work faster and more productively as a result of this division of labour.

4. *Multi-stage production*. A large firm may be able to carry out several stages of the production process on the same site. This yields economies of scale for the firm as it reduces the cost of transporting semi-finished products from one site to another and reduces the risk of delays in the production process. If a firm also produces its own components, it is more able to control the costs associated with this part of the process than if it was buying them in from another firm. It will also be able to ensure that they will be delivered at the time when they are needed.

5. *Organisational economies*. An example of these would arise in the case of a multi-site firm that has one central administrative office employing a range of management specialists instead of having an administrative and general management function at each of its sites. This allows it to recoup economies of scale from the division of labour of its management structure but also allows form filling, ordering and so on to be carried out centrally. This may reduce the overall number of administrative staff employed by the firm, thus reducing its total costs and correspondingly the overhead cost per unit of output.

6. *Financial economies*. These arise because the larger size of the firm gives it more bargaining power. For example, because it is using a greater quantity of raw materials it may be able to get a discount from its supplier for buying in bulk. Alternatively, large firms often find it easier to borrow money at a lower interest rate than small firms, as the former are seen as being a better credit risk given that they have more assets which can be seized in the event of a default on the debt.

External economies of scale may result from:

1. *Improved access to raw materials*. In the case of a large industry, the demand for raw materials will be comparatively high. This will encourage addi-

tional supply of the materials which will be beneficial to all firms operating in the industry.

2. *Agglomeration economies*. These arise when firms within an industry benefit from being located close to each other, as there is some kind of synergistic relationship between them. For example, when component suppliers are located close to the firms manufacturing the finished good the transport costs of moving the components are reduced which benefits both parties.

3. *Input suppliers*. If, for example, an industry has a high demand for a particular type of skilled labour, then there will be an incentive for people to acquire the necessary skills. This will be advantageous for the industry as a whole and for individual firms within it, especially if the cost of this training is borne by individuals rather than the firms themselves. Alternatively, when an industry has quite specialised technological requirements, a large industry may have advantages over a smaller one. Specifically, the greater the amount of a particular type of equipment that is used, the larger will be the number of suppliers and the lower the price of the machinery is likely to be as a result of competition between them.

4. *Support services*. Most firms use business-related services of some type, for example accountancy or computer services. In addition, many firms, especially in manufacturing, also use more specialised services such as research and development. An individual firm may be unable to provide such services itself but if there are a number of similar firms in an industry, then their combined demand may be sufficient to support the establishment of a firm to provide such services. Thus the larger the size of the industry, the more likely it is that services such as these will be sustainable within any given area.

Internal diseconomies may arise as a result of:

1. *Management co-ordination problems*. As the firm expands, and especially if it becomes multi-site, it may be more difficult to co-ordinate the firm's activities. Poor communication between the different levels and functions of the management team or between sites may result in contradictory policies being pursued by different parts of the firm. If this is the case, then the firm will be operating less efficiently than it could do, and time and money will be wasted in dealing with the problems which arise from this lack of co-ordination within the firm. This will increase the firm's costs unnecessarily.

2. *Worker alienation*. It may also be the case that employees within a large firm feel alienated from the firm's decision-making process, for example, if decisions about their future are being made at a distance or there is a lack of communication between different parts of the firm. If such alienation does occur, then the workforce may feel that they have less of a stake in the firm's success and this in turn may make them less productive or more prone to take

industrial action. This would also have an effect on the firm's costs per unit of output which would be higher than if the firm was working more efficiently.

3. *Interdependencies in the production process.* The larger the firm and the more of the production process it carries out, the more likely a disruption in one part of the process is to have knock-on effects on the rest of the firm's work. If, for example, a machine halfway along the assembly line breaks down, the firm may have to halt production further along the line until the machine is repaired. This raises the cost per unit of output as less output is being produced but the inputs (staff and machinery) still have to be paid for.

External diseconomies may arise as a result of a shortage of suitable inputs. In some industries, as the industry expands, the resulting increase in demand for the inputs used raises their price significantly as little or no additional supply of them is forthcoming. In this case, the size of the industry has a negative effect on the firm's costs as it is forced to pay even higher prices for these inputs in order to obtain them. In the case of a particular type of skilled labour, for example, it may be that training new staff takes longer than the firm is prepared to wait and so it 'poaches' staff from other companies. These companies then retaliate by poaching staff from others and so on. As a result, the cost of this type of labour rises steeply because demand is exceeding supply.

Thus from the firm's point of view, the preferred level of production is one where it is reaping economies of scale but is not experiencing diseconomies of scale. There may be little it can do about external economies and diseconomies of scale as they are outside of its control. By monitoring the size of the production site or firm, however, it should be able to find an optimum level of production which allows internal economies to be achieved without allowing internal diseconomies of scale to occur.

Optimal Production in the Long Run

By definition, therefore, the optimal level of production in the long run occurs at the output level at which long-run costs are minimised, that is any possible economies of scale have been achieved and any diseconomies of scale avoided. Consequently, the firm will combine the three factors of production in such a way as to use them in the most efficient (and least cost) way. In order to do this, the firm will look at the MPP of each of the three factors in relation to their respective prices.

The outcome of this is that the firm will choose the method of production for which the ratios of MPP to factor price are equalised, that is:

$$\frac{MPP_L}{P_L} = \frac{MPP_K}{P_K} = \frac{MPP_N}{P_N}$$

At this point, the firm is experiencing 'technical or productive efficiency' as the least cost combination of factors has been achieved for a given level of output, that is, the extra product (MPP) from the last pound spent on each of the factors is equal. Unless either the price or productivity of one of the factors changes, this will remain the efficient position for the firm for that particular level of output. Each output level will have a similar efficient combination of factors based on the above formula.

If the above equality did not exist for a particular output level, it would be in the firm's interests to alter the mix of the factors of production it was using. For example, if the ratio of MPP to factor price was greater for capital than for labour and land, then the firm could substitute capital for labour and land in order to make its production process more efficient. This would enable it to reduce its cost per unit of output and hence allow it either to make a greater profit on the good or to drop its price in order to make the firm more competitive in the market. The firm would therefore keep substituting capital for labour and land until the factor returns were equalised once again.

■ ■ ■ Self-Assessment Question ■ ■ ■ ■ ■ ■ ■ ■ ■ ■ ■ ■

Q5 Give two examples of each of the following:

(a) internal economies of scale

(b) external economies of scale

(c) internal diseconomies of scale

CASE STUDY *easyJet*

In order to establish how to produce its product, easyJet had to consider how much of each of the three factors of production – land, labour and capital – to use and the relationships and/or trade-offs between them in order to maximise efficiency. In terms of the land input, two particular things were required, landing rights/hangar space for the company's aircraft and premises for the company to locate in. While most of the existing UK airlines operated from either Heathrow or Gatwick, easyJet decided to get around the problem of obtaining landing rights at what were already overcrowded airports by basing all of its activities at Luton Airport to the north of London. This had the advantage of ensuring the company had the space that they needed while also keeping costs down. Thus by making a location decision that was different from its competitors, easyJet secured an early advantage.

In relation to its capital input, easyJet began by leasing just two planes, although it has

continued

subsequently acquired more. In order to make more efficient use of them, however, it increased the intensity of their use by scheduling more flights per plane per day than was the industry's normal practice at the time. In addition, the company decided to outsource all of its maintenance in order to avoid the need to invest in the machinery, tools and so on which would be necessary for this part of the business. A further innovation was the focus on internet booking which enabled the company to process customers' requests for flights more quickly than before. Although this required an investment in computer technology – the capital input – it also meant that a smaller number of staff could handle all of the flight bookings, while at the same time travel agents' fees could be avoided as the result of direct selling to customers.

The use of computerisation to reduce the number of staff was just one of the company's innovations which were designed to reduce the amount of labour being used. Apart from the most highly specialised personnel, for example pilots, the company made a point of training its staff to be multi-functional so that they could do a number of jobs in the company as and when needed. An example of this is that the company does not use boarding clerks at its destination airports but instead the cabin crew also perform this function.

In summary, therefore, easyJet chose to supply the airline market using a different combination of land, labour and capital inputs than was the case for the existing airlines. The effect of this on its costs is explored in Section 6.4.

6.3.5 Estimating the Firm's Production Function

Both the general production function for the firm and a specific form of it, the Cobb–Douglas production function, were mentioned in Section 6.3.2. In this section we will use the latter to illustrate how the firm's production function can be estimated using regression analysis.

The Cobb–Douglas production function was written as:

$$Q = AK^aL^bN^c$$

As this is a power function, it can be transformed into a log-linear function:

$$\log Q = \log A + a \log K + b \log L + c \log N$$

This equation can then be estimated using regression analysis in the same way as for its demand equivalent in Chapter 4. In doing so, the same issues arise with respect to the collection and accuracy of the data for Q, K, L and N, and the same techniques and regression statistics can be used to estimate and assess the accuracy of the equation. In addition, however, estimating the production function for a firm has other difficulties associated with it.

To begin with, the capital input into the production process may be difficult to quantify as in the case of indivisibilities, for example, a machine may have to be employed (at the same cost) regardless of how much or how little output is being produced. Thus in this case the explicit link between the level of output produced and the amount of the capital input used is broken. In addition, it is implicitly assumed that the firm will be operating under conditions of productive efficiency, that is for any given level of output, the capital, labour and land inputs are being used in the optimal (most efficient and least cost) way. This may not always be true in practice. If, for example, the firm has to reduce the amount of output that it produces in response to a fall in demand, it may choose not to restructure its production process immediately, especially if it expects this fall to be temporary. This means that the firm will not be operating at least cost, as it is, for example, paying for labour which it does not actually need.

Despite these difficulties, however, the use of the Cobb–Douglas production function has value in terms of the information that it provides for the firm. Specifically, the marginal product of each of the factors of production can be found by differentiating the production function with respect to each of them, for example $MP_K = dQ/dK$; the marginal rate of factor substitution can be found by dividing the relevant marginal products by each other, for example, the marginal rate of factor substitution between capital and labour $MRS_{KL} = MP_K / MP_L$; the elasticity of supply for each input is equal to the coefficient of that input; and returns to scale can be measured by the sum of the coefficients so that if $a + b + c > 1$ then the firm is experiencing increasing returns to scale, if $a + b + c < 1$ then the firm is experiencing decreasing returns to scale, and if $a + b + c = 1$ then the firm is experiencing constant returns to scale. Thus estimation of the Cobb–Douglas production function via regression analysis can give us a significant amount of information about the firm's production process.

CASE STUDY *A Sample Regression Equation*

A firm has estimated its production function in log-linear form using regression analysis with the following result:

$$Q = 1.25 + 0.2\,K + 0.7\,L + 0.1\,N$$
$$(0.05)\quad(0.25)\quad(0.05)$$

$R^2 = 0.97$ adjusted $R^2 = 0.94$ $SE_E = 1.1$

$m = 3$ and $n = 20$ $F = 170$

In this case, all three of the factors of production have an influence on the level of output produced (quantity supplied) but how accurate is the equation? The high R^2 value indicates that the equation is a good fit to the data and this is borne out by the adjusted R^2 statistic. The standard error of the equation (SE_E) and the F-test both confirm this. Calculating the t-statistics for each of the three independent variables gives us indication of how

CASE STUDY *continued*

accurate the individual coefficients are: $t_K = 0.2 / 0.05 = 4$; $t_L = 0.7 / 0.25 = 2.8$; and $t_N = 0.1 / 0.05 = 2$. It is apparent from this that the coefficients for all three factors are reliable (although the *t*-statistic for land is marginal). Consequently, the equation appears to be a good fit to the data and could be used for forecasting purposes. The equation also tells us that the firm is experiencing constant returns to scale as the values of the coefficients add up to one ($0.2 + 0.7 + 0.1 = 1$). The elasticity values indicate that all of the variables are inelastic with respect to supply, but also that quantity supplied is most responsive to changes in the amount of labour being used.

■ ■ ■ **Self-Assessment Question** ■ ■ ■ ■ ■ ■ ■ ■ ■ ■ ■ ■

Q6

(a) What technique was used to estimate the firm's production function?

(b) How are the elasticities of supply for each of the three independent variables obtained in this case?

(c) If $a + b + c < 1$, what type of returns to scale is the firm experiencing?

■ ■

■ 6.4   Cost Estimation

The principal distinction that economists make is between fixed costs and variable costs. Fixed costs are defined as those costs which do not vary with the level of output, that is those which have to be paid by the firm irrespective of the amount of the product that the firm is producing. This category includes things like property costs in the form of rent, maintenance costs and local property taxes. Variable costs, on the other hand, change as the level of output changes. In general, as output rises variable costs increase, for example labour costs rise as more workers are hired to produce additional output, and vice versa. In the short run, the firm will be experiencing a mix of fixed and variable costs, but in the long run all costs (like the factors of production associated with them) are variable. The next two sections examine the costs incurred in these two periods in more detail.

6.4.1   Short-run Cost Estimation

The firm's short-run cost function is also known as its 'operating cost function', that is it measures the firm's day-to-day running costs rather than the firm's overall total costs. The short-run cost function is therefore defined as being 'constrained by prior investment and other multi-period commitments, for example fixed capital and land costs'. Consequently, in the short run, previous investment in premises (the land input) and machinery (the capital input) is viewed as being irrelevant to the firm's operating cost decisions. The relevant costs in this context are the variable costs incurred by the firm, for example wages. Variable costs are therefore the focus of the firm's short-run cost estimation process.

Short-run cost estimation is also often carried out using regression analysis, but some of the issues faced in using it are different from those related to the estimation of the production function. The first issue that arises is what are we trying to estimate? We have already said that it is only the firm's total variable costs which are relevant in the short run. In addition, however, any factors which will result in changes in these costs such as a change in input quality, and hence input prices, or a change in product mix in the case of a multi-product firm, will also need to be included. The second issue relates to the type of data which the firm should use in the cost estimation process. It is likely that the data the firm has available will be in historic rather than future cost form, that is, based on past costs. The first thing the decision maker needs to do, therefore, is to convert these historic data into future cost data if the cost estimation process is to be accurate. Certain assumptions may need to be made in order to do this, for example about the size of any likely wage increases for the workforce over the period in question. There is also the problem of comparing costs over time given that inflation is a persistent phenomenon in many countries. The solution to this is to adjust the data so that costs are measured in real rather than nominal terms in order to ensure that the effects of inflation are removed from the data. This should increase their accuracy. The data should also be adjusted to take account of any leads and lags between cost reporting and output production, for example stockpiling of materials at a time when they are relatively cheap to buy. In this case, the higher costs incurred as a result of this purchase in one period would result in lower costs in the next period as there would be no need to purchase raw materials then. Finally, as with all analyses of this type, the greater the number of data observations the firm has, the more accurate its cost estimates are likely to be.

The third issue relates to the specification of the total variable cost curve which may be either linear, quadratic or cubic. The linear form is perhaps the simplest and is specified as:

$$TVC = a + bQ + \sum_{i=1}^{n} c_i X_i$$

where TVC is total variable cost, Q is the quantity of output and the X_i are any other independent variables (from 1 to n) which are to be included in the equation. They may include, for example, things like expected changes in wage costs, input quality, product mix or product design. If any of these are due to occur during the estimation period then the level of total variable costs will no longer purely be a function of the level of output produced. As before, the a, b and c_i terms are the regression coefficients for the equation which are calculated through the use of the ordinary least squares technique. What is particularly interesting about this equation, however, is that the value of b gives us an approximation to both marginal and average variable costs over the estimation period. The nature of the estimates of these three types of costs – TVC, AVC and MC – is shown in Figures 6.6 and 6.7.

In Figure 6.6 the estimated TVC curve is shown by an upward-sloping dotted line while the true unobserved TVC function a shown as a bold upward-curving line. For simplicity it has been assumed that the equation takes the form TVC = $a + bQ$, that is there are no other relevant factors (the X-values) which need to be included. The estimated function was obtained from looking at a range of cost/output observations between output levels Q_1 and Q_2. This means that any predictions of costs within this range are reasonably accurate, although of course the actual and estimated TVC levels are not necessarily identical. Outside this range, however, the predictive capacity of the estimated TVC function is reduced, so that the estimated function is of little use in estimating costs for levels of output below Q_1 and above Q_2.

In Figure 6.7, the marginal cost curve is shown by the horizontal straight line at point b. This arises from the fact that the MC curve is found by taking the first difference of the TVC equation with respect to Q. Specifically, in this case:

$$MC = \frac{dTVC}{dQ} = \frac{d(a + bQ)}{dQ} = b$$

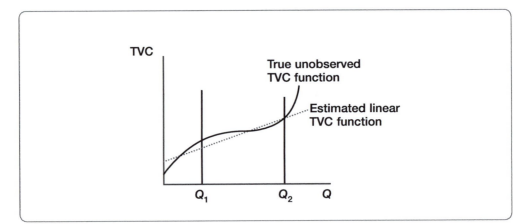

Figure 6.6   The estimated TVC curve

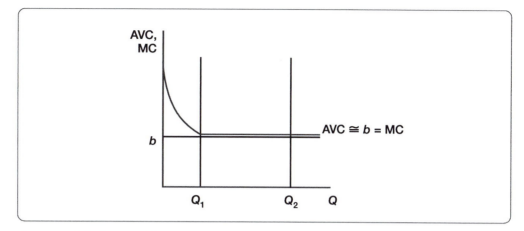

Figure 6.7   Estimated AVC and MC curves

Thus the MC curve is a straight line of constant value.

The AVC curve, on the other hand, is found by dividing the equation for the TVC curve by Q to convert it into an average:

$$AVC = \frac{TVC}{Q} = \frac{a}{Q} + b$$

As the value of Q gets bigger, the value of the first term of this equation gets progressively smaller until eventually it will approximate to b. Thus in Figure 6.7 there is a divergence between the downward-sloping AVC curve and the straight line MC curve at low levels of output, but this is substantially reduced at higher levels of output, in this case those above Q_1. In the case of the quadratic and cubic specifications of the TVC curve, the estimation process is similar but the resulting curves are different. The AVC curve will be U-shaped in each case. The MC curve will be an upward-sloping straight line when the quadratic form is used but will take a j-shape in the case of the cubic form of the TVC curve which conforms more closely with traditional economic theory.

■ ■ ■ Self-Assessment Question ■ ■ ■ ■ ■ ■ ■ ■ ■ ■ ■ ■

Q7

(a) Which of the cost curves are relevant to the firm's short-run cost estimation process?

(b) What forms may the cost estimation equation take?

(c) Identify two possible problems which may arise in obtaining accurate data with which to estimate the equation.

6.4.2 Long-run Cost Estimation

In the long run, all of the inputs into the firm's production process are variable. This means that more radical changes to the firm's cost structure are possible in the long run and that the decisions made by the firm at this time will constrain its activities in the future. For this reason the long-run cost function is also sometimes known as the 'planning cost function', as it can be used by the firm to plan its production operation for some time to come. As all costs are variable in the long run, only the long-run average total cost curve is relevant to the firm's decision-making process during this period. This curve is shown in Figure 6.8.

The long-run average total cost curve is composed of the minimum points of the short-run average total cost curves. Each of the short-run average total cost curves shows the efficient size of firm for a given level of output, and by joining these together the overall shape of the long-run average total cost curve is obtained. Figure 6.8 demonstrates that the optimal size of firm occurs at Q^* where long-run average total costs are minimised. Prior to Q^* the firm is reaping economies of scale, but after Q^* the firm begins to experience diseconomies of scale. It should be noted, however, that while most firms will have the potential to benefit from economies of scale as they grow in size, it is not always the case that they will experience diseconomies of scale. If the firm does not do so then the curve will become horizontal for output levels beyond Q^*. Thus in this instance, efficient, lowest cost production may be sustainable for higher levels of output.

In terms of the estimation process itself, three main methods of long-run cost estimation can be identified – regression analysis, the survivor technique and the engineering technique.

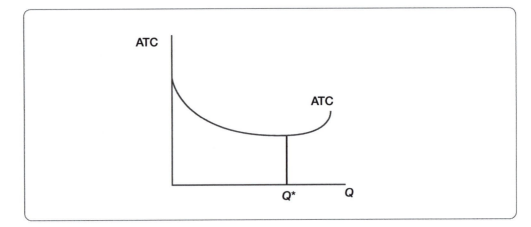

Figure 6.8 Long-run average total cost curve

Regression Analysis

Regression analysis can be used for long-run as well as short-run cost estimation. In this case, the identification of which cost curve to estimate is easy as only the long-run average total cost curve is relevant to the firm's decision-making process during this period. Again, it would normally be assumed that average total cost is primarily related to the level of output produced and the curve could be either linear, quadratic or cubic in terms of its specification. Difficulties in obtaining accurate data mean, however, that the use of regression analysis is more problematic in the short run than in the long run.

To begin with, there is the problem of changes in technology over time. In the case of short-run cost estimation, the need for frequent data observations has led to time-series data being used over weeks, months or years depending on availability. If technology has remained unchanged, this approach is also feasible in the long run, but if not this approach is invalid as we would not be comparing like with like. In order to evaluate the cost effectiveness of the latest technology and to determine the optimal firm size under these new conditions it is necessary to use cross-section data instead. This involves a comparison of different firms using the same technology at one particular point in time. This in itself can generate further problems as firms will be unwilling to pass on commercially sensitive data to potential rivals.

Even where this is not a problem, differences in accounting techniques between firms may make such an analysis more difficult, for example because of the differences in the way in which they depreciate capital investment. In addition, geographical factors may play a role, as in order to obtain sufficient data it may be necessary to include firms in a number of different areas and input prices may differ significantly between them. Finally, this approach will only be truly accurate if all the firms included in the analysis are operating at maximum efficiency. This is a big assumption to make as in practice it is unlikely that all firms will be operating in this way all of the time. If they are not then future costs will be overestimated. In summary, therefore, long-run cost estimation using regression analysis, while possible, is quite difficult to do accurately. Consequently, two other approaches have been developed in order to determine the firm's long-run cost structure (the engineering technique) and the efficient size of firm (the survivor technique) respectively.

The Engineering Technique

The engineering technique is designed to allow firms to estimate the likely cost of a particular new technology. This reduces the level of risk for the firm as it can assess whether it is worthwhile to introduce the new technology or whether the associated costs would be so large as to make this unprofitable. The underlying assumption behind this technique is that the technology remains unchanged throughout the estimation period. The firm then needs to determine the most efficient input combination for each output level, for example how many machines will be required and how many people will be needed to operate them. In effect what the firm is trying to do is to work out the shape of its long-run average total cost curve. It does this by multiplying the number of units of each of the inputs required by their respective prices and summing them to give the total cost of producing a particular level of output in this way. In order to give the average total cost associated with a particular output level it then divides this figure by the number of units of output produced.

Suppose, for example, that the firm wishes to produce 100,000 units of output a year. Assuming that each of the new machines can produce 20,000 units a year then in order to meet its output target the firm will need 5 of them. To run the firm effectively it estimates that it will need 20 people and it will be most efficient to have them based on just one site. Thus in terms of its input levels it will be using 1 unit of land (N), 5 units of capital (K) and 20 units of labour (L). Assuming that each unit of land costs £50,000 (P_N), each unit of capital costs £20,000 (P_K) and the average wage is £15,000 (P_L), then the firm's total costs can then be calculated:

$$\begin{aligned} \text{TC} &= (N \times P_N) + (K \times P_K) + (L \times P_L) \\ &= (1 \times £50,000) + (5 \times £20,000) + (20 \times £15,000) \\ &= £50,000 + £100,000 + £300,000 \\ &= £450,000 \end{aligned}$$

Dividing this figure by the number of units of output produced (100,000) gives us an average total cost of £4.50 per unit of output. The firm can then repeat this calculation for different input and output levels in order to find the most cost-efficient means of production.

This technique has two main advantages. Firstly, by definition, it avoids any errors resulting from changes in technology. Secondly, it uses current input prices so that it is unnecessary to convert the cost data from their historic form as would be the case for regression analysis. On the negative side, however, there is no guarantee that the predictions made using this approach will be accurate in the case of totally new, unproven technologies. A great deal will depend on the assumptions made by the decision maker about the levels of inputs required to run the firm's operations efficiently. Once a particular technology is established, it should become easier to determine what the most efficient size of firm actually is as more information will be available. Exactly how this can be done is shown by the survivor technique.

The Survivor Technique

The basic assumption underlying the survivor technique is that as a result of competition between firms only the most efficient ones, that is those with the lowest average total costs, will survive over time.

In order to use this technique it is first of all necessary to classify the firms in an industry by size, for example small, medium and large. This is often done in terms of the number of people employed by the firm – a small firm, for example, might be defined as one with less than 10 employees. The next stage is to calculate the share of industry output which is accounted for by each size group at several different points in time. If the output share of one of the size groups increases over time then that size of firm is efficient. If the output share of a size groups falls, however, it is inefficient.

Suppose, for example, that in 1991 the small firms in an industry accounted for 50 per cent of that industry's output, the medium-sized firms accounted for 35 per cent and the large firms for 15 per cent. By 2001, these shares had changed to 30, 40 and 30 per cent respectively. What does this tell us? Firstly, the small firms in the industry have suffered a decline in their share of output from 50 to 30 per cent which means that this size of firm is inefficient. Both of the other size groups have increased their share of industry output which means that they are efficient. Of these two groups, the large firms have fared best as they have doubled their share of total industry output compared to a much smaller rise in output share for the medium-size firms. It is reasonable to suggest, therefore, that both large- and medium-size firms are more efficient than small ones. It would be wrong, however, to suggest that large firms are more efficient than medium-size firms on the basis of this evidence as they would both be classified as efficient using this technique.

This latter point highlights one of the problems with the survivor technique which is that it can be used to say whether a firm size is efficient or not, but it cannot be used to measure the relative efficiency of different firm sizes. In addition, of course, it assumes that the firms concerned are operating in a competitive market. If this is not the case then survival within the industry may not be based on having lower average total costs than other firms at all, but instead may be based on things like the existence of barriers to entry into the industry which have prevented the development of meaningful competition. On the positive side, however, this technique can be used to give the decision maker some general guidance with regard to the likely efficient size of operations for the firm in any particular industry. Thus like the other methods we have looked at it has both strengths and weaknesses.

■ ■ ■ Self-Assessment Question ■ ■ ■ ■ ■ ■ ■ ■ ■ ■ ■ ■

Q8

(a) Which cost curve will the firm be trying to estimate in the long run?

(b) Give two reasons why the use of regression analysis to estimate this cost curve may be problematic. What are (i) the engineering technique and (ii) the survivor technique used to measure?

CASE STUDY | *easyJet*

In terms of the estimation of its costs, the company needed to distinguish between its fixed and variable costs and also to decide whether it was interested in looking at its short-run or its long-run cost position. When it was founded, the company was able to take a long-run view in deciding how to produce and what costs to incur (although there is, of course, always some uncertainty regarding whether particular costs will fall or rise in future). Specifically, it decided to reduce its fixed costs by operating out of Luton Airport instead of Heathrow or Gatwick in terms of its land input. In terms of its capital requirements, its decision to lease planes instead of buying them and to outsource its maintenance requirements also reduced its fixed costs substantially. In addition, the cost of investing in the technology to operate its booking system over the internet was offset by the saving in staff and travel agents' fees which it made possible. Finally, the multi-tasking of its staff also reduced its total labour costs as did its decision to provide a 'no frills' product, for example, by not providing free in-flight meals and drinks for its customers. Thus through these measures, easyJet was able to reduce both its fixed and variable costs to below the average for the industry, although it is difficult to say whether or not it reached the point of minimum long-run average cost for the firm. This in turn enabled it to offer cheaper flights to its customers and to obtain a competitive advantage. The success of this strategy is apparent from the company's growth over the last 10 years.

❑ ❑ ❑ End of Chapter SUMMARY ❑ ❑ ❑ ❑ ❑ ❑ ❑ ❑ ❑ ❑ ❑

This chapter began by reviewing supply theory in order to provide a background for a more detailed examination of production and cost estimation. The variables which influence the supply of the product were identified via the supply function, and their effects on the supply curve were also briefly assessed. The nature of, and the relationship between, the factors of production – land, labour and capital – were discussed in the context of both the short and the long run. This was followed by a section covering the estimation of the production function.

With respect to cost estimation in the short run, the firm is constrained by decisions which it has previously made and cannot alter during the period in question. In this case, therefore, the estimation process is concerned with the total variable costs incurred by the firm, and regression analysis is the tool which is used to predict these costs. In the long run, however, it is average total costs which are the focus of attention as far as the estimation process is concerned. Regression analysis can again be used but the difficulties associated with this approach have led firms to adopt alternative methods, specifically the engineering and the survivor techniques. The former is especially useful when the firm is considering the introduction of new technology, while the latter gives it guidance regarding the most efficient size of firm for any given industry.

■ ■ ■ ANSWERS to Self-Assessment Questions ■ ■ ■ ■ ■ ■

Q1   The factors are: the price of the product; the price of related products – substitutes and complements; costs; expectations; the goals of the firm; technology and other factors.

Q2   Law of supply – the higher the price of a product, the greater its supply will be; the lower the price of a product, the lower its supply will be.

(a) The introduction of new technology shifts the supply curve to the right as it increases the amount of the product supplied at every price.

(b) A rise in wage costs shifts the supply curve to the left as it reduces the amount supplied.

Q3   The three factors of production are land, labour and capital. Land is always regarded as being fixed and labour as being variable in the short run.

Q4

APP	0	4	5	6	7	8	8	8	7	6
MPP		4	6	8	10	12	8	8	0	−2

The firm will employ 8 workers as TPP is at its peak of 56 units and MPP = 0.

Q5   Any two from:

(a) internal economies – indivisibilities, greater efficiency of large machines, specialisation and division of labour, multi-stage production, organisational economies and financial economies.

(b) external economies – improved access to raw materials, agglomeration economies, input suppliers and support services.

(c) internal diseconomies – management co-ordination problems, worker alienation and interdependencies in the production process.

Q6   (a) Regression analysis was used to estimate the firm's production function.

(b) The elasticities of supply for each of the independent variables are given by their respective coefficients which are generated by the regression equation.

(c) If $a + b + c < 1$, the firm is experiencing decreasing returns to scale.

Q7   (a) It is the total variable cost curve which is estimated in the short run, although the average variable cost and marginal cost curves can also be derived from the estimated equation.

(b) The equation may be linear, quadratic or cubic in form.

(c) Any two problems from – the need to convert historic cost data into future cost data, adjusting the data for inflation, the time period in which costs are recorded as having been incurred and the frequency of the data observations.

Q8   (a) The firm will be trying to estimate its average (total) cost curve in the long run.

(b) Any two reasons from – changes in technology over time, inaccuracy of cross-sectional data, differences in accounting techniques and inefficiency in the production process.

(i) The engineering technique is used to measure the likely costs of the introduction of new technology.

(ii) The survivor technique is used to determine the most efficient size of firm within an industry.

---

7 Pricing in theory and practice

■ 7.1 Introduction

This chapter considers a range of pricing strategies which may be used by the firm depending upon the circumstances in which it finds itself, the information available to it and its objectives. The chapter begins with a brief review of microeconomic theory in so far as it relates to pricing and then goes on to look at the various forms of pricing which the firm may use in practice instead of those prescribed by the theory. These alternative forms of pricing fall into three broad categories – pricing in established markets, new product pricing and specialist forms of pricing which are only used in certain situations.

Before proceeding any further, it is worth considering the issue of why the firm's pricing strategy is so important. The answer to this is that the wrong price, and by implication the wrong pricing strategy, can have a negative impact on the firm. If the price set by the firm is too high, then it will find it difficult to sell the product and this will have a negative effect on its profitability. If the price is set too low, then the firm is unlikely to have difficulty in selling its product but it may be doing so too cheaply, thus reducing the amount of profit it could otherwise have made. What the firm is generally looking for, therefore, is the highest possible price that the market will bear given the objective it is trying to achieve. For example, if the firm is trying to obtain a reasonably high level of profit over a period of several years and barriers to entry exist which effectively protect its market, then the firm can afford to charge a high price throughout this period and still meet its objective. If there were no barriers to entry, on the other hand, this might not be a good strategy to pursue as although the firm might achieve a high level of profit to begin with, this would have the effect of attracting more firms into the market thus reducing the level of profits to be obtained over the longer term. Consequently, the features of the market in which the firm operates will in part determine its pricing strategy. The next section looks at this in more detail by considering what microeconomic theory has to say about pricing in different market structures.

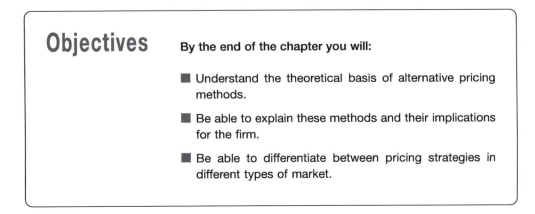

■ 7.2 Pricing and Market Structures

There are four types of market structure – perfect competition, monopoly, monopolistic competition and oligopoly. Each of these can provide the firm with some guidance as to how it should set its price providing that it can identify the type of market in which it operates.

7.2.1 Perfect Competition

This form of market structure is comparatively rare as the assumptions underlying it are quite restrictive – a large number of firms, a homogeneous (identical) product, complete freedom of entry into the market and perfect knowledge of market conditions. The implication of this is that each individual firm is too small to have any influence over price within the market. Thus the price of the good is set by the interaction of market supply and demand. The firm can sell as much as it wants to at that price but cannot set the price of the good itself, that is, the firm is a 'price-taker'. Given that this is the case, there is no need for the firm to choose a particular pricing strategy as in effect the decision has already been made for it – it has no choice.

7.2.2 Monopoly

At the other extreme we have the monopolist. In this case, there is only one firm (or one large dominant firm) in the industry which is protected by the presence of substantial barriers to entry into the market. The firm is now a 'price-maker', that is, it has the freedom to set whatever price it wishes for its product. In practice, of course, its ability to do so may be restricted by government regulation, but subject to this constraint it still has substantial freedom of

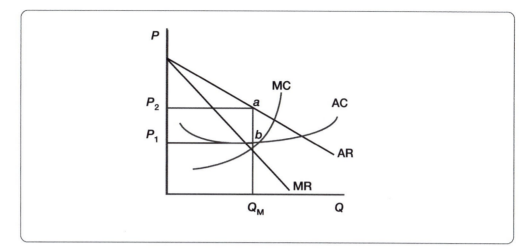

Figure 7.1   Marginal cost pricing under monopoly

action. How will the monopolist set its price? The basic assumption underlying this model is that it will set the price which enables it to maximise its profits. In order to do so it will set the price of its product in such a way as to ensure that marginal cost equals marginal revenue (MC = MR), as shown in Figure 7.1.

The intersection of the MC and MR curves in Figure 7.1 gives the profit-maximising output level Q_M and the corresponding price P_2. The amount of profit made by the monopolist is shown by the area $P_1 P_2 a b$, as in order to make such a profit the firm must cover its average costs. Thus the profit-maximising monopolist will charge a price of P_2 using this approach, which is called 'marginal cost pricing'.

This assumes two things, firstly, that there is no threat of entry into the market so that the firm can get away with charging this comparatively high price and secondly, that it wishes to, or has to, charge the same price to all of its customers. If one of these conditions does not hold then the monopolist may adopt a different pricing strategy. If there is a potential threat of entry it may choose to set a limit price rather than a profit-maximising price. If it does not have to charge the same price to all of its customers, it may operate a policy of price discrimination. Let us look at what such policies imply.

Firstly, in the case of limit pricing, the purpose of the firm's pricing strategy is to set a price which is high enough to make as much profit as possible for the firm but low enough to discourage the entry of new firms into the market. Thus the firm sacrifices some of the profits it could have obtained in the short run in order to protect its profits in the long run. How would this be done? The monopolist by virtue of its size and its experience in the production of the good could reasonably be expected to have lower average costs than any potential entrant. In order to compete with the monopolist, however, any entrant into the market would have to charge the same or a lower price than the monopolist is currently getting its customers to pay in order to encourage them to switch suppliers. This means that the monopolist can stop entry into the market by making it impossible for the new firm to do this. The limit price charged by the monopolist will be at such a level that the new entrant will be unable to make sufficient profit to make it worthwhile entering the industry, that is, the limit price will be set just below the level required for the entrant firm to be able to cover its average costs.

Price discrimination, on the other hand, is targeted towards increasing profits by differentiating between groups of customers. This may be practised whether or not the monopolist is facing the threat of entry into the market concerned. The firm's ability to practise price discrimination rests on its ability to identify distinct sub-markets within its total product market. While price discrimination is not unique to monopoly, the presence of just one dominant firm in the market makes it easier to pursue as customers have little choice other than to buy the product from the firm in question.

In order for price discrimination to work, certain conditions must be fulfilled. Firstly, the difference in prices charged between the different sub-markets must not be wholly attributable to differences in the costs of supplying those markets. Higher prices being charged to customers in geographically remote areas which result from higher transport costs do not, for example, constitute price discrimination. Secondly, the sub-markets must be completely separate so that resale of the good is impossible. This means that consumers buying the good or service at the cheaper price must not be able to sell it on to those who are paying higher prices for it. If this condition does not hold then the consumers being charged the higher prices by the firm could buy their supplies of the product at a discount from those who can obtain it at the lower price rather than buying it direct from the manufacturer. Thirdly, in order for different prices to be charged, the sub-markets must have different elasticities of demand. The firm will be able to charge the highest prices in those sub-markets which have the most inelastic demand. For those sub-markets in which demand is relatively elastic, it will charge lower prices.

There are three forms of price discrimination – first, second and third degree. In the case of first-degree price discrimination, the firm prices each unit of output separately based on what the consumer is prepared to pay for it. This form is comparatively rare, as it assumes that the supplier and purchaser of the good will be bargaining directly with one another over price. Second-degree price discrimination, on the other hand, relates price to quantity purchased. The more the customer purchases, the lower is the average price paid for each unit of the product, for example large business users paying less than domestic users for each unit of electricity consumed. Third-degree price discrimination involves the grouping of consumers into specific sub-markets. A different price is then charged in each market. This assumes that shared characteristics can be readily identified. An example of this might be the practice of charging different prices for adults and children on public transport. Whichever form of price discrimination is being practised by the firm, the effect should be to raise the amount of revenue, and hence profits, that the firm can generate.

7.2.3   Monopolistic Competition

In this case, quite a large number of firms operate in the market, there are no barriers to entry and the industry's product is differentiated rather than homogeneous. What this means is that the firm is able to set the price of its product given that, in the short run at least, it has a monopoly of its own particular version or brand of that product. Thus in the short run the firm sets its price in the same way that a monopolist would do (see Figure 7.1). Limit pricing will not apply in this market, however, as entry cannot be prevented but price discrimination is theoretically possible, if somewhat unusual in practice. Consequently, in the short run, the firm is a price-maker, but in the long run entry by new firms (in response to the relatively high profit levels) turns the firm into a price-taker. This change occurs because as new firms enter the market they take customers away from the existing firms so that the latters' demand (average revenue) curves shift to the left. This process then continues until every firm in the industry is making normal, as opposed to supernormal, profits at which point further entry into the market will cease as there is no longer any incentive for additional firms to move into the industry. At this point, the firm's demand curve will be tangential to its average cost curve and the firm becomes a price-taker as there is now only one market price it can charge if it is to be profitable at all.

7.2.4   Oligopoly

The final market structure is oligopoly. This time a few firms account for a large proportion of the industry's output, although in some cases a number of smaller firms may also operate within the industry. Products within this type of market may be either homogeneous, for example petrol, or differentiated, for example alternative types of soap powder. In the case of the latter, much of the competition between firms may be based upon the branding of goods so as to distinguish them from their closest substitutes. High levels of advertising are consequently often characteristic of this type of market. This in itself can form a barrier to entry for prospective firms as they would need to spend substantial sums of money on advertising in order to ensure consumer recognition of their particular brand. Other barriers to entry may also exist.

The principal difference between this and the other forms of market structure is that each firm will have to take account of the actions of the others, that is, the firms are interdependent rather than independent. A decision made by any one of them will have an effect on the decisions made by the others. How will this affect their pricing behaviour? The answer to this depends on whether the firms choose to compete or to collude with one another. If they choose to compete in order to gain an increased market share then both prices and profits are likely to decrease over time as a result. If, on the other hand, they collude, then they can act as a multi-plant monopolist and maintain relatively high prices and profits. Let us look at some specific cases.

In the case where firms are competing, the effect of being in an oligopolistic market may be to discourage price competition. Instead competition on the basis of advertising and product differentiation may be the norm. This is the result of a phenomenon known as the 'kinked demand curve', that is, under oligopoly the firm does not face the downward-sloping demand curve associated with monopoly and monopolistic competition. The demand curve in this market is made up of two segments with different elasticities, as shown in Figure 7.2.

At levels of output to the left of Q_1 the demand curve is relatively elastic so that if a firm raises its price above P_1 it will lose a large number of its customers to other firms. Thus the other firms have no incentive to follow any price rise as they benefit from an increase in demand if they keep their prices at the original level (P_1). At levels of output to the right of Q_1, however, the demand curve is relatively inelastic. If a firm cuts its price to a level below P_1 then it will attract customers from rival firms. In order to protect their markets, therefore, the rival firms will cut their prices as well. The effect of this is that the market share of each firm will change very little but, because of the lower prices, the firms will be reaping lower profits than before. This can also be seen by looking at the marginal revenue curve. The MR curve now also has two segments corresponding to the two segments of the demand curve. In order to profit maximise the firm must set MC = MR. Thus if the MC curve lies anywhere between MC_1 and MC_2 the profit-maximising price and output levels will be P_1 and Q_1 respectively. Under these circumstances price stability will be the norm and any

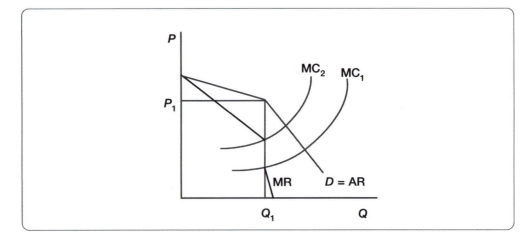

Figure 7.2 The kinked demand curve model of oligopoly

competition which does occur between firms will be on the basis of non-price factors such as advertising and product design.

If, on the other hand, firms decide to collude the effect on prices will be different. Collusion may take one of two forms – formal or tacit. In the case of formal collusion the firms in an industry will join together to form a cartel. This enables them to set a high market price by acting as a multi-plant monopolist. The industry's marginal cost and marginal revenue curves will be determined in order to establish the profit-maximising price and output levels, that is, where MC = MR as in Figure 7.1. Once the profit-maximising price has been determined, all of the firms in the cartel will have to charge that price. They will then choose output levels by setting the firms' marginal costs equal to the industry's marginal costs. The combined profits made by the industry are then divided between the firms. The basis of this division (or quota) may be one of a number of factors such as output levels, market share, capacity or economic power in the market. Alternatively, instead of the use of quotas, the amount of profit each firm obtains may be decided by its success in competing against the others on the basis of non-price factors. Arrangements of this kind are illegal in many countries, and even where they are not the incentive for individual firms to cheat on the agreement in order to obtain still higher profits often leads to them breaking down.

An example of tacit collusion is what is known as price leadership. In this case, one firm within the industry acts as a price-maker by choosing its profit-maximising price and output levels, again by setting MC = MR. The remaining firms in the industry then act as price-takers by accepting this price and choosing their output levels in such a way as to ensure that price equals marginal cost for each firm. The price-maker for the industry may be either the largest firm within it (dominant firm price leadership) or the one which is most typical of the industry as a whole (barometric price leadership). In either case, this approach works the same way. It is worth noting that oligopolistic firms may also co-operate in order to avoid new firms entering the industry through the use of limit pricing.

It is apparent, therefore, that the issue of price setting under oligopoly is less straightforward than for the other forms of market structure as there are a number of alternative methods by which it can be done. What most of the methods we have looked at so far have in common, however, is that they are examples of marginal cost pricing.

7.2.5 Will Firms Use Marginal Cost Pricing in Practice?

The basic assumption underlying marginal cost pricing is that the firm will be seeking to profit maximise regardless of the market structure in which it operates. This raises the question of whether this will always be possible, or even desirable, in practice. The answer to this question is almost certainly no.

To begin with, as was discussed in Chapter 4, the firm's objective may not be profit maximisation at all. While it is reasonable to say that firms will want to be profitable, circumstances may exist in which they are prepared to forgo profits, at least in the short term, in order to protect their market over the longer term. We saw this, for example, in the case of limit pricing where the objective of the firm was to deter entry into the market. The result of this was that the limit price was set at a level below the short-run profit-maximising price. Another example might be where a firm is itself trying to gain entry into a market. In this instance the firm might set a price which is below the profit-maximising price in order to attract more customers to its product. Thus its objective is to maximise sales rather than profits, at least until it has established a strong foothold in the market.

In addition, even if the firm wishes to maximise profits it may not have the information available to do so. It may be, for example, that the firm has introduced a new product on which (by definition) it has no historic cost data. The relevant data will therefore take time to collect. Alternatively, the search costs of obtaining the necessary information about the firm's marginal costs and revenues may be too high to make it worthwhile. In this case, the firm is likely to choose an alternative form of pricing. A number of these are based on so-called 'rule of thumb' techniques which allow the firm to estimate the price it should charge based on the knowledge (however limited) which it has of the market. The rest of this chapter discusses these methods of pricing.

■ ■ ■ Self-Assessment Question ■ ■ ■ ■ ■ ■ ■ ■ ■ ■ ■ ■ ■ ■

Q1 What is meant by the terms price-taker, price-maker, marginal cost pricing, limit pricing, price discrimination and price leadership?

CASE STUDY *The Price of Rail Travel*

As stated previously, third-degree price discrimination involves segmenting the market into different groups of customers, who share certain characteristics, and then charging different prices to each group. This practice is prevalent throughout the travel industry – where it is also known as 'yield management'. The example we will use here, however, is the case of rail travel. If we examine one particular route, from London to Edinburgh, the majority of the train services are provided by two companies Great North Eastern Railways (GNER) and Virgin. Within the context of our market

CASE STUDY *continued*

structure models, this constitutes a special model of oligopoly called duopoly, that is, a market where two firms dominate. (Note: An interesting point arises here in that this is the case when we define the market as rail travel whereas if we defined it as travel between London and Edinburgh, the presence of airlines and coach companies might align it more closely with a more standard model of oligopoly.)

Both companies segment their customers in similar ways through, for example, the use of railcards which offer different discounts to specific groups of customers, for example students, families and pensioners. Similarly, distinctions are made in terms of price for peak and off-peak and first- and second-class travel. Beyond that, however, there can be customers travelling in the same carriage of a train paying a range of fares. A 'bargain' ticket currently costs £35–40, an 'Apex' return £50–55, a 'Value' ticket £60, a 'Super Advance' return £65–75 and a 'Saver' return £82.50. The principal difference between these types of ticket lies in a combination of how far in advance the customer can book their journey and the extent to which they are prepared to be tied to particular trains. This in turn enables the rail companies to manage demand in such a way as to divert customers from peak to off-peak services in order to fill empty seats.

■ 7.3 New Product Pricing

New product pricing was identified above as one of those areas where marginal cost pricing may not be an option due to lack of information about the marginal costs of producing and the marginal revenue which can be obtained from selling the product. How then will the firm set the initial price of the product? This depends on what the firm is trying to achieve at the outset, high profits or high sales. A firm looking for high short-run profits will use the price-skimming approach. A firm wanting a high initial level of sales will use the penetration-pricing approach.

7.3.1 Price Skimming

The idea behind price skimming is that the firm should set the highest possible price for the product when it is first introduced in order to allow it to make a high profit in the short run. The actual price the firm sets will be decided on the basis of a range of factors including the firm's costs, how much profit it wishes to make and its expectations about the way in which the market will develop. This last point is particularly important with respect to the firm's pricing decision.

Price skimming is most often used when one or more of the following market conditions exist: the firm has a short-run monopoly; a 'status' product is being produced; there are substantial barriers to entry into the market; and/or demand for the product is likely to decrease rapidly.

If the firm is the first to produce a particular product then it will have a short-run monopoly for the product for at least as long as it takes for other firms to develop something similar. As it is the sole supplier of the product it can therefore adopt a 'take it or leave it approach' to potential customers and set a high price accordingly. Those customers who will buy the product will be those who are prepared to pay the high price for it. This group will include anyone who believes that it is a 'status' product, that is, one which it is necessary to have to improve, or protect, their social standing.

How long the firm can continue to use this approach will depend upon whether there are barriers to entry into the market which will prevent competition from other firms producing similar or identical products. If, for example, the company can patent its product then it will be able to use this to protect its market and high prices can be charged for some time. A typical case of this would be the introduction of a new prescription drug. Most such drugs are protected from competition in the short run in order to ensure that the company which developed them receives an adequate return on what can be a high investment in terms of research and development costs. Thus until the patent runs out the firm can if it wishes adopt a price-skimming approach. Even if the patent did not exist, however, the developing firm would have an initial advantage as it would be the only firm with the necessary knowledge to produce the drug. It could then wait for other firms to catch up before it lowered the price and in the interim the sales it had already achieved might give it cost advantages over its competitors as a result of economies of scale. If, on the other hand, it had no way of protecting its market at all, or if there was no way it could develop an advantage over its competitors, then this would not be a suitable approach to use.

The final determining factor in the firm's decision whether or not to use price skimming is related to its expectations about demand for the product. If demand is likely to be short-lived then there may be an incentive for the firm to 'cash in' while demand exists and so it will adopt the price-skimming approach. This might be the case for a product, for example a particular form of clothing, which is currently fashionable but will cease to be so in a few months' time. If, on the other hand, demand for a product is expected to last for several years, a longer term pricing strategy may be more appropriate.

7.3.2   Penetration Pricing

In the case where demand for a product is likely to be sustained over a substantial period of time, penetration pricing may prove to be a better alternative than price skimming. In this case, the firm sets a low price initially in order to try to ensure that it will have a large market share in the future. As with price skimming, this strategy is most likely to be used when specific conditions apply. In this case they are: the firm's objective is sales maximisation (at least in the short run); competing products are expected to enter the market fairly quickly; and/or the new product is similar to existing products.

Beginning with the objective of sales maximisation, the firm wants to achieve a high level of sales after the initial introduction of the product as it wishes to obtain the largest possible market share before entry into the market occurs. This is because it wants its product to be bought and used by as many people as possible so that they will identify with the firm's particular brand of the product. Assuming that the product's performance is satisfactory, and the firm must ensure that it is, these initial consumers are likely to be repeat purchasers of it in the future. This allows the firm to secure future demand for its product. As a bonus, branding of the good in this way can make entry into the market more difficult for competitors as they have to be able to attract customers away from the original good. The use of penetration pricing by the established firm presents prospective new entrants with the further problem of the need to be price competitive. If they have higher costs than the original firm, or it now benefits from economies of scale as a result of its initial strategy, then they will again be at a disadvantage. Thus by focusing on sales maximisation in the short run, and accordingly charging a low, penetration price, the firm has actually reaped longer term benefits.

This brings us to the second of the conditions – the case where competing products are expected to enter the market fairly quickly. The sooner entry is expected to occur, the more important it is for the firm to act in such a way as to secure the largest market share that it can. This will then give it the advantages over its competitors of the sort described above.

Finally, there is the situation where the new product is similar to existing products, in which case it is the firm itself which is the new entrant into the market. The easiest way for the firm to draw attention to the new product it is selling is to be competitive in terms of price, that is, to undercut the price of the closest available substitutes for its product. This should enable it to secure a larger market share than it would otherwise obtain over both the short and the longer term. This assumes, of course, that the competing firms will not retaliate by charging lower prices for their products as well.

Thus in setting the initial price of its product the firm has two choices – to set a high (skimming) price in order to maximise profits while the market is protected or to set a low (penetration) price in order to secure future market share. The firm will then adapt its price over time in response to prevailing market forces as the market for the product develops. This brings us to a consideration of the ways in which prices may be set in established markets.

■ ■ ■ Self-Assessment Question ■ ■ ■ ■ ■ ■ ■ ■ ■ ■ ■ ■

Q2 What is the main difference between the price-skimming approach and the penetration-pricing approach to new product pricing?

> ### CASE STUDY | *Penetration Pricing versus Price Skimming*
>
> There is no 'right' answer in terms of which of these two methods of pricing a firm should use when entering a new market for the first time. Referring back to the case of easyJet in Chapter 6, it is apparent that the company was using a penetration-pricing strategy in order to enter the market by branding itself as a low-cost, competitively priced producer. This strategy succeeded at least in part because of the perception by many (potential) customers that air travel was 'too expensive'. Consequently by offering cheaper flights, the company created an additional demand from consumers who had previously felt that air travel was not for them while simultaneously shifting some of the existing demand from the established airlines, for example in relation to business travel.
>
> The opposite case where price skimming tends to be used in order to recoup product development costs can be found in the computer industry. For example, the new Intel Pentium 4 generation of personal computers were clearly priced at the top of the market, originally retailing in the UK for between £1000 and £1500. At the same time, the older Pentium 3 versions of the same computer brands had their prices cut to below £1000. A skimming strategy may be necessary in this and related technological industries in order to recoup the costs of upgrading and redesigning the product as it may be only a short time until the next innovation comes along. For computer companies, this also creates the obvious problem of obtaining enough money from product sales to fund the next generation of research in order to produce another new product with which to stay ahead of the market. There may not be enough time to sell a sufficient volume of computers to justify using a penetration-pricing approach instead.

■ 7.4 Pricing in Established Markets

There are a number of pricing strategies which may be used in established markets. Which one is most appropriate will depend upon the nature of the market in question, the information the firm has at its disposal and what it is trying to achieve. The methods described below also take into account any comparisons which can be made between products in such a way as to allow relative, rather than absolute, prices to be set for a particular good or set of goods. Given that this is the case, some of the methods may lack precision in terms of the final setting of the price as there is an element of subjectivity involved. Six specific methods will be described in this section – mark-up or cost plus pricing, price positioning, pricing to infer quality, product line pricing, pricing product bundles and promotional pricing.

7.4.1 Mark-up (Cost Plus) Pricing

This form of pricing is probably the most precise alternative to marginal cost pricing in established markets. The assumption which underlies it is that even if the firm does not know what its marginal costs are it should be able to work out its level of total variable costs relatively easily. By dividing the figure for total variable costs by the level of output being produced it can then determine the level of its average variable costs. This information can then be used to help the firm to set the price of its product. In order to do so it will use the formula:

$$P = AVC + X\% (AVC)$$

where P is price, AVC is average variable costs and X is the mark-up chosen by the firm to cover its overheads and required profit level.

By using this formula the firm can ensure that it covers the day-to-day running costs of the firm, which is the minimum requirement for the firm to remain in business in the short run. If this was all it was trying to achieve, then the value of X would be zero. Thus the bigger the value of X, the greater the surplus over variable costs the firm is making. The actual size of X will depend on five things – the firm's fixed costs, its objective, the elasticity of demand for the product, the prices being charged by other firms and the rate of inflation.

In order to survive over the longer term, the firm will need to cover its fixed costs as well as its variable costs. It will therefore need to allocate part of its fixed costs to the price of each unit of output produced. It follows from this that the smaller the level of fixed costs and the larger the level of output, the smaller the contribution of fixed costs to the size of X will be. The reverse is also true – the larger the level of fixed costs and the smaller the level of output produced, the bigger the contribution of fixed cost to the size of X will be.

The issue of the firm's objective was raised before in relation to the feasibility of using marginal cost pricing in practice. The argument here runs along basically the same lines. If the firm is trying to gain entry into a market or to increase its market share, then it is likely to want to charge a lower price than it would if maximising short-run profits was the objective. Thus if its objective is sales maximisation it is likely to charge a smaller mark-up on its product than if it is trying to achieve the highest possible level of profit.

The firm cannot, however, decide upon its mark-up without taking into account market conditions. If the price it charges is too high, then potential customers will be discouraged from buying the product. Any changes in the price charged for the product will have to allow for this as well, which is where the issue of elasticity of demand arises. If the product is in a market in which demand is relatively inelastic with respect to price, then the firm can afford to raise its price by increasing the mark-up without any particularly damaging negative effects on its revenue and profits. If, on the other hand, demand is very elastic then this will not be the case and the effect of a higher mark-up will be a significant drop in demand for the firm's product, its revenues and its profits.

This in turn cannot be wholly separated from the behaviour of other firms in the market. In highly competitive markets in particular, no firm can afford to be too far out of step in relation to the price it charges in comparison to other firms. This may have the effect of restricting the size of the firm's mark-up if it is to remain competitive. In a market where price competition is less of an issue, this may be of limited concern to the firm. For example, in markets where the products are significantly different from one another, individual firms may be able to charge higher prices, and use a higher mark-up, by virtue of the fact that they can claim that their product is 'better quality' or 'better designed' than their nearest rivals.

Finally, there is the issue of inflation. In order to keep pace with inflation the firm may wish to increase its price each year so that it is charging the same price in real terms as before. It still, however, has to monitor what other firms are doing. If it is the only firm in the market which is behaving in this way then its product will be becoming relatively more expensive over time compared to those sold by other firms. This also raises the question of the actual rate of inflation the firm should use – one which represents the overall increase in prices in the economy or the one which is specific to the firm. These may not be the same. For example, if industry wage inflation is rising at a faster rate than price inflation perhaps because of a skills shortage, the firm may wish to pass on the higher costs it is experiencing. The effect of this is to increase the price of the product over and above the general rate of inflation. The firm's ability to do this will of course in turn depend upon what other firms in the same market are doing in this respect, that is, the degree to which they are passing on this rise in costs to the consumer.

Thus, in summary, there are a range of factors which the firm must take into account in setting the size of its mark-up. It is the combined influence of them which sets the final price for the product, although some may be more dominant than others at different times and in different market situations.

7.4.2   Price Positioning

The second way of setting the price of a product in an established market is through the use of price positioning. Unlike mark-up pricing, there is no one single equation or rule which will determine the price. This method depends very much upon the decision maker's judgement about the way in which the firm's product fits into the market as a whole. Using this approach, the price of the product is set by comparing it to the other similar products in the market. For example, all stereo systems are designed to play music but there are a range of different types of them on the market. If the firm intends to use price positioning it would look at where in this range its product fits. If, for example, the sound quality produced by this new stereo was better than that provided by existing ones, then the firm could charge a higher price for it.

7.4.3   Pricing to Infer Quality

Pricing to infer quality is related to price positioning in the sense that it is a relative rather than an absolute method of pricing. The comparison of the firm's product with other similar products in the market is again the key. The aim underlying this approach is, however, quite specific – the firm is trying to get the consumer to identify the product as being superior to other similar products on the market. It does this by deliberately charging a high price for the product in the belief that this will lead the customer to assume that high price equals high quality. By using this approach, the firm expects to increase both its sales and its profits. This will work as long as the product meets the customers' expectations. If it fails to do so, they will not repurchase it in the future and may discourage others from buying it. Thus if the high price is not justified by the actual quality of the product then this can only be used by the firm as a very short-term strategy. If the product does live up to customers' expectations, however, a high price may be sustained over the longer term.

7.4.4   Product Line Pricing

This form of pricing is used by multi-product firms which produce a range of substitute and complementary goods. It is necessary for them to consider the whole range of products when deciding on their pricing strategy because of the interdependencies between them, that is, the price of one good will affect the demand for the others. Thus in this case quite a complex pricing strategy will be needed due to the knock-on effects of each pricing decision on the sales of the other goods produced by the firm. What are the effects which will need to be considered?

To begin with, let us consider the effects of raising the price of one product in the range. The immediate effect of this rise in price will be to reduce the demand for, and sales of, that particular product. There will, however, be two secondary effects. Firstly, the sales of the closest substitute product that the firm produces will be increased as it becomes relatively cheaper as a result of the increase in price of the original product. Secondly, the sales of any complementary products to the original product will also fall as a result of the fall in demand for that product (unless of course this is completely offset by the rise in sales of the substitute product). Thus the net effect for the firm of the initial price increase is that sales of two (or more) products will fall while the sales of one will increase. The precise effect of this on the firm's profits will depend upon the relative contributions to profit made by each of the different goods. The reverse of course would happen if there was a price cut – the sales of the original good would rise, as would those of any complementary goods while the sales of the closest substitute would fall.

Likewise, an improvement in the image or quality of one product would have knock-on effects even if the relative prices of the goods remained the same. The sales of the original product would increase as it became more popular or was perceived to be better value for money than before. This in turn might be expected to have the effect of decreasing sales of the closest substitute produced by the firm and raising the demand for any complementary products. If the effect of the improved image or quality of one product in the range was to improve the company's image as a whole, however, the effect might be to increase sales of all of its products at the expense of its competitors.

In using a product line pricing strategy, the firm must pay particular attention to certain products within its range which can be viewed as being representative of the range as a whole. These are the firm's loss leaders, bottom of the line and flagship products.

A loss leader is a product which the firm sells cheaply, sometimes below the amount it costs to make, in order to attract customers to its other products. A typical case of this is a supermarket which sells basic food items such as bread at very low prices in order to attract people into the store. Once there, they are likely to buy a number of other products as well and it is on these that the supermarket makes its profits. In this case, it is not uncommon for supermarkets to compete for customers on the basis of which store sells such items cheapest. Thus the pricing of these items is especially important to the supermarkets concerned.

Bottom of the line products are similar in the sense that they are the ones sold most cheaply, but in this case they are not being sold at a loss, although they will often carry a relatively low profit margin. Usually they are the most basic form of the product which the firm produces and lack any particular distinguishing features which would allow the firm to charge a higher price for them. Too high a price in this case may send the signal that the firm's products as a whole are comparatively expensive so that consumers will not buy them. Too low a price may raise questions about the general quality of the firm's products.

A flagship product is one at the other end of the spectrum, specifically the highest specification or best product that the firm sells. In this case the price will be set as high as possible in order to signal the high quality of this particular product, and by implication the company's whole range of products. Thus in a sense the firm is adopting a pricing to infer quality approach for the top product in its range.

7.4.5   Pricing Product Bundles

There may come a time when the firm wishes to sell its products in combination rather than separately. This will mainly be the case for complementary goods or where multiples of the same product are being sold at a reduced price. In this instance, the firm sells two or more goods together as a package (or bundle) at a lower price than it would charge to someone buying them individually. For example, it is not uncommon for electrical goods retailers to sell televisions and video recorders together as a package. The package containing both items might, say, cost £700 whereas bought separately the television would cost £500 and the video recorder would cost £300. Thus by buying the package the customer 'saves' £100. In reality of course if customers only intended to buy a television they have actually spent an extra £200 and the firm has gained the sale of an extra video recorder. This approach is quite often used to sell out-of-date models of the products concerned or to reduce stocks during periods when sales are slow. Another example, this time of sales of multiples of the same product, might be the sale of videotapes. This is often done on the basis of, say, one videotape being sold for £3.00 or four videotapes for £10.00.

7.4.6   Promotional Pricing

Promotional pricing involves a temporary reduction in the price of one or more products. The firm may do this for a number of reasons. Firstly, it may be done in order to clear excess stocks of a good. Secondly, it may be the result of a decision to turn a particular product into a loss leader for the firm. Thirdly, it may be a way of maintaining or increasing the firm's market share in the face of renewed competition within the market. Fourthly, it can be used for what is known as 'product reinforcement', that is, to bring the product back into the public eye or to confirm the consumers' view that it is good value for money.

This pricing strategy does have certain risks associated with it. To begin with, if demand does not increase as expected in response to the cut in price then the firm may experience a fall in the revenue and profits it receives from the sale of the product. It needs to be prepared for this. Another possible problem is that the cut in price may alter the customers' perception of the product, for example if they equate a lower price with a drop in quality. Alternatively, the fact that the firm can afford to offer the product at a lower price than before may alter the customers' longer term behaviour by making them more price conscious. This may be particularly true at a time when a range of firms or retail outlets are cutting the prices of different brands of the same good simultaneously.

7.4.7   Summary

In this section we have looked at six different methods of pricing which may be used in established markets. Which one the firm adopts will be determined by five main factors – the type of good; the availability of substitute and complementary goods; the firm's objective; the availability and/or search costs associated with obtaining the appropriate information; and the pricing strategies adopted by the firm's competitors. Thus there is no clear-cut 'right' or 'wrong' answer to the question of how the firm should price its good in an established market, merely a range of possibilities which may be used when certain conditions prevail in the market place.

■ ■ ■ Self-Assessment Question ■ ■ ■ ■ ■ ■ ■ ■ ■ ■ ■ ■

Q3   What are the six methods of pricing in established markets which may be used by the firm?

 CASE STUDY *ASDA*

Following a period of competition based on 'special offers', the provision of financial services and loyalty cards, UK supermarkets have become increasingly price competitive – perhaps none more so than ASDA. While the company has always emphasised value for money, it is only since its takeover by the US company Wal-Mart that it has really begun to compete much more aggressively on price. Consequently, although the company still uses a combination of the above strategies across its product range such as 3 for 2 offers (pricing product bundles), cut price special offers (promotional pricing) and price positioning in relation to its competitors, it now has a distinct pricing approach all of its own. The company's 'roll back' strategy with its emphasis on 'permanently lower prices' is based on achieving increased profitability by selling a higher volume of goods at lower prices and consequently builds in slimmer profit margins (or mark-ups) per unit of the product sold than some of its competitors. This has at least partly been made possible by the increased buyer power which has resulted from being part of the much larger Wal-Mart chain which is expanding its activities across Europe. Whether it will be successful over the longer term and what response it will provoke from its competitors, including the UK market leaders Tesco and Sainsbury, remains to be seen.

■ 7.5 Specialist Forms of Pricing

This section completes our review of the various pricing methods available to the firm by looking at three 'special cases' which will be used in a relatively restricted set of product markets. These are target return pricing, transfer pricing and competitive tendering.

7.5.1 Target Return Pricing

Target return pricing may be used when the firm needs a specific rate of return on its investment in new product development. It is used in order to ensure that the firm can both recoup its development costs and make sufficient profit to make the risk associated with product development worthwhile.

The firm sets its required level of profit on the investment:

required profit = aK

where a is the target rate of return, which may be a fixed percentage, and K is capital employed, that is the amount of money the firm has invested in developing the product. The margin to be charged over unit cost (m) is then given by the formula:

$$m = \frac{aK}{Q^b}$$

where Q^b is the budgeted or expected level of output.

Thus this equation gives the firm's profit margin per unit of output. It then adds this to the cost of producing each unit of output to give the overall price of the product. This allows the firm to set a stable long-run price for the product which will both cover its production costs and provide the firm with an adequate return on the funds it has invested in developing the product. The size of the margin will of course vary according to what the market will bear – the margin is likely to be higher for an innovative product than for an adaptation of an existing product.

7.5.2 Transfer Pricing

This is a form of pricing which is used internally within the firm. A rise in the number of large multi-product firms has brought with it the need to find a way of pricing transfers of resources between different parts of the firm. Transfer pricing is the mechanism by which this can be done. For example, suppose that the firm produces both a final good and a range of intermediate goods (components) which are incorporated into the final good. Also suppose that these are produced in different factories in different parts of the country. The factories producing the components then 'sell' those components to the factory which assembles the final good. The transfer price is the price for which these components are sold to the factory producing the final good. If there is an external market for the component part, for example if it could have been sold to the manufacturer of a similar final good, then the transfer price will be set equal to the price that could have been obtained by doing this, that is the market price for the component. If, on the other hand, there is no such external market for the component then the factory producing the final good will be charged a transfer price equal to the marginal cost of producing the component.

7.5.3   Competitive Tendering

This method of setting a price is often used in the case of government-related contracts for things like the provision of refuse collection services and road maintenance programmes. Alternatively it may be used by private sector organisations as a means of hiring another company to carry out part of the firm's functions, such as providing catering services. As there is no one standard product involved, each unit of output (project) is priced individually by potential suppliers who then compete against each other on the basis of this 'tender price' for the award of the contract. How then do these firms set the tender price?

Firstly, the price set will depend upon the tender specification which is issued by the client. This contains the information that firms will need in order to set their price, such as how long the contract is to be awarded for, precisely what it involves in terms of the type of work to be done, what quality of materials should be used and so on. Once they have this information the firms will work out how much it would cost them to do the job in terms of labour costs, equipment hire and so on. The firm will then decide how much to charge in addition to this so that it can make a profit on the contract.

This last point is an interesting one in that two projects with identical specifications may end up with very different tender prices purely as a result of the time at which they were awarded. The reason for this will be related to how much the firms need the work. For example, in times of recession the profit margin the firm is prepared to accept is likely to be lower than during a boom as the firm has a greater need to win the contract and so will be more price competitive. When this is the case for many firms, tender prices are likely to be driven down substantially, indeed it is not unknown for firms to deliberately make a loss on a contract in order to generate cash flow for the company until more work becomes available. Thus how much the firm needs the contract will also be a determinant of the price it sets.

A third factor in setting the tender price will be the firm's expectations about the prices which are likely to be set by other firms. If the other firms bidding for a project are likely to set relatively low prices, the firm will have to follow suit if it is to have any chance of winning. This judgement will be based on knowledge of previous bids and tender prices for similar contracts under similar market conditions. This is important because the client will generally accept the lowest tender price submitted, subject to certain quality constraints. Thus firms are continually trying to outbid each other by setting the lowest price.

This form of pricing is different from the ones we have previously looked at in that it relates to the individual unit pricing of a non-standard product. It is also a case of what is known as monopsony, that is, one buyer, many suppliers. In this case, therefore, it is the client who has the market power and so determines the price of the product in terms of its acceptance or rejection of it. This is a complete reversal of some of the cases we looked at earlier, for example monopoly or collusive oligopoly, where the market power rested with the producers of a good, not the consumers of it.

■ ■ ■ **Self-Assessment Question** ■ ■ ■ ■ ■ ■ ■ ■ ■ ■ ■

Q4 Under what particular circumstances will target return pricing, transfer pricing and competitive tendering be used?

■ 7.6 Changing Prices over Time

After the firm has set the initial price of its product that price may remain stable for some time. Sooner or later, however, the firm is likely to want to alter the amount it charges for it. This may be the case for one (or both) of two reasons – the entry of new firms into the market or changes in the demand for the product.

Taking the question of entry into the market first of all, the firm's ability to maintain its price depends upon both its original pricing strategy and how quickly entry into the market has occurred. If, for example, it had used the price-skimming strategy, then the entry of new firms into the market would be more likely to force the firm to lower its price than would be the case if it had adopted the penetration-pricing strategy instead. In the case of the speed of entry, if new firms were slow to enter the market then prices would tend to be more stable than if the amount of competition in the market were to increase very rapidly with the arrival of a large number of new firms. The precise effect of any new firms entering into the market would also depend upon their cost structure. The greatest threat would arise if the new firms in the market had lower costs than the existing ones. In this case, the new entrants could afford to charge less than the current market price for the good while still making a reasonable profit. If they had the same cost structure, however, any attempt to do this would be at the expense of their profitability and would be unsustainable over the longer term.

Turning now to the effect of changes in the demand for the product, it can be said that a rapid increase in demand would have the effect of raising, or at least maintaining, prices while a slow rate of increase in demand would have a dampening effect on the product's price. A drop in demand would of course be likely to result in a fall in price. The precise effect is also, however, related to the entry of new firms into the market. If demand is increasing rapidly and there are few entrants into the market then the result will almost certainly be higher prices. If, on the other hand, this rapid increase in demand brings a flood of new suppliers into the market prices may rise by less, remain the same or even fall, depending upon the balance between demand and supply. Likewise, if there is a slow increase in demand then prices may remain stable as long as the number of new entrants is relatively small, but if the number of entrants rises then lower prices will eventually be the result. Consequently there is no clear-cut answer to the question of what will happen to the level of prices over time; it depends very much upon the conditions prevailing in individual markets and the relationship between demand and supply.

If the price of a product were to fall as a result of entry and/or an insufficient rate of increase in demand, what would be the effect on existing firms in the market? The initial effect would be a loss of profits as prices fell and the existing firms were forced to follow this trend. Their ability to increase their profits again would depend on the extent to which they could capitalise on their experience of supplying the product by finding a way to produce it more cheaply and so increase their profit margin on future units of output.

There are two ways this could occur, either via the learning effect or by the development of economies of scale (or both). The learning effect arises as the firm's workforce become more experienced in producing a product and more experienced in operating the machinery which is used to make it. This means that it takes progressively less time to produce each extra unit of output so that the labour costs associated with it fall and there is less wastage in the form of substandard output. This has the effect of lowering the firm's average costs so that it may either increase its profit margin over time or, if the need arises, lower its price so that it becomes more competitive.

Economies of scale arise as the firm begins to produce higher levels of output in order to meet increased demand. The lower level of costs per unit of output produced which results from the expansion of production can then either be translated into higher profit margins or be passed on to customers in the form of lower prices as before. If an existing firm in a particular market can exploit either or both of these phenomena then it can gain an advantage over the new entrants into the market and use this to maintain its market share. Thus the way in which prices change over time and the firm's ability to adapt to these changes will depend on both the internal and the external influences on the firm. Different markets and different firms will react in different ways. There is no one set pattern which we can identify as being universally applicable.

■ ■ ■ Self-Assessment Question ■ ■ ■ ■ ■ ■ ■ ■ ■ ■ ■ ■

Q5 What would be the effect on price of a slight rise in demand accompanied by a large increase in the number of new entrants into the market? What is the learning effect?

❏ ❏ ❏ End of Chapter SUMMARY ❏ ❏ ❏ ❏ ❏ ❏ ❏ ❏ ❏ ❏ ❏

This chapter has considered a range of pricing strategies which may be used by the firm in different circumstances. It began by reviewing the approaches to price setting dictated by the four models of market structure – perfect competition, monopoly, monopolistic competition and oligopoly. It then went on to look at two particular forms of pricing which are associated with new products – price skimming and penetration pricing. The focus of the chapter was then widened to include the pricing methods which may be used in established markets – mark-up (cost plus) pricing, price positioning, pricing to infer quality, product line pricing, pricing product bundles and promotional pricing. This was followed by an examination of three specialist forms of pricing which are relatively restricted in terms of their use – target return pricing, transfer pricing and competitive tendering. Finally, it looked at some of the issues which arise in terms of the way prices may change over time.

In summary, therefore, this chapter contains quite a comprehensive review of the various pricing methods and the circumstances in which they will be used by the firm. There is no 'right' or 'wrong' method of pricing, just a number of alternatives. The selection of the most appropriate one in any given set of circumstances is a decision which the firm must make in the light of prevailing market conditions.

■ ■ ■ ANSWERS to Self-Assessment Questions ■ ■ ■ ■ ■ ■

Q1 *Price-taker* – the firm has to sell the good at the prevailing market price. It has no discretion in setting its own price.

Price-maker – the firm can set its own price for the good – that is, it does not have to take the market price.

Marginal cost pricing – charging the profit-maximising price by setting marginal cost equal to marginal revenue.

Limit pricing – the firm sets its price below the profit-maximising level in an attempt to discourage other firms from joining the market by ensuring that they cannot make enough profit to make entry into the industry worthwhile.

Price discrimination – the firm charges different prices to different customers for the same product.

Price leadership – one firm acts as a price-maker for the good and the other firms in the market accept this price – that is, they become price-takers.

Q2

The main difference is in the level of price the firm sets. In the case of price skimming, the firm sets the highest possible price in order to obtain high short-term profits, while in the case of penetration pricing, the firm sets a much lower price in order to obtain high levels of sales early on.

Q3

The six methods of pricing in established markets are mark-up (or cost plus) pricing, price positioning, pricing to infer quality, product line pricing, pricing product bundles and promotional pricing.

Q4

Target return pricing is used when the firm needs to be sure of getting a specific return on its investment in new product development.

Transfer pricing will be used when one part of the firm needs to charge another part of the firm for the supply of components.

Competitive tendering will be used when there is one buyer and several possible suppliers, for example for government contracts.

Q5

A slight rise in demand accompanied by a large increase in the number of new entrants into the market will lead to falling prices. The learning effect demonstrates the increasing efficiency of the labour force in producing a good as they become more experienced in its manufacture.

8 Non-price competition

■ 8.1 Introduction

In the previous chapter we looked at pricing in some detail. Price is, however, only one of the four components of the marketing mix or the four Ps. The three others – promotion, product, and place – will be considered in this chapter. While firms in some markets will compete quite vigorously in terms of price, firms in other markets, for example an oligopolistic market with stable prices, may be either unable or unwilling to do so. In this case non-price competition will be the norm. What this means is that firms will compete by using, for example, different advertising or product development strategies rather than on the basis of price.

This chapter begins with an examination of the ways in which the firm will set its advertising budget and how it may use that money to maximum effect. It then goes on to look at how the firm can compete on the basis of the product it produces, for example by distinguishing it in some way from other similar products in the market. This process is known as product differentiation. Finally, it looks at the place element of non-price competition from two viewpoints – the way in which the firm will distribute its product and how it will choose its production site.

Exactly how the firm will behave with regard to each of these factors will depend upon the market in which it operates and hence the necessity (or otherwise) of engaging in non-price competition. The behaviour of other firms will also be important and so again there is an element of interdependency between them in terms of their actions and reactions. The firm's strategy will also depend on what it is trying to achieve, for example a firm which is looking to maximise sales is likely to advertise more heavily than one which is seeking to maximise profits given that advertising represents an additional cost to the firm. It is only in the case of profit maximisation, however, that we can easily define a rule for the setting of optimal levels of each of the four components. If the firm wishes to profit maximise, it should set the marginal contributions of each of the four components to quantity sold to be equal. Specifically:

Profit (π) = TR (Q) – TC (Q)

where TR is total revenue, TC is total cost and Q is the quantity sold. Quantity sold is a function of the four parts of the marketing mix:

$Q = f$ (price, promotion, product, place)

In order to profit maximise, take first differences so that:

$$\frac{d\pi}{d \text{ price}} = \frac{d\pi}{d \text{ promotion}} = \frac{d\pi}{d \text{ product}} = \frac{d\pi}{d \text{ place}}$$

Thus the contribution to profitability of each of the four elements is equal. If this is not the case then the firm could increase its profits by spending more on the element of the marketing mix which is yielding the greatest marginal returns and less on the others. This process of redistribution would then continue until the position of equality specified above was reached. The implications of this approach for the firm's advertising expenditure are discussed in the following section.

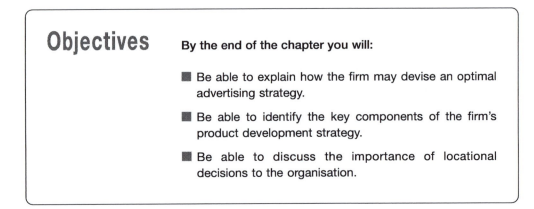

Objectives

By the end of the chapter you will:

■ Be able to explain how the firm may devise an optimal advertising strategy.

■ Be able to identify the key components of the firm's product development strategy.

■ Be able to discuss the importance of locational decisions to the organisation.

■ 8.2   Promotion and Advertising

These two terms are quite often used interchangeably as the main way of promoting the product is generally through advertising. From now on therefore we will treat them as being synonymous and use the term advertising throughout.

Money spent by the firm on advertising (or promoting) its product affects both the firm's demand curve, as its purpose is to stimulate demand, and its costs, as it represents extra spending which the firm would not otherwise be incurring. The effect of this can be seen in the model below.

$$\pi = \text{TR} - \text{TC} - A$$

This equation reflects the fact that advertising (A) is an additional cost to the firm. As a result, the level of profit (π) is now determined by the equation total revenue (TR) minus total cost (TC) minus advertising expenditure (A). Disaggregating total revenue into its component parts, price (P) and quantity (Q), and making explicit the fact that the level of the firm's total costs will depend on Q, allows us to rewrite the equation as follows:

$$\pi = P \cdot Q - \text{TC}(Q) - A$$

Recognising that both total revenue and total costs will depend upon the firm's price and advertising levels gives us a new equation:

$$\pi = P \cdot [Q(P,A)] - TC[Q(P,A)] - A$$

If the firm is now seeking to maximise profit then differentiating the above equation with respect to each of the decision variables, price and advertising, gives us the first-order conditions:

$$\frac{d\pi}{dA} = \frac{P \cdot dQ}{dA} - \frac{dTC}{dQ} \cdot \frac{dQ}{dA} - 1 = 0$$

and

$$\frac{d\pi}{dP} = \frac{P \cdot dQ}{dP} + Q - \frac{dTC}{dQ} \cdot \frac{dQ}{dP} = 0$$

Rearranging the first of these conditions gives:

$$\frac{dQ}{dA}(P - MC) = 1$$

where MC is marginal cost and is equal to dTC/dQ. Multiplying both sides by A/PQ gives:

$$\frac{dQ}{dA} \cdot \frac{A}{Q} \frac{(P - MC)}{P} = \frac{A}{PQ}$$

In this equation the term

$$\frac{dQ}{dA} \cdot \frac{A}{Q}$$

is the advertising elasticity of demand (E_A). The second first-order condition can also be rearranged as:

$$\frac{P - MC}{P} = \frac{-1}{E_P}$$

where E_P is the price elasticity of demand. Combining these last two equations gives what is known as the Dorfman–Steiner condition:

$$\frac{A}{PQ} = \frac{E_A}{E_P}$$

This means that in order to maximise its profits, the firm should set the ratio of advertising expenditure to total revenue (the left-hand side of the equation) equal to the ratio of the advertising elasticity of demand to the price elasticity of demand (the right-hand side of the equation). Given that the firm will usually be able to set the levels of both A and P but not Q, how much of the good it can sell will depend upon the two elasticities of demand. This raises the question: what determines the elasticities of demand for a particular product?

8.2.1 The Price and Advertising Elasticities of Demand

Four main factors influence the price elasticity of demand. These are time, the availability of substitute goods, the degree of necessity, and the level of income. In each case, the higher the value of E_p, the more elastic demand is with respect to price.

As a general rule, the longer the period of time involved the more elastic demand will be with respect to price. This is because it takes people time to adjust their purchasing behaviour in response to a change in the price of the good. If a good is bought infrequently, for example, then it may take some time for knowledge of the price change to be passed on and acted upon. If the good is bought frequently, however, this adjustment time will be significantly shorter.

How quickly demand changes in response to the change in price will also depend upon the availability of substitute goods. This is related to the time factor in the sense that the greater the period of time that has elapsed, the more likely there are to be a number of substitute goods available. The more substitutes there are, and the closer they are to the firm's good, the more elastic demand for it will be with respect to price. This of course is a result of the fact that people will find it easier to switch between the different goods available as their relative prices change.

The third factor, the degree of necessity, can be used to explain why some people will continue to buy a good even when its price rises substantially. If someone habitually buys apples because they prefer them to any other fruit, for example, then a fall in the price of oranges is unlikely to influence them very much. They are unlikely to switch from apples to oranges even though the latter are now relatively cheaper. The apples are 'necessary' to them in the sense that they are habitually bought. A similar line of argument can be applied to most basic foodstuffs such as bread where people tend to purchase roughly the same amounts each week. Demand for these types of products tends to be relatively inelastic, whereas demand for non-essential foodstuffs such as cakes may be more elastic with respect to price.

All of this is, however, in turn related to the level of income someone has or, more specifically, to the proportion of their income that is spent on the good in question. The higher the proportion of someone's income accounted for by a particular good the more elastic demand for it will be, as if the price rises they will have little choice but to reduce their consumption of it. If, on the other hand, the proportion of their income accounted for by the good is very small then a rise in the price of that good can be borne more easily. A combination of these four influences will determine the price elasticity of demand for any particular good.

There are also four main factors which will affect the advertising elasticity of demand (E_A) to varying degrees – the level of advertising expenditure itself, the type of good, the market structure for the good and the state of the economy. Again it is a combination of these factors which will determine the overall size of the advertising elasticity of demand.

Taking the level of advertising expenditure first, it appears that some levels of advertising are more effective than others. To begin with, there may be a threshold level of advertising expenditure which the firm needs to reach before its advertising will be effective at all. If the firm spends less than this, then its advertising will be ineffective, that is the advertising elasticity of demand will be zero. This may, for example, be the case if a firm is seeking to enter a new market, as in order to do so successfully it needs both to make the consumers aware of the new product and to convince them to buy it. If there is strong brand identification within the market then it may require a high level of advertising spending to accomplish this task. Once the firm has passed the threshold level and successfully broken into the market it may then experience a period of increasing returns as any additional advertising spending becomes more effective by increasing the demand for the product at a faster rate. In this case, for example, a 5 per cent increase in advertising expenditure might yield a 10 per cent increase in demand. Once the product becomes firmly established in the market or new rivals to it appear, however, the firm may start to experience diminishing returns as more and more advertising is required to get a much smaller increase in demand. In this case, for example, a 5 per cent increase in advertising expenditure would yield, say, only a 1 per cent increase in demand. Eventually the firm may reach the saturation point for this particular market. If it does, then any additional advertising expenditure is money completely wasted as it yields no increase in demand at all.

In terms of the types of good involved, the advertising elasticity of demand will be higher for new products than for existing ones. The reason for this is the same as the one given above – that for a new product the firm can experience increasing returns on its advertising expenditure while after the product has been on the market for some time decreasing returns become more likely. The demand for luxury items also tends to be more elastic with respect to advertising (as well as price), as expenditure on these types of goods is more flexible than for goods which are viewed as necessities. Thus the demand for the latter will be influenced less by the level of advertising taking place than demand for the former. The advertising elasticity of demand is also higher for durable goods than for non-durable goods. This relates at least in part to the question of frequency of purchase. Durable goods are, by definition, ones which are meant to last for a significant period of time and so are bought relatively infrequently. Thus there is greater scope for purchasing behaviour to be affected by advertising as the consumer will have been exposed to more of it in the time between the original purchase of such a good and the buying of its replacement. In addition, as durable goods are often major purchases, they are more expensive and so more care will normally be taken in choosing them. This will make the customer more receptive to advertising as a way of gathering information. The costs of purchasing the 'wrong' non-durable good are much less serious, however, so that the impact of advertising may be substantially less.

In the case of market structure, the principal determinant of the effectiveness of the firm's advertising will be the size of the firm's market share. The larger the market share the firm has, the lower the advertising elasticity of demand for its product will be as most of those consumers who wish to purchase it are already doing so or have done so. If a firm has a low market share, on the other hand, it has a much greater chance of increasing that share by beginning an intensive advertising campaign. The exact effect of this will, of course, depend upon the response of the other firms in the market. If they retaliate by beginning advertising campaigns of their own then the effect will be muted as the various advertisements start to cancel each other out. In this case the advertising elasticity of demand will be low as few additional customers are likely to be attracted from other firms when those firms are themselves advertising in such a way as to successfully retain the customers' loyalty to their particular brands of the product. If they do not retaliate, however, then the demand for the original firm's product may rise significantly as a result, indicating a relatively high advertising elasticity of demand in that particular market.

Finally, there is the effect of the state of the economy on the advertising elasticity of demand. In times of recession, consumer spending will be relatively low and what spending there is may be focused more towards necessities rather than towards luxury goods. The effect of this will be to reduce the overall impact of advertising, that is to lower the advertising elasticity of demand. As people are spending less, and spending it mainly on essentials, they will be less affected by advertising than when the economy is prospering and consumer spending is higher. When the economy is doing well people will become less cautious about spending their money and may well be attracted to those goods which are being most extensively (or intensively) advertised. Thus, other things being equal, the advertising elasticity of demand for many, if not most, goods will be higher during booms than in recessions.

■ ■ ■ **Self-Assessment Question** ■ ■ ■ ■ ■ ■ ■ ■ ■ ■ ■ ■

Q1

Name two factors which will affect the advertising elasticity of demand.

■■■

8.2.2   Why Will the Firm Use Advertising?

Some of the reasons why the firm will use advertising have already been hinted at above but the purpose of this section is to identify them more specifically. To begin with, there is the effect of advertising on demand. This may take one, or both, of two forms – a shift in the firm's demand curve or a change in its elasticity. In the case of own advertising of the good, the firm is trying to achieve a rightward shift in the demand curve so that more of the good is bought at every price. How successful it is in doing this will depend upon the reactions of other firms, as if several firms are adopting a similar approach then the effectiveness of each firm's advertising is likely to be reduced as the various advertisements cancel each other out in the mind of the consumer. This may be particularly true in the case of goods which are close substitutes for one another. If they are not, however, then the firm may be able to make demand for its product more inelastic with respect to price by using its advertising in such a way as to build up a strong brand loyalty among its customers. Once the customers are loyal to a particular brand of the product, the firm producing that brand can then raise its price without necessarily experiencing a significant drop in demand as a consequence. The basic reason for this is that it has obtained a 'captive market' in the sense that rival brands of the product are viewed as being in some way inferior and so less desirable. They may not really be so in practice but it is the customers' perception of them as being so which is important.

Advertising can also be used as a barrier to entry into an industry. The fact that existing firms in an industry may be able to create buyer loyalty in the way described above can act as a way of preventing new firms from coming into the market. The more firmly buyer loyalty is established, the harder it will be for other firms, even those already established within the industry, to capture any additional demand. This means that unless a prospective entrant has a significant amount of money available to spend on advertising it will be unable to break into the market successfully. This high threshold level of advertising is a particular deterrent to small firms which are unlikely to be able to raise the amount of finance required.

The firm may also use advertising to increase or maintain its market share whether or not entry into the market is occurring. In a market where prices are stable, this may be the most robust form of competition taking place. The effectiveness of such an approach depends upon the reaction of the other firms in the market as before.

Finally, as mentioned previously, the firm will use advertising as a means of boosting its profitability through one or more of the processes described above. As advertising is an additional cost to the firm it is only worthwhile if its effect is to increase the firm's revenue by an amount greater than the advertising actually costs. If this is not the case then profits will be reduced rather than increased as the firm desires.

The relationship between the effectiveness of a firm's advertising and aspects of the market structure in which it operates can therefore be quite complex. Much will depend upon how strong an individual firm is relative to its competitors and also on how many firms actually operate in that particular market.

We can adapt the Dorfman–Steiner condition to take this into account:

$$\frac{A}{PQ} = \frac{E_A}{E_P} = \frac{(E_A + E_{CONJ} \cdot E_{AR})}{(E_M + E_S S_R)/S_F}$$

where:

E_A = the firm's advertising elasticity of demand, given that other firms' advertising remains constant

E_{CONJ} = the responsiveness of rivals' advertising to changes in this firm's advertising

E_{AR} = the elasticity of this firm's demand with respect to rivals' advertising

E_M = the market price elasticity of demand

E_S = elasticity of rivals' supply with respect to changes in the firm's price

S_R = rivals' market share

S_F = the firm's market share

The fewer the number of firms in the industry, the more complex these interactions will be, as each change in advertising will have a greater impact on the other firms than would be the case if there were a large number of firms in the market which might each lose a small proportion of their market share. Moreover, in markets with a large number of firms competition on the basis of price rather than advertising will be the norm. As the number of firms in the market gets smaller, demand will become less elastic with respect to price so that the effect of advertising will be correspondingly greater.

The Dorfman–Steiner condition in either the original or the adapted form will give the firm some indication of the optimal amount of money which the firm should spend on advertising its product. The relative complexity of the calculation, particularly in rapidly changing markets, has, however, led firms to look for alternative approaches to setting their advertising budgets. These are considered in the next section.

■ ■ ■ **Self-Assessment Question** ■ ■ ■ ■ ■ ■ ■ ■ ■ ■ ■ ■

Q2 How can advertising be used as a barrier to entry into the market?

CASE STUDY *Advertising by Universities*

At the time of writing, universities in the UK are not permitted to charge different fees to full-time undergraduate students, that is, a degree in economics costs the same irrespective of the university at which the student is studying for it. Consequently, competing on price in this market is not possible and so non-price competition is the only option available. In order to create and sustain demand for their courses, therefore, many universities are becoming more adept at advertising and marketing them. One of the key parts of most universities' advertising strategies is the creation of a 'brand' which makes them clearly identifiable. While some of the older universities such as Oxford, Cambridge and Edinburgh have a strong brand name based on centuries of tradition, this is not true of the younger universities such as the former polytechnics which were granted university status in 1992. Consequently the latter group probably rely more on advertising than the former.

Advertising by universities tends to be most vigorous in the period from July to October each year. The rationale for this is simple. During September and October, most 17- and 18-year-olds begin to fill in their application forms for entry into university the following year. As a result, it is in the universities' interests to try to gain the attention of prospective students at this point in order to try to fill their courses early. During July and August, on the other hand, the universities will be trying to recruit additional students to fill any remaining vacancies on their courses.

The ways in which universities advertise will vary depending upon their perception of who their customers are most likely to be. Local advertising, for example in local newspapers or on regional television channels, is increasingly being used given the rise in the number of students who prefer to study in their home city. Regardless of the media being used, each university seeks to find 'unique selling points' which will make it attractive to prospective students such as the facilities available, the employability of its graduates and so on. This of course is in turn related to the courses on offer – the universities' product policies – which are discussed in Section 8.3.

8.2.3   Setting the Level of Advertising Expenditure in Practice

There are four alternative methods which the firm may use in order to set its level of advertising expenditure – the objective and task approach, the percentage of sales method, competitive parity and the 'all you can afford' approach.

The objective and task approach requires the firm to identify in advance what it actually wants to achieve via its advertising strategy. For example, the firm might decide that it wants to increase its market share from say 15 to 20 per cent. The next stage is to determine how it can do this. If it decides to use advertising, either alone or in combination with a price cut for example, it then sets its budget on the basis of how much it will need to spend to achieve the required increase in market share. This will of course involve making certain assumptions about the likely effectiveness of its advertising given the market in which it operates – the number of firms, their likely responses and the advertising and price elasticities of demand. The advantage of this approach is that it obliges the firm to be specific about its intentions. It gives the firm a clear target to aim for in terms of what it is trying to do and defines how it can achieve this goal. The main drawback of this approach is that if the firm's market knowledge is insufficient or its assumptions about the reactions of its competitors are incorrect then it could find itself to be way off target. In the worst-case scenario, this could leave it even more poorly off than before in terms of a smaller market share.

The percentage of sales method does not involve setting a specific target in terms of what the firm is trying to achieve. Instead it is merely a way of setting the size of the advertising budget and seeing what happens as a result, although of course if the firm has used this approach in the past it may have some prior knowledge of what the likely effect will be. The firm will initially set aside say 5 per cent of its current or expected sales revenue for advertising the product. It will then either use the same percentage again in later years or vary it on the basis of changes in market conditions. Thus the size of the advertising budget is related to the level of sales which in turn is, at least in part, dependent on the level of advertising. If the firm has a high level of sales which enables it to spend significant sums on advertising then, other things being equal, this will result in still higher sales and more money becoming available for advertising. A firm which is in this 'virtuous circle' may be able to increase its market share substantially. Difficulties arise, however, if the reverse is true, as if sales are low then the amount of money allocated to the advertising budget will also be low which in turn affects the firm's ability to increase its sales and so on. In this case the answer would be either to increase the percentage or to use another method.

Competitive parity is an even simpler method. As its name suggests, the firm merely allocates the same amount of money to advertising as its competitors do. This assumes a certain amount of knowledge about each others' spending but this may not be too difficult to estimate, particularly in a mature market where spending and advertising patterns are relatively fixed. In this case, the effect of advertising may be merely to allow the firm to retain its relative position within the market as the various firms' advertising simply cancels each others' out. If, however, one firm can use its advertising budget more effectively than the others, for example by using a different media combination, then it could gain a competitive advantage. How this might be done will be discussed in the next section.

The 'all you can afford' approach is rather imprecise. This time the firm spends as much as it can on advertising subject to a profitability constraint. The question of how much the firm can afford is of course a subjective one; two firms with the same level of profits may allocate different amounts of money to the advertising budget on the basis of perceived need. Even if a firm is only making a small profit it may still need to spend relatively large sums of money on advertising if it is to remain competitive within its chosen market. Failure to do so may be more damaging over the longer term than a loss of short-term profitability would be.

This concludes the review of the methods which the firm may use to decide upon the size of its advertising budget. The next step is to describe how they can allocate this money in the most effective way possible.

■ ■ ■ Self-Assessment Question ■ ■ ■ ■ ■ ■ ■ ■ ■ ■ ■ ■

Q3 What are the four methods a firm might use to set its advertising expenditure in practice?

8.2.4   Allocating the Advertising Budget

The first step in allocating the advertising budget is to decide which forms of media to use. There are a number of these available to the firm: direct mail, newspapers, posters, leaflets, cinema, television, radio or special displays and exhibitions. The firm may use them either singly or in combination, depending upon its advertising budget and the effect that it is trying to achieve.

There is always likely to be some wastage with each of these forms of advertising as not everyone who is contacted in this way will want to buy the product. The more targeted the advertising is towards potential customers, the more effective it will be. The problem, of course, is to identify the target market and to choose the right media combination to reach it. For example, a small service sector firm based in a particular city might advertise in a local newspaper rather than a national one. Alternatively, the national launch of, say, a new chocolate bar might be advertised on television. This might be more expensive but it would reach a wider audience and therefore more potential customers.

Once the firm has decided which media to use, it needs to ensure that its advertising will be as effective as possible. This can be done by repeating the advertisements over a certain period in order both to attract a wider audience and to reinforce potential customers' awareness of the product. Ideally, from the firm's point of view, this will result in the creation of a strong brand identity for the product. Once this has been done, the probability of repeat sales is increased.

The timing of the advertisement is also important in order to boost sales. It is no coincidence, for example, that most television advertising of toys is done during children's programmes. There may be another aspect to this if the good has a seasonal element. In this case, advertisements for it tend to appear several months before the season in question although this may vary between products. The advertising of summer holidays, for example, tends to be most intensive in the middle of winter.

Assuming that the firm has chosen to use more than one form of media to advertise its product, for example on television and through national newspapers, how will it allocate its advertising budget between them? The answer to this is that it will choose the combination of the two media which gives it the highest possible level of sales given the amount of money that it has to spend on advertising. Or, to put it another way, the optimal budget allocation for the firm is the one where the marginal returns from each pound spent on advertising in each of the two media are equal.

Specifically, it should set

$$\frac{MSR_{NEWS}}{P_{NEWS}} = \frac{MSR_{TV}}{P_{TV}}$$

where MSR is the marginal sales response to a unit of advertising, P is the price of that unit of advertising and the subscripts NEWS and TV stand for newspapers and television respectively. Thus at this point, newspaper and television advertising are equally effective in terms of the amount of extra sales they generate. Any other combination is suboptimal. For example, if the additional sales generated by newspaper advertising are greater than those generated from television advertising then it would be in the firm's interest to spend more of its budget on the former and less on the latter. It would then continue to do this until the returns were equalised. This equation can be used for more than two forms of media; the required condition is still that the returns to each of the forms of advertising should be equal if the budget is to be allocated in the best possible way.

The two-media case can alternatively be shown via the use of iso-sales analysis. Figure 8.1 shows how this is done, again using newspaper and television advertising for one particular firm as our example.

Figure 8.1 shows what happens when the firm sets an advertising budget of £100,000 at a time when television advertisements cost £5000 each and news-

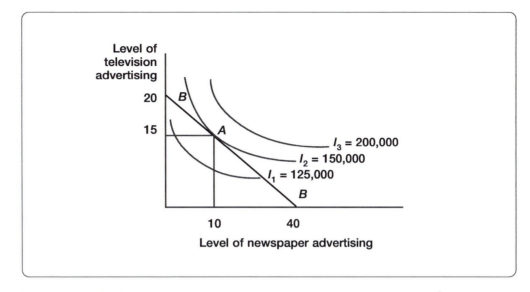

Figure 8.1   Iso-sales analysis

paper advertisements cost £2500 each. Given its budget, the firm can buy either 20 television advertisements or 40 newspaper advertisements or some combination of the two. The line *BB*, the firm's budget constraint, shows the alternative possibilities. Any combination of the two types of advertisement is feasible as long as the firm stays within its budget. The lines marked I_1, I_2 and I_3 are the iso-sales curves which denote equal levels of sales anywhere along their length. The further to the right they are, the higher the level of sales, as shown by the figures associated with each of them.

The optimal combination of the two forms of media for the firm occurs when the budget constraint is tangential to one of the iso-sales curves, point *A* in Figure 8.1. At this point the firm has spent all of its advertising budget, as it is on its budget constraint, and has achieved the highest possible level of sales it can (150,000). Although the firm would like to reach the higher iso-sales curve of I_3 and sell more of its good, it cannot do so given its current advertising budget. Any position to the left of *A*, for example on I_1, would be suboptimal as the firm could achieve higher sales by spending more on advertising. As can be seen from Figure 8.1, the optimal allocation of funds at point *A* is to spend £75,000 on 15 television advertisements and £25,000 on 10 newspaper advertisements.

8.2.5   Summary

So far this chapter has covered the ways in which the firm can set and allocate its advertising budget in order to get the desired result – increased sales of the product. In economic terms, the combined use of the Dorfman–Steiner condition, information about demand elasticities and either marginal sales response or iso-sales analysis should enable the firm to use its advertising most effectively. In reality, however, at least partly as a result of the complexity of the calculations involved, the firm may adopt 'rule of thumb' techniques such as the objective and task approach, percentage of sales method, competitive parity or the 'all you can afford' method as a way of setting its advertising budget. Likewise, in allocating its budget between the different forms of media it may use a 'best guess' approach based on the firm's experience of what has worked for it in the past.

The firm may decide to use advertising as part of its competitive strategy for a number of reasons – to shift or alter the elasticity of its demand curve, to create a barrier to entry into the industry, to increase its market share, to increase its profitability or any combination of these. Its success in doing whatever it sets out to achieve will, however, depend upon the structure of the market in which it operates and this will in turn determine how important the use of advertising will be to the firm. As a general principle, the less competitive an industry is in terms of price, the greater will be the need for the firm to advertise. In a non-collusive oligopolistic market with stable prices, for example, advertising will be crucial to the firm if it is to maintain or increase its market share. None of this will matter, however, if the product fails to live up to the consumers' expectations. This area – the issue of product policy – is discussed in the next section.

■ ■ ■ Self-Assessment Question ■ ■ ■ ■ ■ ■ ■ ■ ■ ■ ■ ■

(a) If the marginal sales response to price ratio is greater for television advertising than for newspaper advertising, what should the firm do to improve the effectiveness of its advertising?

(b) What point on the iso-sales diagram represents the optimal combination of the two forms of advertising?

■ 8.3   Product Policy

Regardless of the amount of advertising being done by the firm it will be unable to increase demand significantly, especially in the form of repeat sales, if the product itself is unattractive to (potential) customers. Every product has six basic characteristics associated with it – quality, design, performance, features, packaging and durability – and it is the combination of these which is important to the firm if it is to sell the product successfully. If, for example, a product gets a reputation for being of poor quality, then consumers will be unwilling to purchase it a second time and they will try an alternative brand instead. This can be termed the primary effect. This may be followed by a secondary effect whereby the unsatisfied customers tell other potential customers about the product's poor quality and so effectively discourage them from buying it as well. This can be very damaging for the firm over the longer term unless it takes steps to remedy the problem which is where its product development strategy becomes important. This will be considered in the next section.

The firm will use a specific combination of the six basic product characteristics in order to separate out its product from other similar ones on the market. This is known as product differentiation. The purpose of this approach is to influence the demand for the product by enabling the consumer to clearly identify it within the market. As in the case of advertising, this may operate in two ways – by increasing demand at every price and hence shifting the firm's demand curve to the right or by reducing the price elasticity of demand and making the demand curve steeper. Varying the product's characteristics may enable the firm to do this in the same way that the appropriate use of advertising does. In both cases, creation of a strong brand identity is basically what the firm is trying to achieve. The difference is that product policy is a matter of substance, whereas advertising is merely a means of promoting an existing product regardless of how good or bad it actually is.

For a multi-product firm the need for each product to satisfy the consumers' requirements is even more important because of the problem of 'guilt by association'. If one product produced by a company gets a poor reputation then the company's name, and hence its other products, may be tarnished as well. If this is the case then the firm may find it very difficult to attract any additional demand for its products. The multi-product firm also has the problem of deciding upon its product mix, that is how much of each product it should produce, as part of its overall strategy. In order to determine this it will need to consider eight criteria and assess the importance of each of them to the prosperity of the firm.

Firstly, there is the issue of the relative prices of the goods. Which ones command the highest prices in the market at any particular time? If a high price is indicative of excess demand for a particular good then the firm should perhaps produce more of it as it will be able to sell the good fairly easily. Secondly, there is the question of the relative costs of the goods. For example, if the firm did produce more of the higher priced good would it incur much higher costs of production as well? These two issues are closely related to the third criterion – what are the respective profit margins on each of the products? While it might pay the firm to switch some of its capacity from a good with a low profit margin to one with a high profit margin, the reverse is not the case. Thus it is the overall balance between costs and revenues which is important in making this decision.

The fourth issue relates to market demand. The firm needs to be sure that there is a demand for the product and that this demand is not just a temporary phenomenon. A high or rising price for a particular good may give the firm an initial signal but there is no guarantee that demand will be sustained. Given that it will take time for the firm to realign its production facilities, it is important that the firm knows that demand for the product will persist once this has been done. Market research will be essential in order to ascertain this. The fifth criterion the firm will have to consider is the actual availability of production facilities. If the firm is already operating at full capacity, the only way, in the short run at least, that it can produce more of one product is by producing less of another one. The firm will have to decide using the other criteria whether or not this is worthwhile. If, on the other hand, it is operating below capacity, increasing the production of one particular product may be relatively straightforward, providing that no major changes need to be made to the machinery and so on. Over the long run of course the firm can be much more flexible in adding extra capacity to its operations. This is related to the sixth of the criteria – the cost of altering the product mix. If changing the firm's production facilities would be expensive then the firm would be more likely to think twice about doing so than if it could do so relatively easily and cheaply. If, for example, the workforce are quite flexible and can produce all of the firm's products then the transitional costs will be less than if specialist workers have to be hired. Likewise if producing more of one particular product requires only minor adjustments to existing machinery, then the costs of altering the product mix will be comparatively low.

The seventh of the eight criteria relates to the extent to which the firm can benefit from interdependencies in the production process. These may take the form of either cost or demand interdependencies or both. In the case of cost interdependencies, the issue is the extent to which the firm's production facilities can be shared between different products. The specific term for this is economies of scope. In the case of demand interdependencies, these would occur if the goods produced by the firm were either substitutes or complements for one another. Additional production and sales of one will have knock-on effects on the others (negative and positive effects respectively). Finally, as always, there is the question of risk. The objective of the firm here, as before, is to minimise risk as far as possible. It can do this by producing a range of goods which have been on the market for varying amounts of time. What we mean by this is that the firm should be aware of market trends in relation to each of the goods it produces and should ideally produce some that are in new or expanding markets in order to offset the effects of the production of any goods for which the market is declining. By doing so it can ensure its long-term future, providing of course that the new products the firm develops are marketable. In order to see how the firm goes about this process, the next stage is to examine the processes of product development within the firm.

■ ■ **Self-Assessment Question** ■ ■ ■ ■ ■ ■ ■ ■ ■ ■ ■

Q5 (a) What are the eight criteria which the firm will use in order to determine its product mix?

(b) What is meant by the term 'economies of scope'?

8.3.1   Product Development

The firm's product development strategy may be based on one or more of three forms of project – speculative, troubleshooting or product differentiation. Speculative projects are those which are designed to help the firm develop new products to replace or complement existing ones. Troubleshooting projects are aimed at eliminating any deficiencies identified in the firm's products such as poor performance under certain conditions. Product differentiation projects, as their name suggests, are undertaken in order to find a niche in the market or to reinforce a brand identity by making the product distinct in some way from other similar ones on the market, for example by changes to its design to make it more 'user friendly'.

Which of these approaches a firm will be using at any particular point in time depends upon four main things. Firstly, it depends upon the firm's objective and the timescale over which it is trying to achieve it. A troubleshooting strategy alone suggests that the firm is being reactive rather than proactive and also that it is taking a relatively short-term view. A focus on speculative project development, on the other hand, suggests that the firm is taking a longer term view, perhaps as a means of ensuring the growth of the firm in future years. This in turn will be related to the second factor which will influence its decision – the firm's history. If the firm has a history of innovation then it is probably more likely to pursue speculative product development in the future than if it has a history of merely adapting existing products, in which case the focus of its development spending may well be on product differentiation. Thirdly, the firm's existing product portfolio will be important. If, for example, the firm has not introduced any new or revised products for some time, then it may find itself in the unfortunate position of being overly exposed in mature or declining product markets. It will need to remedy this by rejuvenating its product line as soon as possible. Fourthly, the nature of the industry in which the firm operates will also be important. The more competitive the industry is in terms of non-price factors, the greater the need to stay ahead of the competition through product development will be.

Whatever the motivation for the adoption of a product development strategy, the question arises of how it can be financed. There are four main methods by which this can be done – on the basis of expected profitability, through the use of industry averages, as a percentage of profit or turnover, or with reference to previous budgets.

The first of these, expected profitability, is fairly self-explanatory. In this case the firm sets and allocates its product development budget on the basis of the return it will get on its spending. Thus if it expects, say, a troubleshooting project to bring significant benefits to the firm in the form of higher profits and an improved reputation for the company's products, then it will be prepared to spend money on it. Likewise, speculative product development will not be undertaken unless it is expected to be profitable. The bigger the expected profit, the more money the firm is likely to spend on its product development strategy.

The use of industry averages to determine the appropriate level of spending on product development is very similar to the competitive parity approach in the case of advertising. Again it is largely a case of keeping up with other firms in the industry so that the firm does not end up at a comparative disadvantage. This type of approach may be used in mature markets where the firm is pursuing a product differentiation strategy. In this case, the product development spending of most, if not all, firms in the industry will be broadly similar.

Setting the product development budget as a percentage of profit or turnover also has similarities to a method which was examined in the context of advertising, this time the percentage of sales approach. It allows the firm to set aside an amount of money for product development which is related to the firm's current position in the market place. By financing product development internally in this way the firm can avoid the risks associated with borrowing money but, on the other hand, if the firm is experiencing declining profits or turnover, this can be a severe restriction on product development at a time when the need for it may be comparatively great.

The fourth method of setting the product development budget, with reference to previous years' budgets, provides an element of continuity but may not allow for major changes in the firm's circumstances such as a need to develop a new product in order to replace one which has now become obsolete. For a firm with a history of high product development budgets this is probably less of a problem than for a firm with a history of spending minimal sums on product development, as the former should be able to reallocate funding within the overall budget to allow for this which the latter may not be able to do.

Whichever of the four methods the firm chooses, it has to make sure that its product development budget is both sufficient for its needs and allocated in the best possible way between the various projects it is undertaking. In order to do this, it may compare the expected rates of return on these projects and channel the most money into those which are expected to yield the highest returns, that is to be the most profitable. This in itself is a highly speculative approach, however, as there is no guarantee that things will work out as expected. For example, a small, inexpensive change to an existing product may end up being more rewarding to the firm in terms of extra sales and profits than the more costly development of a major new product. There is no way of knowing for sure and hence any product development strategy is associated with quite a high degree of risk.

The question then arises of how the success, or otherwise, of a firm's product development strategy may be measured. There are three main possibilities – the number of new or improved products developed, the impact of these new products on the market and the effect of them on the firm's profit level. Assessing success on the basis of the number of products developed is flawed, as just because a product has been developed it does not automatically mean that it is marketable. It may be well designed and presented but, even with the added impetus of a strong advertising strategy, it does not follow that consumers will necessarily want to buy it. In order to avoid this problem, the firm should of course have tried to estimate likely demand for the product at an earlier stage in its development. If the demand was not there then no further development of the product should have taken place. Consequently, more is not necessarily better in terms of the firm's product development strategy; it is preferable to develop one highly profitable product than several mediocre or poor performing ones.

Given that this is the case, evaluating the impact that the products have on the market may be a better approach to use. This is bound up with other parts of the firm's competitive strategy, particularly with respect to pricing and advertising. If the price(s) of the new product(s) are set at a level which is right for the market then they will have a greater impact on it than if they are over-priced. Likewise, particularly with a totally new product, the firm may have to spend a significant amount on advertising and carry out that advertising in the most effective way possible in order to generate a high level of sales. This is in turn related to the effect on the firm's profit level of the introduction of a new product or products. Regardless of the number of new or amended products introduced, the net effect should be to improve the firm's profitability so that it gets a satisfactory return on its investment in product development. Thus the success of the firm's product development strategy can also be measured in terms of how much extra profit it generates for the firm. The main problem here of course is to separate out the effects of the product development strategy from the other effects which may be operating in the market simultaneously. For example, a rise in prices as a result of demand exceeding supply for a particular generic type of good may be responsible for the firm's improved profitability rather than necessarily the firm's own improved brand of it. At a time when the market is changing rapidly it can be quite difficult to attribute these effects to their actual causes. Thus there are a number of problems involved in determining the success of the firm's product development strategy.

8.3.2   Summary

The previous two sections have demonstrated that there are a number of issues which the firm will need to address in determining its product policy. The focus of such a policy will always be on producing products which are attractive to the consumer. The problem is that this will change over time, so that the firm will need to adapt in order to keep pace with market trends. As this is the case, the firm will need to make certain choices about how it is to pursue its product strategy.

In the case of a multi-product firm, its decisions regarding how much of each product to produce will be important to its overall performance. The criteria which may be used to determine the optimal product mix for such a firm were discussed above. The firm will also need to consider a range of options with respect to its product development strategy. These include the types of project it may undertake, how it may set its product development budget and how the success of its product development strategy will be measured. As with all of the firm's activities, there is an element of risk involved in making these decisions which the firm will seek to minimise as far as possible. A good, well thought through product strategy is likely to be beneficial to the firm, whereas the failure to adopt such a strategy is likely to be damaging, particularly over the longer term.

■ ■ ■ **Self-Assessment Question** ■ ■ ■ ■ ■ ■ ■ ■ ■ ■ ■ ■

Q6

(a) What four factors will influence the firm's choice of product strategy?

(b) What are the four methods by which the firm can finance its product development strategy?

(c) How can the firm measure the success of its product development strategy?

CASE STUDY | *University Product Policy*

In order to attract new students, universities must have products, that is, degree courses, which people want to do. Thus courses need to be developed/adapted to suit the needs of the market. This is not always easy. Even if changes in demand can be clearly identified, supplying that demand can take longer as there may be a need, for example, to hire new lecturers with a particular subject specialisation. This takes time and money which brings us to the issue of resources. As is the case

CASE STUDY *continued*

with any organisation, a university's product development strategy is in part determined by what it can afford to do. In particular, if there are competing needs for resources for new course development, then policy choices have to be made regarding which developments should be allowed to proceed and which ones should not. It is at this point that the 'product features' such as design, quality and so on will be taken into account, as well as the expected contribution to university revenues and profits of each of the available options. In addition, at the other end of the product policy

spectrum, decisions may also need to be made about whether or not to withdraw courses for which there is low demand, particularly if they are expensive to run. While this has the advantage of allowing any money saved to be reallocated to new courses, internal opposition to such a move is likely to be quite strong. Thus the university will need to continuously review its portfolio of courses to ensure their viability, bringing new courses on stream when necessary and dropping those which it is no longer feasible to run.

■ 8.4 Product Distribution and Production Site Location

The distribution network set up by the firm and the location of its production site are interrelated decisions in that they both form part of the place component of the marketing mix. Such decisions are important to the firm as they affect its ability to supply its customers efficiently. Failure to do so can have a negative effect on the firm's profitability as it results in an unsatisfactory level of service and on occasion a lack of responsiveness to the customers' needs. This, as in the case of poor product performance, can lead to a firm getting a bad reputation among potential customers. Given the importance of the 'place' element, therefore, the next two sections examine product distribution and production site location in more detail.

8.4.1 Product Distribution

The firm has three main decisions to make regarding the way in which it intends to distribute its product – how long the supply chain should be, where to sell the product and how to get it to the retailer.

In terms of the length of the supply chain, the question is how many people or organisations handle the product before it reaches the final consumer? This is also known as the marketing configuration associated with the product. At the most basic level, there is the case where the manufacturer sells direct to the final consumer with no one else being involved. This is the zero-level marketing configuration. The one-level marketing configuration, on the other hand, includes a retailer in this process. The manufacturer sells to the retailer who then sells the product to the final consumer. The two-level marketing configuration takes this a stage further. The manufacturer now sells the product in bulk to a wholesaler who then sells it in smaller amounts to the retailer who in turn sells it to the final customer. Finally, the three-level marketing configuration includes another group known as jobbers who act as intermediaries between the wholesalers and the retailers. At each level in the hierarchy more people become involved in selling the product all of whom will want to take a share of the profits to be made from it. The result of this, where the market can bear it, may well be higher prices in order to allow this to occur. If not, then the firm will have to decide how much of its potential profit it is willing to forgo in order to get others involved in the supply of the product.

The question of where to sell the product has two distinct aspects. Firstly, there is the issue of the geographical region in which the product should be sold, that is will the firm be selling the product at local, national or international level? This will, of course, partly depend upon the size of the firm in terms of its production level and how great the demand for the product is in any given area. The more it can produce, the more customers it can sell to, but if these customers are highly concentrated in one particular area then it may have a relatively local market in geographical terms. If, on the other hand, the firm produces a relatively small amount of a highly specialised product then it may be selling to a wide geographical area in order to find sufficient customers to keep it in business. Secondly, there is the problem of choosing the retailers of the product in any given area. This will involve finding suitable outlets and negotiating prices and in-store advertising strategies with them. Once the retailers have been chosen, the next question arises of how to get the product to them. What type of transport is to be used? How frequently are deliveries to be made? There are many possibilities.

In order to help it to make any decision, the firm is likely to break its decision-making process into stages. In the case of product distribution, eight distinct stages can be identified. These are research, promotion, contact, matching, negotiation, physical distribution, financing and risk taking. An individual firm may go through any number of these, and possibly even do so in a different order, depending upon its individual circumstances.

The first stage, research, is a basic information-gathering exercise to find out as much as possible about the nature of the market, its geography and the potential outlets for the product. The more information the firm has, the more able it will be to take the best possible decision about the way in which it should distribute the product. Once the firm has done this and identified the areas in which it wishes to sell the product, it needs to find retailers who are prepared to stock it. This is the promotion stage. In order to be able to place the product with suitable retailers, the firm needs to let them know about the product. It then has to convince them to sell it. This is the contact stage where the firm makes specific arrangements with the sellers of the product and through them gets the product to the final consumers of it. This will quite often take the form of a temporary arrangement in order to see how the product sells. Once this has been put into place, the firm will obtain feedback from the retailers about how well the product is being received in the market. This will enable it to adapt the product if necessary to the needs of the consumers – the matching stage. It may be, for example, that a particular defect within the product has been identified which had not been identified before. This is the firm's chance to remedy this before the product goes on sale to a larger market. The negotiation stage involves discussions between supplier and retailer over things such as the price to be charged in order to give both sides their required profit margin. Another aspect of this might be to agree the product placement within the store which will help to determine how well the product sells. A good display position within the store, for example, may increase sales as the product is drawn to the notice of the consumer much more strongly than if it is given a less favourable position. Once this has been done, the question of the physical distribution of the product will need to be addressed. The answer to this will depend upon the resources which can be called upon by each side. If, for example, the manufacturer has a fleet of lorries of its own, it may agree to transport the product direct to the retailer. If, on the other hand, the manufacturer does not have access to such facilities but the retailer does, then the arrangement may instead be that the retailer will collect it from the manufacturer. Alternatively, they may share the costs of moving the product, with the manufacturer being responsible for moving it to the retailer's central stores and the retailer moving it from there to its individual outlets. The seventh and eighth stages, financing and risk taking, are related. To begin with, there is the question of how the goods should be paid for. There are two main options. Firstly, the retailer may pay for the goods when they are delivered so that the only way to recoup this outlay is to ensure that they are sold. Secondly, the two sides may use a 'sale or return' agreement whereby any goods which are not sold by the retailer can be returned to the manufacturer without having to be paid for. These options are related to risk in the sense that the risk of being left with unsold stockpiles of the product varies according to which approach is used. In the first case, the retailer is taking all of the risk while in the second case the risk lies with the manufacturer. In any event, there is an element of risk throughout the distribution process that the wrong strategy may be being used.

To summarise, the firm's decisions regarding the distribution of its product will be influenced by five main factors. The first of these is the location and purchasing patterns of the customers. The firm will have to find a market which is geographically large enough to allow it to sell as much of its product as possible. The size of this market will also depend, however, upon the frequency with which customers buy the product. If, for example, the average duration between purchases is six months then the firm will need a larger number of initial customers than if the average duration is six weeks, as in the latter case repeat purchases occur more often, that is, each individual consumer will buy more of the product. This is related to the second of the factors, the product's characteristics, for example its durability or how easy it is to transport. A durable good, such as a car, is obviously bought less frequently than a non-durable good, for example a loaf of bread. In the case of ease of transportation, this will be an important determinant of how close to the market the firm will want, or have, to be. Manufactured goods are relatively easy to transport, for example, but many services are bought and consumed simultaneously and so cannot be transported at all, for example a meal in a restaurant. In the case of the latter, proximity to the market is crucial whereas in the case of the former it is not, unless the costs of transportation are so high as to leave the firm with no alternative. This is, of course, in turn related to the third of the factors influencing the firm's distribution decision, its resources. This might take the form of either whether it can afford to pay high transportation costs or whether it has its own means of transport, for example a lorry fleet, as mentioned previously. The final factor which the firm will need to take into consideration is the competitiveness of the market in which it operates. If it is very price competitive then the firm will need to minimise its transport costs as far as possible in order to avoid having to charge a higher price than other firms on the market. If, on the other hand, non-price competition is the norm, then the distribution decision may become even more important to the firm as it is in itself a way of gaining a competitive advantage. This might result, for example, from shorter waiting times for delivery than for its competitors' goods.

Overall, therefore, the firm has much to consider in relation to the way in which it will distribute its product. Some of these factors will also influence the location of its production site – this is examined in the next section.

8.4.2   Production Site Location

There are many factors which will determine the firm's production site location. They can, however, be divided into three broad groups – proximity to the market, cost factors and policy influences.

Taking proximity to the market first of all, there are three main factors which will determine how close the firm needs to be to its customers. These are the availability of market information, the marketing configuration the firm has decided to use and the maintenance requirements of the product. If market information is easy to obtain and is easily transportable, perhaps by electronic means, then the firm will not need to be as geographically close to the market as would be the case when it needs day-to-day contact with its customers. The manufactured goods versus services distinction may apply here in the same way as it did for product distribution, with proximity to the market being more important for the latter than for the former. In the case of the marketing configuration, the more intermediaries the firm involves in the distribution process, the more remote from the final consumer it will be. This suggests that a firm which has, say, adopted a three-level marketing configuration believes that proximity to the market is less important to it than would be the case for a firm which had adopted a one-level marketing configuration. Finally in terms of maintenance requirements, this may depend upon the nature of the product and whether or not the manufacturer chooses to get involved in this area. Most durable goods, for example, will need to be serviced and/or repaired at some time during their working lives and some, such as cars, may need to have this done more often than others, for example washing machines. The manufacturer will have to decide how to deal with this. If it chooses to carry out these functions itself then it will need to be relatively close to the market which it serves, compared to the case where the manufacturer either subcontracts such work or refuses to get involved in it at all. Thus the question of how close to the final market the firm will want, or need, to be is related to other decisions it has made, or will have to make, for example with respect to the distribution process.

This relationship between the firm's location decision and its other decisions is also exemplified in the case of costs. How it is going to produce the good will influence its cost structure which in turn will have an impact on its choice of production site. This brings us to the second group of factors it will have to consider, those related to cost. These include the cost of transporting raw materials, the cost of transporting the product, the price and availability of suitable premises, and labour costs.

If the raw materials being used are difficult or expensive to transport then it is in the firm's interest to locate as close to the supply of those raw materials as possible. Alternatively, if the raw materials are imported by sea, for example, then the firm might locate close to a port so that further transport costs are reduced. If, on the other hand, it is the product which is relatively expensive to move then the firm may prefer to be close to the market in order to reduce its transport costs. The choice of site may, therefore, be at least partly determined by the relative transport costs of the raw materials and the product. This decision will be constrained, however, by the availability of suitable premises at the right price. The more specific the firm's needs are, however, the more difficult it may be to find such premises. The effect of this may be to raise the firm's total costs as it has little choice but to pay higher property costs in order to get the type of site it needs. If, on the other hand, the firm does not have specialised requirements, it can be more flexible in its choice of location and reduce these costs accordingly. The next factor in the firm's location decision will be labour costs which are in turn related to the availability of the right type of workers for the firm's needs. In cases where the firm uses specific types of skilled labour, for example, it will be more constrained in its choice of location than if it only requires unskilled labour. Once it has identified areas which have the right sort of staff, it will then look for the area with the lowest wage rates for that type of worker in order to reduce its labour costs. This will be especially important for a firm which has a very labour-intensive production process as wages will form a substantial part of its overall costs. Its ability to choose the lowest cost site in terms of transport costs, property costs or labour costs will, of course, be constrained by the other factors influencing its location decision which we have already discussed. It may even be the case that the firm has to trade-off different types of cost, for example if low-rent premises suited to its needs are only available in an area without a supply of affordable skilled labour. In this case, the firm will have to decide which of the two – property costs or labour costs – is more important to its efficient operation and profitability.

In some cases, the firm's choice of location may be influenced by government policy. Most European governments, for example, operate some form of regional policy designed to attract firms to depressed areas with relatively high levels of unemployment. The ways of doing this vary, but the provision of labour subsidies, investment grants and tax concessions are fairly common regional policy tools. In the case of labour subsidies a relocating firm may, for example, be offered a fixed amount of money per job created. Investment grants may be given to help to pay for the cost of premises or equipment which reduces the firm's initial set-up costs. In terms of running costs, exemption from local property taxes for a certain period is a possibility. There may be a number of variations on these themes which are the subject of negotiation between firms and government agencies. Another factor which may influence the firm's location on an international scale is the presence of trade restrictions. An example of this would be an American or Japanese firm which has set up a production site in one of the European Union (EU) countries in order to avoid the trade barriers which have been constructed against non-EU firms. Such firms often also locate in such a way as to take advantage of the incentives provided by the different regional policy initiatives within the EU member states.

To summarise, therefore, the firm will have a number of, often competing, factors to consider when making its location decision. The final choice of site will depend upon the relative importance of each of these factors to the firm. For some, the question of the firm's proximity to the market may be the most important, for others it may be labour costs and so on. In many cases, it will be necessary to come to some sort of compromise in choosing the firm's site, as one which is clearly 'better' than all the others may not be readily identifiable. If so, an element of subjectivity on the part of the decision maker may be inevitable.

■ ■ ■ Self-Assessment Question ■ ■ ■ ■ ■ ■ ■ ■ ■ ■ ■ ■

Q7

(a) What are the three basic decisions which the firm has to make about the way in which it will distribute its product?

(b) What are the three groups of factors which will influence the firm's production site location decision?

CASE STUDY

'Place' Decisions for Universities

Product distribution and production site location decisions also have to be made by universities. In terms of site location, most UK universities are based in one city but within that city may have several campuses. Some universities also have subsidiary bases in other towns or overseas in order to cater for specific geographical markets.

In terms of product distribution, there are also alternative ways of reaching the customer. Traditionally most students study on campus at one particular university but they may be doing so on either a full-time or a part-time basis. Alternatively, students may study on a distance learning basis with on-line support and/or occasional tutorials.

As was the case for universities' product policies, the decisions taken about where to locate and how to distribute the product may vary between universities, courses and over time. Thus each university will need to take this into account both in terms of its advertising and, more generally, in terms of its overall competitive strategy. Getting the mix of these factors right may be difficult to achieve but it will potentially reap significant dividends for the organisation.

❏ ❏ ❏ End of Chapter SUMMARY ❏ ❏ ❏ ❏ ❏ ❏ ❏ ❏ ❏ ❏ ❏

This chapter has examined the firm's promotion, product and place decisions. With respect to promotion it looked at the firm's approach to setting and allocating its advertising budget, the factors which determine the advertising elasticity of demand and the ways in which advertising can affect the firm's market. In terms of the firm's product policy, the importance of finding the 'right' product for the market was discussed together with the issues faced by a multi-product firm in choosing the optimal product mix. Some time was also spent looking at the various product development strategies which the firm may adopt, the ways in which the firm will set its product development budget and how it can measure the success of its chosen approach. Finally, the place element was broken down into two parts – product distribution and production site location – and in each case the principal factors influencing those decisions were identified and discussed.

■ ■ ■ ANSWERS to Self-Assessment Questions ■ ■ ■ ■ ■ ■ ■

Q1   Any two factors from: the level of advertising expenditure, the type of product, market structure and the state of the economy.

Q2 Advertising can be used as a barrier to entry into the market if the threshold level of advertising needed to break into it is high. It may be difficult for prospective entrants to pay for the amount of advertising needed in order to break into the market. If they cannot afford to do so then in effect this is a barrier to entry.

Q3 The four methods are the objective and task approach, percentage of sales method, competitive parity and the 'all you can afford' approach.

Q4 (a) If the marginal sales response from television advertising is greater than that from newspaper advertising, then the firm should spend more on television advertising and less on newspaper advertising. This process should be continued until the returns from each of them are equal.

(b) Point *A* on the iso-sales diagram, where the indifference curve is tangential to the budget constraint, represents the optimal combination of the two forms of advertising.

Q5 (a) The eight criteria which the firm will use in order to determine its product mix are: the relative prices of the products; the relative costs associated with the products; their relative profit margins; market demand; the availability of production facilities; the costs of altering the product mix; the existence of interdependencies in the production process; and the degree of risk associated with changing the product mix.

(b) The term 'economies of scope' refers to the case where production facilities can be shared between different goods and different amounts of each of them produced accordingly.

Q6 (a) The four factors which will influence the firm's choice of product strategy are the firm's objective, the firm's history, its existing product portfolio and the nature of the market or industry in which it operates.

(b) The four methods by which the firm can finance its product development strategy are on the basis of expected profitability, industry averages, as a percentage of profit or turnover and with reference to previous budgets.

(c) The firm can measure the success of its product development strategy on the basis of the number of new or improved products developed, the impact of these products on the market or their effect on the firm's profit level.

Q7   (a)   The three basic decisions the firm faces in relation to its product distribution strategy are how long the supply chain should be, where to sell the product and how to get it to the retailer/customer.

   (b)   The three groups of factors which will influence the firm's production site location decision are those relating to the firm's proximity to its market, its costs and any policy influences which are exerted on the firm.

9 Managerial decisions and the firm's competitive strategy

■ 9.1 Introduction

In this chapter we explain how the firm can combine its decision-making processes in order to develop an overall competitive strategy. Earlier chapters of the book covered five main areas – the business environment, business objectives, demand and cost estimation, price and non-price competition, and investment appraisal. Some of the links between these areas have been mentioned previously but this chapter is designed to make them more explicit. It is not, however, comprehensive, as one of the ways in which a firm can gain a competitive advantage over its rivals is to arrange the components of its strategy differently from its competitors. As a result, some firms will find themselves in a unique position relative to others in the same industry, although the extent to which this can be achieved will differ between industry types and over time. An additional consequence of the number and range of choices to be made in devising a competitive strategy is that there may also be significant variations between companies in terms of their implementation of broadly similar strategies. Section 9.2 identifies the main generic types of competitive strategy which exist while Section 9.3 examines the ways in which they may be put into operation.

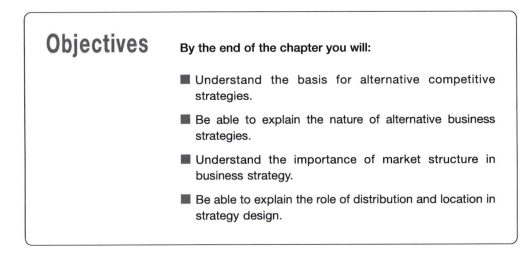

Objectives

By the end of the chapter you will:

■ Understand the basis for alternative competitive strategies.

■ Be able to explain the nature of alternative business strategies.

■ Understand the importance of market structure in business strategy.

■ Be able to explain the role of distribution and location in strategy design.

CASE STUDY

Strategic Choices in the Pharmaceutical Industry

A pharmaceutical company has developed a new drug on which it has taken out a patent. As long as this patent is in force, the firm is in a unique position of being the only one which may produce it. Once the patent has expired, however, it will be faced with the arrival of a number of competing brands of the drug. The consequences of this for the firm will depend on what it has been doing in terms of the various elements of its strategy in the intervening period. Its choices may, hypothetically, be as follows:

■ *Option 1* – develop and patent another drug on the assumption that its sales of the original drug will fall and it needs a replacement revenue earner (a product innovation strategy).

■ *Option 2* – attempt to convince customers that its brand of the drug is superior to the others available in order to maintain its sales (a product differentiation strategy).

In each case, the implications of the decision for the company are different:

Option 1 will require the firm to invest in new product development which, given the nature of the industry, is potentially a long-term investment. Appropriate investment appraisal criteria – for example payback or discounted cash flow methods – will need to be used in order to decide whether this type of investment should be undertaken and whether or not it is likely to be profitable. A complication in this particular case is that there is no guarantee of success in terms of either the development of the new drug itself or the company's ability to bring it to market successfully – for example a competitor may develop and patent a similar drug first. Thus this option may be potentially the most rewarding but also carries the

highest level of risk. There is also the question of how to finance this new development. If the firm wishes to finance it out of existing funds rather than by borrowing, then the implication of this is that it will have to make higher profits than might otherwise be necessary and retain more of them rather than distributing them to shareholders. In order to achieve the higher profits, it might in turn be necessary to exploit its monopoly position by charging a high price for its existing drug, that is to use marginal cost pricing rather than an alternative pricing strategy. At the same time, however, by retaining more of its profits, it runs the additional risk of shareholder dissatisfaction unless it can convince them that this particular strategy is in their interests too. Thus we return to the issue of manager–shareholder conflict which is apparent in many of the models of business objectives.

Option 2, on the other hand, may be perceived to be a relatively lower risk choice. Given that by the time the patent on the drug expires, it will be well known to its customers, this may in itself be a source of competitive advantage. The firm cannot, however, just assume that this will be the case in the face of increased competition. Consequently the firm will need to divert resources towards its promotional activities in order to convince doctors to continue prescribing the drug and/or patients to continue to demand it. This may involve advertising in medical journals or magazines, attendance at medical conferences and so on. At the same time, however, the firm may need to rethink its pricing strategy in the face of increased competition and lower the price it charges for the product. This may, for example, involve a shift from marginal cost pricing to mark-up pricing with the size of the mark-up being at least partly related to the number of competitors who have entered the market. The extent to which the price and non-price elements

continued

of its competitive strategy are important will also depend upon the precise nature of the market, which brings us back in turn to demand estimation and forecasting. The firm's use of these techniques will enable it to gain and analyse market information in order to ascertain what the most effective strategy is likely to be and how it should be implemented. If, for example, this analysis were to reveal that price competitiveness was going to be the key determinant of success, the firm would then need to turn its attention to how it could reduce the price of the drug without eroding the firm's profitability. This would lead it to consider its current and future cost structure so that cost estimation would have a role to play. The need to reduce its costs might in turn lead to investment in new more efficient equipment and so on.

In summary, therefore, the firm's choice between the two options involves making a range of sub-decisions about the nature of the firm's competitive environment; the firm's objectives and its attitude to risk, demand and cost conditions; the relative importance and mix of the price and non-price competition elements of its strategy; and the appropriate investment appraisal techniques to use. If the firm is to be successful, it must combine these decisions in a coherent, logical and consistent way in order to form its overall competitive strategy. Of course, in an ideal world, the firm would have sufficient resources to pursue both options so that it would not have to make this choice. While this may be a feasible solution for some firms, it is unlikely to be so for the majority. Consequently, the more thorough the analysis of the options that the firm is able to undertake, the more likely it is to find the optimal solution to its particular problem. Once again, however, the firm's ability to do this will be constrained by the amount of time and resources available.

◼ 9.2　The Firm's Competitive Strategy

The firm's competitive strategy should be designed in such a way as to combine all of the elements of the firm's activities into a coherent whole. It should give the company a clear sense of direction in terms of both what it wants to achieve and how it is going to achieve it. This is, of course, an ideal, as some firms may not be able to manage this, for example, because of an absence of relevant information or organisational politics. In terms of the choice of competitive strategy, we can identify four main ones for the firm to select from – the cost leadership strategy, the differentiation strategy, the cost focus strategy and the differentiation focus strategy (Porter, 1980). Again it should be noted that these are generic strategies and the detailed implementation of them may vary between firms in practice. Before discussing each strategy in more detail, it is useful to summarise the relationships between them – see Figure 9.1.

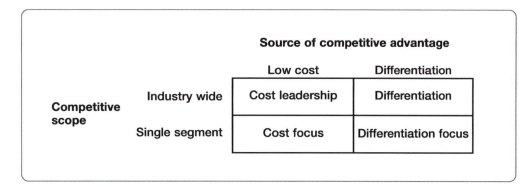

Figure 9.1   Porter's generic strategies

The matrix in Figure 9.1 defines each of the four strategies in terms of a combination of (a) how the firm seeks to achieve competitive advantage – either by producing a differentiated product or by obtaining lower costs than its competitors – and (b) the size of the market it is trying to reach – its competitive scope – which may span either the entire market or a particular part (segment) of it. The firm's choice of strategy from these four alternatives will depend on two main factors – the type of product involved and what other firms in the same market are doing.

In terms of product type, for example, products such as coal or wheat are difficult to differentiate, so that a cost-based strategy is likely to be the most feasible. The producer would then need to decide whether to supply, say, a national or a local market (geographical segment) for the product. This would be the difference between a cost leadership and a cost focus strategy respectively. Other products, on the other hand, such as cosmetics or chocolate bars, are quite easy to differentiate via branding. In both of these cases, the firm would face the same issue as to whether to try to cover the whole market or to focus on just part of it. This might in turn also depend upon whether the company was an established player or a new entrant into the market. In the case of the latter, a differentiation focus strategy might enable the firm to succeed by gaining a foothold in the market on which it could build, whereas a differentiation strategy might lead to failure because it placed too great a strain on the resources of the company.

With respect to what other firms in the same market are doing, competitive advantage may be obtained either by doing the same as everyone else but doing it better, or by doing something different. For example, if all of the firms in a particular industry were attempting to achieve a cost leadership strategy, only one could be the cost leader at any particular point in time. If the other firms in the industry were confident that they could undercut the costs of the leader at some point in the future then they might well continue with that strategy. At some point, however, one or more of them may decide to change to a differentiation strategy in order to change the rules under which the industry is operating. This could lead to a significant competitive advantage for the firm which produces the most innovative differentiation strategy.

Having discussed the strategies in broad terms, the following sections examine them in more detail beginning with the cost leadership strategy.

9.2.1   The Cost Leadership Strategy

As its name suggests, the basis of the cost leadership strategy is that the firm seeks to produce the lowest cost version of the product on the market. In order to do this it will need either to achieve large volume sales or to use the latest production technology (or both). In the case of the former, it will be able to take advantage of economies of scale which are not available to smaller lower volume competitors. Alternatively, by using the latest production technology it will be more efficient than at least some of its rivals who are using older machinery. In both cases the firm can gain a competitive edge by producing the good more cheaply than other firms in the market.

This approach does of course have implications for other parts of the firm's operations, and the decision to adopt a cost leadership strategy will constrain the decisions the firm can make in other areas. To begin with, it is necessary to ensure that the firm can sell all of the output which it produces. In order to do so the firm may have to set a relatively low price for the product. This may in turn adversely affect the profit margin which the firm can make on each unit of the product sold, although the extent to which this is the case will depend upon how successful the firm is in lowering its costs. The overall effect of this strategy on the firm's profits will therefore depend upon how successful it is in creating additional demand for the product at this lower price. What this approach also does, however, is effectively rule out the use of some pricing methods, for example pricing to infer quality. It would also restrict the size of the mark-up which the firm could use if it had chosen a cost plus pricing strategy. Thus the fact that the firm has adopted this strategy restricts its freedom of choice in this area.

Alternatively, the firm could address the problem of the need to sell large amounts of the product by using advertising. In order to achieve the desired effect, however, the firm might need to set aside a substantial amount of money to make its advertising campaign as intensive as possible, at least in the short term. This again would have an impact on its profitability, although it is perhaps more difficult to quantify in this case. The firm would also need to consider the effects of large-scale production on the product itself. Would the need to produce it ever more cheaply lead to a drop in quality, for example, perhaps as a result of inferior materials being used? If so, how will this affect demand?

It is because of considerations of this type that this particular strategy is generally, although not always, associated with particular types of market. Firstly, demand for the product needs to be elastic with respect to price, as the ability to be price competitive as a result of having lower costs than other firms in the market is crucial to the successful implementation of this strategy. Secondly, the product needs to be relatively homogeneous. In order to encourage customers to make the switch from other manufacturers' versions of the product the firm's product must be very similar to theirs. It would be difficult to implement such a strategy in a market where strong brand identification existed. In markets where there are strong brand identities, an alternative approach may be necessary.

9.2.2   The Differentiation Strategy

This alternative approach may take the form of a differentiation strategy. In this case, the firm tries to compete on the basis of the quality of a product rather than its price. This makes the need to cut costs less of a priority although, of course, the firm will still want to operate as efficiently as possible. The basis of the differentiation strategy is to set the firm's product apart from the others on the market in some way. One way in which this can be done is by improving its quality so that the firm can charge a higher price for the product than its competitors do and so raise its profit margin.

In order to make this strategy work, however, the firm must make sure that it provides a high-quality product relative to the price charged. If the product is found by customers not to be of suitable quality then they will not make repeat purchases. Improvements in the quality of other similar products in the market will have to be monitored regularly in order to ensure that the firm retains its competitive advantage over time. This means in turn that the firm will need to spend money on product development, both to improve and differentiate its product and also to develop new ones as the market changes.

If the firm is using this particular strategy, then brand names will be at a premium as they provide the firm with a clear way of distinguishing its product from others on the market. In order to reinforce this the firm will have to carry out an intensive and persuasive advertising campaign. The firm may also place greater emphasis on the 'product package', that is it would use things such as after-sales service as a means of promoting the product.

As was the case for the cost leadership strategy, the differentiation strategy is associated with certain types of markets. To begin with, given that the firm is likely to charge higher prices than its competitors, demand for the product must be relatively inelastic with respect to price. In addition, the less homogeneous the product is the better, as this allows much easier brand identification. Thus which of the two strategies discussed so far the firm will adopt depends upon both the type of product and the nature of the market in which it finds itself.

9.2.3 The Focus Strategy

Up to now we have implicitly assumed that the firm has decided upon a strategy which covers the entire market for the product. In reality, however, it has the alternative of concentrating on specific parts of the market rather than the market as a whole. This is what is known as a focus strategy, that is it concentrates on a particular market segment. One form this could take would be to sell the product within a particular geographical area, for example London, rather than on a national or international scale, the UK or the EU, even though potential markets also exist in these areas. Another possibility is that the firm might concentrate on producing one particular version of the product, for example personal compact disc players, while its competitors produce a range of substitute and complementary goods from personal compact disc players through to complete stereo systems and beyond. A third alternative is that the company might focus on a particular, clearly identifiable sub-group of potential customers, for example only selling holidays to people over 50 years of age – which is the focus strategy pursued by Saga holidays in the UK. A focus strategy is often, but not solely, used when the firm is trying to enter a new market, and thus in some respects has similarities to the demand estimation method of test marketing. It allows the firm to try out different combinations of the factors within the marketing mix before, if it wishes, beginning to sell the product on a wider scale.

The focus strategy can be subdivided into two alternative parts, the cost focus and the differentiation focus strategies. In the case of a cost focus strategy, the firm attempts to minimise the cost of supplying the market segment and hence to compete mainly on the basis of price. In the case of the differentiation focus strategy, however, the emphasis is on non-price competition particularly in terms of quality and branding. Thus these two forms of focus strategy correspond to the cost leadership and differentiation strategies respectively, and the methods of achieving them are similar, but they operate on a smaller scale. This can of course be problematic in the case of the cost focus strategy in particular, as the firm may not be producing enough of the product in order to drive down costs below those of other firms which are supplying the entire market rather than just one particular segment of it. In this case the differentiation focus strategy may well be a better alternative.

9.2.4 Summary

In Section 9.2 we have looked at the competitive strategies the firm may use in order to gain an advantage over its competitors. We have also discussed the implications of these strategies for the decision-making process of the firm, noting that the choice of strategy will in effect constrain the alternatives open to it. In the case of the cost leadership strategy, for example, the need for the firm to control its costs will mean that the cost estimation process and the related decisions arising from it in terms of the use of different input mixes will be especially important. The fact that the firm wishes to minimise costs will also influence the amount it spends on advertising, product development and its distribution process, all of which will be minimised as far as possible.

In the case of the differentiation strategy, on the other hand, cost estimation is relatively less important. Demand estimation techniques will have a greater role to play as the firm will need to more clearly identify what the customer wants from the product, what will influence their choice and how the product can be adapted and promoted to take this into account. Thus the firm is likely to spend more money on market research, advertising and product development than if it had adopted the cost leadership strategy instead. This is possible because the firm pursuing the differentiation strategy will be able to charge a higher price for its product and so recoup these extra costs more easily. Thus the choice of strategy also influences the price the firm will set and possibly its choice of pricing method as well.

■ ■ ■ Self-Assessment Question ■ ■ ■ ■ ■ ■ ■ ■ ■ ■ ■ ■

Q1 What is the difference between the cost leadership strategy and the different-iation strategy?

■ 9.3 Implementation of the Firm's Competitive Strategy

Once the firm has decided which of the strategies to adopt it needs to find a way to implement it. For the cost leadership strategy, the question would be: how can the firm lower its costs? For the differentiation strategy, how can the firm distinguish its product from others on the market? For the focus strategy the main question would be: how does the firm identify the market segment? Depending on which of the two forms of the focus strategy was used, there would then be the secondary questions of how to cut costs and how to distinguish the product from others in the market in the case of the cost focus and the differentiation focus strategies respectively. Given that these are the same questions which would be asked for the first two strategies we will not mention them separately again.

There are three routes through which the firm's competitive strategy can be implemented – internal development, acquisition and via joint ventures. Let us look at each of these in turn.

9.3.1   Internal Development

The firm's ability to adopt this line of approach will depend upon its existing structure in terms of its production facilities and the nature of the product(s) it produces. These may in turn affect its decision regarding the best competitive strategy to pursue. Let us look at production facilities first of all.

In order to be able to produce at least cost, the firm must be efficient, particularly if its competitors are attempting to pursue a similar strategy. This means that its equipment must be at least technologically equal to that used by other firms and preferably better. If this is not the case then the firm's ability to pursue a cost leadership strategy through internal means may be substantially reduced, unless of course it can afford to replace its machinery. It must also be using the labour and land inputs efficiently as well, and it cannot afford to spend too much on things like advertising and product development, although the question of how much is too much is a difficult one in itself. This also assumes that the firm is producing enough of the product to benefit from economies of scale in the production process. While it may have the capacity to do so, there will be little point in producing large amounts of the good, even to lower costs, if the firm is left with stockpiles of it which it cannot sell. This brings us to the nature of the product itself and what is known as the product life cycle. For the moment we will assume that the firm only produces one product.

Every product has a limited life before it becomes obsolete, although this may be months, years or decades. During its lifetime the product will go through four stages. Firstly there is the introductory stage immediately after the product is brought onto the market. During this time sales will tend to be low and demand will be relatively inelastic with respect to price. In order to get the product known to the customer the firm will need to advertise and, if the product is poorly received, adapt it to meet the customers' requirements more closely. Thus at this stage in the product life cycle use of the differentiation strategy may be more appropriate than a cost leadership strategy as it will take time for a sufficient volume of sales to be reached to make the latter feasible. There may of course be some exceptions to this. One example would be if the firm was entering a market with a homogeneous product but the firm had the advantage of having the latest technology which no other firm in the market had yet introduced.

The second stage of the product life cycle is the growth phase. By this time in the cycle greater product awareness has led to rising sales, and at this point the cost leadership strategy becomes more feasible as the larger volume of the goods produced and sold allows the firm to reap economies of scale. Competing on the basis of price may also become more important as there is likely to have been additional entry into the market. The more similar any new entrants' products are to the firm's product, the more price, and hence cost, competitive it will need to be. If, on the other hand, there is a high degree of product differentiation then the firm may decide to carry on with a differentiation strategy as reducing costs in order to reduce price will become less of a priority.

By the time the product reaches its third stage, the maturity or saturation phase, the rate of growth of sales of the product will have slowed considerably (maturity) or fallen to zero (saturation). Demand will be more elastic with respect to price than before and lowering the price of the product may be a necessity if the firm is to generate any increase in sales volume at all. At this point the firm will have the choice of either reducing its profit margin on the good or retaining its existing profit margin by reducing costs further. If it has been following a cost leadership strategy in the previous period the latter may be far more difficult to achieve than if it has been operating a differentiation strategy. Thus the strategy the firm has been following previously may determine what it can do in the current period. This is yet another example of how a decision made in one time period can limit the firm's options later on.

In the fourth, decline, stage this problem becomes more acute as the volume of the product sold begins to fall and demand becomes even more price elastic. Unless the firm has found some means of offsetting this through the creation of a strong positive brand identity it will have little alternative to cut the price of the good further, perhaps through the use of promotional pricing. The choice regarding its profit margin is the same as before, but its options are equally, if not even more, limited. By this time the firm should already have introduced, or at the very least thought about introducing, a new product to offset the decline in sales and revenue from the existing one. This will of course necessitate the setting aside of money for product development to create the new product and for advertising to promote it. Thus the cycle will begin again for the new product.

This brings us to the case of multi-product firms which will be producing several products at different stages in their life cycles. In this case, the choice of the appropriate strategy becomes even more difficult, as what may be appropriate for one product might not be appropriate for others. For example, the growth stage products may be selling in high enough volumes for a cost leadership strategy to be feasible, but the new products may need nurturing and would benefit from a differentiation strategy at least in the early stages of their development. Alternatively, if the firm was not absolutely sure that a new product would work then it might use a focus strategy for that product and sell it within a limited geographical area. Given this conflict, the choice of an overall strategy for the firm, as opposed to for an individual product, will be that much more difficult. What this illustrates is that co-ordinating the different parts of the firm's activities and hence its decision-making process can be quite a complex matter.

Whichever of the strategies the firm chooses, however, as long as it has sufficient production capacity of the right type and a suitable product(s) it can implement that strategy through internal development, that is, by altering its own activities accordingly. There will, however, be cases where this is not true, which is where acquisition and joint ventures can be seen as a means to the required strategic end.

9.3.2   Acquisition

If the company is currently producing a mature product (or products) which is near to the end of its product life cycle then it will need to introduce a new product to replace it. While it can take the internal development route discussed above by reorientating or expanding its production, this may not always be easy to do, especially if it would involve setting up a completely new production plant as this will take both time and money. The easier, and sometimes cheaper, solution may be to take over a firm which is already oper- ating in the market which the firm wants to enter. This will be especially true if the new product the firm wishes to develop is very different from its existing product(s). By taking over a firm producing that product it will be buying not only physical production capacity but also experience of the way in which that particular market operates. This will be advantageous to the firm as it will waste less time and money in getting the product, the produc- tion facilities and the combination of the components of the marketing mix right. Another reason for adopting this approach might be the existence of barriers to entry into the market because of things like knowledge of the production process and economies of scale. If, for example, price competition as a result of low costs (perhaps arising from economies of scale) is a feature of this market, then a new firm may only be able to enter the market by buying one of the existing firms. There may be no other way that the new firm could produce and sell enough of the product to be competitive given the current level of market demand. In a sense, therefore, acquisition is a short cut for the firm. Once a firm has got a foothold in the new market and some experience of producing the good it can then decide what its compet- itive strategy should be, that is whether it should be the same as that being adopted by existing firms or whether it could benefit by doing something different, perhaps producing an adapted form of the product for which it could generate a stronger brand identity.

9.3.3   Joint Ventures

The basic principle of entering into a joint venture is similar to that for an acquisition, that is, to minimise risk by 'buying' experience from another firm or firms. In this case, the risk of entering a market is spread between a number of firms which co-operate to produce a particular product (or products). It also allows the firms involved to pool their skills so that each of them benefits from the others' participation in some way. This approach, although probably rarer than the other two, is quite often associated with a focus strategy which involves the development of a new geographical market. In this case a firm might choose to link up with a firm which already has a knowledge of the market in that area. In return the firm would share its knowledge of operating in a different area. Thus both sides have something to gain from this type of approach. The exact strategy they would use in each market would of course be a matter of negotiation between them.

■ ■ ■ Self-Assessment Question ■ ■ ■ ■ ■ ■ ■ ■ ■ ■ ■ ■

Q2 What is meant by the terms 'internal development', 'acquisition' and 'joint ventures'?

9.3.4　Summary

Any of the strategies identified in this chapter – cost leadership, differentiation, cost focus and differentiation focus – can be used to give the firm a competitive advantage over other firms in any particular market. The choice of strategy in any given situation will be determined by the firm's current production operations, the nature of its products and the market for them, and the activities of the firm's competitors.

The firm's choice of strategy may also at least partly determine the way in which the firm implements it, through internal development, acquisition or a joint venture. In any case, whichever competitive strategy is chosen and however it is implemented, there will be further implications for the firm's entire decision-making process. This will include things like how crucial cost and demand estimation are to the firm, how the pricing and advertising of the product should be done, how important product development is to the firm and so on. Thus, each decision taken will have a knock-on effect on the rest of the firm's decision-making process. No one decision can be taken in isolation from the others.

■ 9.4　The Applicability of Competitive Strategies and Managerial Decision-making Tools to Different Industries

This chapter illustrates that there are a number of alternative competitive strategies which the firm can pursue in its search for competitive advantage within the market. An important point to remember, however, is that there are no clear 'right' or 'wrong' answers in terms of which strategy should be selected and how it should be implemented within a particular industry. A significant influence on this decision will, of course, be the firm's perception of the general economic and competitive environment in which it operates, as was discussed in Chapters 1–3. Similarly, throughout the book we have stressed that managerial economics and decision making is about *choice* and not about being prescriptive regarding what the firm should do, or the decision-making tools it should use, when faced with a particular set of circumstances. Much of this choice will depend upon the constraints imposed by the firm's history, the resources it has at its disposal, the nature and attitudes of the management team and the ability of the firm to adapt to changes in its environment. The case studies which are presented in the earlier chapters act as illustrations of the types of issues which organisations can face in their operations, and demonstrate some of the choices which can be made in particular situations. Different organisations in similar situations at different points in time may, however, choose to do things differently, depending upon their perception of the industry in which they operate and whether they believe competitive advantage can be obtained by competing on the same basis as other firms in the market or by doing something different.

❏ ❏ ❏ End of Chapter SUMMARY ❏ ❏ ❏ ❏ ❏ ❏ ❏ ❏ ❏ ❏ ❏

While it is true that many of the techniques we have discussed were originally designed for application to manufacturing industries, we would argue that they can be applied across a range of service industries as well. Indeed the case studies presented throughout the book demonstrate this. In terms of investment appraisal, for example, Chapters 10–12 examine the types of investment decisions which are made in both the private and the public sectors. Chapter 8 showed that universities, even though they are not-for-profit institutions, use non-price competition in the forms of product (course) innovation and advertising in order to attract customers (students). Production and cost issues arising within the airline industry were discussed in Chapter 6, while the problems faced by retailers in estimating demand and setting prices were discussed in Chapters 5 and 7 respectively. Similarly the ways in which a construction firm might change its business objective over time were the subject of the case study in Chapter 4. In summary, therefore, the strategies and techniques which we have described can be used across a range of industries; it is up to the organisation's management team to decide which ones are most appropriate in which situation.

Reference

Porter, M.E. (1980) *Competitive Strategy*, Free Press, New York.

■ ■ ■ ANSWERS to Self-Assessment Questions ■ ■ ■ ■ ■ ■

Q1   The cost leadership strategy is based on the firm being able to produce and sell its product more cheaply than its rivals, while a firm following the differentiation strategy seeks to compete on the basis of the nature of the product itself rather than its price, for example in terms of its quality or brand name and image.

Q2   Internal development is where the firm either reduces its own costs or changes the nature of its existing product depending on which strategy it is following – that is, it relies on changing its existing activities in some way. Acquisition occurs when the firm takes over another firm in order to achieve what it has set out to do, for example to expand its product range. Joint ventures occur where two or more companies join together to develop a new product or to enter a new market in order to minimise the risk of doing so.

Investment Decisions

You already know from previous chapters that business decisions on pricing, advertising and competitive strategy are closely linked to the nature of the market a firm operates in and to what extent that market is competitive. In addition, the source of competition may be local, national or even global – or all three. It therefore follows that the key decisions relating to expansion, new product development, staff training and any other aspect of management represent an attempt to remain competitive or become more competitive. All such decisions are essentially investment decisions. In this part of the text we consider why firms invest, how management can decide on the 'best' investment alternative and to what extent these decisions are similar as between the private and public sectors of the economy. This section is also designed to enable you to apply concepts and techniques from economic analysis to practical decision making in management and to develop your critical and analytical skills in the context of investment-related management decisions. Chapter 10 introduces the concept of investment appraisal and some techniques which are widely used in investment decision making. Chapter 11 goes on to discuss these techniques in the context of risk and uncertainty – a context which is typical in a globalising world and fairly typical of most of the market structures you have met in Part II. The final chapter looks more closely at the public sector in terms of the nature of public sector investment and the requirement that it meets value for money for the taxpayer – an increasingly important aspect of EU public policy.

Further reading for Part III

Chapters 10, 11 and 12

Irvin, G. (1995) *Modern Cost-benefit Methods: An Introduction to Financial, Economic and Social Appraisal of Development Projects,* Macmillan – now Palgrave Macmillan, Basingstoke.

Keat, P. and Young, P.K. (1992) *Managerial Economics: Economic Tools for Today's Decision Makers,* Macmillan, New York.

Lumby, S. (1994) *Investment Appraisal and Financial Decisions*, 5th edn, Chapman & Hall, London.

Maddala, G.S. and Miller, E. (1989) *Microeconomics: Theory and Applications,* McGraw-Hill, Singapore.

Petersen, H. and Lewis, W. (1990) *Managerial Economics*, 2nd edn, Macmillan – now Palgrave Macmillan, Basingstoke.

10 Investment appraisal

■ 10.1 Introduction

This chapter aims to provide you with the tools to undertake investment appraisals and to use the results to arrive at efficient management decisions regarding the utilisation of capital funds. Not every available investment appraisal technique is covered, but the main techniques used widely today are given detailed treatment in the chapter. You will find in other books of the course that some of these crop up again but in a different context – the context in which they are set in this book is very much from an economics perspective. That is, they are utilised within the economic framework of *opportunity cost*. This is the underpinning basis for this part of the book. Some of the techniques involve mathematical formulae but these are explained in detail and many examples are given in addition to self-assessment questions to enable you to see and understand clearly how they actually work.

In earlier chapters of this book you studied the various aspects of the macroeconomy, business cycles, pricing theory, cost analysis and competitive strategy. All of these are inextricably linked to management decisions on the utilisation of both private and public capital funds. A fairly obvious link is in relation to pricing – the price or cost of any product or service is not simply determined by supply and demand or marketing strategy – it must also be related to the cost of the investment required to produce the product or service in the first place so as to generate an 'acceptable' rate of return or even to minimise loss. In general, if private and public sector investment decisions are being taken so as to maximise return then the rate of growth of the macroeconomy will be enhanced. Thus, microeconomic investment decisions are also closely linked with the subsequent performance of the economy as a whole. This point was explained in some detail in Part I of the book.

The question which therefore arises is quite a simple one:

How do (or should) decision makers go about maximising the return/benefits of capital investment?

The answer, unfortunately, is not quite so simple! Basically there are many techniques which are available to assess whether a particular investment is the 'best' one available at a given time. However, different techniques can very easily produce different answers. This is simply because the theoretical and mathematical bases of the techniques also differ. It is therefore crucial that we understand first the *nature* of these different techniques and second the *meaning* of the results they actually produce. Only then are we in a position to select the most appropriate technique for a given problem and thus be able to correctly interpret what the results are actually telling us. This chapter proceeds as follows:

In order to help you through the remaining chapters of the book you will need a working calculator with a memory storage and retrieval function. There are a number of calculations involved in the self-assessment questions and exercises.

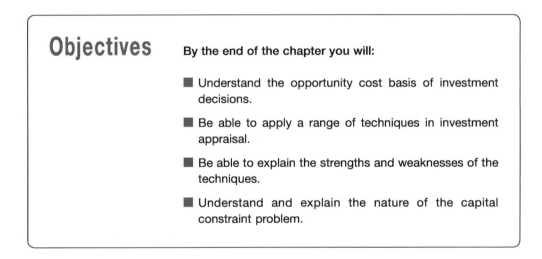

Objectives

By the end of the chapter you will:

- Understand the opportunity cost basis of investment decisions.

- Be able to apply a range of techniques in investment appraisal.

- Be able to explain the strengths and weaknesses of the techniques.

- Understand and explain the nature of the capital constraint problem.

■ 10.2 The Economic Nature of Investment

We need to understand how investment decisions are made and why alternative investment decisions were not made! In other words, we need to understand the nature of investment. One thing is certain – whatever past investment decisions were made by a firm these will continue to strongly influence the costs the firm faces, its efficiency levels, its prices and its profits. At any given point in time a firm's productive capacity is necessarily its inherited capacity from past investment decisions. These past investment decisions must have been taken on the basis of the expected *future state of the market* the firm operates in or was perhaps planning to operate in.

Such investment decisions, it must be stressed, are not restricted to acquiring capital equipment or buildings but also include training of the workforce, product development or enhancement, reorganisation and production process changes. All of the latter represent an investment problem in that they are expected to produce a return for the firm. A basic question here of course is whether such investment will produce a return and whether the return is the best possible in the firm's circumstances.

It therefore follows that any investment decisions made in the present will largely determine all of these parameters in the future. It should be clear to you now that one of the most important decisions management face is the decision to invest since, it is no exaggeration to say, this decision ultimately will affect everything else the management of a firm can achieve. So, exactly what is the economic nature of investment? Does it have a rationale of its own or is it linked to other economic decisions?

Many different and perfectly valid reasons can be put forward on why investment occurs. However, in the end, there is only one reason which has any meaning: it is to *raise* the *consumption* of goods and services in the *future* beyond the level currently enjoyed. In other words, it is intended to raise our standard of living, the future value of the firm and the future wealth of the individuals who choose to make their capital available for investment purposes.

This means there is necessarily a trade-off between consuming goods and services now and consuming more goods and services in the future – the link between the two is investment. It is commonly referred to in economics as the *consumption–investment trade-off*. In general, people (including the owners of firms) prefer to consume now rather than later, so they need to be given an incentive to forgo some portion of potential present consumption – that incentive is simply the 'promise' of higher levels of consumption in the future. A standard model used to explain this link is the single-period consumption decision shown in Figure 10.1.

Imagine you are asked to lend someone £1 for one year. Assuming you could afford to lend the money (that is, you did not need to spend it now) you

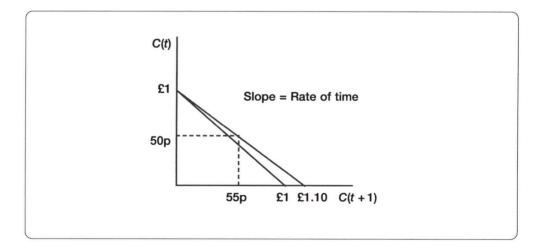

Figure 10.1 The single-period consumption decision

would still *prefer* to spend it now. In order to persuade you to lend the money the person would need to give you an incentive – at minimum that when he or she gives you the money back the amount will be enough not only to repay the £1 but also to compensate you for giving up the chance of being able to spend it now! In other words, you would expect payment of the initial sum plus interest.

In Figure 10.1 it is clear that the interest required is 10 per cent – but what does this actually mean? Strictly speaking the interest rate of 10 per cent which you require is simply a reflection of *your* time preference for consumption – in order to forgo the chance of spending the money now you are willing to wait for a year in order to spend £1.10.

The other side of this coin is that the borrower is *not* willing to wait a year to spend the pound but wants to spend it now and hence is *willing* to pay a price, that is, 10 pence in interest. If your time preference for consumption was zero, that is you were not concerned about when you spend your money, then you would be a very unusual person indeed – in economic terms you would be irrational!

Given that people are generally rational in their economic decisions, what we have described above is generally applicable – lenders wish to be compensated while borrowers are willing to compensate. If this were not the case there would be no capital markets and there would be no investment undertaken – in fact all wealth would be consumed as soon as it was produced!

From the above discussion you have probably already gathered that any individual's rate of time preference is simply the rate of interest they are willing to accept for forgoing consumption in the present. The concept underlying this rationale is that of opportunity cost. If a person gives up the chance to consume all of his or her income now he or she incurs the opportunity cost of doing so.

So the rate of time preference is the rate of interest acceptable to the lender and reflects the opportunity cost to the lender of not spending his or her money *now*.

■ ■ ■ Self-Assessment Question ■ ■ ■ ■ ■ ■ ■ ■ ■ ■ ■ ■ ■

Q1 Explain why it is considered economically irrational if a lender is prepared to accept a rate of interest which is less than his or her time preference for consumption.

It therefore follows that the single-period consumption decision above captures all the salient features of the nature of the investment decision itself. That is, it demonstrates that not all individuals (or firms) will have the same rate of time preference for consumption, that this rate is just the interest rate acceptable to them and that it is intended to cover the opportunity cost of their capital. Thus, another way of thinking about this is that the rate of time preference *is* the rate of interest and that this is simply the opportunity cost of capital. In our example above the opportunity cost (to you) of lending the £1 is 10 pence. It is also important to realise that this additional 10 pence is not a profit – it is merely compensation for the loss of opportunity to consume the £1 in an earlier period.

The 10 pence would only constitute a profit, in economic terms, if the nearest alternative of the £1 could only generate *no* interest at all. The key element here is once again opportunity cost and it relates directly to the concept of profit: we can identify two definitions of profit, one of which is commonly used and the other which is less well understood. The two definitions relate to *accounting profit* and *economic profit*.

■ Accounting profit is the financial surplus over all accounting costs, excluding opportunity costs – it is essentially reported profit.

■ Economic profit is the financial surplus over all accounting *and* opportunity costs – it is the true measure of an investment's added value.

This distinction is very important since it explains the nature of profit more clearly, in that opportunity cost of an adopted decision can only be fully known where the decision maker is aware of most of the alternatives available. Opportunity costs are those perceived as being relevant to future actions whereas accounting costs are financial costs incurred from past actions. Thus, whereas accounting profit is a reporting device, economic profit is a decision-making device.

For example, supposing a small firm earned an accounting profit of £40,000 in a particular year and the firm's capital asset value was £500,000. This is a (simple) return on capital of 8 per cent. However supposing the owner(s) of the firm liquidated the firm's assets and put the money in a bank account at a prevailing interest rate of 10 per cent – the profit generated would be £50,000. From an economic point of view the firm's owner(s) have incurred an *opportunity cost* of £10,000 even though they have still made a profit of £40,000! That is, they have made an accounting profit but incurred an economic loss.

If we reverse the outcome so that the profit from operating the firm was £50,000 while the prevailing interest rate was 8 per cent, then we can say that the firm has made an economic profit of £10,000, that is, it has covered its opportunity cost (£40,000) and added £10,000 of value. This of course assumes that the best possible alternative use for the capital was in a bank account at 8 per cent – it may well be the case that the firm's owner(s) could have liquidated the firm and put the money into another enterprise which produced a 15 per cent rate of return.

This is a rather laborious example to highlight a fairly straightforward concept. However, it is important that the meaning of economic profit is clearly understood since all the investment appraisal techniques you will use from Part III depend on that concept being properly understood.

We can briefly summarise the economic nature of investment. First, it is for the purpose of raising future consumption levels. In practice this means expanding the productive capacity of organisations in order that the higher levels of consumption can be met. Second, in order to maximise these higher levels of future consumption and wealth, appropriate techniques need to be employed which minimise the opportunity costs that exist with any capital expenditure. The rest of this chapter is devoted to a number of techniques widely employed in investment appraisal.

■ ■ ■ Self-Assessment Question ■ ■ ■ ■ ■ ■ ■ ■ ■ ■ ■ ■

 Q2 Briefly state, in your own words, what you understand by the concept of opportunity cost.

■ 10.3 Traditional Techniques

There are essentially two of these – the *return on capital employed* (RoCe) and *payback method* – and they each utilise a particular *decision criterion* for the selection of investment projects.

10.3.1   Return on Capital Employed

There are a number of definitions of this technique which simply confuse matters – that is, there is no single definition of what RoCe actually is. Indeed even the name varies between textbooks. It is sometimes referred to as the book rate of return and sometimes the accounting rate of return as well as the return on capital employed! Irrespective of what it might be called it further suffers from the weakness that there are different ways of calculating it. That in itself would not be a major problem except for the fact that these different calculation bases usually produce very different results.

The one certain thing about this technique, however it is used in practice, is that there is agreement on what the decision criterion is – to accept the investment alternative which provides the highest rate of return on capital employed and which simultaneously meets the organisation's own 'target rate of return'.

We will return to the 'target rate of return' issue shortly, but for the moment there are essentially two ways in which the RoCe can be calculated – first on the basis of the initial capital employed as defined in the formula below:

$$\left[\left[\dfrac{\sum\limits_{t=1}^{N} P}{N}\right]/K_0\right] * 100$$

where P = annual profit, N = years and K_0 = the initial capital employed. Second, on the basis of the average capital employed given below:

$$\left[\left[\dfrac{\sum\limits_{t=1}^{N} P}{N}\right]/K\right] * 100$$

where P = annual profit, N = years and $\bar{K}$ = average capital employed.

These look very similar but in fact are very different. For example, suppose a firm is considering investing in retooling one of its production lines. This will require an initial capital outlay of £30,000 plus perhaps £3000 of working capital to be made available for the new facility if it is accepted. Over the expected life of the production line (say five years) depreciation will produce a 'scrap value' of £2000. The latter data and the information in Table 10.1 can be used to calculate both versions of the RoCe.

Because the cash flows in Table 10.1 are net then the profit here is simply the net cash flow minus the depreciation. To find the depreciation amount each year we simply subtract the scrap value from the initial capital outlay and divide by the project's economic life so that we get:

(£30,000 – £2000)/5 = £5600 per year

Table 10.1 Net cash flow

Year	Net cash flow £ (revenue – cost)
1	12,000
2	10,000
3	8,000
4	5,000
5	2,000

So the annual profit is simply:

Year	NCF		Depreciation		Profit
1	12,000	–	5,600	=	6,400
2	10,000	–	5,600	=	4,400
3	8,000	–	5,600	=	2,400
4	5,000	–	5,600	=	–600
5	2,000	–	5,600	=	–3,600

So the average annual profit is £9200/5 = £1840. The initial capital employed is the £30,000 plus the £3000 working capital so the average capital employed is given by:

$$[(£30,000 – £2000)/2] + £2000 + £3000 = £19,000$$

Notice that the denominator is 2 because there are two 'units' of capital employed in the project – the initial outlay and its scrap value. However, the scrap value needs to be added on at the end since it represents capital tied up in the project which is realisable through selling the equipment as scrap, that is, it has an opportunity cost. Similarly the working capital is also money tied up in the project so it needs to be added as well.

So, now we have our annual average profit figure and our average capital employed figure we are in a position to calculate the RoCe using both definitions of the method, that is, the initial capital employed only (£33,000) and the average capital employed (£19,000). Using only the initial capital employed the technique gives the following:

$$\frac{\text{Average Annual Profit}}{\text{Initial Capital Employed}} \times 100$$

(£1840/£33,000) × 100 = 5.575%

The investment would generate a RoCe of just under 6 per cent. But using the average capital employed we get a very different result:

$$\frac{\text{Average Annual Profit}}{\text{Average Capital Employed}} \times 100$$

(£1840/£19,000) × 100 = 9.68%

Clearly there is a difference in the two RoCe's yet they come from exactly the same project! This is one of the drawbacks of the technique – its definition is too ambiguous and therefore is open to manipulation. For example, a manager may want an investment to be approved for his or her own reasons and may therefore prefer to use the average capital employed version. Even worse, suppose a tiny investment of a few hundred pounds (unforeseen) was needed in year 3 – this would produce a denominator in the average method of 3 instead of 2, thus raising the RoCe even higher than 9.68 per cent.

In addition, it is quite clear that the rate of return in the RoCe method is unlikely to bear any strong relationship with the actual profitability of an investment since profit is an absolute number, whereas the rate of return is a percentage and easily manipulated. So this method could easily select the 'wrong' project from several competing projects.

Note too that it treats each pound, no matter when it arrives (year 1, 2 and so on), as if it is worth the same to the firm. This fundamentally breaks the rationale behind the investment–consumption trade-off since each pound has an opportunity cost. And finally, suppose the firm in this example had a target rate of return of 10 per cent – would it accept this project? It totally depends on which version of RoCe it used. If it used the initial capital employed version it would reject the project, but it would accept it if it used the average capital employed version! Quite clearly this is illogical.

There is one other problem associated with the method. It uses average annual profit in both versions but the longer a project's economic life is, the higher this average will tend to be – it is simply an arithmetical fact that the average will rise if a number greater than 1 is added to the numerator but only 1 is added to the denominator. This means the RoCe method will always tend to favour projects which have a longer time span and means that the method is arguably open to a higher risk element being involved since it favours longer term projects.

There are, however, a number of advantages to the approach in general. First of all, it is simple to understand what a 'percentage return' is. Most managers are comfortable with the notion of a 'rate of return' and second, from a manager's point of view, his or her salary and/or bonuses are often related to the 'profitability' of the firm and 'profitability' is so often measured in terms of a firm's return on capital employed!

Finally there is the issue of the 'target rate of return'. It is often the case that the 'target' is simply a function of historical performance in that if past investments have generated, say, a 22 per cent return then the management expect future investments to do the same. Of course this is also very questionable since economic conditions change, markets change and technology changes over time. Hence there is no reason to expect the past to be a guide to the future.

It could be argued that in fact this 'target return' setting may lead to reduced competitiveness since firms will necessarily need to adjust prices in order to achieve the 'target return' on their investments.

From an economic perspective the advantages of this 'traditional' technique in no way compensate for the underlying lack of economic rationality which the technique exhibits.

▦ ▦ ▦ Self-Assessment Question ▦ ▦ ▦ ▦ ▦ ▦ ▦ ▦ ▦ ▦ ▦ ▦

Q3 Identify the key weaknesses in the RoCe technique. Why might management still prefer this approach to investment appraisal?

▦ ▦

10.3.2 The Payback Method

This second 'traditional' technique of investment appraisal essentially boils down to a very simple decision criterion which is: select the project which returns the capital outlay in the *shortest* time and does so within the organisation's *payback horizon*. Unfortunately it also suffers from the same problem as RoCe in that it tends to be given different names such as the capital recovery period, the pay-off period and the payback period. Unlike RoCe, however, all of these are calculated in the same way. Consider the information in Table 10.2.

Project 1 will pay for its capital outlay in under 3 years and this can be calculated quite simply as shown in Table 10.3.

Since the capital outlay required to be paid back is only £100,000 it is clear that year 3 revenues are in excess of what is actually required. Hence the payback period for project 1 is simply:

2 (years) + (1000/4000) = 2.25 years

that is, the payback period for project 1 is 2 years and 3 months. For project 2 the same calculation gives:

£5000 (year 1) + £6000 (year 2) + [(£18,000–£11,000)/£8000]
= 1 + 2 + (£7000/£8000) = 2.875 years

that is, 2 years and 10½ months.

Table 10.2 Capital outlay and project revenues

	Capital outlay £	Project revenues £				
	Year 0	Year 1	Year 2	Year 3	Year 4	Year 5
Project 1	10,000	5,000	4,000	4,000	2,000	
Project 2	18,000	5,000	6,000	8,000	6,000	4,000

Table 10.3   Cumulative revenue

Annual revenue £	Cumulative revenue £	Still to be recovered by end of year £
Year 0 = −10,000	0	10,000
Year 1 = 5,000	5,000	5,000
Year 2 = 4,000	9,000	1,000
Year 3 = 4,000	13,000	0

Given the decision rule employed in the payback method the choice between the two projects is straightforward – project 1 recovers its capital outlay the fastest and therefore should be selected while project 2 is rejected. Unfortunately this very simple decision rule leaves much to be desired. If we consider the economic life of each of the above projects it is clear that over project 1's life it will generate a cumulative revenue of £15,000 which is 50 per cent more than its capital outlay. In the case of project 2 it will generate a cumulative revenue of £29,000 which is 61 per cent above its outlay, yet project 2 would be rejected using the payback rule!

This problem is not simply restricted to the 'rule' itself. It is also a function of a very common practice in the private sector which is to impose a 'payback horizon' on investment capital. That is to say, many firms will only invest if the capital outlay can be recovered within a specified period – the firm's payback horizon. In the case of the example above let us suppose the payback horizon is 3 years. In this case both projects are acceptable but which one should be chosen? On the basis of the decision rule it would be project 1 yet again even though project 2 is clearly superior.

An additional problem here is that project 1's economic life clearly ends in year 4 but project 2 looks as though it will continue to generate revenues even beyond year 5. Indeed it is a feature of the payback method that revenue occurring beyond the imposed payback horizon tends to be ignored since it exists 'outside' the framework of the simple decision rule. These criticisms of course can only be levelled at the method where management are using it in the strictest form.

But even so there remains the problem that the method itself leads to ambiguity in decision making since it is not robust or objective enough to identify the correct project other than through chance! Why is this? Put simply, the method is open to misuse since it is a conscious decision to impose an arbitrary payback horizon and to ignore revenues which occur beyond it.

In addition suppose a project requires additional capital inputs at some point during its economic life – when should the payback period be calculated from? This is not at all clear. Because of the arbitrary nature of the method and its openness to misuse it can also be used to justify investments which are not necessarily in the interests of the firm but rather in the interests of the decision maker. In short, it is far too subjective and open to manipulation.

Finally, the method if used widely in firms carries a serious economic danger: because of its nature the decision maker will almost always select the alternative investment which recovers the capital in the shortest period of time. Hence it is an implicitly risk-averse approach to investment decision making. It is not a method which is likely to thrust a firm to the forefront of product development or technology since these take time! Therefore firms which use payback as the main appraisal method run the serious risk of becoming less competitive over time if they will only support investments which effectively have a short economic life.

Although the method is simple to apply and to understand and is 'good' for risk-averse firms, it does suffer from a number of serious problems, one of which you have already seen, that is, it tends to ignore anything outside the payback horizon and therefore ignores cash inflows which exist outside that time period but which may be very significant. But more importantly, it ignores the time value of money itself despite the fact that it puts greater emphasis on early cash flows – this is because it does not use the opportunity cost of capital to discount any of the cash flows of any of the competing projects.

Thus, in terms of achieving value for money for the investing firm it leaves too much to chance and cannot be seen as an operational tool within the context of a fully worked out investment strategy. This is mainly because it ignores opportunity costs and the fundamental meaning of profit.

The payback method has the problem of being: arbitrary; unrelated to the cost of capital; it discourages innovation (because it is basically a risk-averse method); and ignores cash flows which lie beyond it. Its strengths are its simplicity and interpretation, and it is risk-averse and useful for initial screening of proposals.

However, these cannot outweigh the fact that the method fails totally to take account of the time value of money and hence, only by chance, will it select an investment project which does maximise the wealth of the firm.

■ ■ ■ Self-Assessment Question ■ ■ ■ ■ ■ ■ ■ ■ ■ ■ ■ ■ ■

 Q4 Despite all the weaknesses of payback, why might small firms be more inclined to use the method?

One way round this problem for firms is to set a payback horizon and a target rate of return so that the tendency to favour short-term projects (payback) is compensated for by the tendency to favour longer term projects (RoCe). This of course does not deal with the problems of manipulation and the time value of money.

Two approaches to investment appraisal which do explicitly take account of the time value of money (that is, the opportunity cost of capital) are the net present value method and the internal rate of return method. We consider these below.

■ 10.4 Discounted Cash Flow Techniques

The fact that a potential opportunity cost is always linked to alternative uses of capital, including its consumption, suggests that over time money carries with it a *time value* which has nothing whatsoever to do with inflation. That is, given that people do have a time preference for consumption, then it follows that the money they could spend now instead of lending must have a time value! What is this time value of money? The answer completely depends on the rate of time preference of consumption, that is, it is simply the interest rate the lender is willing to accept – and that interest rate needs to be sufficient to cover the lender's opportunity cost. A lender may provide one pound to a friend at a rate of 10 per cent so that after one year it is worth £1.10 to the lender. But note that since the extra 10 pence merely compensates the lender for the opportunity cost incurred then the £1.10 after one year is equivalent in value *to the lender* of the pound now. To put this another way, the *present value* of the £1 to the lender is identical to its *future value* of £1.10. This also means therefore that the present value of £1.10 (receivable after one year) is £1. There is thus a connection between the future value of money and the present value of money which has nothing to do with inflation but is controlled via the time value of money itself. So we can say that each pound has a present value (PV) and a future value (FV). The process of discounting is an explicit attempt to take full account of this and is written as:

$$FV(£) = PV(1 + i)^t$$

where i reflects our time preference (opportunity cost of forgoing present consumption) for consuming goods and services. Thus i is simply the interest rate. As an example we can say that the future value of £1.00 in 5 years' time, at an interest rate of 6 per cent is:

$$£1.00(1 + 0.06)^5 = £1.00 \times 1.3382 = £1.34$$

and this is irrespective of the rate of inflation since the latter affects all values and not simply your £1. Reversing this process implies that in order to give up £1.00 now the FV must at least equal the PV of the £1.00: that is, the FV must be *discounted* at the same rate of interest. So:

$$PV(£1.34) = £1.34(1 + 0.06)^{-5} = £1.34 \times 0.747 = £1.00$$

When we do this we call the interest rate a *discount rate*. The term in brackets is referred to as the discount rate $(1 + 0.06)$ and when this is put to the power of $-t$ (in this case 5), the whole term $(1 + 0.06)^{-5}$ is referred to as the *discount factor*. Alternatively we could discount the £1.34 using a different approach.

$$PV(\pounds1.34) = \pounds1.34/(1.06)^5$$

This means exactly the same thing but note that the power numeral in this formulation does *not* have a negative sign. Tables of discount factors and future value factors are provided as an Appendix at the end of this book.

■ ■ ■ Self-Assessment Question ■ ■ ■ ■ ■ ■ ■ ■ ■ ■ ■ ■

Calculate the discount factor which needs to be applied to £1 for the following discount rates: 8 per cent over 6 years; 12 per cent over 3 years; 20 per cent over 20 years; 6 per cent over 40 years. What can you ascertain about the relationship between the discount rate and the time period?

Now that we are clear on the numerical method used to relate future values to present values we can begin to investigate the two DCF techniques of net present value and internal rate of return.

10.4.1   The Net Present Value Technique

The discounting process explicitly takes account of the time value of money, that is it explicitly takes account of the opportunity cost of the investor's capital. This is exactly what the DCF methods of investment appraisal do, by utilising the theoretical relationship (which we have already established) between the present value of money receivable in the future and its current opportunity cost. The concept of present value is the logical end to the process of discounting and can easily be defined as *the discounted cash flows arising from the economic life of a project minus the capital outlay of the project*.

With this definition the present value of a single cash flow (A) arriving at time (t) in the future is simply $A_t (1 + i)^{-t}$. Notice it is just the discounting formula but this time with a cash flow associated with it. As is usual, the term i is the discount rate. So the latter equation tells us the present value of A after a certain time and at a certain discount rate, but to complete the picture we need to establish the net present value (NPV) and this is simply: $PV - K_0$, where K_0 = the capital outlay.

The capital outlay has a subscript of zero to indicate that it occurs in year zero, that is, at the start of an investment project (by definition!). Usually the capital outlay is not subject to discounting, since it is being spent immediately and not over time, unless it actually is spread over a sizeable period of time which can be the case with very large projects and/or projects which simply cannot be undertaken immediately and require the capital to be entered at specific and crucial stages. The formula for NPV is given as:

$$\left[\sum_{A=1}^{N} A(1 + i)^{-t} \right] - K_0$$

where the terms have already been described as above. Here we will be assuming that the capital (K_0) is in fact injected at the start of a project's economic life. Let us consider an example of a single project which is not competing for resources with any other possible investment other than a financial one such as a bank account and it has an expected economic life of 4 years. The capital outlay is £10,000 and the cash inflow expected is given in Table 10.4.

Table 10.4 Cash flow

Year	Cash flow £
0	−10,000
1	4,000
2	5,000
3	3,000
4	2,000

Assuming the investment has no scrap value at the end of the 4 years the total monetary value of the cash inflows is £14,000. If the opportunity cost of capital for this firm is just the going rate of interest it could get (say 8 per cent) by putting the £10,000 in the bank then the cash inflows need to be discounted by 8 per cent. Using the formula given above this gives:

$$£4000(1.08)^{-1} + £5000(1.08)^{-2} + £3000(1.08)^{-3} + £2000(1.08)^{-4}$$

$$= £3703.7 + £4286.7 + £2381.5 + £1470$$

So the present value of the cash inflows is £11,841.9. And the NPV is (£11,841.9 − £10,000) = £1841.9. Now, the alternative available is for the firm to put the money into the bank. If it chose to do this it would receive, after 4 years, a terminal value given by £10,000(1.08)^4 = £13,605, that is, a financial 'profit' of £3605 which is clearly better than the 'profit' receivable from the project – or is it? The 'profit' from the project is *real* profit in the sense that it is an *economic* profit whereas the 'profit' from the bank is an *accounting* profit. To see this all we need do is discount the terminal value of the £10,000 sitting in a bank account for 4 years at the firm's opportunity cost of capital of 8 per cent so that we get:

$$£13,605(1.08)^{-4} = £10,000$$

In other words, there is a financial surplus from the bank alternative but there is no economic surplus. It therefore follows that the best alternative for the £10,000 is to put it into a physical investment instead of the only available financial investment, a bank account. Every series of cash flows, when discounted, generates an NPV graph associated with it. The graph is usually referred to as the NPV profile of the stream of cash flows relevant to a given project. We can construct an NPV profile (Figure 10.2) for the example above.

There is no reason to expect a straight line but most NPV profiles will not be too dissimilar to this one. As is clear from the above, NPV is a *negative function* of the discount rate. We already know the project gives a total cash inflow of £14,000 and that the capital outlay is £10,000; therefore, discounting all the cash flows at a *zero* discount rate gives an NPV of £4000. That is, the intersection of the NPV profile with the *y*-axis is the monetary value of the cash flows once the capital outlay has been deducted. It is only the monetary value because a zero discount rate means, by definition, that the cash flows have not been discounted at all! If we then discount the cash flows by 8 per cent, as we have, we move down the line to an NPV of £1842. If we raise the discount rate above 8 per cent the NPV falls again and, eventually, if the discount rate is high enough the NPV will fall to zero. It is perfectly possible that the NPV could be less than zero – that is, it could be negative. This would mean the project was incurring opportunity costs and making an economic loss whereas at every point above the interest rate axis the project returns an economic profit. At the point where the NPV line meets the interest rate axis all opportunity costs of the capital have been covered and a zero economic profit has been made.

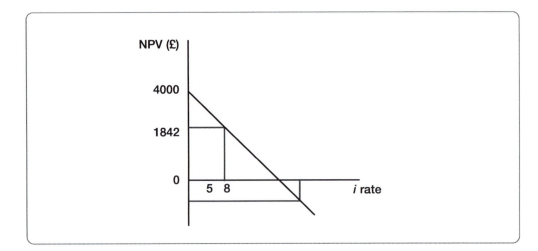

Figure 10.2 NPV profile

■ ■ ■ Self-Assessment Question ■ ■ ■ ■ ■ ■ ■ ■ ■ ■ ■ ■

Q6 Apply a discount rate of 15 per cent to the project's cash inflows and calculate the resulting NPV. Provide a very brief economic interpretation of the answer.

So, to find the NPV of a stream of cash inflows is simply a matter of applying the correct formula in the correct way to the relevant data. It is also usually a good idea to try a number of discount rates, including high ones, so that the NPV profile can be plotted against these rates. It also enables us to check how sensitive the NPV is to the discount rate as it rises – this is important if we assume a given discount rate applies for the whole of a project's life since, if it does change at some point (upwards) the NPV falls faster. This can be seen from Figure 10.3.

The sensitivity of the NPV to the discount rate is also a quick way of determining the risk to the project if the discount rate were to rise at some point. The NPV of project A loses the majority of its economic value if the discount rate rises from *x* to *y* per cent, while in the case of project B a much smaller loss in economic value occurs for the identical increase in the discount rate. Thus we can see that project A is much more sensitive to discount rate changes than project B. Hence project A is a more risky project with respect to the discount rate. Another way of interpreting this is that we can define the relationship here simply as an elasticity (which you met in Chapter 5). That is, the steeper the slope of an NPV line, the lower its elasticity and the higher a project's exposure to risk.

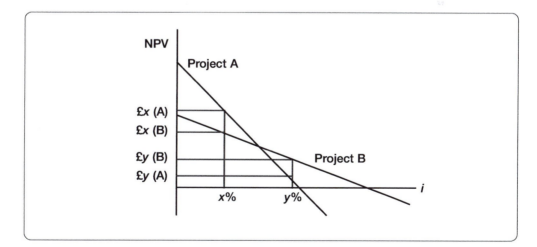

Figure 10.3 NPV sensitivity to the discount rate

We will consider risk in much more detail in Chapter 11. In the meantime let us return to the numerical example we used to highlight the weaknesses of the payback technique but this time apply the NPV technique to the same data. If we assume that the market rate of interest is 10 per cent then we can use that rate to discount the relevant cash flows and find the NPV of both projects in Table 10.5.

Project 1 $5K/(1.1)^1 + 4K/(1.1)^2 + 4K/(1.1)^3 + 2K/(1.1)^4$

Project 2 $5K/(1.1)^1 + 6K/(1.1)^2 + 8K/(1.1)^3 + 6K/(1.1)^4 + 4K(1.1)^5$

PV of project 1 = £12.22K
PV of project 2 = £22.1K

NPV (project 1) = PV – K_0 = £12.22K – £10K = £2.22K
NPV (project 2) = PV – K_0 = £22.1K – £18K = £4.1K

The NPV method produces a very different result from the payback method. Whereas the latter suggested that project 1 is preferable, the former is quite clearly indicating that in fact project 2 is the best project since it maximises economic profit. Of course this type of NPV calculation can only be correctly applied if projects 1 and 2 are *mutually exclusive*, that is, if they do not depend on each other. There are investment alternatives which are not always mutually exclusive even though they may appear so. For example, the decision to build a new hospital rests on past decisions to invest in training medical staff – these are clearly interdependent investment decisions. However, if the investment choice was between training medical staff and training teachers this would represent a mutually exclusive choice set. In practice most investment decisions do actually involve having to decide between competing mutually exclusive alternatives. There is, however, one aspect to the example above which unfortunately complicates matters. If you look at the two projects they do not exhibit the same time profiles – that is, they clearly have different economic lives. This raises a problem.

Table 10.5   Cash flows for NPV calculation

	Capital outlay £	Project revenues £				
	Year 0	Year 1	Year 2	Year 3	Year 4	Year 5
Project 1	10,000	5,000	4,000	4,000	2,000	
Project 2	18,000	5,000	6,000	8,000	6,000	4,000

The Replacement Cycle Problem

Many projects have an economic life which is less than required, that is the investment, or part of it, must be replaced at some time in the future – often within the time frame of a strategic plan. In this case, a project's NPV is measured in annual equivalent terms, that is, equivalence in terms of x replacements during the desired time frame. So how does this work in practice?

Project 1 has an economic life of 4 years whereas project 2 has an economic life of 5 years. This means we cannot compare the NPVs of these choices since they are not strictly comparable – that is, the opportunity cost of capital applies to each one over a different period of time. Or to put it more simply, each £ arriving in year 1, 2 and so on for project 1 has a different opportunity cost and this is also true for project 2. However since project 2 has an additional year of revenues then we cannot compare its NPV with that of project 1. To do so would be to completely invalidate the theoretical basis of the time value of money. It would be a non-rational comparison. Hence we need to put them on the same 'time' footing in order to compare them properly. To do this we begin with the project which has the longest economic life and then calculate the number of times each of the others would need replacing within that longest time period if one of them was to be selected.

Project 2 takes 5 years (longer than project 1) so that is the number we need to use in relation to the comparison. To do this we must find the lowest common multiple into which project 2 and project 1 can be divided. Obviously this is 20. So, over 20 years project 2 would need to be replaced three times and project 1 four times. That is, to correctly compare these competing projects we need to do so on the basis that there are four project 2s and five project 1s! Unfortunately it is not just a simple matter of 'adding up' the four project 2s or the five project 1s to see which has the highest combined NPV. This is because with the first replacement of project 2 its revenues need to be discounted in years 6 to 10, not years 1 to 5 again.

So, we need to account for the fact that the replacement cycle of three times or four times or however many times requires the discounting to be applied for different years. This process produces an equation which takes account of the replacement cycle problem and is given below and generates the annual equivalent NPV (AENPV):

$$\text{AENPV} = \left[\frac{i}{1- (1 + i)^{-t}} \right] \times \text{NPV}$$

(The expression in brackets is referred to as the annual equivalent factor)

So AENPV = AEF × NPV

Tables already exist to transform NPVs into annual equivalent NPVs – and this is useful even if a project is not to be replaced, that is, the AENPV tells us how the project compares with others of different economic lives – a crucial piece of data. A table for annual equivalent factors is given in the Appendix at the end of this book.

Using the table provided (or the equation above) we can check if project 2 really does produce the best economic value for the firm's investment funds. Looking *along* the interest rate row in the AEF Table in the Appendix to 10 per cent and then *down* the years columns to the relevant economic life we get:

Project 1 lasts for 4 years so its annual equivalent factor is: 0.31547

Project 2 lasts for 5 years so its annual equivalent factor is: 0.26379

Using the definition of AENPV above, that is AEF * NPV, we get the following:

Project 1 AENPV = 0.31547 × £2.22K = £0.7K

Project 2 AENPV = 0.26379 × £4.1K = £1.08K

As you can see, in annual equivalent terms project 2 is still preferred, but notice that in these terms its AENPV is 54 per cent above that of project 1 whereas in straightforward NPV terms it is nearly 85 per cent higher than project 1. Hence the difference between these projects in economic value is not as great as the 'normal' NPV calculation would indicate. This demonstrates the danger of using 'normal' NPV analysis in the case where alternative investment projects have different economic lives – it is quite commonly the case that the true value of a project in annual equivalent terms is quite different than in NPV terms. As pointed out above, it is often better to express NPVs in annual equivalent terms even where alternatives have the same economic life since it is a good 'habit' just in case we forget to do so when they do have different economic lives!

A Quicker Approach to NPV

In the examples so far we have been using the same procedure to calculate the PV of revenues. That is, we have been discounting each of the revenues separately. This was necessary because in the above examples the revenue streams contained non-identical values. What if the expected revenues from a project were the same over its expected economic life? That is to say that instead of £50,000 in year 1 and £42,000 in year 2 and so on the revenues were £40,000 for each year of the project's economic life. In this case (and it is quite common due to simplifying assumptions which are made by management) we can use what is known as the PV factor formula – this uses the fact that if all cash flows are the same then we are dealing with a constant stock as opposed to a variable flow of cash which varies in different years. The formula is given below:

$$PV \text{ factor} = \left[\frac{(1 + i)^t - 1}{i\,(1 + i)^t} \right]$$

Suppose a firm is seeking to establish whether a positive NPV will be generated from an investment project which requires a capital outlay of £100,000 and is expected to produce a constant net revenue stream of £15,000 over its 10-year life. We simply substitute the relevant data (discount rate and time period) into the above formula and multiply this by the constant revenue stream then subtract the capital outlay from the total. Again we use a 10 per cent discount rate:

$$\left[\frac{(1.1)^{10} - 1}{0.1(1.1)^{10}} \right] * £15K$$

$$= 6.1445 * £15K = £92.17K - £100K$$

$$= -£7.83K$$

Thus, the NPV from this project will be negative! It must be rejected because although the cash inflows amount to £50K more than the capital outlay (an accounting profit) in reality it makes an economic loss of nearly £8K. This is seen more clearly in Figure 10.4.

At a zero discount rate the NPV of this project is £50K. However at a discount rate of 10 per cent the NPV is negative. Notice that if the discount rate was 8 per cent the NPV would be zero. Does this mean zero profit is generated? The answer is no – it simply means there is no economic profit but there will be an accounting profit. To put it another way, if 8 per cent was the best available rate of interest then the £100K capital could have been put into a financial investment (deposit account, bonds and so on) and over the period of 10

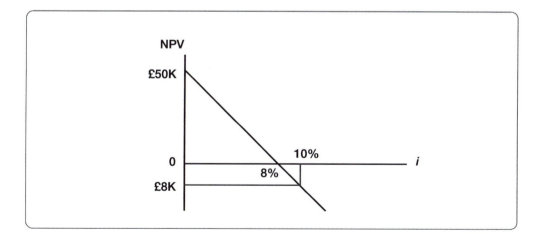

Figure 10.4   An NPV profile with economic losses

years it would have produced £100K(1.08)^{10} = £215.89K which is a financial (or accounting) profit of £115.89K. If we reverse this process and calculate what the present value of £215.89K receivable after 10 years is *today* we get:

£215.89K(1.08)$^{-10}$ = £100K

In other words, in economic terms the project would incur a zero opportunity cost if the interest (and so discount rate) was 8 per cent even though it still generates a financial return. But in this case the discount rate is actually 10 per cent so what has actually happened? At 10 per cent over 10 years the capital would accumulate (in a financial account) to £259.4K but in this project a real loss is occurring. To check this we need only take each of the project's cash inflows as they arrive and reinvest them in a financial account over the remainder of the project's life. Thus the first cash inflow of £15K would be in an account at 10 per cent for 9 years, the second for 8 years and so on. At the end of the 10 years the terminal value of these cash inflows would be £239.07K. Now, if we discount this terminal value back to a present value we find the following:

£239.07K(1.1)$^{-10}$ = £92.17K

that is, exactly the NPV we have already calculated above. Therefore in economic terms the project has incurred an opportunity cost of £7.83K and in purely financial terms it has incurred (a non-discounted) loss of:

(£259.4K – £239.07K) = £20.33K

What this reveals is the true nature of the NPV technique and of its theoretical rationale in that it is exclusively considering the alternative to the project, that is, instead of putting the £100K into the project the money could be loaned to the capital market as a financial investment.

■ ■ ■ Self-Assessment Question ■ ■ ■ ■ ■ ■ ■ ■ ■ ■ ■ ■ ■

Q7 Explain why it makes sense to use the PV factor formula to calculate the present value of a constant stream of cash flows.

In summary we can now state explicitly what the set of decision rules for the NPV technique must be:

- ■ If NPV > zero a project is 'acceptable' because it gives an economic profit.

- ■ If NPV < zero a project is not 'acceptable' because it gives an economic loss.

- ■ If NPV = zero a project is 'acceptable' because it incurs zero opportunity costs.

The Effect of Inflation

We have already established that the opportunity cost of capital is nothing to do with price inflation. However this does not mean that the latter can be ignored! Most investment appraisals require future revenues (cash inflows) to be forecast – this means running the risk that the purchasing power of these revenues will be reduced by inflation (see Chapter 2 for an explanation of inflation and purchasing power). In some way this needs to be accounted for. Either we can *deflate* expected future revenues using an appropriate price index, for example a consumer or a producer price deflator, or alternatively we can build anticipated inflation into our discount rate in order to produce a *real discount rate*. This is given as:

$$R_i = [(1 + M_i)/(1 + P)] - 1$$

where R_i is the real rate of discount, M_i is the market rate of interest, and P is the price index deflator. If this is not done over a project's estimated economic life a positive NPV result may in fact prove to be misleading and an opportunity cost for the firm could be incurred. It is very often the case that the opportunity cost of capital to a firm is the prevailing market rate of interest, and hence this is the rate it will use as the appropriate discount rate for NPV analysis. If the market rate of interest is 10 per cent and the expected rate of inflation is 3.5 per cent the real rate of discount to be used is $[(1.1)/(1.035)] - 1 = 0.0628$, that is, it is 6.28 per cent. It is important to note here that the commonly held belief that the real rate of interest is just the market rate minus the inflation rate is wrong! Obviously, in an economy where inflation is (or may be) a problem it is very important for firms to be thinking in terms of the real NPV of projects and/or the real annual equivalent NPV of projects. So far we have considered the NPV method, the annual equivalent value of an NPV and the role of inflation in project appraisal. You should be clear now on how to use these concepts and methods and how to interpret them in terms of economic profit or loss. You should also be able to construct an NPV profile, suggest if it is sensitive to the discount rate and assess whether it may therefore be too 'risky'. You now also have the conceptual and practical tools to undertake an investment appraisal covering payback, RoCE, NPV and AENPV. There is, however, another discounted cash flow technique known as the internal rate of return (IRR) and we now turn to examining this as an approach to investment appraisal.

10.4.2 The Internal Rate of Return Technique

The IRR of a project is that discount rate which would be required to reduce a project's NPV to zero. That is,

$$\text{IRR } 1 \quad \sum_{A=1}^{N} A(1 + i) - K_0 = 0$$

This simply means if we sum (add up) all the cash flows discounted by i from the first cash flow ($A = 1$) in year 1 to the last cash flow ($A = N$) in year N and subtract the capital cost (K_0) we will get an NPV of zero because i is the unique value to achieve this outcome. That is, we need to find a value for i which reduces the NPV of a stream of cash inflows to zero. Let us go back to our NPV example, where if the discount rate had been 8 per cent instead of 10 per cent the NPV would have been zero instead of −£7.83K. Figure 10.4 is repeated as Figure 10.5 but with some additional information.

At an 8 per cent discount rate this project generates a zero NPV. Since the definition of IRR is simply that discount rate which produces a zero NPV then it follows that the above project has an IRR of 8 per cent. What does this mean? It means that the project's cash inflows relative to its capital outlay, over the 10-year period, will produce a rate of return of 8 per cent, and when compared to the discount rate which has been applied (that is, the market interest rate) it is clearly *less* than this and so this project, in IRR terms would be rejected. Thus if we choose a particular discount rate, at random, and it produces a zero NPV then that discount rate is known as the project's *own* internal rate of return. Of course it is only by chance that this ever happens in project appraisal but nevertheless it is often the case that management prefer projects to be expressed in terms of a rate of return. One of the problems with NPV is that management often do not know what it actually means! For this reason it is good practice to provide IRR information as well. Many private sector firms use a *'hurdle'* IRR – that is, if a project's IRR < the hurdle rate it will be rejected. The hurdle rate is often seen as the organisation's risk assessment of the project. In the public sector a test rate is often used (and set by government) to assess the public viability of a proposal. Note, however, that the IRR of a project is *not* the same as a project's return on capital employed! The latter is merely a ratio of profit to outlay and, like payback, totally ignores the opportunity cost of capital.

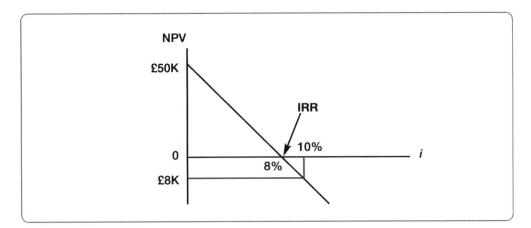

Figure 10.5   The IRR of an investment project

So, if the IRR is just a discount rate which reduces the NPV to zero is it really a separate method at all? Some economists and finance specialists would argue that it is just a special case of the NPV method and nothing more. To see this we can construct a set of decision rules for IRR which in fact are perfectly consistent with those for NPV. Since we already know that the IRR of a project is just a certain discount rate which reduces the NPV of the project to zero the IRR is simply the point of intersection of the NPV profile and the *i*-axis. Therefore there is an unambiguous relationship between NPV and IRR as follows:

- If IRR > real market rate of interest a project is 'acceptable' since this means the project is generating an economic profit.

- If IRR < real market rate of interest a project is not 'acceptable' since the project must be generating an economic loss.

- If IRR = real market rate of interest a project is 'acceptable' since the project is covering the opportunity cost of capital.

To see why some argue that the IRR is just a special case of the NPV method we can put the decision criteria of both together so that we get the following:

Decision Rules

If NPV > 0 then IRR > real market rate of interest   *accept*

If NPV < 0 then IRR < real market rate of interest   *reject*

If NPV = 0 then IRR = real market rate of interest   *accept*

■ ■ ■ Self-Assessment Question ■ ■ ■ ■ ■ ■ ■ ■ ■ ■ ■ ■

Q8 Explain why the RoCe is not the same as the IRR of a project.

The relationship between NPV and IRR is an exact one in terms of the decision rules they both use. However, although we know from theory that the IRR of a project is just that discount rate which reduces its NPV to zero there is still the matter of actually calculating it. In practice this is not as straightforward as Figure 10.5 suggests. Indeed, where a project produces cash flows for more than 3 years the calculation of the IRR becomes a problem of finding the 'answer' using complicated polynomial equations! This is outside the scope of the present book. However, there is a method we can use *to estimate* the IRR of a project and this is known as *proportional linear interpolation*. The equation for this is as follows:

$$\text{IRR} = (i_1) + \left[\frac{\text{NPV}_1}{\text{NPV}_1 + \text{NPV}_2} \right] \times (i_2 - i_1)$$

where NPV_1 is the NPV of a project using discount rate i_1 and NPV_2 is the NPV using discount rate i_2. Note that i_2 must be larger than i_1 and so NPV_2 will be smaller than NPV_1. It is a question of trial and error. Basically the method is based on choosing a discount rate i_2 which we 'guess' will produce a much lower (or even negative) NPV_2 in order that we can interpolate between the two NPVs and estimate where it cuts the i-axis. Note that if the NPV_2 is negative we still use it in the formula as a positive number.

Supposing a project has an NPV of £2000 at a discount rate of 8 per cent. If we want to know what its IRR is we can choose a higher discount rate to apply to the project's cash flows so as to deliberately produce a negative NPV. Let us choose a rate of 12 per cent and suppose this gives an NPV of £1000: this is not very good since it does not give us a negative NPV! So, let us try a rate of 15 per cent and suppose this gives an NPV of –£400. Now we have our two values – one NPV above the i-axis and one below it so we can interpolate between the two and estimate where on the axis the NPV line actually goes through.

Using the linear interpolation formula we get the following:

$$\text{IRR} = (0.08) + \left[\frac{£2000}{£2000 + £400} \times (0.15 - 0.08) \right]$$

$$= (0.08) + [0.833 \times (0.07)]$$

$$= (0.08) + 0.05831$$

$$= 0.1383$$

So the IRR is 13.83 per cent.

This approach to finding the IRR of a project is more accurate the narrower the gap between the positive and the negative NPV. So, in the presence of unstable discount rates firms may wish to use the IRR rather than the NPV to assess which one of alternative investment projects they should accept. To that extent the IRR has an advantage over the NPV method. However, this is the only advantage it has since the IRR can in fact produce very strange results depending on the nature of a project's cash flows.

■ ■ ■ Self-Assessment Question ■ ■ ■ ■ ■ ■ ■ ■ ■ ■ ■ ■ ■

Q9 Find the IRR of a project where its NPV is £400 at a discount rate of 6 per cent, and at a discount rate of 9 per cent its NPV is –£150.

Basically any investment project can have either of two types of cash flow – conventional and unconventional. A conventional cash flow is one where either all the cash flows are *positive* with no or no more than *one* negative cash flow or all the cash flows are *negative* with no or no more than *one* positive cash flow.

For example, consider the choice between six projects.

```
project 1 CF   £100   £200   £220   £120    conventional
project 2 CF   £100   £200   £150  -£220    conventional
project 3 CF  -£100  -£200  -£150  -£120    conventional
project 4 CF  -£100  -£200  -£150   £120    conventional
project 5 CF   £100  -£200   £150  -£120    unconventional
project 6 CF  -£100   £200  -£150  -£120    unconventional
```

Projects 5 and 6 exhibit unconventional cash flows because they both exhibit more than one change of sign. Project 5 goes from positive to negative to positive to negative (three changes of sign) and project 6 goes from negative to positive to negative (two changes of sign).

The basis of a 'non-conventional' cash flow is essentially one which produces an nth degree polynomial. Thus four changes of sign in the cash flow stream will produce four IRRs, for example £100, –£200, £150, –£120 gives three changes of sign so there will be three IRRs. There are numerous patterns which can be produced if the cash flows behave in an unconventional manner.

The main IRR 'patterns' are illustrated in Figure 10.6. In A we can see that the NPV profile actually gives three IRRs. In this case there is no way of knowing which one is the true IRR of the project – it could be the lowest one. In B the NPV profile in fact produces no IRR at all but it does show that the project appears to

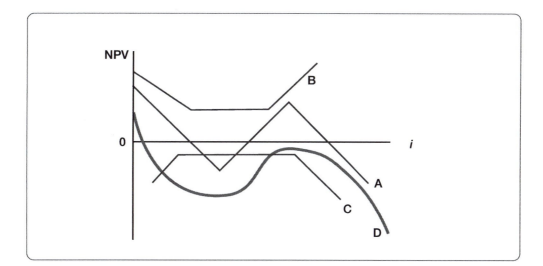

Figure 10.6 The problem of multiple IRRs

produce a positive NPV whatever the IRR might be. Even so, in terms of the IRR decision rules we could not make a decision since we do not have an IRR to compare with the real market rate of interest. In C we have a similar problem except that the NPV will always be negative – but again, with no IRR, we have no basis for comparison with the real market rate of interest. Finally, D is a special case: notice that after the NPV line goes through the i-axis the first time it then appears to 'try' to get through it again but does not quite manage to – this turns out to be a complex number, that is, it has no economic interpretation.

Quite clearly, unless a project (or all projects under consideration) produces conventional cash flows then management would find it very difficult indeed to make a rational decision on investment based on the IRR method. For this reason, it is generally considered that the NPV method is more robust, more reliable and more informative than IRR and therefore should always be the preferred method of investment appraisal over payback, RoCE and IRR. So far we have examined four techniques of investment appraisal and identified their advantages and disadvantages in relation not just to methodological issues but, more importantly, in relation to their interpretation and meaning for management decision making.

10.4.3   Revisiting Payback

The fundamental weakness of the payback technique was identified as its failure to take account of the opportunity cost of capital. This criticism needs to be amended. Consider the nature of payback – it will always select the investment alternative which recovers the capital outlay the fastest. If you think about it this means that the technique, despite its simplicity, is actually attempting to account for the opportunity cost of capital, albeit in a very simplistic manner. This is simply because the technique puts greater emphasis on earlier cash inflows than on later cash inflows. In other words it is *implicitly* discounting the cash inflows! To that extent payback is not quite as useless as the standard theoretical critique would have us believe. In addition we can explicitly account for the opportunity cost of capital within the payback technique itself. It is very straightforward.

Suppose a firm which operates a 3-year payback horizon is considering a capital investment of £200K and the expected useful economic life of this investment is 5 years so that the project's profile is as follows:

Year 0	1	2	3	4	5
–£200K	£90K	£90K	£94K	£48K	£40K

The payback period will be 2 years plus $(20/94) = 2$ years and 77 days and it would therefore be accepted as a feasible investment for the firm. But what is the payback period if we discount these cash inflows by the prevailing interest rate of say 10 per cent? This is done below:

PV of cash inflows $= 81.81 + 74.38 + 70.62 + 32.78 + 24.83$

and payback is in 2 years plus (43.81/70.62) = 2 years and 226 days. That is, 147 days longer than under the simple payback technique. However the project would still be acceptable because it still manages to produce a discounted payback period which is within the firm's payback horizon. Hence, the worst feature of the technique can be overcome in this way even though its other undesirable aspects will remain!

All of the foregoing analysis implicitly makes two key assumptions: first, that management have sufficient capital funds to enable a rational choice between competing investment possibilities, and second that the revenue forecasts from such possibilities are themselves reliable. This latter issue is pursued in the next chapter, but for the moment we wish to focus on the problem of availability of funds – that is, the capital constraint problem.

■ 10.5 Capital Constraint Problems

So far an assumption has been made that when a firm is considering its investment choices it will always (if rational) opt for that investment which maximises the present value of the profit it eventually receives from the investment. In the real world, however, it is the case that it is simply not possible for management always to know all the possible investment opportunities available to the firm simply because they do not possess perfect knowledge. In any case even strenuous attempts to investigate the many possibilities available would be costly in terms of time and money.

It is generally the case that firms will seek to investigate those investment possibilities which more easily present themselves and are consistent with the nature of the business. However, this (necessarily) constrained choice is not the only constraint on a firm's investment choices – there is the small matter of investment funds to be considered! It may well be the case that a firm has spotted an excellent investment opportunity, for example a revolutionary new way of producing its product, and the management may well consider such an investment to be the best possible use of the funds available. However, the firm may simply not have the funds and/or is not in a position to borrow them. In other words, all firms will always face *capital constraints* which, in many cases, act to limit the range of possible investments which the management can even begin to consider. It follows that the choice of 'best' investment project must take place within the context of rationing the available capital among one, several or all of the feasible projects, feasible in the sense that any single project can actually be funded within the present capital constraint. There are a number of very different capital rationing problems which may face an individual firm.

In this chapter we will focus on two, the single-period problem and the multi-period problem.

10.5.1 Single-period Capital Rationing

As single-period capital rationing suggests, all we are concerned with here is the decision to allocate investment funds in a single period (say one year) across a number of competing projects. Supposing a firm has a total of £1m available for investment and has five possible projects in mind. The prevailing interest rate in the capital market is 7.5 per cent. The cost and expected returns from each are shown in Table 10.6 (all figures are in £000s).

How should this firm decide to invest its £1m? Immediately we can see that it does not have enough funds to invest in all the projects since this would cost £1.9m so there is clearly a capital rationing problem. The problem is how to maximise the return on all feasible investments within the capital constraint. However, in the above example the capital constraint is not quite as binding as it appears. This is because a decision not to invest in some of the projects is easy – for projects B and E putting the money into a bank gives a better return and without any risk! So, we can take B and E out of the decision problem immediately. However projects A, C and D provide a better return than the financial market and so we need to look at these a bit more closely.

Project A gives a profit of £12,000 whereas C produces double this and D produces just over four times this amount. On the face of it project D appears the best alternative since it has the highest rate of return and the highest absolute profit. However, it will absorb 80 per cent of the capital funds available, making project C impossible to fund this year. Even so, enough funds will be left for project A so that total profit could reach £112,000 – this of course gives the combined rate of return of 12.17 per cent which is *less* than project D on its own.

We might consider combining projects A and C: this gives a total profit of £36,000 with a combined rate of return of 8.57 per cent which is better than C on its own but worse than A on its own. So it does appear that the choice is between project D *only* and project D combined with project A. However, another way of considering the capital rationing problem is to look at the relative improvement in profit per pound invested. The 'cheapest' project is A at £120,000 while C costs £300,000 and D costs £800,000. The profit per project rises from £12,000 to £24,000 to £100,000.

So, raising investment from A to C by 2.5 times only raises the profit by two times. Raising investment from A to D by 6.7 times raises the profit by 8.3 times

Table 10.6 Single-period capital rationing

Project	A	B	C	D	E
Capital outlay	120	400	300	800	300
Profit	12	25	24	100	15
Return (%)	10	6.25	8	12.5	5

and going from C to D, a 2.7 times increase, raises the profit by 4.16 times! It is clear therefore that A is preferred to C in relative terms and that D is preferred to C in relative terms. This is because the *benefit–cost ratio* of these two projects is better than for C, that is, 12/120 = 0.1; 24/300 = 0.08 and 100/800 = 0.125.

Thus, in this example, the capital is best rationed between projects A and D. Project C needs to wait for the firm to amass more capital for investment. The above is a very straightforward example of capital rationing in a single period, but it can be the case that the 'best' alternative, on the face of it, turns out not to be when we ask a few more questions, particularly in terms of the relative contribution per pound a given project makes. In other words, the capital rationing problem forces us to think a little deeper about the true merits of any given set of alternative investments.

■ ■ ■ Self-Assessment Question ■ ■ ■ ■ ■ ■ ■ ■ ■ ■ ■ ■

Q10 In a single sentence, summarise why a firm must normally ration capital across competing projects. What is the main objective of this rationing process?

■■

A much more complex problem arises when possible investment projects are interdependent, that is not mutually exclusive. This is because the expected profit from any one project is dependent on the expected profits from one other or perhaps even more than one other project. In this case the capital needs to be rationed over the expected lifetime of the interdependent projects in such a way that the possible range of joint profit from these projects is maximised.

This is a multi-period capital rationing problem and will normally require a sophisticated computer program to solve. However, for a broad range of such problems a simple linear programming solution will often exist. We want to consider this type of capital rationing problem below.

Important Note
Students who wish to skip this section may do so – it is intended merely
to show that capital constraint problems can be highly complex. The 'real'
world is more akin to this than the previous example!

10.5.2   Multi-period Capital Rationing

Suppose the NPV per £ of capital invested in two projects (A and B) is expected to be £3 for A and £1 for B. However, these two projects are interdependent and not mutually exclusive. The management have to decide how to apportion the firm's available funds over the 3-year economic life of these two projects in order that the joint NPVs are maximised. However, the firm faces capital constraints each year so it must ration the capital funds over the 3-year period. In addition, due to the interdependency of these projects their respective NPVs per £ invested also vary over the time period. In other words, a fairly common investment decision problem facing management! The relevant data are shown in Table 10.7.

The objective is to achieve the expected levels of NPV/£ invested therefore we can set out an objective function which we are trying to meet as: maximum NPV = £3A + £1B. Note that the expected NPV per £ invested is not the sum of the column data since a present value of £1 receivable after the first year is less by the time we get to the end of the third year.

In year 1, A produces £1 of PV per £1 invested and B produces £3 of PV per £ invested but these are constrained by available funds of £90 so the question is simply this: how many £s should be given to A and how many to B in each year? In year 2 the constraint on money allocation is £80 and in year 3 the constraint is £60. We can write these in mathematical terms as follows.

Maximise the joint expected NPV (£3A + £1B) subject to:

$$£1A + £3B \leq £90 \qquad \text{Year 1 constraint}$$
$$£2A + £2B \leq £80 \qquad \text{Year 2 constraint}$$
$$£2A + £0B \leq £60 \qquad \text{Year 3 constraint}$$

All we need do now is restate the above inequalities as equations and solve each equation using iteration. Thus we get:

$$£1A + £3B = £90$$
$$£2A + £2B = £80$$
$$£2A + £0B = £60$$

First Iteration: we can solve for A or B by simply removing one of them. We can see that project A in year 2 is twice the value compared with year 1 therefore we can try to remove A from the problem by using the number 2. However, we need to use –2 to achieve this since the value of A in both years is a posi-

Table 10.7 Multi-period capital rationing

Year	Project A's PV per £ invested	Project B's PV per £ invested	Capital funds (£)
1	1	3	90
2	2	2	80
3	2	0	60
Expected NPV/£1	3	1	

tive number. So, by multiplying the year 1 constraint by –2 and adding this to the year 2 constraint we should be able to remove A from the problem in this first iteration. This gives:

$$- £2A – £6B = –£180$$
$$+ £2A + £2B = £80$$
$$= £0A – £4B = –£100 \quad \text{hence} \quad £4B = £100 \quad \text{and} \quad B = 25$$

Substituting this value into the first equation gives the following:

$$£1A + £3(25) = 90 \quad \text{and so} \quad A = 15 \quad \text{and} \quad B = 25$$

Now we can move on to the second iteration.

Second Iteration: £2A + £2B = £80 (year 2) and £2A + £0B = £60 (year 3), hence by visual inspection we know that A must be 30 (that is, 60/2) and so B must be 10. However we now have two sets of values for A and B which satisfy all three constraints! Which particular set will achieve our goal of maximising the joint NPV? To answer this question we have to 'test' both sets of values in our objective function which was £3A + £1B. This gives:

For solution pair (15, 25)   3(15) + 1(25) = £70 and
For solution pair (30, 10)   3(30) + 1(10) = £100

Clearly the allocation of the available capital between these two projects in each year should be £30 to A and £10 to B since this allocation will maximise the joint NPV. But this needs to be checked to test if indeed this allocation is within the capital constraint which the firm is facing. Consider Table 10.8.

As we can see from the table there is a binding constraint on the capital allocation between the two projects in years 2 and 3. What does this mean? Two things – first the capital rationing problem has been solved for these years since the total allocation just meets the binding constraint and second, more importantly, it means that if this allocation were to be changed the firm would definitely incur an opportunity cost since, by definition, this is the allocation which maximises the joint NPV, that is, it is an optimal allocation. Any deviation from this would produce a sub-optimal solution. In year 1, however, there would be no opportunity cost incurred since there remains £30 of capital which could be allocated to another investment project (say project C) without affecting the profit (NPV) for projects A and B.

Table 10.8   Capital constraint

Year	Project A	Project B	Total spend	Constraint	Type
1	1 * 30	3 *10	£60	£90	non-binding
2	2 * 30	2 *10	£80	£80	binding
3	2 * 30	0 *10	£60	£60	binding

What the above examples illustrate is that determining the best investment choice is not simply a matter of using the most appropriate investment appraisal technique – it is also a management decision problem which needs to be addressed in the context of capital constraints, whether the constraints operate in a single year or over a number of years.

❏ ❏ ❏ End of Chapter SUMMARY ❏ ❏ ❏ ❏ ❏ ❏ ❏ ❏ ❏ ❏ ❏

The rationale for private sector investment spending must address the key issues of opportunity cost and economic profit. If these are not addressed then strictly speaking there is no rationale for the use of the firm's capital for investment purposes. The payback method is completely inappropriate as a tool for investment decision making in the private and public sectors and should only be used as a screening device. Although it is redeemed somewhat with the use of discounted payback it still carries many problems. The discounting process, the 'time value of money' and the concept of 'present value' are all underpinned by the basic concept of opportunity cost. This is the crucial idea behind all discounted cash flow methods of investment appraisal. The IRR method is only workable in the context of conventional cash flows. However even here it implicitly assumes all cash flows are earning the same IRR. In general the IRR method is not to be preferred to the NPV method. There can be a significant difference between real and nominal market rates of interest. It is important that this is taken account of by either deflating the cash flows by a price deflator and then discounting by the real rate or discounting by the market rate but not deflating the cash flows. The RoCe is not the same concept or method as the IRR and should not be confused with it. The main point you should have understood from the chapter is the relationship between NPV, IRR and economic profit. This relationship, as described in the NPV/IRR decision criteria, is the conceptual heart of the discounted cash flow approach to investment appraisal.

■ ■ ■ ANSWERS to Self-Assessment Questions ■ ■ ■ ■ ■ ■ ■

Q1

The notion of economic rationality simply implies that individuals will wish to maximise *utility*. It follows that if an individual has a preference rate for consumption which is higher than the best prevailing interest rate then he or she will choose to consume now rather than save or invest. So giving up consumption now for what would effectively be the same or even lower level of consumption in the future will produce *disutility* – knowingly doing so could justifiably be regarded as economically irrational.

Q2

You should have said something along the following lines: basically the opportunity cost of any action is the value of the forgone alternative action. In financial terms, if there existed a perfect capital market, no investment could possibly be better or worse than any other – there could be no opportunity cost in such a world. But because resources are not infinite and no economic market is perfect there must always exist an opportunity cost associated with any decision, economic or otherwise.

Q3
There are several weaknesses involved in the use of RoCe as a method of investment appraisal but we would expect you to identify the more important ones as:

■ It completely ignores the time value of money.

■ It uses accounting profit in the calculation, which is not a decision-making tool.

■ It has several 'versions', not just two, and therefore is very ambiguous.

Q4
This is because the method puts greatest emphasis on the early cash inflows of the firm's investments. In many small firms the greatest constraint is cash flow – hence the use of payback by the management of small firms represents a very rational approach to investment appraisal given their (often) main problem is one of cash flow.

Q5
The question asks you to calculate factors, therefore you should not use the table provided but instead use one of the PV equations. We would suggest the following:

$$PV(£1) = £1/(1 + i)^t$$

So, in each case we get:

$£1/(1.08)^6 = 0.63$ that is, the £'s present value is 63 pence.

$£1/(1.12)^3 = 0.71$ that is, the £'s present value is 71 pence.

$£1/(1.2)^{20} = 0.026$ that is, the £'s present value is 2.6 pence.

$£1/(1.06)^{40} = 0.097$ that is, the £'s present value is 9.7 pence.

From the above it is clear that the shorter the time period the greater is the present value of money, but the higher the discount rate the less it will be. This means that a relatively low discount rate combined with a long time period is likely to produce a higher PV than a high discount rate over a shorter time period. So the present value of any investment is fundamentally determined by the interaction of the discount rate and the time period.

Q6
At a rate of discount of 15 per cent the calculation is as follows:

$$£4000(1.15)^{-1} + £5000(1.15)^{-2} + £3000(1.15)^{-3} + £2000(1.15)^{-4}$$
$$= £10,375 - £10,000$$
$$= £375$$

The result means that even at a high discount rate of 15 per cent this project still returns an economic profit of £375.

Q7   A single formula need only be used once to find the present value of cash flows which are the same every year. We could use the simpler formula and calculate the PV of each separate cash flow, but this is much more time consuming and completely unnecessary where the cash flows are constant. Where they are not constant, however, we must use the simpler formula.

Q8   This is a very important question because most managers, when they hear a phrase such as 'the rate of return is 12 per cent', think this is a return on capital employed, almost automatically. If in fact it is an IRR then it means something completely different. It means the project is economically worthwhile as long as the opportunity cost of capital (which is usually the real market rate of interest) is *less* than 12 per cent. However, the RoCe means no such thing – it is just a simple accounting ratio which has no connection whatsoever with the opportunity cost of capital and in fact is likely to grossly overstate the true value of an investment project to a firm.

Q9   Using the linear interpolation formula and substituting the values into it gives:

$$\text{IRR} = (0.06) + \frac{£400}{£400 + £150} \times (0.09 - 0.06)$$

$$= (0.06) + [0.727 * (0.03)]$$

$$= 0.818$$

that is, the IRR is 8.18 per cent.

Q10   A firm must normally ration capital across competing projects because at any one time it will rarely have sufficient capital to be able to invest in all possible projects. The main objective behind the rationing process is to maximise the economic profit achievable by selecting that combination of projects which exhibit the best benefit–cost ratios.

See also tables in the Appendix at the end of the book.

Investment appraisal under risk and uncertainty

■ 11.1 Introduction

One of the key assumptions which we were implicitly making in Chapter 10 was that the expected cash flows from the projects were in some sense guaranteed. That is we did not question whether the *actual* outcome of a project would indeed be the *expected* outcome. Quite clearly since we do not live in a completely riskless or certain world this kind of assumption is not tenable – especially where firms are thinking of investing significant amounts of their own capital or of borrowing from the banks. It is crucial therefore that any investment appraisal (apart from very small projects) needs to explicitly take account of the fact that both risk and uncertainty are likely to surround all the parameters of any investment project.

In Chapter 10 you studied the methods of NPV, AENPV and IRR. Although these approaches to project appraisal are far superior to the traditional methods (which we looked at in Chapter 10), on their own they cannot deal with risk and uncertainty. First of all we have to explicitly define what we mean by risk and uncertainty before we can proceed to using any of the risk analysis techniques in the context of NPV or IRR. The plan of this chapter is firstly to discuss the concepts of risk and uncertainty and then to look in some detail at the various techniques we can apply in the context of investment appraisal.

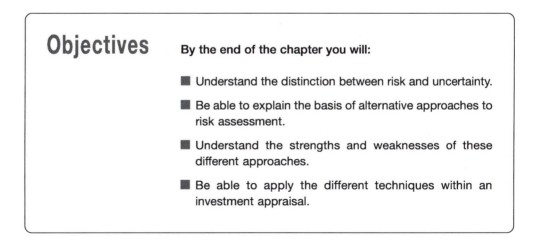

Objectives

By the end of the chapter you will:

■ Understand the distinction between risk and uncertainty.

■ Be able to explain the basis of alternative approaches to risk assessment.

■ Understand the strengths and weaknesses of these different approaches.

■ Be able to apply the different techniques within an investment appraisal.

■ 11.2 Risk versus Uncertainty

The terms 'risk' and 'uncertainty' are often used interchangeably in everyday language to mean the same thing. In fact they never mean the same thing for a very simple reason: the former requires the existence of prior knowledge while the latter, in its purest form, only exists in the absence of knowledge. For example, a card player takes risks when implementing a gambit in poker even though the player is operating under some level of uncertainty. This, however, is a level of uncertainty which is minimised due to the player's (partial) knowledge of the other players' strategies and his prior knowledge of which cards have already been tabled.

In other words, the existence of some knowledge means he is taking a risk by definition. If we compare this situation with a non-poker player who joins the game one hour after it has started we are then in a scenario of pure uncertainty! Not only can he not play poker he also has no knowledge at all of existing strategies in the game or of the cards previously tabled! This is a situation where the decisions of the new player are being made in the context of uncertainty.

Thus the fundamental nature of risk is that people and organisations are said to be taking a risk when they are operating in a situation of some information which enables them to make a reasonably informed choice. Or to put it another way, risk itself is quantifiable – we can measure it (within limits) and therefore we can assess whether the measured risk associated with a decision is one worth taking. However, if someone chooses to join a poker game and cannot play poker they have no basis upon which to assess the risk of losing. They are operating in a situation of pure uncertainty and you have no information available to convert that uncertainty into a knowable risk.

Therefore uncertainty is the situation where people and organisations simply have no way of measuring, forecasting or assessing the likelihood of future outcomes or events. It is very different from the concept of risk where some information does exist. We can sum up what we mean by risk and uncertainty as follows:

> The essential fact is that 'risk' means in some cases a quantity susceptible of measurement, while at other times it is … distinctly not. [Thus] a 'measurable' uncertainty, or risk proper … is so far different from an unmeasurable one that it is not in effect an uncertainty at all. (Knight, 1921)

We can therefore define risk as follows:

Risk = Quantifiable Uncertainty

and quite clearly uncertainty is not the same as risk.

There are two types of risk – *systematic* and *specific*. The first relates to the environment in which a project is to be assessed and implemented, while the second relates to the specific nature of a project itself – that is, it is the risk involved irrespective of the environment. It is often the case, however, that they are strongly related in practice. A *systematic risk* is associated with the environment within which a project is to be implemented. A *specific risk* is associated with the project in hand, that is, it is a degree of risk which will pertain irrespective of the environment – for example in the case of new product launches or the development of industrial and retail sites for which little prior experience on the part of developers or operators exists.

■ ■ ■ Self-Assessment Question ■ ■ ■ ■ ■ ■ ■ ■ ■ ■ ■ ■

Q1 Explain why a firm is unlikely to have much, if any, influence over sources of systematic risk compared with sources of specific risk.

■ 11.3 Risk Assessment Methods

There are a number of fairly simple methods available to assess the degree of risk and we will consider the three most popular below:

- ■ The risk-adjusted discount rate (RADR)

- ■ The test discount rate or hurdle rate

- ■ Expected NPV (ENPV)

In the context of investment the issue of risk is simply one of the likelihood that an opportunity cost to the firm or shareholders or in the public sector, the taxpayer, will be incurred if a project is implemented. The purpose of risk assessment is to minimise this likelihood.

11.3.1   The Risk-adjusted Discount Rate

The risk-adjusted discount rate (RADR) allocates possible investment projects into risk classes ranging from risk-free to high risk. Each risk class has a risk premium attached to it. Suppose, for example, that the market rate of interest is 8 per cent then a medium risk project may be allocated a 2 per cent risk premium, while a high risk project may be allocated a risk premium of 4 per cent. So, the RADR for each class of project will be as follows:

risk-free = 7%   medium risk = 10%   high risk = 12%

In the case of a medium or high risk project the discount rate which is applied to the future cash flows would be 10 and 12 per cent respectively – if the NPVs were still positive then it is assumed that the actual outcome will indeed be a positive NPV.

This is very much an intuitive or experience-based approach to assessing risk. In that sense it *does* deal with the problem of risk but in a very subjective manner more linked to an organisation's history or even the decision makers' preferences. Three main problems arise in its use:

1. The allocation of alternative or competing projects into risk categories is bound to be subjective since no attempt at an analytical solution will be made in this method.

2. The risk premium used is by definition subjective or it may be linked to past performance which is no longer relevant if the systematic risk conditions have changed, that is if the environment is now different compared to that which pertained when similar projects were completed.

3. The perceived risk tends to be associated with the project as a whole as opposed to its individual components, that is, the actual exposure to risk is more likely to be connected to one or two crucial parameters than to every parameter which will determine the actual outcome. This 'deeper' look at risk is ignored using the RADR.

11.3.2   The 'Test' or 'Hurdle' Discount Rate

A 'test' discount rate (TDR) is simply a risk-adjusted discount rate if it is greater than the real rate of interest. It is often applied in the context of public sector investment proposals where taxpayers' money is to be used. Basically it represents an attempt to protect the taxpayer from exposure to unnecessary risk by applying an IRR test to public sector investments. The size of the TDR will depend on the attitude to risk and the budget constraint of the public agencies involved and whether the venture is to include private sector finance. Where the government places a high emphasis on achieving value for money for the taxpayer, the TDR will generally be higher than otherwise.

For example, suppose the real rate of interest in the economy is 6 per cent, then 'public' money should not be invested in projects which return an IRR of less than 6 per cent, otherwise the taxpayer is incurring an opportunity cost. In fact if the TDR is set at, say, 7 per cent then the government is effectively attaching a risk premium to the taxpayers' money. The rationale behind this approach to risk is simply that each pound of taxpayers' money is worth as much to the taxpayer as each pound of shareholders' money is worth to the shareholder. Hence the taxpayers' money needs to be treated with the same respect in the context of investment.

In the private sector a similar approach to risk involving the IRR is commonly used, the so-called *'hurdle'* rate. Here a firm may simply take the view that unless a possible investment project can deliver a 10 per cent IRR then it will not invest in it – indeed under this approach a firm will not invest in any project which cannot produce a 10 per cent IRR.

If you think about it this is very similar to the 'target' rate of return used in the RoCe method we looked at in Chapter 10 and suffers from a similar problem – it can be set in an arbitrary manner so that the 'risk' implied by it bears no relation whatsoever to the true risk involved in any given project. It is also usually based on 'past' experience and of course suffers from the problem that this will not always be a good guide to future performance.

One other point is worth mentioning here – the hurdle rate can be set far too high if the firm concerned is essentially risk-averse. This means the management are unlikely to enter into investment projects which could strongly enhance the worth of the firm in the future and therefore will lose opportunities which are in fact very good for the firm.

■ ■ ■ Self-Assessment Question ■ ■ ■ ■ ■ ■ ■ ■ ■ ■ ■ ■

Q2 If the real rate of interest in the economy was 5 per cent and a firm was using a 12 per cent hurdle IRR what can you deduce about this firm's attitude to risk?

11.3.3   Expected NPV (ENPV)

It will always be the case that future cash inflows from any investment project will be subject to some uncertainty. However it is also the case that a reasonable grasp of the wider economic environment will enable management to quantify that uncertainty in order to ascertain as far as possible the *knowable risk* associated with future cash inflows. There are many parameters which expose investments to risk. For example price inflation, development costs, operating costs, capacity utilisation/demand, and legislative and policy changes are only some of the sources of risk which can affect the economic value of an investment project. So how does the ENPV method attempt to deal with this problem?

Essentially it is a very simple and rather intuitive method in that it merely allocates a *subjective probability of occurrence* to each cash flow. A subjective probability is simply based on management experience of dealing with similar projects – it is basically a judgemental approach to attaching risk. For example, management may be considering investment in a new heating system for a hospital and the savings to be made compared with the current (outdated) system are thought to be in the range of £5000 to £10,000 per annum.

What the savings will actually turn out to be will depend on a number of factors such as the utilisation rate of the system, the weather, changes in fuel prices and how effectively the new system is managed. There will be other parameters which could also affect the actual savings made but the point is a straightforward one: given prior knowledge of other similar systems the hospital management will be aware that the savings will be subject to variability which is being generated by the above 'uncertainties'. Using such prior information we can attach a subjective probability to the potential savings within the already known range. Thus a possible savings profile can be constructed as follows.

Savings range (from prior knowledge) = £5K to £10K per annum and we can divide this range into any number of savings amounts and allocate a probability to each of them. Let us divide it into four possible outcomes using our prior knowledge of this type of heating system so that we get:

£5K   or   £7K   or   £9K   or   £10K

Also using prior knowledge we can allocate a probability of occurrence to each potential savings amount. Suppose these probabilities are as follows:

0.25   0.4   0.25   0.1   Note they must add to 1!

that is,

25%   40%   25%   10%

So, the expected savings per annum is the weighted average of these amounts and is given by:

0.25(£5K) + 0.4(£7K) + 0.25(£9K) + 0.1(£10K) = £3200

and its EPV = $3200(1.08)^{-1}$ = £2963

We would then need to go on and calculate the expected second, third and last cash flows from the project using the same approach. Note that if we ignored the subjective probabilities for the first cash flow and used just the simple average we would get:

£5K + £7K + £9K + £10K = £7.75K

and its PV = $£7.75(1.08)^{-1}$ = £7.176K, that is, 142% higher!

There is clearly a major difference when we can use our experience of similar investments to 'guess' at the likely outcome of the future cash flows and use the attached probabilities to calculate this. If we do not use the probabilities then we are implicitly assuming that there is an equal chance of the first cash flow being £10,000 as there is of it being £5000 – clearly this kind of assumption is unrealistic.

So using ENPV is simply a matter of finding the weighted average of a set of alternative future outcomes which are based (usually) on managerial experience of similar projects. As an approach to risk assessment it has one major weakness – managerial experience is based on the past but the past is rarely a guide to the future. In addition, the ENPV technique cannot tell us the degree of risk involved because all of the risk information is 'captured' in the subjective probabilities. It has the advantage of being very simple to use but cannot really tell us what the probability is of a project delivering, for example, a negative NPV – yet this is precisely the kind of information management would really want to know.

What ENPV actually does is give an estimate of the average value of a project's performance – it does not really account for risk at all because it is about expected performance or outcomes, whereas risk would indicate by how much the actual outcome is likely to deviate from the expected outcome! Most applications of this method ignore this basic problem. The other problem is that several projects may exhibit the same ENPV but possess very different variances and standard deviations – that is they will possess different probabilities of the actual outcome deviating from the expected outcome. This point is also commonly ignored. For project appraisal purposes ENPV is not a recommended way of assessing risk simply because it does not actually do this!

In general it is not a good idea to base a firm's risk assessment of any investment project on ENPV, RADR or a hurdle rate of IRR since these simple techniques are essentially a 'blind' approach to capturing risk. Indeed it could be argued, as pointed out above, that they are not really risk assessment techniques, particularly ENPV, but rather screening devices which should only be used as an *initial* assessment.

■ ■ ■ **Self-Assessment Question** ■ ■ ■ ■ ■ ■ ■ ■ ■ ■ ■ ■

Q3 Calculate the ENPV of a project with a capital cost of £5000, an economic life of 2 years and the following cash flow range (discount rate = 7 per cent).

Year 1 CF = £2000 or £3000 or £6000 and the probability for each is 0.2, 0.6 and 0.2 respectively.

Year 2 CF = £1000 or £3000 or £4000 and the probability for each is 0.3, 0.4 and 0.3 respectively.

To summarise so far, we can see that risk can be captured in the use of a RADR and/or a test or hurdle rate but, like the ENPV method, these do not explicitly tell us what the actual risk associated with an investment project failing is. To do this we need to be a little more sophisticated in our technique and this means we need to go back to the fundamental nature of risk discussed earlier – that is, risk is all about attaching probabilities to future outcomes and events so we need to turn to probability theory to help us do this.

■ 11.4 Probability Analysis in Investment Appraisal

This technique is used where management have sufficient information on all the various aspects of a potential investment project's cash flows so that they can utilise the properties of the normal distribution curve to attach a *definite* probability of 'success' or 'failure' to a proposed investment. The standard normal curve is an extremely useful tool in assessing the riskiness of a project, and the essential feature of this approach to risk assessment is in the simple question which it asks. What is the probability that the NPV of this project will be negative? In other words, what is the chance that the firm will incur an economic loss if it invests in this project? This is clearly the key question confronting a firm when it is considering investing a large amount of its own capital (or borrowed capital) in a major project. Before we go on to look at the use of probability in the context of investment appraisal, it is useful to remind ourselves what the properties of the normal distribution are (Figure 11.1).

The curve shows that 68 per cent of all observations of any given variable which has a normal distribution will lie within plus or minus one standard deviation (sd) of the mean (centre line) and 94 per cent will lie within plus or minus two sds of the mean. As the number of observations on most variables increases, the whole sample more closely fits a normal curve such as above.

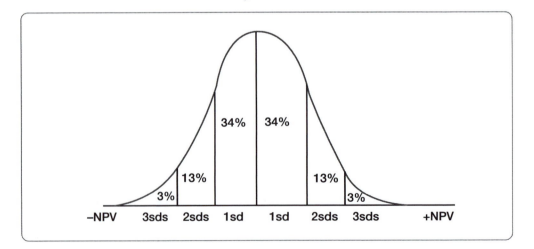

Figure 11.1   The normal distribution

Now why would we be interested in this from a risk analysis point of view? Consider what it would mean if a project's NPV were to lie towards the left-hand side of the figure and the average of its expected NPV was only £100 – there is a good chance that the true value of the NPV could be negative since to the extreme left of the mean must exist a negative area under the curve. If we can pinpoint where an NPV might actually be, in terms of the graph, then we can determine its likelihood of being negative. In order to do this we need to know something about a project's NPV in terms of two things – the variance of the NPV and the standard deviation of the NPV.

These are defined as follows:

$$\text{Variance} = \sum_{t=1}^{N} (Xi - \bar{Xi})^2 \quad \text{and} \quad \text{Standard deviation} = \sqrt{\text{Variance}}$$

We will be shortly using a case study to clearly illustrate this technique and in addition to apply sensitivity analysis to the results. As discussed above, a key question to ask of any potential investment project is whether it may turn out to give a negative NPV. A negative NPV means a value which is less than zero, hence we can say that the probability that any NPV will be negative is given by the formula:

$z = (0 - \text{ENPV})/\text{sd} = \text{sd units}$

where the ENPV is the weighted mean (as in the ENPV discussed before). So, the above equation is simply measuring how far from its expected mean value an NPV might be in the left-hand direction of the normal curve. Before we go on to actually calculate this let us give you an example of how it needs to be interpreted. Suppose we know that the expected NPV of a project is £160 and the standard deviation associated with this is £135, then by using the above equation we can find the number of sd units by which this varies from the mean relative to zero as our 'reference' point. This gives:

$z = (0 - 160)/135 = -1.185 \text{ sd units}$

What we need to do now is to find the probability associated with this number of sd units from the normal distribution function itself. However, we do not need to calculate it from the function since there are tables which allow us to read off the probability directly as long as we know the value of z. Using the relevant table (provided in the Appendix) reading down the column to 1.1 and then across to 0.08 to give us 1.18 (note that the table gives 1.18 but not 1.185 – the difference is not significant) we see that the value in the table is 0.3810. Is this our probability value of a negative NPV? The answer is no because we are only interested in the left-hand side of the normal curve, that is, in finding a probability that the NPV will be negative. To do this we need to subtract our table

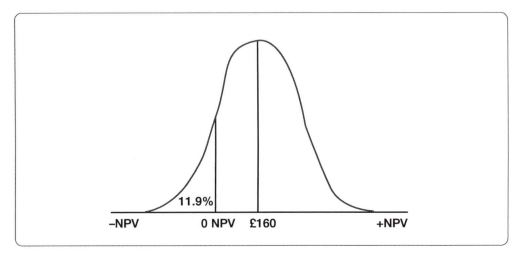

Figure 11.2   A normal distribution curve showing negative NPV

value from 0.5 (that is, we are only concerned with the left-hand tail of the distribution) so that the probability that the NPV will be negative is given in the table as:

(0.5 – table z)→(0.5 – 0.3810) = 0.119 which is 11.9%

So, there is an 11.9 per cent probability that the NPV for the above project will be negative. In terms of the normal curve we can see this more clearly (Figure 11.2).

The graph shows the area where the NPV might lie under the curve given its standard deviation and expected value. This means that this project has a 1 in 10 chance of generating an economic loss for the firm. This is a fairly good risk since it also means such a project has a 9 in 10 chance of generating a positive NPV and therefore an economic profit.

■ ■ ■ Self-Assessment Question ■ ■ ■ ■ ■ ■ ■ ■ ■ ■ ■ ■ ■

Q4   Find the probability of a negative NPV where the expected NPV is £1200 and its standard deviation is £1020.

Now that we can see how to use the normal distribution table and how to interpret what the 'number' actually means we can go on to find the probability of a negative NPV using a full-scale case study.

■ 11.5 A Case Study in Risk and Sensitivity Analysis

It is intended that you learn and understand the principles and methods involved in applying probability and sensitivity analysis through the following case study. All the analysis is fully worked out in order that you can follow the process clearly.

Although, in many cases, companies and other organisations use standard spreadsheet or other computable formats to undertake the calculations involved, it is nevertheless the case that, for most people, the procedures involved in the calculations remain a 'black box' unless they have had some experience in actually doing the 'number-crunching' for themselves.

This case study demonstrates how such an analysis can be undertaken. It is not a test of arithmetic, cleverness or ability of any kind whatsoever – it is a learning vehicle and by the end of the case study you will know:

1. How to specify the nature of this type of problem

2. Which procedures and sequence in calculations are needed

3. What questions need to be asked

4. How to interpret the results

The actual problem in the example is real, although names and actual numbers are changed for obvious reasons. The problem has also been somewhat simplified so that it can be done without too many complications; however, all the salient features of the problem are present.

CASE STUDY *Alarms R Us*

Alarms R Us plc is a firm which began operating in the UK in 1984 and manufactures alarm systems for business premises exclusively. However, since 1990 the firm has witnessed a threefold expansion in the sale of alarm systems to the domestic household market which it puts down to an increased fear of burglary among householders. Whether real or perceived, this development has been driving up total market sales fairly rapidly. The management are considering whether they should diversify the firm's activities into the household market. However, due to rapid change in the manufacturing technology of alarm systems, use of existing production lines is ruled out as an option for the household product. A new production line will be required. A very brief assessment of comparable systems operated by other manufacturers and approaches to a number of suppliers suggests this would require an initial capital investment of approximately £400K. The firm

CASE STUDY *continued*

operate with a 3-year payback horizon and a target rate of return of 20 per cent.

Although this segment of the market has been expanding it is not an area the management are familiar with and they decide to hire an economic consultant to analyse the proposed investment. The terms of reference given to the consultant are as follows:

Determine likely future sales scenarios
Determine the payback period
Determine the RoCe
Determine the NPV, AENPV and IRR
Determine the probability of an economic loss
Determine the risk sources
Determine the sensitivity of the investment to
   these risk sources
All analyses to be restricted to a 4-year
   timescale due to expected obsolescence
Recommend a course of action

From the terms of reference above it is clear that management are looking for as full an investment appraisal as possible. The consultant's task is first to establish why total market sales of household alarms have been increasing. Second, to undertake the various calculations necessary. Third, to identify any key assumptions which have been made in the calculations and in the sales trends and finally to make a recommendation to the management of Alarms R Us.

As an economist, the consultant is well aware of the debate surrounding unemployment and crime. Most of the economic literature in this area suggests there is a positive correlation between the two. Using published data sources the consultant is able to test the hypothesis that unemployment and crime are related in a statistically significant manner and produces the following regression equation (remember you met regression theory in Chapter 6):

$$\text{Reported Crime} = 120{,}000 + 1.24 \text{ Unemployment} + 0.92 \text{ Time}$$
$$(7.7) \qquad\qquad (4.2)$$

$$R^2 = 0.89$$

This suggests that there is a positive and direct connection between reported crime and unemployment. Basically, if unemployment were to rise by 1 per cent then we should expect to see reported crime rise by 1.24 per cent plus 0.92 per cent. The latter is due to a time trend identified by the equation as being statistically significant. That is, even if unemployment did not rise or if it stayed constant, reported crime would still rise year on year at a rate of 0.92 per cent. The reasons for this will be myriad. The consultant is also aware that unemployment tends to rise in periods of economic downturn – thus the

Table 11.1 Alternative scenarios – Treasury forecasts

Real GDP growth forecast	Unemployment change	Impact on reported crime	Sales conditions
3% (Optimistic)	−2%	−2.48% (+0.92T)	Awful
2% (Moderate)	−1%	−1.24% (+0.92T)	Poor
1% (Central)	−0.5%	−0.62% (+0.92T)	Weak
0% (Low)	+1%	+1.24% (+0.92T)	Good
−1% (Poor)	+1.5%	+1.86% (+0.92T)	Excellent

volatility in reported crime would appear to be (at least partly) a function of the business cycle (which you met in Chapter 3). To summarise, it appears that future sales will be directly related to trends in reported crime and de facto related to future economic conditions.

Using HM Treasury forecasts of future real GDP, the scenario alternatives shown in Table 11.1 are produced.

If real GDP growth turns out to be poor over the next 4 years we would expect to see reported crime rising from its present level by $(0.0186 + 0.0092)$ = $(1.0278)^4$ = 11.6 per cent. If on the other hand the economy were to enter a period of rapid expansion we would expect to see a reduction in reported crime over a 4-year period of approximately 6 per cent, that is, the market in household alarms would most certainly shrink. Considering past studies of GDP growth the consultant estimates that the chances of the alternative sales scenarios are as follows:

Excellent (10%) Good (20%) Weak (40%) Poor (20%) Awful (10%)

Using current market sales data and an estimated penetration level by Alarms R Us of 6 per cent combined with the known operating costs of the new production line, a series of net cash flow estimates are produced based upon the alternative sales scenarios (Table 11.2). These do not account for future price

Table 11.2 Net cash flows for alternative sales scenarios

Sales scenario	NCF (Year 1)	NCF (Year 2)	NCF (Year 3)	NCF (Year 4)
Excellent	250	200	200	150
Good	200	180	180	130
Weak	170	150	150	120
Poor	150	130	130	100
Awful	100	80	80	50

Table 11.3   Payback and RoCe calculations

Year 1 NCF = 250(.1) + 200(0.2) + 170(0.4) + 150(0.2) +100(0.1) = £173K
Year 2 NCF = 200(.1) + 180(0.2) + 150(0.4) + 130(0.2) + 80(0.1) = £150K
Year 3 NCF = 200(.1) + 180(0.2) + 150(0.4) + 130(0.2) + 80(0.1) = £150K
Year 4 NCF = 150(.1) + 130(0.2) + 120(0.4) + 100(0.2) + 50(0.1) = £114K

Total net cash flow (over 4 years) = £587K

Payback period   = [£400K − (£173K+£150K)]/£150K = 2.5 years

RoCe   = [£587K/4]/£400K = 0.367, that is **36.7%**

inflation. Note also that the NCFs are given by gross cash inflow minus operating and maintenance costs of the new production line on a per annum basis. Thus they represent the forecast accounting profit from the new production line per annum. All figures are in £K.

Under the terms of reference it is straightforward to calculate both the payback period and the RoCe. But first we need to calculate the expected NCF using the weightings shown in Table 11.2. These are given in Table 11.3.

Note that no 'scrap value' has been included in the calculation of the RoCe and the calculations also exclude depreciation effects. This is merely to simplify since the RoCe is, by definition, not a particularly reliable appraisal method and therefore there is no real need to go much further into it.

These data demonstrate two things. First, the expected payback period falls within the firm's 3-year payback horizon and it adequately meets the target rate of return of 20 per cent. Note that we do not calculate payback and RoCe for each scenario since this would be a pointless exercise – this is because the chances of any single scenario occurring are much less than that associated with their weighted distribution.

Now we need to move on to the calculation of NPV, AENPV and IRR. We already know the distribution of the expected NCFs, therefore we can simply apply these. However the NCFs do not include inflation and this has to be dealt with. Again using Treasury forecasts the annual rate of price inflation is forecast to not exceed 3.0 per cent and not fall below 2.0 per cent over the next 4 years. A simple (but reasonable) device here is to take the mean forecast value which clearly will be 2.5 per cent per annum.

Other than the present proposal, the firm is not considering any alternative investments therefore the next best alternative for its capital of £400K is to 'lock' it up in a long-term government securities (non-accessible for 4 years) at a guaranteed return of 10.7 per cent per annum. This represents the opportunity cost of the capital to the firm. However, we still need to identify an appropriate discount rate to apply to the expected NCFs. Since we must account for inflation and the firm's opportunity cost of capital it is quite clear we need to use the formula for the derivation of the real interest rate. This has already been given as:

$$R_i = [(1 + M_i)/(1 + P)] - 1$$

and using the data on inflation and the opportunity cost of capital this will give a real discount rate of:

$$[(1.107)/(1.025)] - 1 = 0.08, \text{ that is } 8\%$$

This will capture the effects of future inflation and explicitly address the firm's opportunity cost of capital. We are now in a position to determine the NPV, AENPV and the IRR of this proposal.

We already know that the expected NCFs are as follows:

£173K, £150K, £150K and £114K

It is therefore a simple matter to apply our real discount rate and determine the expected present value of the NCFs and hence the ENPV of the proposal. These are given as:

$$173(1.08)^{-1} + 150(1.08)^{-2} + 150(1.08)^{-3} + 114(1.08)^{-4} = £491.65K$$

and hence the ENPV of the proposal is simply £491.65K – £400K = £91.65K. This is clearly a very strong indicator that the proposed new investment will generate an economic surplus for the firm over the 4-year period.

In annual equivalent terms the project would generate the following:

$$AENPV = AEF * NPV$$

The AEF for 4 years at 8 per cent is given in the relevant table (see Appendix) as 0.30192 so the AENPV will be 0.30192*£91.65K = £27.67K per annum. Again a very healthy indicator of an efficient investment.

Turning to the project's IRR, we already know that at a real discount rate of 8 per cent it produces a strong ENPV. It thus follows that the real interest rate in the capital market would need to rise quite significantly to produce a negative ENPV. To arrive at the IRR we need to resort to our formula for proportional linear interpolation. From Chapter 10 you will remember that this is given by:

$$IRR = (i_1) + \left[\frac{NPV_1}{NPV_1 + NPV_2} \times (i_2 - i_1) \right]$$

We already have i_1 at 8 per cent and NPV1 at £91.65 so it is simply a matter of trial and error with a higher i value. Let us try an i value of 12 per cent. Applying this to the NCFs gives an ENPV of £53.26K. We need to try a higher i value! One approach to this is to check by how much the ENPV fell given our new discount rate. We raised it by half (from 8 to 12 per cent) and the ENPV almost halved.

If we use this as a guide it suggests that raising the discount rate by half again (from 12 to 8 per cent) we should be able 'lose' our positive ENPV. So, applying a discount rate of 18 per cent to the NCFs we get an ENPV which is very close to zero and we can sensibly use it in the interpolation formula. Thus we get:

$$\text{IRR} = (0.08) + \left[\frac{91.65}{91.65 + 4} \times (0.18 - 0.08) \right]$$

$$= 0.08 + (0.9582 * 0.1)$$

$$= 0.176, \text{ that is } 17.6\%$$

This tells us that the proposal appears a very sound one indeed because its IRR is considerably above the firm's opportunity cost of capital of 10.7 per cent. Note too that the IRR is considerably less than the figure obtained for the RoCe! In graphical terms the new production line proposal can be summarised as shown in Figure 11.3.

All the relevant information of the foregoing NPV, IRR and AENPV analyses is captured in Figure 11.3. Note that the IRR is above the firm's opportunity cost of capital (OCC) and also note that it must be the case that the firm would earn an economic profit from the new production line.

This is because at a discount rate equal to the firm's OCC (that is, 10.7 per cent) the NPV is approximately £60K – this means that an additional £60K will be generated over and above the surplus the firm could earn by locking the capital away in government securities for 4 years.

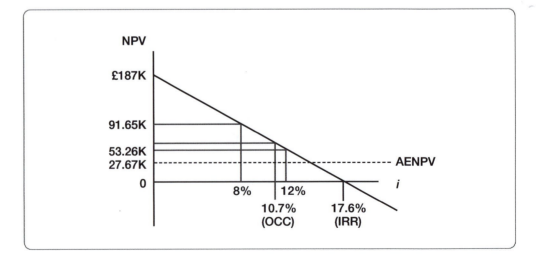

Figure 11.3 The NPV profile for Alarms R Us's proposed investment

■ ■ ■ Self-Assessment Question ■ ■ ■ ■ ■ ■ ■ ■ ■ ■ ■ ■ ■

Q5 Explain why the NPV begins at £187K.

Thus, on the grounds of payback, RoCe, NPV, AENPV and IRR this would appear to represent an efficient investment for the firm. However, there is the small matter of risk to be contended with. Part of the terms of reference include a requirement that the risk of failure be assessed.

11.5.1   Determining the Probability of Failure

We have already defined the probability of failure as the chance that an expected (positive) NPV could in fact turn out to be negative, that is less than zero. We already know how to find the variance and standard deviation associated with alternative outcomes and how to apply these in the context of the normal distribution. The following analysis does all of this in detail.

We know that the expected NPV from this investment is approximately £92K. However we also wish to know what the chances are that this healthy NPV could in fact turn out to be negative. In order to assess this risk we need to return to our scenario table of NCFs.

This is because we have to calculate the NPV for each and every alternative scenario. We will calculate for the first scenario in detail but only enter the results for the others. As an exercise you might consider calculating the others to check that you understand how the data are arrived at.

Scenario (Excellent Sales Conditions):

$$250(1.08)^{-1} + 200(1.08)^{-2} + 200(1.08)^{-3} + 150(1.08)^{-4}$$

PV = 231.5 + 171.4 + 158.8 + 110.25 = £671.95K and the NPV is given by the PV minus the capital outlay of £400K, that is, the NPV under excellent sales conditions will be £271.95K. For the other sales conditions we get:

Good = £177.93K   Fair = £93.27K   Poor = £27.03K   Awful = −£138.57K

Now we have to apply our variance formula to calculate both the variance in these data and the standard deviation. Remember that these were defined earlier as:

$$\text{Variance} = \sum_{t=1}^{N} (Xi - \bar{X}i)^2 \quad \text{and} \quad \text{Standard deviation} = \sqrt{\text{Variance}}$$

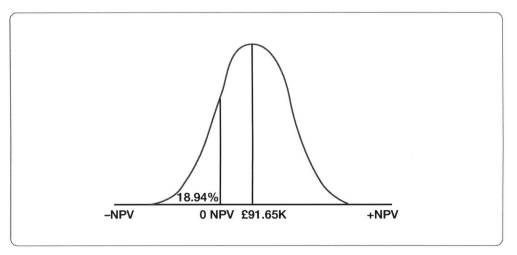

Figure 11.4 Risk profile for the proposed investment

Substituting our NPVs into the variance formula and subtracting the mean NPV from these gives:

$$\text{Variance} = \sum_{t=1}^{N} (\text{NPV} - \overline{\text{ENPV}})^2$$

$(271.95{-}91.65)^2 + (177.93{-}91.65)^2 + (93.27{-}91.65)^2$
$+ (27.03{-}91.65)^2 + (-138.57{-}91.65)^2 = £10{,}875.91$

Now substituting this variance into the standard deviation formula gives:

$$\text{Standard deviation} = \sqrt{10{,}875.91} = 104.287$$

We are now in a position to determine the probability that the new production line will make a loss, that is, that its expected NPV of £91.65K will actually turn out to be less than zero – that is, that an economic loss will be incurred. Remember to do this we need to find the z value and this is given as $z = (0 - \text{ENPV})/\text{sd} = \text{sd}$ units. Substituting our ENPV and standard deviation into this gives:

$z = (0 - 91.65)/104.287$

$= 0.879$ standard deviation units

If we look up the normal distribution table given in the Appendix we find that the z value for this number of standard deviation units is given as 0.3106, and noting that we are only concerned with the left-hand tail of the distribution we need to employ $(0.5 - \text{table } z) = (0.5 - 0.3106) = 0.1894$, that is, 18.94 per cent. What does this mean?

Simply that, despite the proposed investment looking very strong indeed, there is nevertheless nearly a 1 in 5 probability that it will fail! This can be seen clearly in Figure 11.4.

Now we have a problem. This is a high level of risk. Would the firm's management be prepared to accept such exposure to risk? The answer to this question depends on what it is that lies behind this risk profile. In other words we now need to try to establish the *sources* of this risk and to conduct a *sensitivity analysis* of the NPV to these risk sources. This we already know is part of the terms of reference and involves identifying the most likely sources of *systematic* and *specific risk* associated with the project.

■ ■ ■ Self-Assessment Questions ■ ■ ■ ■ ■ ■ ■ ■ ■ ■ ■ ■

Q6 How applicable is the normal distribution where some of the variables are correlated with each other?

Q7 (a) Write down the probability of a negative NPV where the *z* value is 0.85, 1.09 and 2.56.

(b) What can you say about the probability values as the *z* value increases?

11.5.2 A Sensitivity Analysis of the Proposed Investment

In the case of *systematic risk* the obvious source is the probability distribution itself, that is, suppose the distribution is not 1/20/40/20/1 but could be 2/8/80/8/2 or 15/20/30/20/15 or another distribution. All the calculations would need to be done from scratch and this is an extremely tedious operation, which is why it is not done here. However, with a computer many iterations can be done quickly. Another obvious source of systematic risk is the *rate of interest* used and it is very easy to analyse by how much this would need to rise to 'wipe out' the positive NPV of the project. Another source of systematic risk is the economy itself.

Changes in national and/or international economic conditions may lead the Treasury to downgrade its growth forecasts so that, for example, an excellent scenario may be cut from the previous 3 per cent to, say, 2 per cent and the 'awful' scenario may be cut from −1 per cent to −3 per cent. All the sales conditions scenarios would then need to be re-estimated. A further source of systematic risk is the regression equation used to determine the association between unemployment and reported crime. This may well be in error since it is totally dependent on the data sample used and only utilises reported crime as the dependent variable.

Additionally, it could be argued, the regression equation fundamentally ignores the social, environmental and cultural basis of crime. Finally an implicit assumption in the equation is that reported crime and household burglary are synonymous – in fact the association between unemployment and burglary may be very different. Another equation incorporating more variables (especially sociological ones) and using a different data set and a more accurate dependent variable could easily produce a very different interpretation of the relationship between crime and unemployment.

Sources of *specific risk* include the operating costs of the new production line – they may turn out to be higher than those expected – and of course whether the firm might face stiffer competition from other firms in the sector. Another source of specific risk (but is also linked to systematic risk) is the *capital cost* of the production line itself – this may turn out to be higher than expected and to some extent will depend on the required specification set down by the management. A specific risk parameter which the firm will have control over is the *timescale* of the evaluation itself, that is by how much this could be reduced before threatening the viability of the project.

Other sources of specific and systematic risk could be picked out but, generally speaking, it is the systematic risk parameters which tend to be the most important since they are outwith the control of the firm and, often, cannot be anticipated. Nevertheless the above type of analysis always helps to shed significant light on where the key risk of project failure is likely to come from. We will not get involved in the sensitivity of the NPV to all of the above risk parameters but rather will concentrate on the more important ones. These are:

- Interest rate sensitivity

- Capital cost sensitivity

- Timescale sensitivity

In each case we want to ask a very simple question:

1. How high could the interest rate go before threatening the viability of the production line?

2. How high could the capital cost go before wiping out the expected positive NPV?

3. If the timescale of the appraisal had to be reduced at what point in the project's economic life would the expected NPV cease to be positive?

■ ■ ■ Self-Assessment Question ■ ■ ■ ■ ■ ■ ■ ■ ■ ■ ■

Q8 Identify potential sources of risk to the above project which have not been mentioned already.

■■

Interest Rate Level

The initial appraisal of the project used a discount rate of 8 per cent and at this rate the expected NPV was £91.65K. However we also calculated the IRR to be 17.6 per cent. Since, by definition, the IRR is the rate that would need to apply in order to reduce the NPV to zero it follows that the interest rate would need to rise to at least 17.6 per cent before a positive NPV is threatened. In other words, the interest rate would need to more than double to produce a negative NPV and therefore an economic loss.

Capital Cost

The sensitivity of the NPV to capital cost variability is simply given as:

[(Expected PV of the NCFs – Capital Cost)/Capital Cost] * 100

This gives:

[(£491.65K – £400K)/£400K] * 100 = 22.9%

In other words, the capital cost of the project would need to rise by nearly one-quarter before the positive NPV is threatened. Now we turn to the evaluation period. A rationale for considering timescale as a risk source is provided since it is not at all clear why the timescale of an evaluation should matter – but it does!

Before going into this you might wonder why the timescale of the evaluation is relevant. If you think about it, each cash inflow is being discounted by a larger and larger discount factor the longer the period of the evaluation. So if the period is reduced this will in turn reduce the effects of the discounting process on the more distant cash inflows. Therefore there are very good reasons why we would wish to check for timescale sensitivity in project appraisal.

Timescale

At 4 years the expected NPV is £91.65K. We already know that the expected NCFs are as follows:

£173K, £150K, £150K and £114K

Visual inspection tells us that the first 2 years will definitely return a negative NPV since they cannot possibly add up to £400 (even before discounting!). We can use this fact to determine just how negative the NPV will actually be if the evaluation period is reduced to just the first 2 years. This will simply be:

$$173(1.08)^{-1} + 150(1.08)^{-2} = £288.8K$$

and the NPV will therefore be

$$(£288.8K - £400K) = -£111.2K$$

Thus at some point during the 4-year evaluation period the NPV of this project shifts from negative to positive. We need to find that point. Again we can use proportional linear interpolation to help. Remembering that we are using 2 years as the 'test' period, this gives:

$$T = 2 + [91.65/(91.65 + 111.2) \times (4 - 2)] = 2.9 \text{ years}$$

where T is the 'test' time over which the project will still produce a positive NPV. Or to put it another way, T represents the economic life of a project over which it continues to remain economically viable. Alternatively, you can think of this as the discounted payback period for the project.

From a sensitivity point of view it means that even if the new production line had to be scrapped, for whatever reason, after only about 3 years the firm will still have made an accounting surplus from it and incurred zero opportunity costs.

Now we have the data we need to draw up a sensitivity table upon which, along with all the other aspects of this appraisal, the management of Alarms R Us can base a decision to invest in the new production line or not.

Selected sensitivity parameters for the new production line	
Parameter	Change required to produce a negative NPV
Interest rate	To more than double over a 4-year period
Capital cost	Would need to rise by nearly one-quarter
Timescale	Could be reduced by one-quarter

The probability analysis determined that there is a 1 in 5 chance of an economic loss being made. Although this is a high level of risk, if we consider the above three risk sources it would appear that the investment is reasonably safe. This is because the NPV is not particularly sensitive to a key parameter, the interest rate. In addition, for the interest rate to more than double in 4 years would probably require the 'excellent' GDP growth scenario to occur.

Given that there is only a 10 per cent chance of this happening then it is extremely unlikely that interest rates could more than double. In addition this means that any one of the sales conditions which produce a positive NPV (four out of five of them) would be acceptable. On the basis of the foregoing analysis the economic consultant would recommend that the management go ahead with the investment.

However, it must be stressed that no matter how detailed a project appraisal is it remains a management decision to accept or reject the proposal. The appraisal merely provides useful information upon which a clear and, more importantly, rational economic decision can be arrived at.

■ ■ ■ Self-Assessment Question ■ ■ ■ ■ ■ ■ ■ ■ ■ ■ ■

Q9 Identify any weaknesses in sensitivity analysis.

This has been a fairly long and detailed case study incorporating all the salient features of an investment appraisal. Through this you should now have a clear understanding of how to undertake such calculations and how to interpret the results. However it must be remembered that the approaches to risk discussed above fundamentally depend on a very crucial piece of information – the probability that a particular economic/sales scenario will occur. What if there is no such information? The launch of a brand new product which has no history (by definition) or has no similar substitutes from which data can be derived is one such example. In cases like these the decision maker is not dealing with risk per se but is dealing with uncertainty. One approach to this investment decision problem is the application of game theory. In this chapter only an introduction to a few game theory methods is given, but it will be sufficient for you to understand the nature of investment decision making when the core problem is uncertainty rather than calculated risk.

■ 11.6 Investment Decisions under Uncertainty

Consider a firm which is thinking of entering a new overseas market with a product which has been and continues to be successful in its domestic market. The marketing department has assessed the situation and produced the following possible outcomes for the product.

If it is successful in the new market the firm can expect average net profits of £200K per year in the first 3 years, thereafter settling down to approximately £150K per annum. However, there are a large number of unknowns such as: cultural and consumer preference differences may not in fact be overcome; local firms could introduce a similar product; exchange rates have been known to be very volatile in the past. There are other unknowns but it is not essential to go into these. Because of these uncertainties an alternative outcome for the product is that it will fail in its first year and cost the firm £100K, that is, entry into the new overseas market will lead to losses which are unsustainable even in the short run. Entry into any new market, even with an existing product, carries several investment requirements such as extra production requirements, distribution networks, training of management and staff overseas and so on. Therefore it represents an investment decision proper. We have no probabilities to go on here and therefore we need another approach to assessing the risk.

Two approaches used in game theory can deal with this problem: the maximin criterion and the minimax regret criterion. Both operate on the basis of a 'pay-off matrix' which can be constructed from the limited data above.

11.6.1   Maximin Method

Taking the above data we can construct the pay-off matrix as shown in Table 11.4. What this method focuses on is how to determine the worst possible outcome for the investment decision. That is, it looks for the maximum minimum pay-off. Thus, if the management decide to invest in the new market the minimum pay-off in the first row is −£100K but if they decide not to invest then the minimum pay-off is £0. Given that the maximin criterion is to choose the alternative with the maximum of these minima (that is, £0 > −£100K) it follows that management would decide not to invest in the new market. As can be seen, this game theory approach to decision making is highly risk-averse. It concentrates solely on the worst outcome associated with each of the alternatives.

Nevertheless in the context of almost pure uncertainty it remains a very useful tool for firms which simply could not absorb unanticipated losses. An alternative approach is to attempt to minimise any regret associated with making the wrong decision.

Table 11.4   Maximin pay-off matrix

Pay-off matrix		
Maximin criterion	Successful	Failure
Enter new market	£200K	−£100K
Do not enter new market	£0	£0

Table 11.5   Minimax pay-off matrix

Pay-off matrix		
Minimax regret criterion	Successful	Failure
Enter new market	£0	−£100K
Do not enter new market	£200K	£0

11.6.2   Minimax Regret Method

This is an attempt to move away from the ultra risk-averse nature of the maximin method. Once again we construct a pay-off matrix using the same data (Table 11.5). The first thing to note is that cells in the second column have been swapped. This is because we are now attempting to determine the regret (opportunity cost) to the firm if it makes the wrong decision. Thus, if the firm enters the new market and it is a success then there is zero regret (that is, a loss of £0)! Hence the entry of zero in the first cell. Similarly if it chooses not to enter the market and subsequent developments show that it would have been a failure then again there is zero regret. We can now analyse the alternative 'regrets' associated with the invest and do not invest decisions. The maximum regret associated with the decision to invest will be −£100K but the maximum regret associated with a decision not to invest is the failure to earn £200K! However, the minimum regret associated with a decision not to invest in the new market is zero, therefore once again the management would opt not to invest in the new market. Although the same decision has been arrived at there is no reason that this will always be the case. The minimax regret method will often produce a different decision from the maximin method. This is because the fundamental approach to uncertainty being taken is quite different between the methods. There are severe weaknesses in both methods but as stated above, in the absence of other data, they do provide a useful (albeit limited) basis upon which management can arrive at investment decisions where information is either non-existent or very unreliable.

■ 11.7 Investment Analysis: Implications for Economic Efficiency

In this chapter and in Chapter 10 we have covered (in detail) several investment appraisal methods and considered how some of them can be applied in the context of risk. This section considers the implications for the economic efficiency of firms and other organisations where risk assessment and/or a structured approach to uncertainty is focused primarily on a risk-averse and/or minimum regret philosophy.

We have already established the difference between an economic and an accounting profit. Basically the wealth of a firm will be maximised if its investments are selected on the basis of NPV, IRR and AENPV and if a rational approach to the risk involved has been taken. Using payback or RoCe will only by chance maximise a firm's future returns.

It therefore follows that since payback is very risk averse in its approach and RoCe is highly dubious as a method at all, firms using these methods are much more likely to be less efficient. We already know from Chapter 3 that there is a strong positive correlation between past investment decisions and profitability. This is hardly surprising but it also implies that if investment decisions are made using the more sophisticated methods then firms are much more likely to raise future profitability.

This has serious implications for new product development and long-term profit. Such development is highly likely not to occur where a risk-averse investment method is being employed and/or where a proper risk analysis is not undertaken. An obvious implication of this is that the technology gap between firms will grow and, where risk aversiveness is endemic, this gap will tend to increase between whole economies. Chapter 3 demonstrated this.

It therefore follows that the competitiveness between firms and economies can quite easily widen, leading to lower efficiency levels in relative terms. This process has been witnessed in the case of many European economies compared with Japan, the USA and several SE Asian economies. The advent of the 'euro' currency is partly one attempt to raise efficiency levels and the competitiveness of EU economies in the face of increasing competition from other parts of the global economy.

In terms of technology, pricing, quality, consumer 'care', marketing and all other aspects of the competitive market, investment decisions (or non-decisions!) lie at the heart of future performance. Such decisions and the methods used to arrive at them are not simply a matter of management efficiency but fundamentally a matter of the economic health of firms, public sector enterprises and economies as a whole. A failure on the part of management to utilise rational investment appraisal methods is more likely to lead to the long-term failure of the business in question even where short-term success is the goal. The conflict between short-termism and long-term planning is a serious one. The increased use of many of the methods discussed in this chapter will enable management to more clearly demonstrate the importance of the long term over the short term.

❏ ❏ ❏ End of Chapter SUMMARY ❏ ❏ ❏ ❏ ❏ ❏ ❏ ❏ ❏ ❏ ❏

Risk and uncertainty, although related concepts, are not the same thing. Risk may be divided into systematic and specific components and only then can an attempt be made to quantify it. Uncertainty on the other hand is not so amenable to quantification and is simply a fact of life in all aspects of project appraisal. Of the numerous approaches to risk assessment in project appraisal, the most useful (but still relatively simple) is probability analysis. Although it suffers from some drawbacks, that is it uses ENPV and is open to misinterpretation, it provides more relevant information for decision makers than the other methods identified in the chapter.

However, in the end, the process of risk assessment necessarily involves a significant degree of subjective assessment. That is, the decision to accept or reject a project proposal in the light of its risk profile will always be a judgemental one. Only then are we in a position to determine which of the alternatives is exposed to the higher degree of risk of failure.

■ ■ ■ ANSWERS to Self-Assessment Questions ■ ■ ■ ■ ■ ■

Q1

Systematic risk arises from the economic environment in which we all live (local, national and global) and so an individual firm (unless it is a giant monopoly) cannot hope to have a major influence on factors such as interest rates, exchange rates, aggregate demand and many other factors which, directly and indirectly, can influence the success or otherwise of investment projects. In the case of specific risk this simply refers to parameters over which an individual firm may have some influence such as their own wage levels, output levels, prices, capacity utilisation and so on, all of which may be important to the eventual success or failure of any given investment project.

Q2

It would seem to be a highly risk-averse firm. This is because it is only prepared to invest in investment projects which produce an extremely high rate of return, that is, a very large economic profit. Thus, in using such a high IRR hurdle it is effectively attempting to 'screen out' any risk whatsoever and is very likely to be missing out on good investment opportunities which, although below 12 per cent, could still be well ahead of 5 per cent!

Q3

The ENPV can be calculated as follows.

Expected CF (year 1) = 0.2(2000) + 0.6(3000) + 0.2(6000) = 3400

Expected CF (year 2) = 0.3(1000) + 0.4(3000) + 0.3(4000) = 2700

So the EPV = £3400$(1.07)^{-1}$ + £2700$(1.07)^{-2}$ = £5535.85

Hence the ENPV = EPV − K ⇒ £535.85

Q4 $z = (0 - 1200)/1020 = 1.176$ standard deviation units. Hence the probability of a negative NPV (using the table provided) is:

(0.5 – 0.3790) = 0.21, that is 12.1%

Q5   This is because this is the value of the NCFs minus the capital outlay if the NCFs are discounted at zero, that is, if they are not discounted at all.

Q6   If some of the variables (such as NCFs, likely sales conditions and so on) are correlated with each other the normal distribution will lead to an incorrect evaluation. This is because we would actually be dealing with joint distributions. A correlated variable is one where its 'behaviour' is being partly determined by other variables in the problem. In the case of the risk of a negative NPV it may well be the case that the positive NPV we expect from a given project is only positive as long as one of the other elements in the calculation continues to behave in the same fashion. A correlated variable which is crucial to NPV but not normally distributed would make the interpretation of the z value extremely difficult.

Q7   (a) The answers are: 19.77, 13.79 and 0.523 per cent.

(b) As the value of z increases we see that the value of the associated probability rises towards an asymptotic value of just below 1 but never quite reaches 1.

Q8   You may have identified several other sources of risk involved in the project. They could include unanticipated variability in any of the following: operating and maintenance costs of the new production line; price inflation may be higher than 2.5 per cent; changes in legislation could affect material input costs and many others. You have probably identified some which we do not mention here but do not worry about that. The key point is that identifying sources of risk to any project is a major but crucial part of the risk analysis.

Q9   The main weakness is that it only checks sensitivity of one variable at a time. This is unrealistic in many cases since it will often be the case that a change in one of the risk sources causes a change in another. For example, if price inflation rises then interest rates tend to rise. In other words, many of the risk sources are themselves correlated with others. Another weakness of sensitivity analysis is that it is merely a 'snapshot' at a given time. It is not dynamic in its treatment of the interaction of risk sources. For these two reasons sensitivity analysis should always be interpreted with a degree of caution on the part of management.

See also tables in the Appendix at the end of the book.

12 Public sector decisions

■ 12.1 Introduction

This chapter is essentially an introduction to the nature of investment decisions in the public sector. A number of concepts are introduced which relate directly to many of the techniques already covered in Chapters 10 and 11.

At the root of public sector investment decisions is the basic idea of achieving 'value for money' for the taxpayer in a project where, for reasons of 'market failure', the private sector cannot or will not undertake the project on its own. In other words, some form of investment appraisal should be conducted whenever the government feels it necessary to 'intervene' in the economic development process. The concept of market failure is fundamental to the rationale for public sector intervention in a free market economy. We will deal with this important idea in the next section. Due to its wide-ranging nature an investment appraisal in the public sector tends to go beyond the type of investment appraisal methods we have already looked at and attempts to consider the full economic implications of an investment proposal, including locational issues, environmental issues and social impacts.

The decision to proceed with a particular project is (generally) taken by representatives of the community, such as government, health trusts, local councils and so on and therefore needs to be evaluated in relation to the community's preferences. That is, if the community could make an investment decision would it necessarily choose the same project or projects as its representatives?

A basic question therefore arises: whether or not we can assign the concept of *economic rationality* to a community or its representatives as we do in the case of the individual. Economic theory makes the assumption that all individual decisions are rational in the sense that any individual will always choose that option which maximises utility and/or minimises costs. We can simply extend this reasoning to the 'community' so that we can add the utilities of the individuals to produce a social preference which will reflect the *collective rationality* of the community.

In doing this what we are looking for is to identify not only the direct economic costs and benefits of an investment project but also its indirect economic and social costs and benefits. This being the case, we need to identify what social costs and benefits might be involved in the decision to proceed with a project. If we add up all the social costs and benefits and this produces a net social benefit (NSB) then a project is worth undertaking. This is the crux of a cost–benefit analysis (CBA). It is an appraisal framework which is wider than NPV or IRR and attempts to identify all the economic, social and environmental impacts (positive and negative) of public sector investment. The overall aim therefore of investment (and other) decisions in the public sector is to determine whether in fact there will be a net social benefit or a net social cost (NSC) arising from any given investment decision. If the discounted benefits and costs produce a positive NSB, in NPV terms, then the public's money has been well spent, albeit not necessarily best spent. It is issues such as these which the current chapter focuses upon. However before entering into any detail of the nature of appraisal in the public sector it is first essential that we understand why the public sector should be involved in the provision of any goods or services.

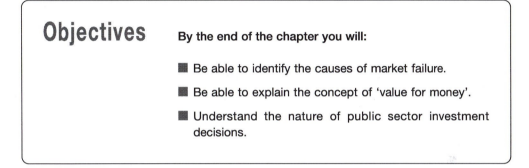

Objectives

By the end of the chapter you will:

■ Be able to identify the causes of market failure.

■ Be able to explain the concept of 'value for money'.

■ Understand the nature of public sector investment decisions.

■ 12.2 Market Failure

Standard neoclassical economic theory puts forward the proposition that markets operate efficiently and effectively and that disequilibrium can only ever be a temporary state of affairs. If private capital is not forthcoming in a particular market this is because the rate of return is below the opportunity cost of capital and/or there is so little effective demand in that market that investment is not viable. There is, however, a serious flaw in this view of the world: it assumes that markets are perfectly competitive and have perfect knowledge and foresight. It also assumes that all risks are rationally and accurately assessed.

We know that these assumptions are untenable in the real world and that firms do not compete in perfect markets, do not have perfect knowledge and therefore cannot possibly assess all opportunities and risks accurately. In other words, firms may actually miss good investment opportunities due to lack of information, poor planning, a weak competitive strategy and many other reasons. One of the roles of government is to 'fill' gaps in the market economy where it appears that the free market mechanism is not working (or cannot) due to the presence of one or more market failure phenomena. These include:

■ Unequal access to investment funds

■ The lack of information

■ The existence of barriers to entry

■ An unjustified level of risk aversion

■ An inability to adjust due to rigid prices

■ An inflexible labour force

■ Poorly trained management

There are many other types of market failure, but those listed above tend to be the main obstacles to private sector investment. Where one or more of these appear to exist the public sector may seek to step in and correct the market failure through subsidies such as capital grants, management and worker training, improved information and transport systems and more favourable tax systems.

Many of the sources of market failure above apply to the most obvious of cases such as mass health care, mass education systems, national pension funds, road systems, defence and many others. In general there will be a need for public sector intervention where we are able to make a clear distinction between two types of commodity – public goods and private goods. In the case of a purely private 'good' where consumption (the benefit) is restricted to the purchaser of the good and payment (the cost) is similarly so there is no requirement per se for public intervention, since this represents a market where an equilibrium price is capable of being established. However this does not apply in the case of a pure public 'good' where consumption (the benefit) is non-excludable and non-rivalrous (not competed for) and payment (the cost) is normally made through general taxation. Most public goods are not pure in the sense that they may be priced at the point of use and/or they break the rules of non-excludability and non-rivalry in consumption. In these circumstances they are 'impure' public goods.

Education and health care are examples of 'impure' public goods. However, it will *always* be the case that pure private and public goods impose costs and/or benefits on both users and non-users as will 'impure' public goods. For example, the provision of roads leads to congestion for non-users and pollution for both users and non-users. That is, the congestion and pollution are social costs generally not reflected in the 'private' cost incurred in car or public transport use. On the other hand, the *rapid availability* of goods and services is a social benefit of the existence and use of the roads. It thus follows that the production and consumption of both private and public goods generate 'by-products' which are either unintended and/or unavoidable. These we refer to as externalities of production and consumption. An externality is a by-product of the main activity. We can characterise externalities as follows:

■ A positive externality is a social benefit.

■ A negative externality is a social cost.

There are two crucial problems with externalities in CBA: putting a value on their generation and determining who receives them and who pays for them since it will *not* be at all obvious in many cases. A major problem underlying the valuation of positive and negative externalities is that of the *impossibility* of interpersonal utility comparisons. That is to say it is simply not possible to allocate to any given individual a 'value' for the loss of an amenity or the gain of an amenity which truly reflects that individual's own valuation.

■ ■ ■ Self-Assessment Question ■ ■ ■ ■ ■ ■ ■ ■ ■ ■ ■ ■

Q1 Identify two other public goods which you consider to be 'impure' and explain your reasoning.

If this is true for every individual then it follows that we cannot 'add up' all the 'bads' and all the 'goods' associated with a project and come to a definitive *social value* for that project. In other words, we cannot identify a *social welfare function* which truly accounts for all the utility and disutility associated with public sector investment and/or with the externality effects of a private sector investment. In other words, the measurement of both positive and negative externalities remains as much an act of faith as it ever did. However this does not mean they should be ignored, but rather that they need to be incorporated into a CBA for a project in a more judgemental way – that is, they are more easily dealt with from a political and social perspective than an economic one, even when a 'number' can actually be associated with them.

The great danger in valuing social costs and benefits is that they are likely to be either overvalued or undervalued. Neither is a problem if both costs and benefits are subject to the same error – but it is mere chance that they would be. A common solution to this problem is to simply ignore it by measuring only (in value terms) those social consequences which are 'easily' measured. In this way, the non-measurable consequences (goods and bads) cannot be over- or undervalued and so cannot inordinately affect project choice. These problems are addressed later in the chapter. In the meantime a more practicable approach to public sector investment appraisal will be discussed.

■ 12.3 Making a Difference?

Whatever the specific reason for public sector intervention and whatever the problems in measuring positive and negative externalities, it will always be the case that two fundamental objectives should be aimed to be achieved. These are the achievement of *additionality* and the minimisation of *displacement* effects. The notion of additionality is a straightforward one in public investment appraisal and evaluation. It simply means that, in the presence of one or more market failures, the public sector's involvement will lead to one or more of the following:

■ An economic, social or environmental activity actually being implemented

■ Being implemented but on a larger scale

■ Being implemented faster

■ Being focused on a group and/or spatial area of policy concern

■ Being implemented earlier than would otherwise have been the case

■ A larger social and economic benefit

It does not follow that the above are only possible where the public sector is exclusively implementing a project. More often than not, these additional 'outputs' will arise where the private sector is 'levered up' by public sector funds and/or expertise. As stated above, if the rate of return without public sector involvement is not a sufficient incentive for private sector activity and the proposed project is deemed socially desirable then (part) public assistance may be sufficient to enable the proposal to be implemented. It should only be so of course if there is a demonstrable additionality from doing so.

The issue of additionality is therefore this: the justification for public sector investment in the first place is that a market failure exists, hence the involvement of the public sector should produce an outcome which would not have happened otherwise. In other words, the public sector's involvement should show a demonstrable addition to the economy in the form of new firms, more output and more jobs.

In the case of displacement we simply mean that public sector involvement may lead to economic activity which is merely substituting for the same activity already taking place. For example, if government provides employment subsidies to some firms and not others then the firms receiving the subsidy are likely to recruit more workers but those without the subsidy may lose workers. Thus many of the 'new' jobs are in fact only displaced jobs.

Similarly, supported firms may gain market share at the expense of non-supported firms – no extra output has occurred, simply a rearranging of market shares. In this extreme case displacement would be 100 per cent.

A further problem in the appraisal of public sector investment is the counterfactual problem – that is, what would have happened if the public sector had not been involved in trying to solve a market failure problem? This raises the issue of 'deadweight' – that is, economic activity which would have taken place anyway. Obviously this is a difficult concept to measure, but it is significant since private sector recipients of taxpayers' money are unlikely to admit they would have invested in a given project even without the taxpayers' help. Clearly the identification of potential deadweight loss is an important element in public sector investment appraisal.

If we have a combination of significant deadweight, high displacement and weak or zero additionality associated with a public sector investment then it is very difficult to justify such investment in terms of value for money (VFM) for the taxpayer. On the other hand if we are dealing with a potential involvement of public sector funds where deadweight will be minimal, displacement minimal and additionality high then VFM will be more or less guaranteed. We can combine these elements to produce a formula which attempts to measure *net* additionality as follows:

$$A = (Q - D)*(1 - d)$$

where

A is net additionality, Q 'output', D deadweight and d the displacement factor.

Suppose the government wished to boost the competitiveness of the UK electronics firms through an injection of £10m into the research and development activity of indigenous UK firms. This would also aid in the employment of new and unemployed electronics graduates. If the total number of new jobs created is expected to be 2500 but the estimate for deadweight is 400 jobs and the displacement factor is 0.25 (that is, 25 in every 100 jobs are just 'moved around') then clearly the net number of jobs is only:

$$(2500 - 400)*(1 - 0.25) = 1575$$

and the cost to the government of these jobs is simply £10m/1575 = £6349.

■ ■ ■ Self-Assessment Question ■ ■ ■ ■ ■ ■ ■ ■ ■ ■ ■ ■

Q2 Briefly explain what the two CBA concepts of displacement and additionality mean.

However, as you have seen in Chapter 2, every new expenditure brings with it a multiplier effect, therefore we also need to consider not just the impact of this extra £10m on the expenditure multiplier but also its impact on business itself. Two multiplier effects will take place: the effect on firms which supply inputs to the firms receiving the R&D grant and the effect on household incomes as more people are employed. However we know that not all additional supply inputs will come from UK firms and not all of additional incomes will be spent on UK goods. Therefore the true net additional effect of the £10m will be given as:

$$A = (Q - D) * (1 - d) * (1 + s) * (1 + k)$$

where *s* and *k* are the supplier and income multipliers respectively. If even 20 per cent of the new inputs are purchased from UK firms and 80 per cent of extra income is spent on UK goods, then the additionality effect is raised significantly:

$$A = (2500 - 400) * (1 - 0.25) * (1.2) * (1.8) = 3402 \text{ jobs}$$

and the cost per job reduces to £10m/3402 = £2939. If the average earnings from these jobs is £15K per year then the economy is better off to the tune of £12,061 per job per year. With this level of economic benefit it is quite clear that the NPV would be positive. In addition the government will generate a surplus over cost per job through the income tax applied in each case. This of course would be an ideal outcome for this type of investment. In the real world the net effects are never as strong because deadweight and displacement are usually on the high side and supplier and income multipliers on the low side. Nevertheless the combination of all of these elements is crucial in producing a fuller analysis of public sector investment in terms of value for money.

■ ■ ■ Self-Assessment Question ■ ■ ■ ■ ■ ■ ■ ■ ■ ■ ■ ■

Q3 Why would the existence of high displacement and low additionality pose a threat to value for money in public sector investment projects?

■ 12.4 Objectives in Public Sector Decision Making

Many public sector organisations are required to achieve multifaceted 'outputs'. For example, in delivering health care, education, social services and other public 'goods' they are not simply required to achieve 'targets' but also to do so as efficiently as possible. This means that cost effectiveness in delivery is of prime importance, and therefore the minimisation of cost in itself becomes a prime aspect of public sector performance. An obvious example of this is in the area of compulsory competitive tendering (CCT) where the public sector provider is required to tender, in competition with the private sector, for the service they are already supplying. In theory, CCT is designed to produce the 'cost minimisation' effect shown in Figure 12.1.

You have already met cost curves such as these in Chapter 6. In Figure 12.1 we can see two things happening. First, prior to CCT the delivery cost per 'unit' of a public service is C_1 and the community receive Q_1 units for this. With the introduction of CCT we find that not only does the cost per 'unit' fall but the number of 'units' of the service now being received by the community increases to Q_2. This is what is fundamentally meant by cost effectiveness in

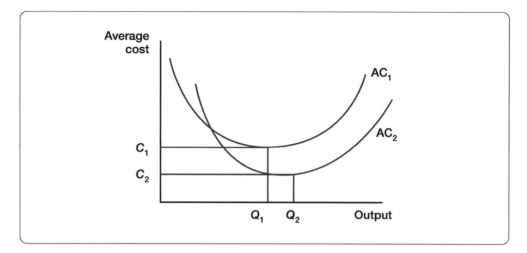

Figure 12.1 Cost minimisation in the case of CCT

public sector provision, that is, an ability to deliver either the same or more of a service at a lower cost than was previously the case. This is clearly only possible if the level of efficiency in delivery is increased.

It thus follows that a crucial component of value for money to the customer (that is, the taxpayer) is cost effectiveness. We already know from previous chapters that the chances of increasing cost effectiveness are significantly greater where correct investment decisions are taken. It thus follows that investment decisions in the public sector need to include an awareness of the goal of cost effectiveness. To put it simply – if we view each pound of taxpayers' money as being as important as each pound of (private) shareholders' money then we would expect our representatives to seek to maximise the 'return' from public sector investments. How this 'return' is measured is an issue we will come to later.

A second requirement on public sector organisations is that they do actually select from competing investment choices the best possible alternative. That is, they need to consider the opportunity costs of their investment decisions. For example, a local authority may decide to invest £12K in a town centre 'facelift' when it could have invested the money in a new set of textbooks for local primary schools or in upgrading play areas or many other 'desirable' public 'goods'.

The question which arises in this context is not simply whether the alternative decided on is delivered cost effectively but also whether it is the alternative which provides the greatest 'return' to the taxpayers. In this sense there will always be a potential opportunity cost in public sector investment decisions. Finally the public sector must also consider the issue of effectiveness itself. This does not relate to cost effectiveness but to the achievement (or otherwise) of the objective(s) behind any given decision.

For example, the government may introduce a policy of subsidising firms to employ unemployed young people, but in a later evaluation of the policy finds that only 20 per cent of the 'new' workers are below the age of 21 and the rest are older with more useful experience to firms. For all the individuals employed this has been a success and it may also have been the most cost-effective way of reducing unemployment, but in terms of effectiveness it will be deemed a failure. That is, the project will have failed one of the fundamental tests of value for money. Taking these three elements of appraisal produces the strict definition of value for money in the public sector.

■ 12.5 The Meaning of Value for Money in the Public Sector

Value for money in the public sector is composed of three criteria:

- *Economy* – opportunity cost
- *Efficiency* – cost effectiveness
- *Effectiveness* – objectives met

Taking 'economy' first this relates to the question, 'will an opportunity cost be incurred?'. The answer is 'yes' if additionality is likely to be minimal or even zero. If we consider 'efficiency' this relates to the question, 'is the implementation system the best we can have, that is, is there a better (cheaper) way of delivering this project?'. The answer is 'yes' if displacement is likely to be high and additionality low. The third criterion, 'effectiveness', relates to the objective(s) of the project and poses the question, 'can the main objective(s) be achieved with this *particular* project?'. The answer is 'no' if displacement is likely to be high. A value for money analysis is therefore an essential ingredient not only in appraising the worth of a possible project prior to a decision to implement it but also in evaluating the actual outcomes of a project once it has been implemented.

A full CBA of a proposed public sector investment or a public/private partnership would attempt to capture the value of the investment in terms of all of the above concepts. That is, externalities generated, additionality, deadweight, displacement, multiplier effects and the distribution of the costs and benefits across the affected population. All of the crucial elements of this process can be appreciated in Figure 12.2.

Following the links on the left-hand side of the diagram we can see that if VFM is not present then there is not a justification for the use of public funds. However, on the right-hand side we can see that the criteria do exist which justify the use of public funds, even as a leverage in an essentially private sector project.

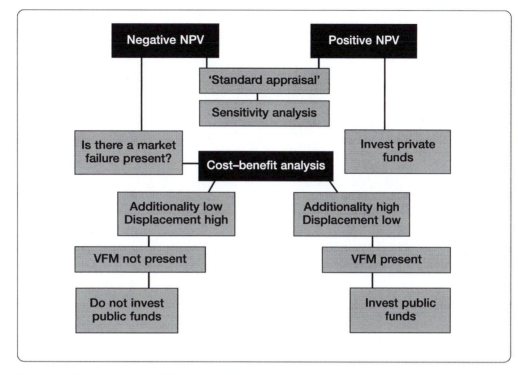

Figure 12.2 Investment appraisal in the public sector

■ ■ ■ Self-Assessment Question ■ ■ ■ ■ ■ ■ ■ ■ ■ ■ ■

Q4 Why might a practical solution to valuing social costs and benefits simply be to ignore them?

If we take three examples for consideration we can more clearly see how an appraisal of public sector investment might be undertaken. The three examples are from the education sector, the health sector and the transport sector respectively.

12.5.1   The Education Sector

Why do most countries operate mass education systems which are almost exclusively publicly funded? This may seem an odd question, but the fact is we need a very sound rationale for such large public resources to be committed to only one category of public expenditure. In the absence of such a rationale we should expect private individuals to fund their own education. So, what is the rationale for the public to do so? For this we need to return to our understanding of market failure. In the case of education which market failures must be present to justify public sector involvement? Remember these were listed as:

1. Unequal access to investment funds

2. The lack of information

3. The existence of barriers to entry

4. An unjustified level of risk aversion

5. An inability to adjust due to rigid prices

6. An inflexible labour force

7. Poorly trained management

In the case of mass education systems it is quite clear that the first four would apply to most of any country's population. Given the existence of all four (or any of them in fact) we could not, by definition, have a mass education system. A school place would be a matter for the 'market' which in practice would leave access to education as a matter of chance or as a matter of the parents' income or as a matter of where one actually lived. In other words, whether an individual received even basic schooling would be dependent on many factors totally outwith the control of that individual. By the same argument many individuals would simply not receive an education at all. Would this matter? The answer depends on what an education is supposed to do both for the individual and for society and the economy as a whole. In other words, it is very much a social cost–benefit problem.

In the absence of public sector provision it is unlikely that schooling, en masse, would otherwise take place, hence there is likely to be minimal deadweight involved. In addition the displacement factor, almost by definition, will be extremely small. However, additionality is likely to be very large. In other words, the provision of mass education would appear to contain the ingredients which are ideal for public investment. Not only does it involve many new jobs (teaching, ancillary services) but the nature of education lends itself very much to the domestic generation of textbooks, schools, furniture and all the other basic needs of a school system. Hence we would expect the relevant multipliers to be quite significant and therefore net additionality to be very strong.

These factors in themselves serve to provide a strong rationale for the public provision of mass education. But we can go much further than this in the case of education. There are other outputs which need to be considered. Some of these are not amenable to measurement in a CBA but they are nevertheless important. For example, a mass education system is expected to (at least) contribute to the following:

1. A more productive workforce

2. A higher income workforce

3. A better educated population

4. A more informed voting base

5. Better social skills

6. Political stability

7. Social stability

8. Reduced crime

Clearly a monetary value can be allocated to (1) and (2) and to (8), whereas the others represent in a very real sense positive externalities where the prime purpose of education is to improve the functioning of society as a whole. This means that all members of society gain positive social and economic benefits from the fact that all members of society receive an education.

It is not necessary to put a monetary value on these externalities since they are patently positive. In the case of the first two, however, we can identify a definite 'return' to the taxpayer associated with the investment. One method of doing this is through the evaluation of investment in human capital.

The concept of human capital simply means the quantity and quality of education, training and experience which a given individual accumulates over the lifespan. In general those who accumulate more human capital will tend to be more productive and to earn higher incomes over the lifespan compared with individuals who accumulate less human capital. If this is generally the case then we can use the concept to appraise the economic value of investing in education and training and to identify the return to the taxpayer. Consider the equation below:

$$R = \frac{Y_L - Y_C}{C_{YL}}$$

where R is the return to education, Y_L represents the income associated with any given level of education, Y_C represents income associated with the minimum (compulsory) level of education, C_{YL} is the cost associated with the extra education beyond the minimum. To see how this works let us take the case of someone who only undertakes the minimum level of education, that is, up to the number of compulsory years, and compare this with someone who goes all the way through to become a graduate. In this case the equation becomes:

$$R = \frac{Y_H - Y_C}{C_{YH}}$$

where H and C represent higher and compulsory levels respectively. In terms of age exit points the school leaver exits at the age of 16 and the graduate at the age of 21. Suppose the graduate's average earnings over the working life are £30K per annum and the school leaver's average earnings over the working life are £17K per annum. If the costs associated with the extra education are the direct cost of higher education (that is, a taxpayer cost of say £16K, including 2 extra years of schooling) plus the opportunity cost to the individual of not earning £17K per annum during higher education, then the total cost of the extra education is £16K plus 5* £17K assuming 2 extra years are spent at school and 3 years are spent studying for the degree. This is a total investment of £101K.

The difference in average earnings over the working life is £13K per annum. Assuming the school leaver and the graduate retire at the age of 65 then the former will work for 49 years and the latter for 44 years. This means the difference in their average lifetime earnings needs to be discounted to provide the NPV of investing a further 4 years in education. Using the PV factor formula from Chapter 10 we get:

$$£13K*\left[\frac{(1.08)^{44} - 1}{0.08(1.08)^{44}}\right] - £101K = (£13K*12.077) - £101K = £56K$$

So, the NPV of the additional earnings is about £56K in total at an 8 per cent discount rate. The IRR is about 13 per cent (you can check this as an exercise!) – that is, the rate of return to the extra education is about 13 per cent per annum. Now we need to make an important distinction. This is the return to the individual, not society. The return to the rest of society is the extra tax generated from the graduate's higher earnings and the additional income multiplier effect which it will generate.

The rate of return to the individual is always higher than to society. This is one of the justifications in many countries for a graduate income tax which is 1 or 2 percentage points higher than 'normal' income tax. To summarise, we know that there are non-quantifiable benefits from public sector investment in education and there are direct economic benefits which are measurable in terms of IRR. In this particular case the achievement of value for money is almost always guaranteed.

This type of human capital appraisal can be undertaken for all levels of education and for training programmes operated by firms. It will demonstrate whether in fact there are economic gains to be made from additional education or additional training. A note of caution is relevant however – it is generally the case that the more education and training received by any one individual the lower will be the rate of return. This is simply due to the fact that the direct and opportunity costs of these rise significantly with both level and age. Hence the importance in any economy of providing most of the education and most of the training to those who are about to enter the labour market is at the early point of their working lives.

The non-quantifiable benefits become more important in relative terms as age proceeds, thus providing an important rationale for lifelong learning. That is, education or training undertaken at any age will always generate a positive return to society. Figure 12.3 summarises the effect on earnings over the working life.

A person leaving school after the compulsory years (age 16 in most countries) begins to earn an income immediately. However those staying on for 2 years beyond the post-compulsory years lose those earnings (indicated by –6–18) while those staying on into higher education lose earnings of –16–22. However, the higher earnings (indicated by **++**) represent the gain from those investments. Most age–earnings profiles generate a peak around the ages of 45 to 50 in most countries. It is also the case that the type of profile above can be found in almost all economies.

If you consider the shapes of the three curves in Figure 12.3 it is quite clear they follow a type of quadratic pattern, that is, rising then falling. Knowing the mathematical 'shape' of these profiles we can also use regression methods to determine the rate of return to education.

A typical regression model for investment in education or training is as follows:

$$Y = a + b_1 S + b_2 \text{Exp} - b_3 \text{Exp}^2$$

where Y is average income, S is years of schooling and Exp is experience. This type of regression captures all the salient features of the age–earnings curves above. If we express the whole equation in logarithmic terms then the coef-

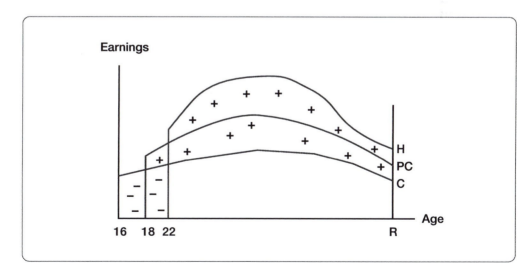

Figure 12.3 A typical age–earnings profile from education investment

ficients (the bs) can be interpreted as: b_1 = rate of return to education; b_2 rate of return to experience and b_3 is also a rate of return to experience. The coefficient b_3 is negative since this captures the effect of age and additional experience on labour productivity. That is, as we get older we become less productive, and as we gain more and more experience in work each additional year of experience tends to add less and less to our productivity.

In other words, our marginal productivity falls, hence average earnings tend to fall in later working years. A similar type of analysis can be undertaken for youth training programmes, apprenticeship systems and any type of education or training provided in both the private and public sectors. However in the case of the public sector the wider benefits are of real significance.

12.5.2   The Health Sector

Can we or should we apply a similar set of criteria to investment in health care? Only a minority of countries in the world operate a mainly (or wholly) publicly funded health service from cradle to grave. In most cases the private sector delivers health care just like any other market. So why would the public sector be involved at all? We can identify several very good reasons for this. In the interests of wider public health it may be viewed as essential that communicable diseases be minimised through, for example, vaccination programmes.

It may also be considered in the interests of society as a whole (and not just a few) that access to health care is a fundamental right or a basic need which only the state can guarantee. If this view holds it is invariably the result of a consensus arrived at through a democratic process. Whether the reason(s) is primarily one of public health considerations or linked to a political consensus, there will be positive externalities associated with public sector health provision.

One of the most obvious of these is the maintenance of a more productive labour force. If the population in general does not have access to primary health care provision (at least) then labour productivity will be lower due, for example, to increased working days lost, less effective performance at work and retirement at an earlier age than would otherwise be the case.

These represent the positive production externalities associated with public health provision. In other words, a strong and rational case for public sector investment in health can quite easily be made. Even in the case of specific disease control there will be positive externalities involved.

For example, consider the case of the simple medical treatment for the prevention of polio. In most situations this is nothing more than a small lump of sugar coated with the polio vaccine. It takes a few minutes to administer and therefore has a minimal cost in staff time and in patient working hours lost or school hours lost. The benefits, however, are substantial. Even as far back as the 1960s US economists were able to demonstrate the cost–benefit justification in purely economic terms while ignoring the psychological and social benefits entirely. They produced the following framework for the cost–benefit analysis of polio vaccination:

$$\sum_{t=0}^{T} R - [B(N - W) - C]/(1 + r)^t$$

where R is the cost of the research into the vaccine, B is the benefit per case prevented, N is the number of polio cases to be expected if there were no vaccination programme, W is the number occurring after the implementation of the programme, C is the cost of the programme and $t \to T$ is any given year (t) up to the period (T) over which the programme is evaluated. In the 1960s it was estimated that the IRR of this programme was between 11 and 12 per cent (Westbrod, 1971). Clearly this type of cost–benefit application could be applied to many health care programmes in the public sector. What it reveals is that investing public resources (in the presence of market failure) in health care (or illness prevention) can and does produce a measurable and definite return to the taxpayer.

■ ■ ■ Self-Assessment Question ■ ■ ■ ■ ■ ■ ■ ■ ■ ■ ■ ■

Q5 List three positive externalities you think may be associated with a mass child vaccination programme.

There is of course a potentially negative side to this type of approach. If taken to the extreme it could be used as a justification for not intervening in the health 'market'. That is, there is likely to be a smaller (if not zero) return to public sector health care for a range of incurable illnesses, for the aged and infirm and for any other group which either the State or the health service deems unlikely to 'benefit' from treatment. This is the dilemma in the context of resource constraints. Hence we need a different approach to evaluating public health care which is not exclusively steeped in the framework of rate of return analysis.

This has been done through 'value of life' studies which attempt to estimate the benefit in saving a human life. Although lost earnings are part of this accounting procedure it also includes values for emotional loss, insurance payouts, loss of carers (for example parents, grandparents) and other associated costs of premature or avoidable death. The values obtained are often estimated from survey data based on questionnaires in which the survey respondents are typically asked what they would be willing to pay to avoid either their own or a relative's early demise. In the USA the estimates produced range from £650K to over £7.5m depending on age and expected future earnings. The lost earnings component of the higher end of the life-value range continues to dominate the calculations as would be expected.

The nature of the cost–benefit studies conducted in the context of health care will always be open to criticism since, in general, people do not like a monetary value being attached to either disease prevention or loss of life. However, if the public sector is required to demonstrate value for money, in all spheres, then these types of calculations are unavoidable. Although any numerical assessment of the costs and benefits of health care will, almost by definition, be in error, they nevertheless are derived from a clear and unambiguous basis in theory. This is best understood in terms of Figure 12.4.

If society was composed of only three people (a, b and c) and the private costs of a vaccination to each were given by the marginal cost curve MPC while the expected private benefits to each were mba, mbb and mbc respectively, then none of these individuals would be vaccinated! This is because the starting cost is higher than the best expected benefit for person c. However, the avoidance of an epidemic is a social benefit hence the true benefit for the society is the sum of all the private benefits. If we 'vertically' add these in the graph we produce a marginal social benefit curve which cuts through the MC curve at point Q_0. This is the optimal level of provision for the vaccination programme, that is, the point at which the benefits to society are just equal to the costs at C_0.

In an ideal world we would know exactly where the optimum provision (Q_0) should be, but in practice we can really only generate a 'guesstimate' of the type discussed above. Simply because we cannot put an exact value (monetary or otherwise) on the social and economic benefits of health programmes and services is not a reason not to attempt some form of evaluation exercise. We

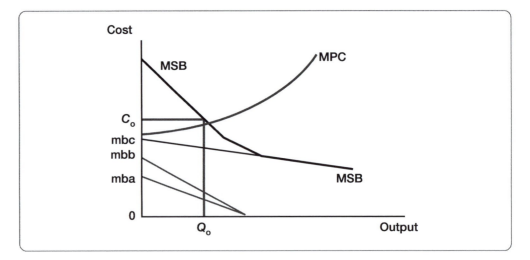

Figure 12.4   The provision of a public good

know from theory that an 'optimum' does exist – it is simply a matter of refining the appraisal techniques over time to try and get as close to that point as possible. In this way public expenditures on health care are more likely to be delivering the three criteria of value for money and more likely to minimise deadweight and displacement effects.

Let us now consider the application of these concepts to another area of significant public sector investment, the road transport sector.

12.5.3   The Road Transport Sector

Road transport is a major benefit to any economy since it allows the faster movement of goods and people and therefore enables the economy to function at a higher level than would otherwise be the case. However, although the prime function of roads is an economic one, the very use of the roads brings significant social costs. These include air pollution, congestion, accidents, illness and the removal of land which could have been used for other purposes.

The cost to the car or lorry owner is the purchase price, fuel price, maintenance costs and any road tax he or she might need to pay. This is the private cost to the individual. However, the individual does not directly pay for the negative externalities listed above (congestion, pollution and so on). Instead, society has to 'pick up the bill', so to speak. We can see this in Figure 12.5.

If the only factor to be considered in the demand for road usage were the benefit it gave to the private individual then people would use their vehicles up to the point where the marginal private benefit (MPB) to them eventually fell to zero at P_0. That is, at that point the cost to the individual exceeds the benefit. However, at P_0 the negative externalities associated with this level of road usage

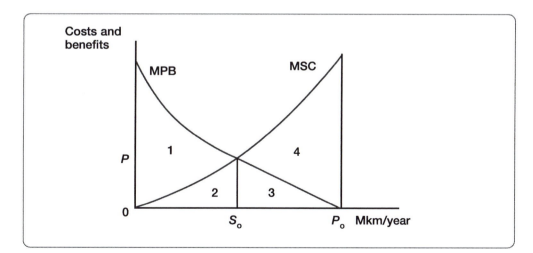

Figure 12.5   Private versus social demand for road travel

(millions of km per year in total), measured by the marginal social cost curve (MSC), are very high.

In other words, a total negative externality of areas (2 + 3 + 4) is being generated, whereas a total benefit of area 1 is being generated. Clearly (area 1) < (areas 2 + 3 + 4). It is therefore important that some of the negative externality is removed in order that the social benefit can be made positive.

The only solution to this problem is to remove areas (3 + 4) since these represent an amount of externality which is well above the socially optimum amount (S_0). This would involve a tax equivalent to the vertical distance between S_0 and the intersection of the MPB and MSC curves, thus restricting private demand to S_0. If this is done we generate a net social benefit of areas (1–2) which will be greater than zero, even though we still have the remaining externality of area 2. This then passes at least some of the externality costs to the vehicle owner, thus minimising the social cost and the direct cost to society. From this type of analysis we can define exactly what we mean by social cost as follows.

We know that the marginal cost to the individual car driver of another 1 kilometre is definitely not the only cost to be incurred. To this we need to add the extra congestion, pollution and so on. Therefore there will be a marginal social cost incurred from this extra kilometre of travel – this is the marginal externality cost (MEC). In some way this needs to be reflected in the 'price' the car user pays for using the available road space, so it follows that the price should include this: this produces the following price for road usage:

$$P = MC + MEC = MSC$$

where MSC is the true marginal social cost associated with road usage. If price is set at MSC then it follows that any 'tax' on road usage must cover the MEC, so we can say that the negative externality imposed on society by road usage could be covered by a 'tax' which is equal to the social cost involved.

Although we can define exactly what a positive and negative externality means, it is still the case that they are very difficult to measure in practice, especially those which are indirect. This is why taxation is often the most common method of dealing with negative externalities, that is, even if we cannot assign a *definite* value to an externality we still *know* that it exists, hence a tax can be used to 'sweep up' what we estimate the cost to be. It is a blunt instrument for dealing with externalities but so far the best and most cost-effective we have. In the case of road transport this is the reason the tax 'disincentive' is widely used around the world.

All economic activity involves some positive and negative externalities, that is, social 'goods' and social 'bads'. The role of investment appraisal in the public sector is to identify these and, as far as possible, evaluate them in monetary terms. Where public sector involvement in economic activity is warranted it is usually because the government considers that a market failure of some kind is operating to prevent the free market economy from functioning as it should. A standard appraisal is purely about the easily measurable costs and benefits (in money terms) of individual project proposals – and possibly the least complex aspect of public sector project appraisal. CBA goes beyond standard project appraisal and tries to measure all foreseeable costs and benefits by explicitly considering the social aspects of project implementation.

■ 12.6 Public Sector Investment

12.6.1 Introduction

We have discussed the wider issues of appraising investment (or any expenditures) by public sector agencies. These tend to require that attention is paid to the likely social benefits and social costs that might be created by such investment. We can now investigate further the implications for such investment using the example of building commercial 'space' for small companies. However, this time we will use numbers. Not only do we need to establish the usual basis for investment (NPV and so on) but we also need to test how sensitive this will be to key systematic and specific risks. In addition, since this is a public sector investment we must also consider both additionality and displacement.

 CASE STUDY *The 'NEWSITE' Project*

Suppose a local government agency wishes to put unused land to industrial use via small business development and decides to construct 16 new premises (units of varying size) on part of the unused acreage. This is seen as a 'pump-priming' investment with low rents to maximise occupancy. Over a 10-year period the agency expects *rental income* to cover all *opportunity costs*, that is, to produce at least a zero NPV. However, the occupancy rate will clearly depend on general economic conditions over that period – so a *systematic risk* is involved over which the agency has no control!

And of course in assessing the risk to value for taxpayers' money the appraisal must make assumptions about the future 'environment'.

12.6.2 Data for Case Study – The 'NEWSITE' Project

Total floor space available for rent = 14,000 sq.ft. when the units are completed (construction time = 10 months).

The capital cost (including drainage, access, building services and unit construction) is estimated at an average of £9000 *per unit* = 16 units * £9000 = £144,000.

The current real interest rate (risk-free rate) is 4 per cent and the rental rate is expected to be £2/sq.ft. Using the data provided complete the spreadsheet analysis below:

Economic conditions	Very good	Good	Moderate	Poor	Very poor
Rental take-up (%)	95	85	75	60	50
Square feet	13,300	11,900	10,500	8,400	7,000
Annual rent (£)	26,600	23,800	21,000	16,800	14,000
PV of rent over 10 years^	215,750	193,040	170,329	136,263	113,553
NPV over 10 years	71,750	49,040	26,329	−7,737	−30,447
Probability of condition	0.1	0.2	0.4	0.2	0.1
NPV* Probability	7,175	9,808	10,532	−1,547	−3,045

Note (^) is Annual Rent * Present Value Factor.
All numbers have been rounded to the nearest decimal point.

To find the expected net present value (ENPV) we simply sum across the final row in the table. This gives an ENPV of £22,923. Note that if we take the weighted average rental income but do not apply a discount rate it comes out at £20,520 per annum. So, the 'NEWSITE' scheme appears to be a worthwhile one. However, what is the chance that this strong ENPV could turn out to be a *negative NPV*? To answer this we need to calculate the variance and standard deviation contained in the NPV and ENPV data. Remember from Chapter 9 that:

Variance = Sum(NPV–ENPV)^2 * Probability of Condition

and

Standard deviation = SQRT(VAR)

and that the probability that *any* NPV will be *negative* is given by the formula:

(0 − ENPV)/STD = y STD units

Let us begin with calculating the variance of the NPVs over the range of economic conditions:

$(71,750 − 22,923)^2 * 0.1$ + $(49,040 − 22,923)^2 * 0.2$ +

$(26,329 − 22,923)^2 * 0.4$ + $(−7,737 − 22,923)^2 * 0.2$ +

$(−30,447 − 22,923)^2 * 0.1$

= 637,743,441.5 (this is the variance)

The standard deviation is the square root of this which is: 25,254. Now we need to find the number of standard deviation units associated with the above relative to the project's ENPV and to our 'baseline' of the chance of a negative NPV. To do this we simply set the baseline at zero. This gives:

$z = (0 - 22{,}923)/25{,}254 = 0.9076$ standard deviation units

Now we look up the value of z in the normal distribution table (provided in the Appendix) and this gives a value for z of 0.3340. Since we are only interested in the probability of a negative NPV then we should only be concerned with the left-hand side of the normal distribution. This means we must subtract out table z *value* from 0.5 and this gives us the probability that the NPV for the 'NEWSITE' project will be:

$(0.5 - \text{table } z) \rightarrow (0.5 - 0.3340) = 0.166 \rightarrow 16.6\%$

Hence, there is nearly a 17 per cent chance that this project will *in fact* return a negative NPV. Notice that we used the term 'in fact' in the previous sentence. This is because it is important to understand what a probability actually means. If we divide 16.6 per cent into 100 per cent we get a value of 6. This means that out of every six projects with a similar NPV profile and under similar conditions one will definitely return a negative NPV. The question that needs to be asked is: is this an acceptable risk to taxpayers' money? If the answer is no, then we need go no further with the appraisal. If it is yes then we need to conduct a sensitivity analysis of the project in order to be more certain that the risk is minimised.

12.6.3 Sensitivity Analysis of the 'NEWSITE' Project

First we have to identify the systematic and the specific risks associated with this project.

We know that the discount rate (in real terms) is 4 per cent but the local government has no influence over interest rates in the economy therefore the interest rate is clearly a source of systematic risk. Similarly, the rental take-up (and so rental income) will depend on future economic conditions and the local government has no influence over that either – hence another source of systematic risk. What about the specific risks? We know that the appraisal was conducted over a 10-year period therefore the local government could try to reduce the timescale of the appraisal period to test how sensitive the NPV is to time – this is under its control therefore it is a source of specific risk. Similarly, the capital cost of the project is to a large extent dependent on the effectiveness of the local government's project management team – hence this too is a source of specific risk. We can list the risks as follows:

■ *Systematic risks:* real interest rates and future economic conditions (rental income)

■ *Specific risks:* capital costs and timescales

Real Interest Rates

Since the ENPV at 4 per cent is £22,923 (that is, the PV(F) = 8.11) it follows that the PV(F) required to reduce this to zero will be given as:

$$(CF * F) - K_0 = \text{zero, that is } (£22,923 * 8.11) - £144,000 = 0$$

hence:

$$F = £144,000/£22,923 = 6.28$$

Now, let the *real* interest rate over the 10-year period be 6 per cent (instead of 4 per cent) producing a PV(F) of 7.36. Using proportional linear interpolation:

$$R_i = 0.04 + [8.11 - 6.28]/[8.11 - 7.36] * (0.06 - 0.04) = 0.0888$$

Thus, the real interest rate would need to rise to nearly 9 per cent before the NPV would be negative. (Note that this value of 8.88 per cent is really the project's IRR.)

Rental Income

The capital cost is £144,000 and the PV Factor (F) = 8.11, thus the lowest annual (average) income which could be acceptable (to give a zero NPV) will be given as:

$$144/8.11 = £17,756 \text{ per annum}$$

This should be compared with the £20,520 weighted (non-discounted) average income predicted. Thus, the project could 'absorb' a 13.5 per cent reduction in its rental income before it would become uneconomic.

Capital Costs

At a risk-free real rate of 4 per cent the expected PV of the investment is £166,923 (that is ENPV plus capital cost of £144,000).The capital cost would need to rise above this value to produce a negative ENPV, implying that a capital cost overrun of just under 16 per cent would be required before value for money is threatened. That is:

$(166{,}923 - 144{,}000)/144{,}000 = 15.8\%$

Timescale

The ENPV was calculated on a 10-year life but what is the minimum appraisal period necessary to protect value for money? At 10 years the ENPV is £22,923 so, try a year timescale:

At 7 years the PV Factor (F), that is, 7yrs @ 4%, = 6.01, hence, the ENPV will be 6.01 * Annual Rent * Probability for Each Rental Condition minus the capital cost. This gives an EPV of £123,686 and so the ENPV is £123,686 − £144,000 = −£20,314.

Using *proportional linear interpolation* we get:

$T = 7 + [20{,}314]/[22{,}923 + 20{,}314] * (10 - 7) = 8.41$ years

So, all opportunity costs are covered by the end of 8½ years. Or alternatively, cutting the project's 'life' by nearly 16 per cent (10 years to 8.41 years) still leaves it as a viable economic venture. Taking these risk sources together we can construct the project's risk profile:

Sensitivity table for the 'NEWSITE' project

Source of risk	Original value	Min/max value	Variation (%)
Capital cost	£144,000	£166,923	+15.9%
Timescale	10 yrs	8.41yrs	−15.9%
Annual income	£20,520	£17,756	−13.5%
Real *i* rate	4.00%	8.88%	+122%

Quite clearly, the riskiest parameter is project income (because it shows the least variation). From an assessment point of view this is a 'good' result since it is a parameter specific to the project which is most likely to affect it – therefore some detailed attention to this would be worthwhile. Of course it may be considered that the variation needed to threaten this project is such that there is a low risk to value for money and so the project should, *on financial grounds*, be implemented. However, we also need to consider the issues of displacement and additionality. To do this we need to consider if any of the firms moving into the new premises have simply moved away from another location and we need to know how many are new firms. This information will tell us how many jobs the public sector investment has created.

❏ ❏ ❏ End of Chapter SUMMARY ❏ ❏ ❏ ❏ ❏ ❏ ❏ ❏ ❏ ❏ ❏

In essence CBA requires the existence of an identifiable and measurable 'social' welfare function – this rarely, if ever, exists and hence principles of compensation need to be invoked as part of the cost side in a full CBA. However, identifying the actual costs involved is almost impossible and further weakens the CBA as an objective instrument of project appraisal. The role of CBA needs to be seen in the wider context of project appraisal. That is, as part of a larger picture in which several different aspects of project appraisal are interconnected.

If an investment project is being considered for public sector funding (either wholly or in part) but the standard appraisal reveals that a positive NPV is highly probable, then there is little additionality which public sector funding can bring to the project, in which case it ought to be funded by the private sector. Where negative externalities are likely to result from this these need to be included in the project costings, and if the NPV is still positive then the project ought to go ahead under private funding. On the other hand if a project is not likely to return a positive NPV, due to some form of market failure, but is still a desirable project, then a CBA can be conducted to weigh up the effect of public sector involvement in terms of social 'goods and bads' including the displacement and additionality effects.

Where these effects are favourable then it will usually be the case that such funding will represent VFM, but if they are unfavourable then it is probably the case that not only should public funding be withheld but the project itself should not (and is likely not to) be allowed to go ahead. The role of a CBA is therefore to test whether there really is merit in a weak investment proposal from the private sector being 'pump-primed' by the public sector and to test whether a wholly public sector-funded project is good value for the taxpayer.

In practice, however, it will often be the case that such projects are approved for political, aesthetic, strategic or other reasons even though on a VFM basis they would not be. As in the case of the standard approach to investment appraisal, it is quite clear that the final decision to invest in any project on the part of the public sector will always be a fundamentally subjective one. Indeed a cynical view of the function of CBA would argue that a decision to invest public money has often already been taken and the CBA is only conducted afterwards in order to provide an apparent 'justification' for that decision. Irrespective of how and why it is used in practice by government, the fact remains that a CBA is an *extension* of standard appraisal methods and provides very useful and informative insights into the total effect of investment projects which we would otherwise be unaware of. To that extent the real value of a CBA is that it will always generate more information upon which decisions can be taken.

Reference

Westbrod, B.A. 'Costs and Benefits of Medical Research: A Case Study of Poliomyelitis' *Journal of Political Economy*, May–June, 1971 pp. 527–44.

■ ■ ■ **ANSWERS** to Self-Assessment Questions ■ ■ ■ ■ ■ ■ ■

Q1
You may have suggested public goods other than the two here. If we consider two generally accepted public goods – the police service and the law itself – we find that both tend to be impure on a number of accounts. In the case of the police service we cannot say this is a public good universally available to everyone simply because of resource constraints. It is often argued that such services tend to be very differential in their effectiveness dependent on locality, local budgets, recruitment levels and on the nature of the area to be policed. Crime prevention is not the sole function of the police service – it is also a responsibility of each citizen. To that extent the police service cannot be considered a pure public good. Similarly in the case of the law itself this requires individuals to pay their own expenses very often and is not funded exclusively from general taxation.

Q2
Displacement refers to the situation where a new economic activity does not generate *additional* economic activity at all (absolute displacement) or to the situation where a new economic activity absorbs some of the resources which were already being productively used in another sector of the economy or in the same sector but at another location (partial displacement).

Additionality explicitly refers to the situation where *public* funding leads to an economic activity (for example higher output, more jobs) which would otherwise have not occurred at all or would have occurred but at a lower level of activity. The presence of both the displacement and the additionality effects of new investment is a key indicator in CBA of whether the final outcome is likely to be a net social benefit or not.

Q3
If any public sector project appeared likely to produce high displacement and low additionality this would mean that it would be taking resources away from current economic activity and thus adding little or nothing to total economic output. This being the case, at least one or more of the three criteria behind VFM would not be met – economy, efficiency and effectiveness – and hence value for money could not be demonstrated.

Q4

It could be argued that the difficulty involved in measuring such costs and benefits makes it impossible to arrive at an accurate or even approximately accurate figure. Hence major assumptions would need to be made in the construction of any monetary figure for these costs and benefits. Given that we cannot measure the comparative levels of utility of those who receive the benefits and incur the costs it is better not to even attempt to undertake such evaluations. The problem with this approach, however, is that it focuses CBA to a very narrow 'yardstick', monetary values, which we know cannot possibly capture the intrinsic value to the community of many social benefits (or costs) which are incurred. Just because we cannot measure something is no reason to ignore the fact that it exists!

Q5

The purpose of a vaccination programme is to prevent the contraction of a specific illness or illnesses and therefore its prime purpose is to enable children to be healthier than they otherwise might be. This will produce a number of attractive positive externalities. You have probably identified many different positive externalities. We have listed below those which seem particularly relevant to the economy.

- Fewer school absences
- A healthier future labour force
- Hence, higher future productivity
- Lower future health care costs

Compared to the direct cost of a vaccination programme, it is extremely likely that these externalities will produce a strong net social benefit.

See also tables in the Appendix at the end of the book.

Discount tables and the normal distribution table

How to Use the Tables

Future Value Table: Supposing you want to know what £1 will be worth in 9 years' time at an interest rate of 12 per cent. If you look along the top of the future value table to 0.12 and follow the column down to the 9th year you will see the entry is 2.77. This means that £1 invested for 9 years at an interest rate of 12 per cent will be worth £2.77 at the end of the ninth year.

Present Value Table: If you wish to know the present value of £1 receivable after 12 years at a discount rate of 14 per cent simply look along to the 14 per cent column and down to the cell which corresponds to 12 years: the entry is given as 0.20755, that is, the £1 has a present value of just over 20 pence.

Present Value Factor Table: If you look at the table you can find the discount factor associated with a given discount rate over a given period of time. For example, the present value of £1 receivable each year over 8 years at a discount rate of 12 per cent is given by the discount factor (4.967) × £1, that is, the PV of £1 receivable each year for 8 years at a 12 per cent discount rate is £4.967.

Annual Equivalent Factor Table: If an NPV amount needs to be converted to an annual equivalent amount then this table is very useful. For example, suppose the NPV from a project is calculated to be £50K using a discount rate of 6 per cent and it has an expected economic life of 10 years. We need to find the AEF for the combination of 10 years and 6 per cent. Again, looking along the table to the 6 per cent column and down to the corresponding 10-year cell we get the AEF as 0.13586. Hence our NPV of £50K is £6793 in annual equivalent terms.

Normal Distribution Table: Once we know the value for z we can use the table to calculate a probability value. Suppose $z = 1.13$ we need to go down the z column to 1.1 and along to 0.03 where the entry is given as 0.3708. Since we are only using half of the distribution then the probability value will be $(0.5 - 0.3708) = 0.1292$, that is, 12.92 per cent.

Future Value Table

The future value of £1 = £1$(1 + i)^t$

| Years | Interest rate → | | | | | | | | | |
	2%	4%	6%	8%	10%	12%	14%	16%	18%	20%
1	1.02	1.04	1.06	1.08	1.1	1.12	1.14	1.18	1.18	1.2
2	1.0404	1.0816	1.1236	1.1664	1.21	1.2544	1.2996	1.3924	1.3924	1.44
3	1.06120	1.12486	1.19101	1.25971	1.331	1.40492	1.48154	1.64303	1.64303	1.728
4	1.08243	1.16985	1.26247	1.36048	1.4641	1.57351	1.68896	1.93877	1.93877	2.0736
5	1.10408	1.21665	1.33822	1.46932	1.61051	1.76234	1.92541	2.28775	2.28775	2.48832
6	1.12616	1.26531	1.41851	1.58687	1.77156	1.97382	2.19497	2.69955	2.69955	2.98598
7	1.14868	1.31593	1.50363	1.71382	1.94871	2.21068	2.50226	3.18547	3.18547	3.58318
8	1.17165	1.36856	1.59384	1.85093	2.14358	2.47596	2.85258	3.75885	3.75885	4.29981
9	1.19509	1.42331	1.68947	1.99900	2.35794	2.77307	3.25194	4.43545	4.43545	5.15978
10	1.21899	1.48024	1.79084	2.15892	2.59374	3.10584	3.70722	5.23383	5.23383	6.19173
11	1.24337	1.53945	1.89829	2.33163	2.85311	3.47854	4.22623	6.17592	6.17592	7.43008
12	1.26824	1.60103	2.01219	2.51817	3.13842	3.89597	4.81790	7.28759	7.28759	8.91610
13	1.29360	1.66507	2.13292	2.71962	3.45227	4.36349	5.49241	8.59935	8.59935	10.6993
14	1.31947	1.73167	2.26090	2.93719	3.79749	4.88711	6.26134	10.1472	10.1472	12.8391
15	1.34586	1.80094	2.39655	3.17216	4.17724	5.47356	7.13793	11.9737	11.9737	15.4070
16	1.37278	1.87298	2.54035	3.42594	4.59497	6.13039	8.13724	14.1290	14.1290	18.4884
17	1.40024	1.94790	2.69277	3.70001	5.05447	6.86604	9.27646	16.6722	16.6722	22.1861
18	1.42824	2.02581	2.85433	3.99601	5.55991	7.68996	10.5751	19.6732	19.6732	26.6233
19	1.45681	2.10684	3.02559	4.31570	6.11590	8.61276	12.0556	23.2144	23.2144	31.9479
20	1.48594	2.19112	3.20713	4.66095	6.72749	9.64629	13.7434	27.3930	27.3930	38.3375
21	1.51566	2.27876	3.39956	5.03383	7.40024	10.8038	15.6675	32.3237	32.3237	46.0051
22	1.54597	2.36991	3.60353	5.43654	8.14027	12.1003	17.8610	38.1420	38.1420	55.2061
23	1.57689	2.46471	3.81974	5.87146	8.95430	13.5523	20.3615	45.0076	45.0076	66.2473
24	1.60843	2.56330	4.04893	6.34118	9.84973	15.1786	23.2122	53.1090	53.1090	79.4968
25	1.64060	2.66583	4.29187	6.84847	10.8347	17.0000	26.4619	62.6686	62.6686	95.3962
26	1.67341	2.77246	4.54938	7.39635	11.9181	19.0400	30.1665	73.9489	73.9489	114.475
27	1.70688	2.88336	4.82234	7.98806	13.1099	21.3248	34.3899	87.2597	87.2597	137.370
28	1.74102	2.99870	5.11168	8.62710	14.4209	23.8838	39.2044	102.966	102.966	164.844
29	1.77584	3.11865	5.41838	9.31727	15.8630	26.7499	44.6931	121.500	121.500	197.813
30	1.81136	3.24339	5.74349	10.0626	17.4494	29.9599	50.9501	143.370	143.370	237.376
31	1.84758	3.37313	6.08810	10.8676	19.1943	33.5551	58.0831	169.177	169.177	284.851
32	1.88454	3.50805	6.45338	11.7370	21.1137	37.5817	66.2148	199.629	199.629	341.821
33	1.92223	3.64838	6.84058	12.6760	23.2251	42.0915	75.4849	235.562	235.562	410.186
34	1.96067	3.79431	7.25102	13.6901	25.5476	47.1425	86.0527	277.963	277.963	492.223
35	1.99988	3.94608	7.68608	14.7853	28.1024	52.7996	98.1001	327.997	327.997	590.668
36	2.03988	4.10393	8.14725	15.9681	30.9126	59.1355	111.834	387.036	387.036	708.801
37	2.08068	4.26808	8.63608	17.2456	34.0039	66.2318	127.490	456.703	456.703	850.562
38	2.12229	4.43881	9.15425	18.6252	37.4043	74.1796	145.339	538.910	538.910	1020.67
39	2.16474	4.61636	9.70350	20.1152	41.1447	83.0812	165.687	635.913	635.913	1224.80
40	2.20803	4.80102	10.2857	21.7245	45.2592	93.0509	188.883	750.378	750.378	1469.77

Present Value Table

The present value of £1 = £1$(1 + i)^{-t}$

Years	Interest rate →									
	2%	4%	6%	8%	10%	12%	14%	16%	18%	20%
1	0.98039	0.96153	0.94339	0.92592	0.90909	0.89285	0.87719	0.86206	0.84745	0.83333
2	0.96116	0.92455	0.88999	0.85733	0.82644	0.79719	0.76946	0.74316	0.71818	0.69444
3	0.94232	0.88899	0.83961	0.79383	0.75131	0.71178	0.67497	0.64065	0.60863	0.57870
4	0.92384	0.85480	0.79209	0.73502	0.68301	0.63551	0.59208	0.55229	0.51578	0.48225
5	0.90573	0.82192	0.74725	0.68058	0.62092	0.56742	0.51936	0.47611	0.43710	0.40187
6	0.88797	0.79031	0.70496	0.63016	0.56447	0.50663	0.45558	0.41044	0.37043	0.33489
7	0.87056	0.75991	0.66505	0.58349	0.51315	0.45234	0.39963	0.35382	0.31392	0.27908
8	0.85349	0.73069	0.62741	0.54026	0.46650	0.40388	0.35055	0.30502	0.26603	0.23256
9	0.83675	0.70258	0.59189	0.50024	0.42409	0.36061	0.30750	0.26295	0.22545	0.19380
10	0.82034	0.67556	0.55839	0.46319	0.38554	0.32197	0.26974	0.22668	0.19106	0.16150
11	0.80426	0.64958	0.52678	0.42888	0.35049	0.28747	0.23661	0.19541	0.16191	0.13458
12	0.78849	0.62459	0.49696	0.39711	0.31863	0.25667	0.20755	0.16846	0.13721	0.11215
13	0.77303	0.60057	0.46883	0.36769	0.28966	0.22917	0.18206	0.14522	0.11628	0.09346
14	0.75787	0.57747	0.44230	0.34046	0.26333	0.20461	0.15970	0.12519	0.09854	0.07788
15	0.74301	0.55526	0.41726	0.31524	0.23939	0.18269	0.14009	0.10792	0.08351	0.06490
16	0.72844	0.53390	0.39364	0.29189	0.21762	0.16312	0.12289	0.09304	0.07077	0.05408
17	0.71416	0.51337	0.37136	0.27026	0.19784	0.14564	0.10779	0.08020	0.05997	0.04507
18	0.70015	0.49362	0.35034	0.25024	0.17985	0.13003	0.09456	0.06914	0.05083	0.03756
19	0.68643	0.47464	0.33051	0.23171	0.16350	0.11610	0.08294	0.05960	0.04307	0.03130
20	0.67297	0.45638	0.31180	0.21454	0.14864	0.10366	0.07276	0.05138	0.03650	0.02608
21	0.65977	0.43883	0.29415	0.19865	0.13513	0.09255	0.06382	0.04429	0.03093	0.02173
22	0.64683	0.42195	0.27750	0.18394	0.12284	0.08264	0.05598	0.03818	0.02621	0.01811
23	0.63415	0.40572	0.26179	0.17031	0.11167	0.07378	0.04911	0.03292	0.02221	0.01509
24	0.62172	0.39012	0.24697	0.15769	0.10152	0.06588	0.04308	0.02837	0.01882	0.01257
25	0.60953	0.37511	0.23299	0.14601	0.09229	0.05882	0.03779	0.02446	0.01595	0.01048
26	0.59757	0.36068	0.21981	0.13520	0.08390	0.05252	0.03314	0.02109	0.01352	0.00873
27	0.58586	0.34681	0.20736	0.12518	0.07627	0.04689	0.02907	0.01818	0.01146	0.00727
28	0.57437	0.33347	0.19563	0.11591	0.06934	0.04186	0.02550	0.01567	0.00971	0.00606
29	0.56311	0.32065	0.18455	0.10732	0.06303	0.03738	0.02237	0.01351	0.00823	0.00505
30	0.55207	0.30831	0.17411	0.09937	0.05730	0.03337	0.01962	0.01164	0.00697	0.00421
31	0.54124	0.29646	0.16425	0.09201	0.05209	0.02980	0.01721	0.01004	0.00591	0.00351
32	0.53063	0.28505	0.15495	0.08520	0.04736	0.02660	0.01510	0.00865	0.00500	0.00292
33	0.52022	0.27409	0.14618	0.07888	0.04305	0.02375	0.01324	0.00746	0.00424	0.00243
34	0.51002	0.26355	0.13791	0.07304	0.03914	0.02121	0.01162	0.00643	0.00359	0.00203
35	0.50002	0.25341	0.13010	0.06763	0.03558	0.01893	0.01019	0.00554	0.00304	0.00169
36	0.49022	0.24366	0.12274	0.06262	0.03234	0.01691	0.00894	0.00478	0.00258	0.00141
37	0.48061	0.23429	0.11579	0.05798	0.02940	0.01509	0.00784	0.00412	0.00218	0.00117
38	0.47118	0.22528	0.10923	0.05369	0.02673	0.01348	0.00688	0.00355	0.00185	9.79744
39	0.46194	0.21662	0.10305	0.04971	0.02430	0.01203	0.00603	0.00306	0.00157	8.16453
40	0.45289	0.20828	0.09722	0.04603	0.02209	0.01074	0.00529	0.00264	0.00133	6.80378

Present Value Factor Table

Present value factors: $£1* \left[\dfrac{(1 + i)^t - 1}{i(1 + i)^t} \right] = \text{PV of } £1$

Years	Interest rate → 5%	8%	10%	12%	15%
1	0.95238	0.92592	0.90909	0.89285	0.86956
2	1.85941	1.78326	1.73553	1.69005	1.62570
3	2.72324	2.57709	2.48685	2.40183	2.28322
4	3.54595	3.31212	3.16986	3.03734	2.85497
5	4.32947	3.99271	3.79078	3.60477	3.35215
6	5.07569	4.62287	4.35526	4.11140	3.78448
7	5.78637	5.20637	4.86841	4.56375	4.16041
8	6.46321	5.74663	5.33492	4.96763	4.48732
9	7.10782	6.24688	5.75902	5.32824	4.77158
10	7.72173	6.71008	6.14456	5.65022	5.01876
11	8.30641	7.13896	6.49506	5.93769	5.23371
12	8.86325	7.53607	6.81369	6.19437	5.42061
13	9.39357	7.90377	7.10335	6.42354	5.58314
14	9.89864	8.24423	7.36668	6.62816	5.72447
15	10.3796	8.55947	7.60607	6.81086	5.84737
16	10.8377	8.85136	7.82370	6.97398	5.95423
17	11.2740	9.12163	8.02155	7.11963	6.04716
18	11.6895	9.37188	8.20141	7.24967	6.12796
19	12.0853	9.60359	8.36492	7.36577	6.19823
20	12.4622	9.81814	8.51356	7.46944	6.25933
21	12.8211	10.0168	8.64869	7.56200	6.31246
22	13.1630	10.2007	8.77154	7.64464	6.35866
23	13.4885	10.3710	8.88321	7.71843	6.39883
24	13.7986	10.5287	8.98474	7.78431	6.43377
25	14.0939	10.6747	9.07704	7.84313	6.46414
26	14.3751	10.8099	9.16094	7.89565	6.49056
27	14.6430	10.9351	9.23722	7.94255	6.51353
28	14.8981	11.0510	9.30656	7.98442	6.53350
29	15.1410	11.1584	9.36960	8.02180	6.55087
30	15.3724	11.2577	9.42691	8.05518	6.56597
31	15.5928	11.3497	9.47901	8.08498	6.57911
32	15.8026	11.4349	9.52637	8.11159	6.59053
33	16.0025	11.5138	9.56943	8.13535	6.60046
34	16.1929	11.5869	9.60857	8.15656	6.60909
35	16.3741	11.6545	9.64415	8.17550	6.61660
36	16.5468	11.7171	9.67650	8.19241	6.62313
37	16.7112	11.7751	9.70591	8.20751	6.62881
38	16.8678	11.8288	9.73265	8.22099	6.63375
39	17.0170	11.8785	9.75695	8.23302	6.63804
40	17.1590	11.9246	9.77905	8.24377	6.64177

Annual Equivalent Factor Table

Annual equivalent factors = $i/1 - (1 + i)^\wedge -t$

Years	Interest rate →								
	2%	4%	6%	8%	10%	12%	14%	16%	18%
1	1.02	1.04	1.06	1.08	1.1	1.12	1.14	1.16	1.18
2	0.51504	0.53019	0.54543	0.56076	0.57619	0.59169	0.60728	0.62296	0.63871
3	0.34675	0.36034	0.37410	0.38803	0.40211	0.41634	0.43073	0.44525	0.45992
4	0.26262	0.27549	0.28859	0.30192	0.31547	0.32923	0.34320	0.35737	0.37173
5	0.21215	0.22462	0.23739	0.25045	0.26379	0.27740	0.29128	0.30540	0.31977
6	0.17852	0.19076	0.20336	0.21631	0.22960	0.24322	0.25715	0.27138	0.28591
7	0.15451	0.16660	0.17913	0.19207	0.20540	0.21911	0.23319	0.24761	0.26236
8	0.13650	0.14852	0.16103	0.17401	0.18744	0.20130	0.21557	0.23022	0.24524
9	0.12251	0.13449	0.14702	0.16007	0.17364	0.18767	0.20216	0.21708	0.23239
10	0.11132	0.12329	0.13586	0.14902	0.16274	0.17698	0.19171	0.20690	0.22251
11	0.10217	0.11414	0.12679	0.14007	0.15396	0.16841	0.18339	0.19886	0.21477
12	0.09455	0.10655	0.11927	0.13269	0.14676	0.16143	0.17666	0.19241	0.20862
13	0.08811	0.10014	0.11296	0.12652	0.14077	0.15567	0.17116	0.18718	0.20368
14	0.08260	0.09466	0.10758	0.12129	0.13574	0.15087	0.16660	0.18289	0.19967
15	0.07782	0.08994	0.10296	0.11682	0.13147	0.14682	0.16280	0.17935	0.19640
16	0.07365	0.08581	0.09895	0.11297	0.12781	0.14339	0.15961	0.17641	0.19371
17	0.06996	0.08219	0.09544	0.10962	0.12466	0.14045	0.15691	0.17395	0.19148
18	0.06670	0.07899	0.09235	0.10670	0.12193	0.13793	0.15462	0.17188	0.18963
19	0.06378	0.07613	0.08962	0.10412	0.11954	0.13576	0.15266	0.17014	0.18810
20	0.06115	0.07358	0.08718	0.10185	0.11745	0.13387	0.15098	0.16866	0.18681
21	0.05878	0.07128	0.08500	0.09983	0.11562	0.13224	0.14954	0.16741	0.18574
22	0.05663	0.06919	0.08304	0.09803	0.11400	0.13081	0.14830	0.16635	0.18484
23	0.05466	0.06730	0.08127	0.09642	0.11257	0.12955	0.14723	0.16544	0.18409
24	0.05287	0.06558	0.07967	0.09497	0.11129	0.12846	0.14630	0.16467	0.18345
25	0.05122	0.06401	0.07822	0.09367	0.11016	0.12749	0.14549	0.16401	0.18291
26	0.04969	0.06256	0.07690	0.09250	0.10915	0.12665	0.14480	0.16344	0.18246
27	0.04829	0.06123	0.07569	0.09144	0.10825	0.12590	0.14419	0.16296	0.18208
28	0.04698	0.06001	0.07459	0.09048	0.10745	0.12524	0.14366	0.16254	0.18176
29	0.04577	0.05887	0.07357	0.08961	0.10672	0.12466	0.14320	0.16219	0.18149
30	0.04464	0.05783	0.07264	0.08882	0.10607	0.12414	0.14280	0.16188	0.18126
31	0.04359	0.05685	0.07179	0.08810	0.10549	0.12368	0.14245	0.16162	0.18107
32	0.04261	0.05594	0.07100	0.08745	0.10497	0.12328	0.14214	0.16139	0.18090
33	0.04168	0.05510	0.07027	0.08685	0.10449	0.12292	0.14187	0.16120	0.18076
34	0.04081	0.05431	0.06959	0.08630	0.10407	0.12260	0.14164	0.16103	0.18064
35	0.04000	0.05357	0.06897	0.08580	0.10368	0.12231	0.14144	0.16089	0.18055
36	0.03923	0.05288	0.06839	0.08534	0.10334	0.12206	0.14126	0.16076	0.18046
37	0.03850	0.05223	0.06785	0.08492	0.10302	0.12183	0.14110	0.16066	0.18039
38	0.03782	0.05163	0.06735	0.08453	0.10274	0.12163	0.14096	0.16057	0.18033
39	0.03717	0.05106	0.06689	0.08418	0.10249	0.12146	0.14085	0.16049	0.18028
40	0.03655	0.05052	0.06646	0.08386	0.10225	0.12130	0.14074	0.16042	0.18024

Normal Distribution Table

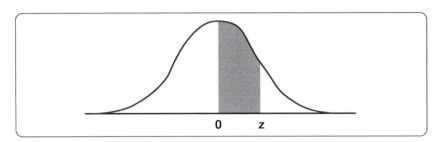

Entries in the table give the area under the curve between the mean and z standard deviations above the mean. For example for $z = 1.02$, the area under the curve between the mean and z is 0.3461.

z	0.00	.01	.02	.03	.04	.05	.06	.07	.08	.09
0.0	0.0000	0.0040	0.0080	0.0120	0.0160	0.0199	0.0239	0.0279	0.0319	0.0359
0.1	0.0398	0.0438	0.0478	0.0517	0.0557	0.0596	0.0636	0.0675	0.0714	0.0753
0.2	0.0793	0.0832	0.0871	0.0910	0.0948	0.0987	0.1026	0.1064	0.1103	0.1141
0.3	0.1179	0.1217	0.1255	0.1293	0.1331	0.1368	0.1406	0.1443	0.1480	0.1517
0.4	0.1554	0.1591	0.1628	0.1664	0.1700	0.1736	0.1772	0.1808	0.1844	0.1879
0.5	0.1915	0.1950	0.1985	0.2019	0.2054	0.2088	0.2123	0.2157	0.2190	0.2224
0.6	0.2257	0.2291	0.2324	0.2357	0.2389	0.2422	0.2454	0.2486	0.2518	0.2549
0.7	0.2580	0.2612	0.2642	0.2673	0.2704	0.2734	0.2764	0.2794	0.2823	0.2852
0.8	0.2881	0.2910	0.2939	0.2967	0.2995	0.3023	0.3051	0.3078	0.3106	0.3133
0.9	0.3159	0.3186	0.3212	0.3238	0.3264	0.3289	0.3315	0.3340	0.3365	0.3389
1.0	0.3413	0.3438	0.3461	0.3485	0.3508	0.3531	0.3554	0.3577	0.3599	0.3621
1.1	0.3643	0.3665	0.3686	0.3708	0.3729	0.3749	0.3770	0.3790	0.3810	0.3830
1.2	0.3849	0.3869	0.3888	0.3907	0.3925	0.3944	0.3962	0.3980	0.3997	0.4015
1.3	0.4032	0.4049	0.4066	0.4082	0.4099	0.4115	0.4131	0.4147	0.4162	0.4177
1.4	0.4192	0.4207	0.4222	0.4236	0.4251	0.4265	0.4279	0.4292	0.4306	0.4319
1.5	0.4332	0.4345	0.4357	0.4370	0.4382	0.4394	0.4406	0.4418	0.4429	0.4441
1.6	0.4452	0.4463	0.4474	0.4484	0.4495	0.4505	0.4515	0.4525	0.4535	0.4545
1.7	0.4554	0.4564	0.4573	0.4582	0.4591	0.4599	0.4608	0.4616	0.4625	0.4633
1.8	0.4641	0.4649	0.4656	0.4664	0.4671	0.4678	0.4686	0.4693	0.4699	0.4706
1.9	0.4713	0.4719	0.4726	0.4732	0.4738	0.4744	0.4750	0.4756	0.4761	0.4767
2.0	0.4772	0.4778	0.4783	0.4788	0.4793	0.4798	0.4803	0.4808	0.4812	0.4817
2.1	0.4821	0.4826	0.4830	0.4834	0.4838	0.4842	0.4846	0.4850	0.4854	0.4857
2.2	0.4861	0.4864	0.4868	0.4871	0.4875	0.4878	0.4881	0.4884	0.4887	0.4890
2.3	0.4893	0.4896	0.4898	0.4901	0.4904	0.4906	0.4909	0.4911	0.4913	0.4916
2.4	0.4918	0.4920	0.4922	0.4925	0.4927	0.4929	0.4931	0.4932	0.4934	0.4936
2.5	0.4938	0.4940	0.4941	0.4943	0.4945	0.4946	0.4948	0.4949	0.4951	0.4952
2.6	0.4953	0.4955	0.4956	0.4957	0.4959	0.4960	0.4961	0.4962	0.4963	0.4964
2.7	0.4965	0.4966	0.4967	0.4968	0.4969	0.4970	0.4971	0.4972	0.4973	0.4974
2.8	0.4974	0.4975	0.4976	0.4977	0.4977	0.4978	0.4979	0.4979	0.4980	0.4981
2.9	0.4981	0.4982	0.4982	0.4983	0.4984	0.4984	0.4985	0.4985	0.4986	0.4986
3.0	0.4986	0.4987	0.4987	0.4988	0.4988	0.4989	0.4989	0.4989	0.4990	0.4990

Index